Thank you very much for picking up
this graphic novel. I'd love to continue
making a living drawing manga.
(Check out the photo of the
Cake of Doom I made last year!)

—KOUHEI HORIKOSHI, 2012

KOUHEI HORIKOSHI

was born in Aichi, Japan, in 1986.
He received a Tezuka Award Honorable
Mention in 2006, and after publishing
several short stories in *Akamaru Jump*,
his first serialized work in *Weekly Shonen
Jump* was *Oumagadoki Doubutsuen* in 2010.
Barrage is his second series in
Weekly Shonen Jump.

BARRAGE

VOLUME 2

SHONEN JUMP Manga Edition

Story and Art by
KOUHEI HORIKOSHI

Translation | TETSUICHIRO MIYAKI
Touch-up Art and Lettering | JAMES GAUBATZ
Design | FAWN LAU
Editor | HOPE DONOVAN

SENSEI NO BARRAGE © 2012 by Kouhei Horikoshi
All rights reserved. First published in Japan in 2012 by SHUEISHA Inc.,
Tokyo. English translation rights arranged by SHUEISHA Inc.

Printed in the U.S.A.

Published by VIZ Media, LLC
P.O. Box 77010
San Francisco, CA 94107

10 9 8 7 6 5 4 3 2 1
First printing, April 2013

www.viz.com   www.shonenjump.com

BARRAGE

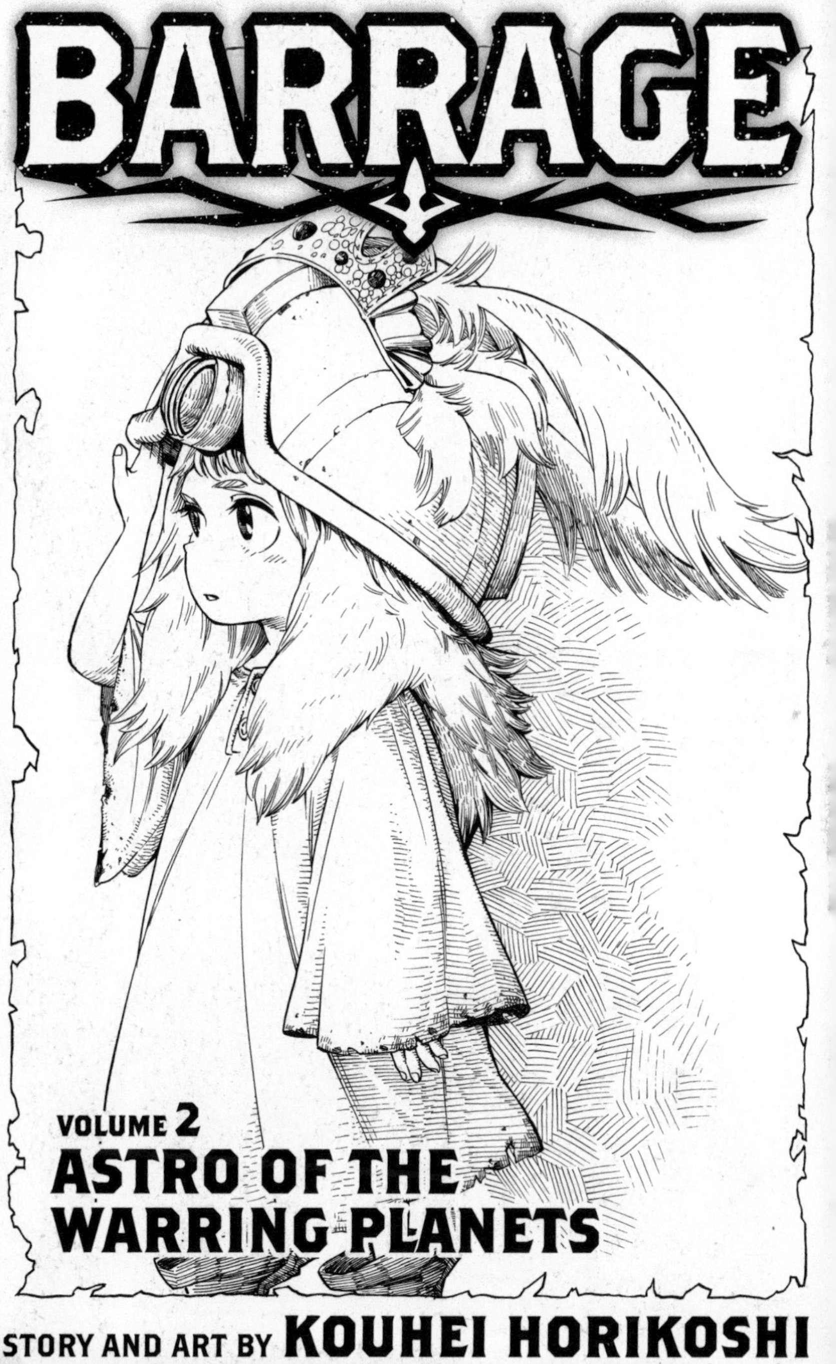

VOLUME 2

ASTRO OF THE WARRING PLANETS

STORY AND ART BY **KOUHEI HORIKOSHI**

CHARACTERS

ASTRO

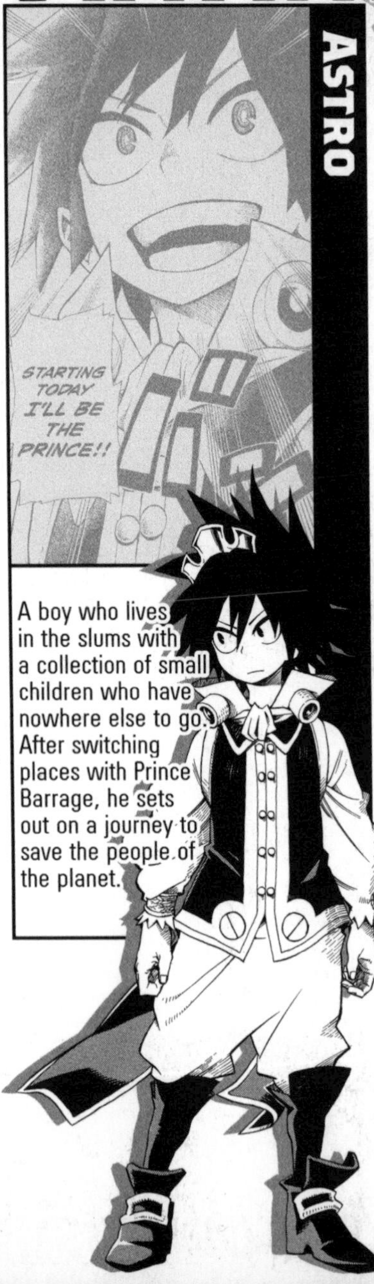
STARTING TODAY I'LL BE THE PRINCE!!

A boy who lives in the slums with a collection of small children who have nowhere else to go. After switching places with Prince Barrage, he sets out on a journey to save the people of the planet.

TIAMAT

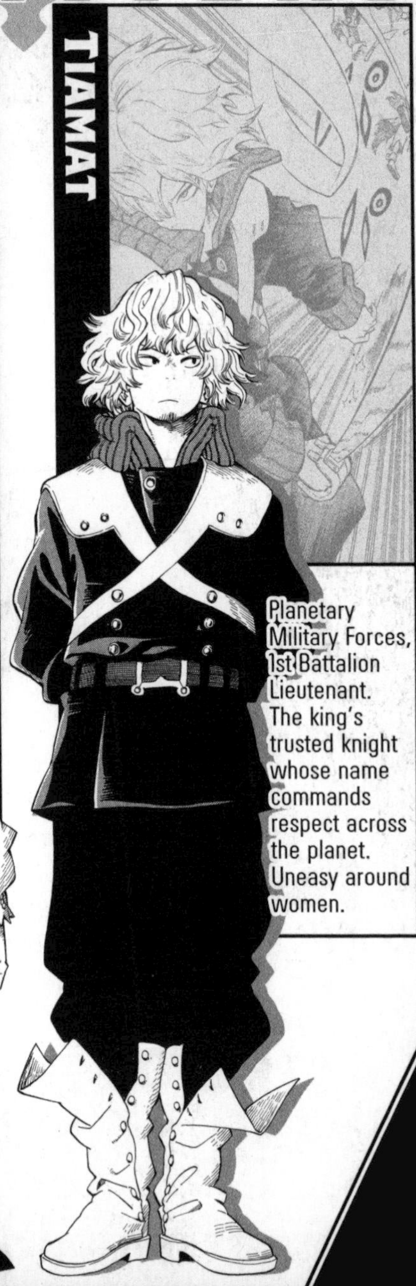

Planetary Military Forces, 1st Battalion Lieutenant. The king's trusted knight whose name commands respect across the planet. Uneasy around women.

STORY

The planet Industria, once united under the peaceful rule of the royal family, is currently overrun by aliens. One day, Prince Barrage switches places with a slum kid named Astro, who is hauled off to the castle by mistake. After the king learns of the real prince's death, he asks Astro to take his place and bring peace to the war-torn planet. After all, Astro can wield the Orgue—a weapon that can only be used by those with the qualifications to be king. In order to protect his family, Astro agrees to set out on a journey to save the planet. But the moment he and Tiamat reach Maseille, they're attacked!

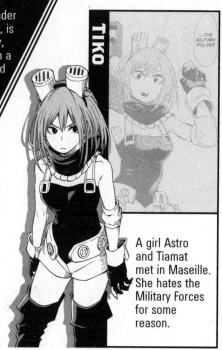

TIKO

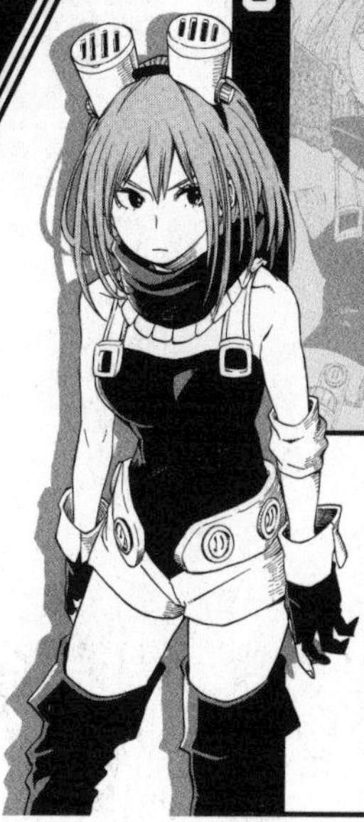

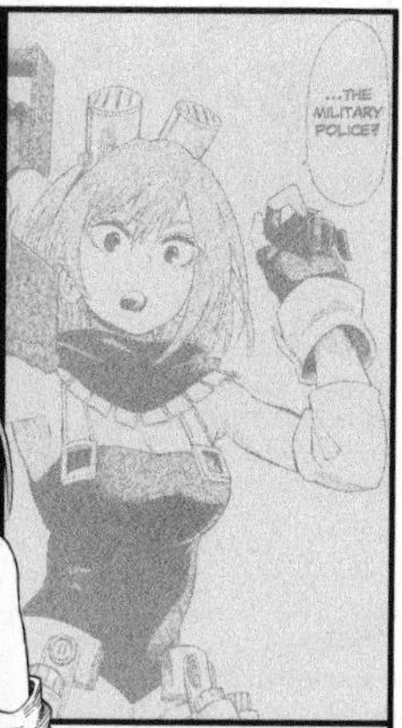
...THE MILITARY POLICE?

A girl Astro and Tiamat met in Maseille. She hates the Military Forces for some reason.

KIDS

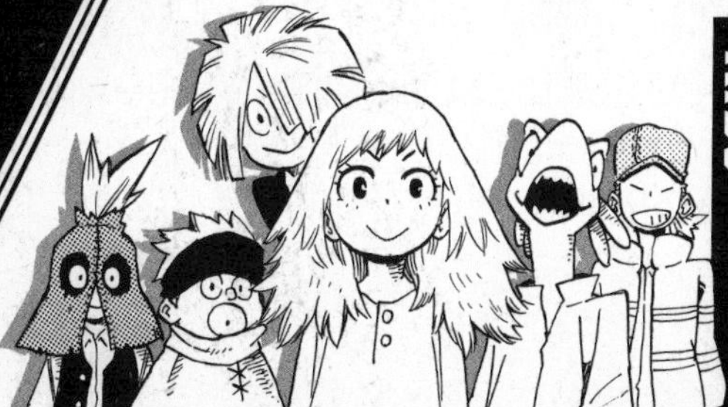

Astro's happy family. From the left, their names are Okikuna, Sho, Little, Chima, Suntara, and Macro.

KING

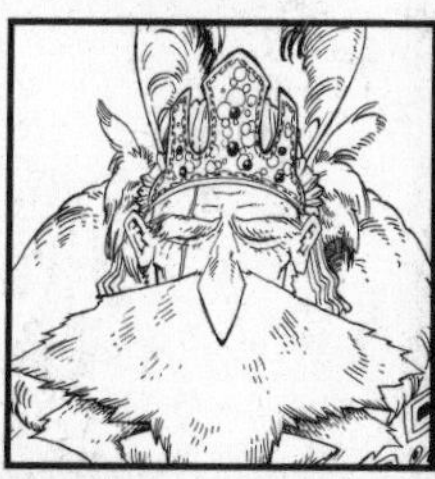

The King of Industria. Reigned over Industria with the power of the Orgue. He asked Astro to take the prince's place.

BARRAGE

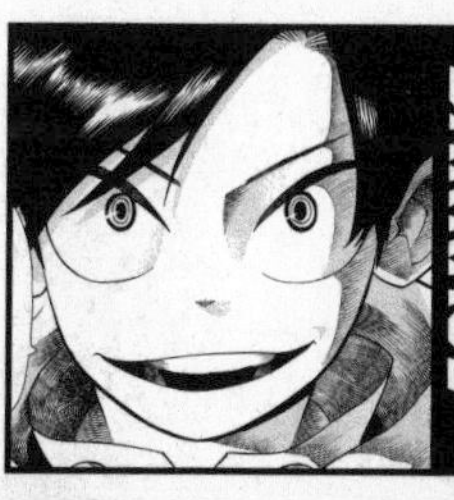

The Prince of Industria. He ran away from the castle and forced the Orgue on Astro before being assassinated.

BARRAGE

VOLUME 2 | **ASTRO OF THE WARRING PLANETS**

CONTENTS

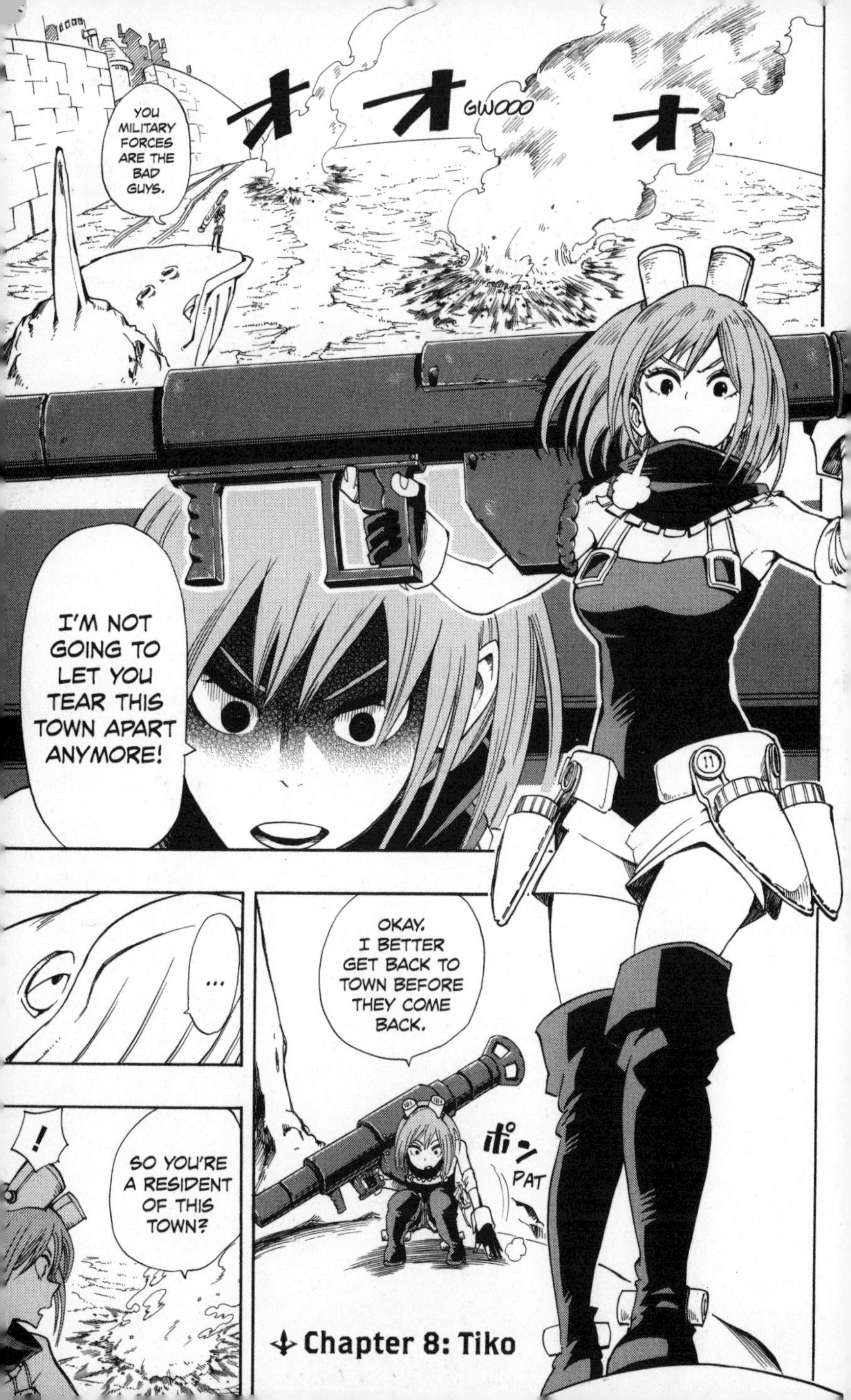

オオオ
GWOOO
YOU MILITARY FORCES ARE THE BAD GUYS.
I'M NOT GOING TO LET YOU TEAR THIS TOWN APART ANYMORE!
OKAY. I BETTER GET BACK TO TOWN BEFORE THEY COME BACK.
ポン
PAT
...
!
SO YOU'RE A RESIDENT OF THIS TOWN?
Chapter 8: Tiko

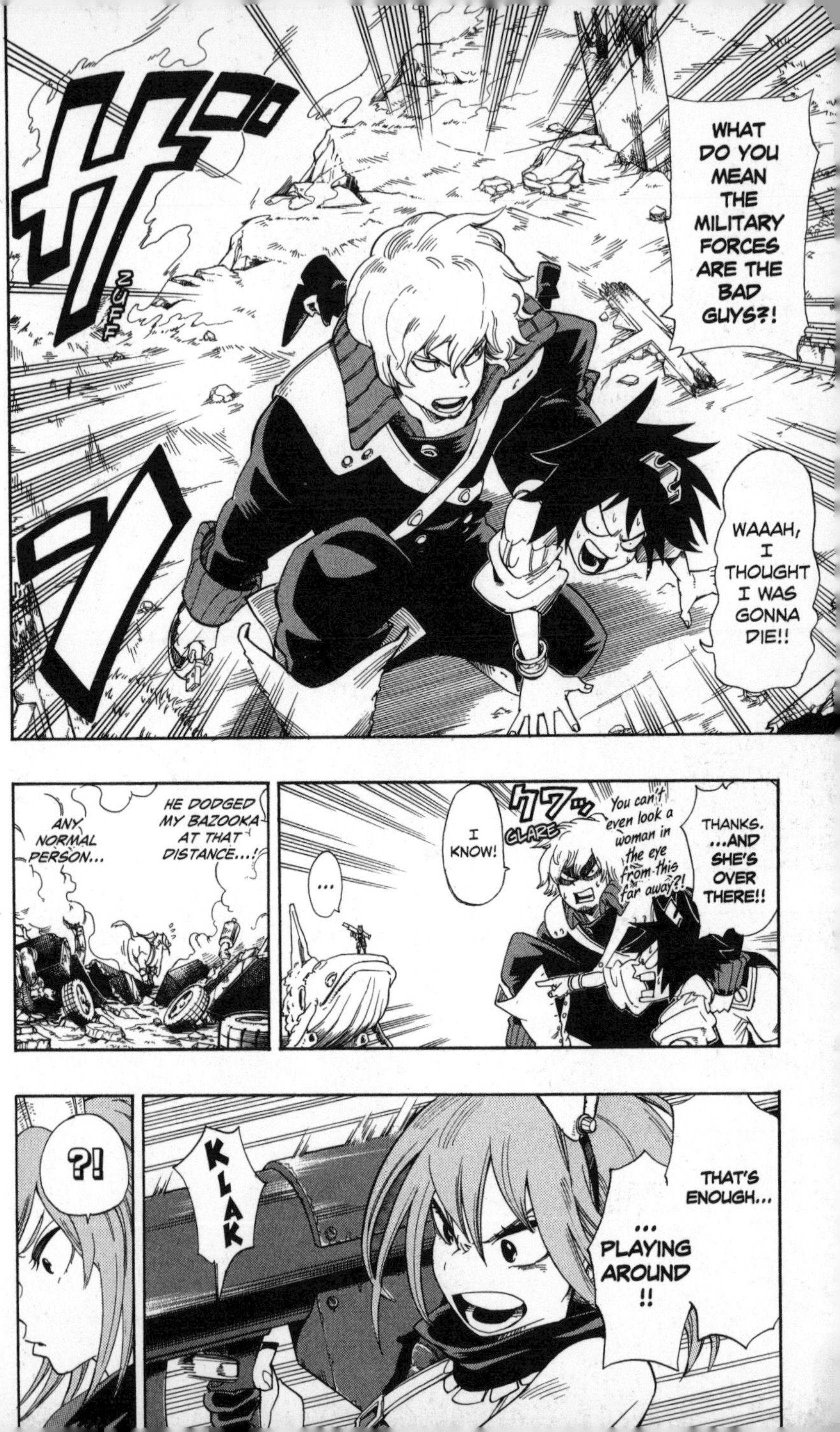

WHAT DO YOU MEAN THE MILITARY FORCES ARE THE BAD GUYS?!
ZUFF
WAAAH, I THOUGHT I WAS GONNA DIE!!
THANKS. ...AND SHE'S OVER THERE!!
You can't even look a woman in the eye from this far away?!
GLARE
I KNOW!
...
HE DODGED MY BAZOOKA AT THAT DISTANCE...!
ANY NORMAL PERSON...
THAT'S ENOUGH...
... PLAYING AROUND !!
KLAK
?!

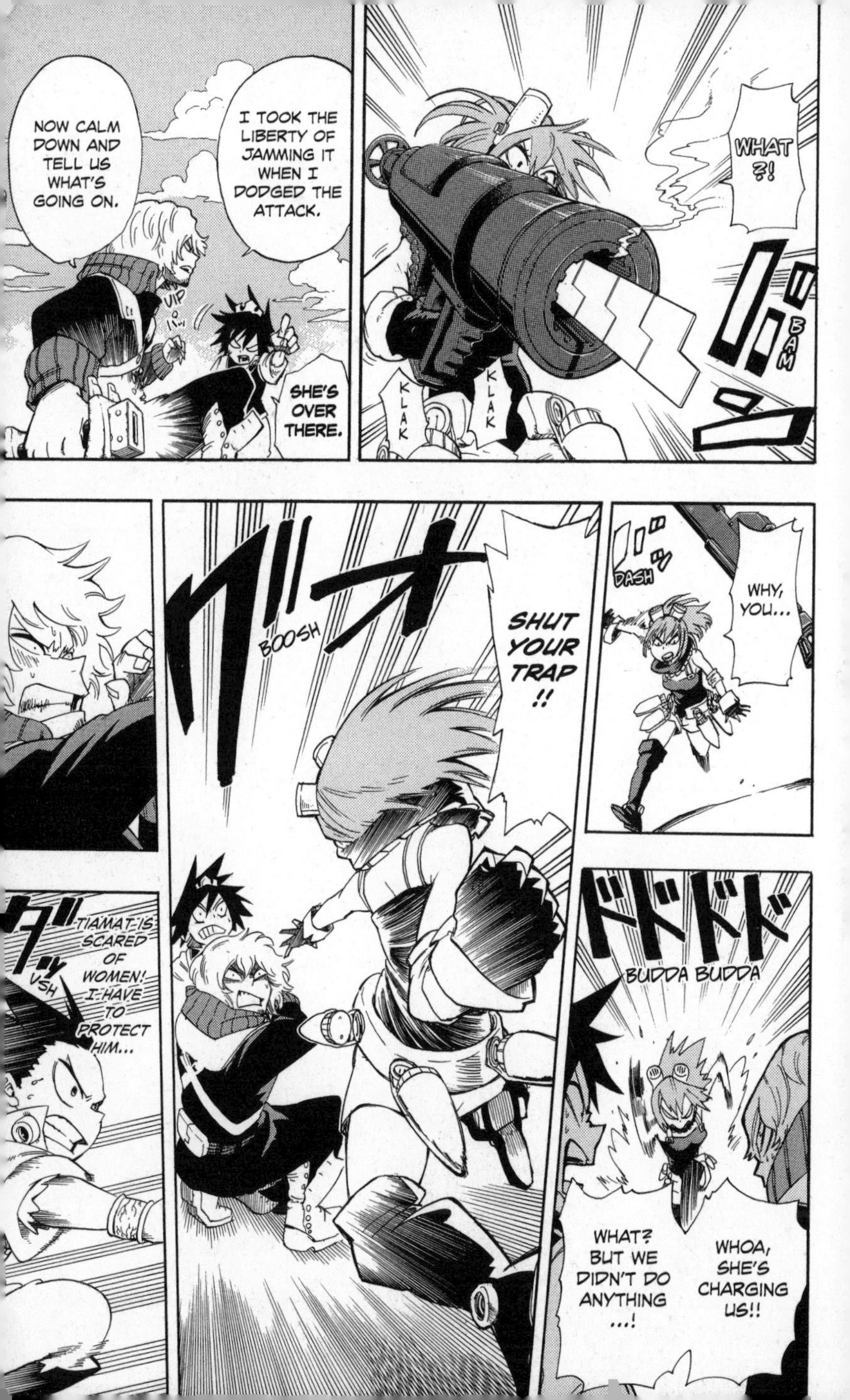
WHAT ?!
BAM
KLAK
KLAK
I TOOK THE LIBERTY OF JAMMING IT WHEN I DODGED THE ATTACK.
NOW CALM DOWN AND TELL US WHAT'S GOING ON.
UIP
SHE'S OVER THERE.
DASH
WHY, YOU...
SHUT YOUR TRAP !!
BOOSH
BUDDA BUDDA
WHOA, SHE'S CHARGING US!!
WHAT? BUT WE DIDN'T DO ANYTHING ...!
TIAMAT IS SCARED OF WOMEN! I HAVE TO PROTECT HIM...
VSH

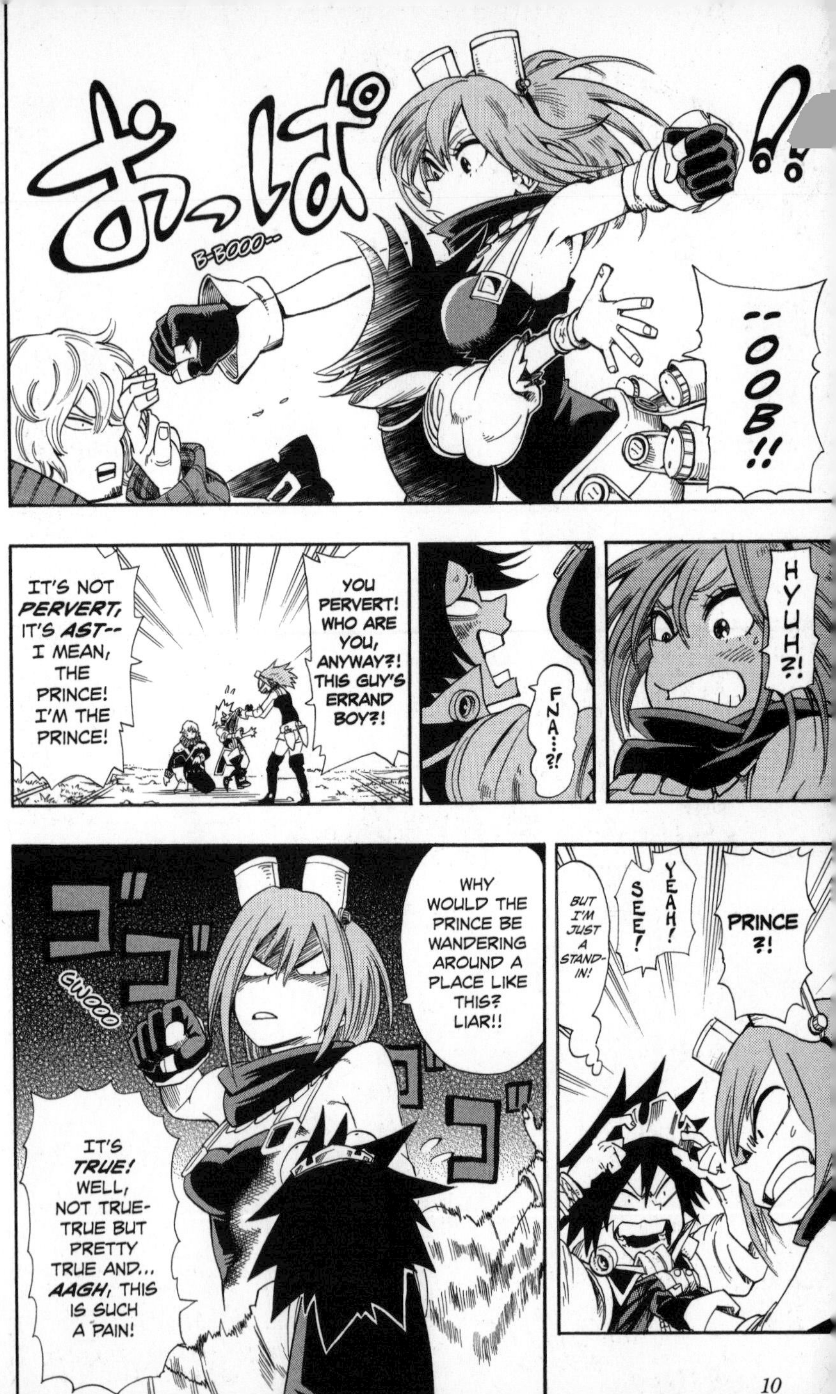
!?
--OOOB!!
おっぱ
B-BOOO--
HYUH?!
FNA...?!
YOU PERVERT! WHO ARE YOU, ANYWAY?! THIS GUY'S ERRAND BOY?!
IT'S NOT PERVERT, IT'S AST-- I MEAN, THE PRINCE! I'M THE PRINCE!
PRINCE?!
YEAH! SEE!
BUT I'M JUST A STAND-IN!
WHY WOULD THE PRINCE BE WANDERING AROUND A PLACE LIKE THIS? LIAR!!
ゴゴゴ
GNOOO
IT'S TRUE! WELL, NOT TRUE-TRUE BUT PRETTY TRUE AND... AAGH, THIS IS SUCH A PAIN!

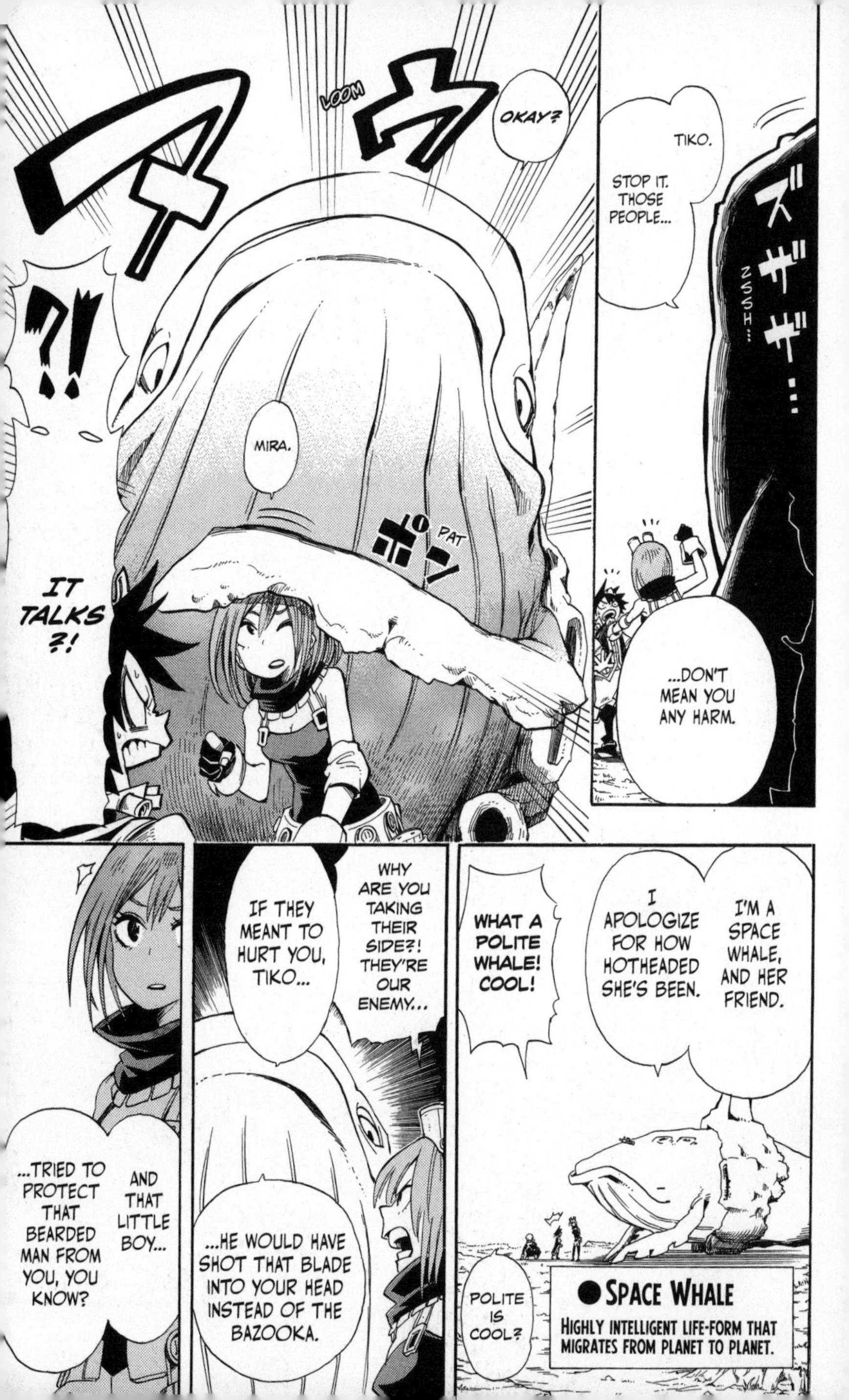
TIKO.
STOP IT. THOSE PEOPLE...
ZSSH...
...DON'T MEAN YOU ANY HARM.
OKAY?
LOOM
MIRA.
PAT
?!!
IT TALKS?!
I'M A SPACE WHALE, AND HER FRIEND.
I APOLOGIZE FOR HOW HOTHEADED SHE'S BEEN.
WHAT A POLITE WHALE! COOL!
POLITE IS COOL?
● SPACE WHALE
HIGHLY INTELLIGENT LIFE-FORM THAT MIGRATES FROM PLANET TO PLANET.
WHY ARE YOU TAKING THEIR SIDE?! THEY'RE OUR ENEMY...
IF THEY MEANT TO HURT YOU, TIKO...
...HE WOULD HAVE SHOT THAT BLADE INTO YOUR HEAD INSTEAD OF THE BAZOOKA.
AND THAT LITTLE BOY...
...TRIED TO PROTECT THAT BEARDED MAN FROM YOU, YOU KNOW?

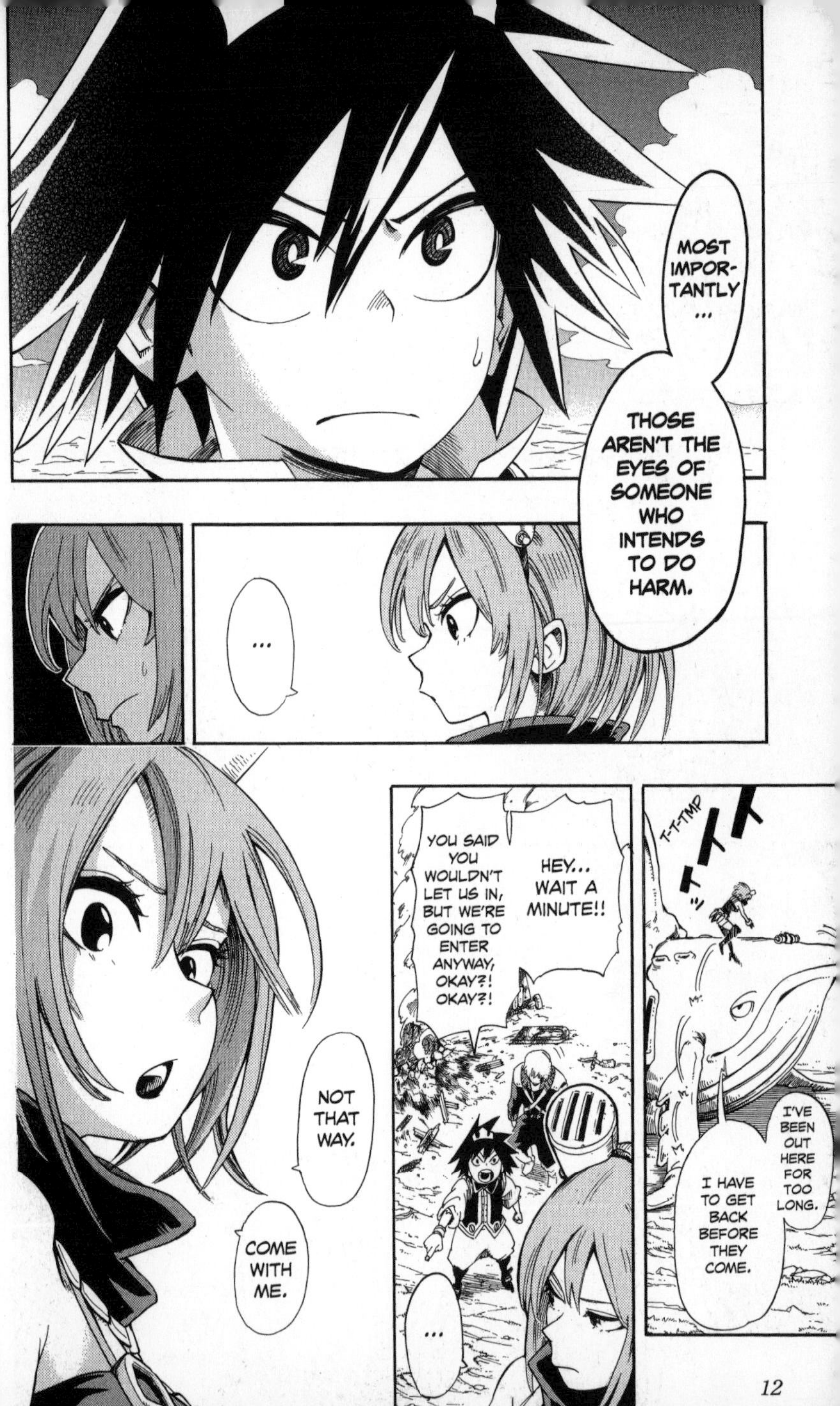
MOST IMPOR-TANTLY ...
THOSE AREN'T THE EYES OF SOMEONE WHO INTENDS TO DO HARM.
...
T-T-TMP
I'VE BEEN OUT HERE FOR TOO LONG.
I HAVE TO GET BACK BEFORE THEY COME.
HEY... WAIT A MINUTE!!
YOU SAID YOU WOULDN'T LET US IN, BUT WE'RE GOING TO ENTER ANYWAY, OKAY?! OKAY?!
...
NOT THAT WAY.
COME WITH ME.

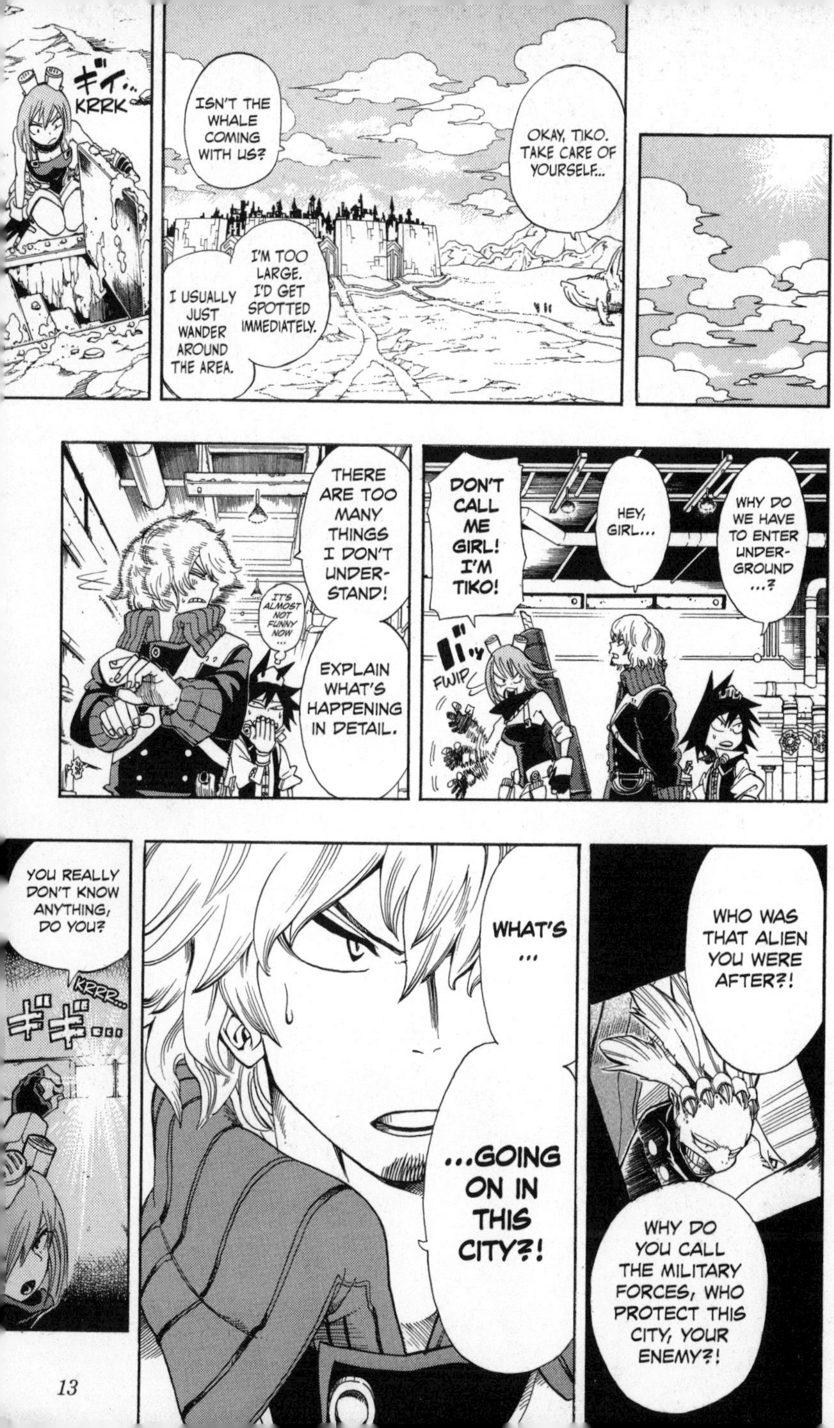

OKAY, TIKO. TAKE CARE OF YOURSELF...
ISN'T THE WHALE COMING WITH US?
I'M TOO LARGE. I'D GET SPOTTED IMMEDIATELY.
I USUALLY JUST WANDER AROUND THE AREA.
ギイ… KRRK
WHY DO WE HAVE TO ENTER UNDER-GROUND ...?
HEY, GIRL...
DON'T CALL ME GIRL! I'M TIKO!
FWIP
THERE ARE TOO MANY THINGS I DON'T UNDER-STAND!
IT'S ALMOST NOT FUNNY NOW ...
EXPLAIN WHAT'S HAPPENING IN DETAIL.
WHO WAS THAT ALIEN YOU WERE AFTER?!
WHY DO YOU CALL THE MILITARY FORCES, WHO PROTECT THIS CITY, YOUR ENEMY?!
WHAT'S ...
...GOING ON IN THIS CITY?!
YOU REALLY DON'T KNOW ANYTHING, DO YOU?
KRRR...
ギギ…

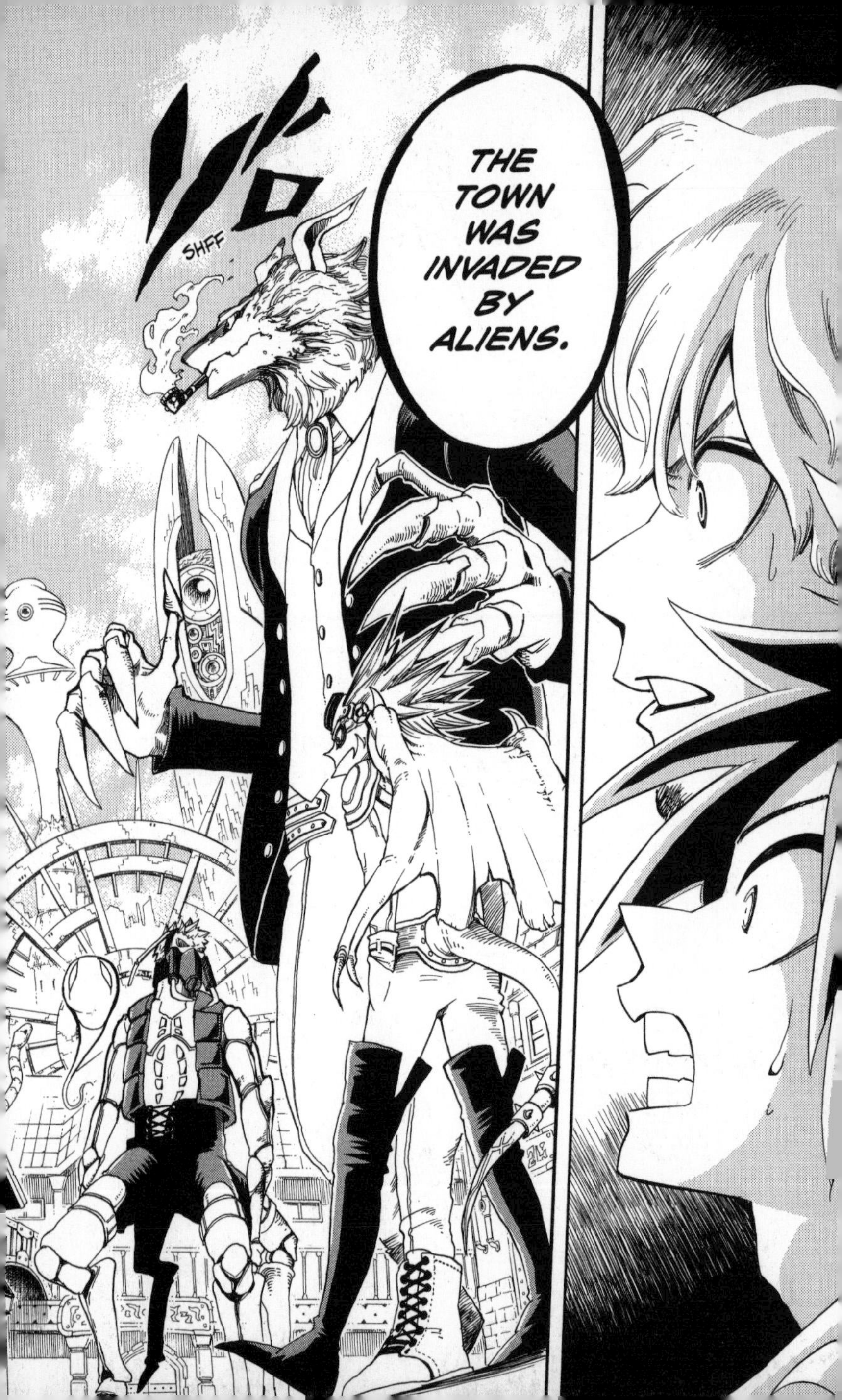
THE TOWN WAS INVADED BY ALIENS.
SHFF

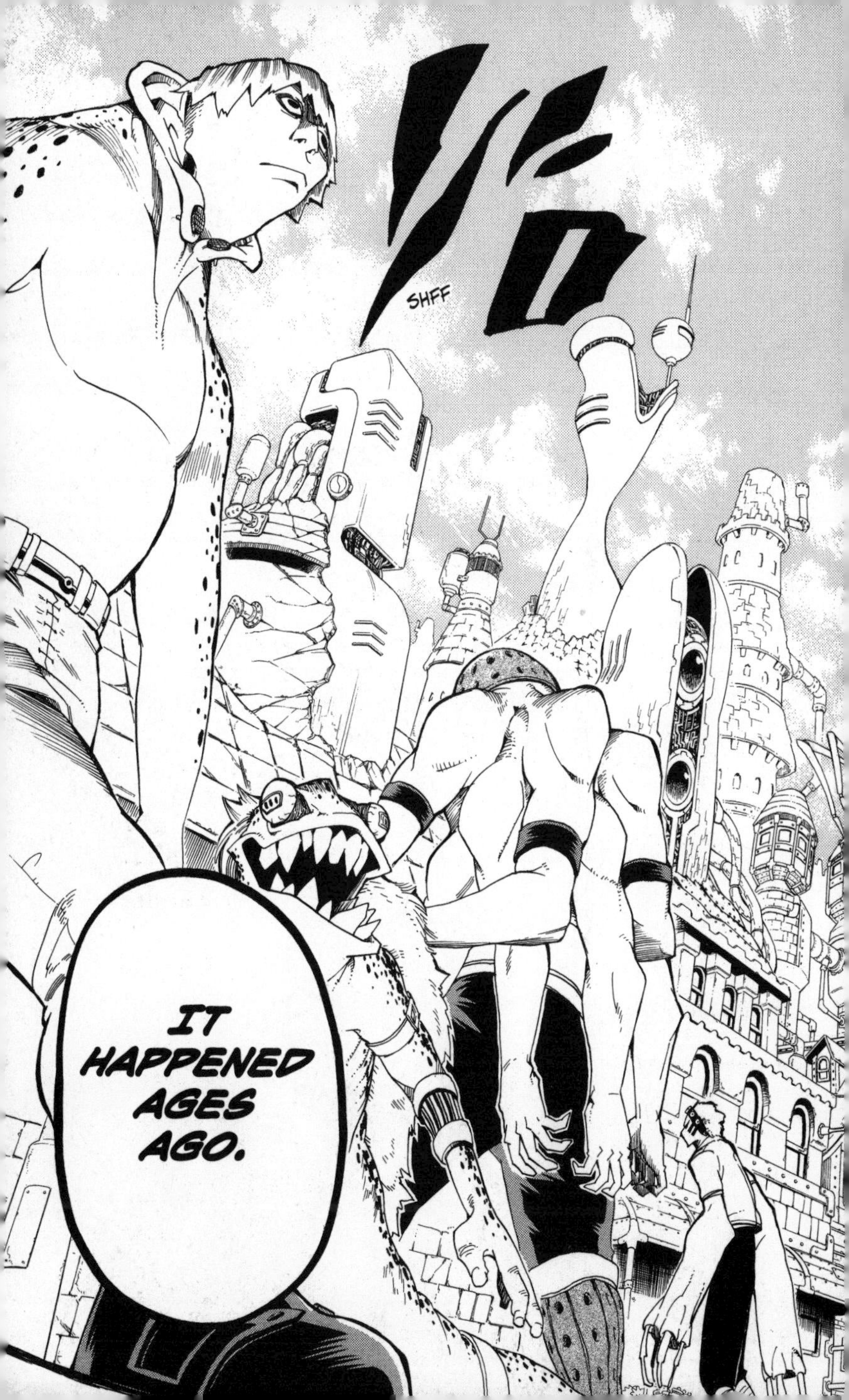
SHFF
IT HAPPENED AGES AGO.

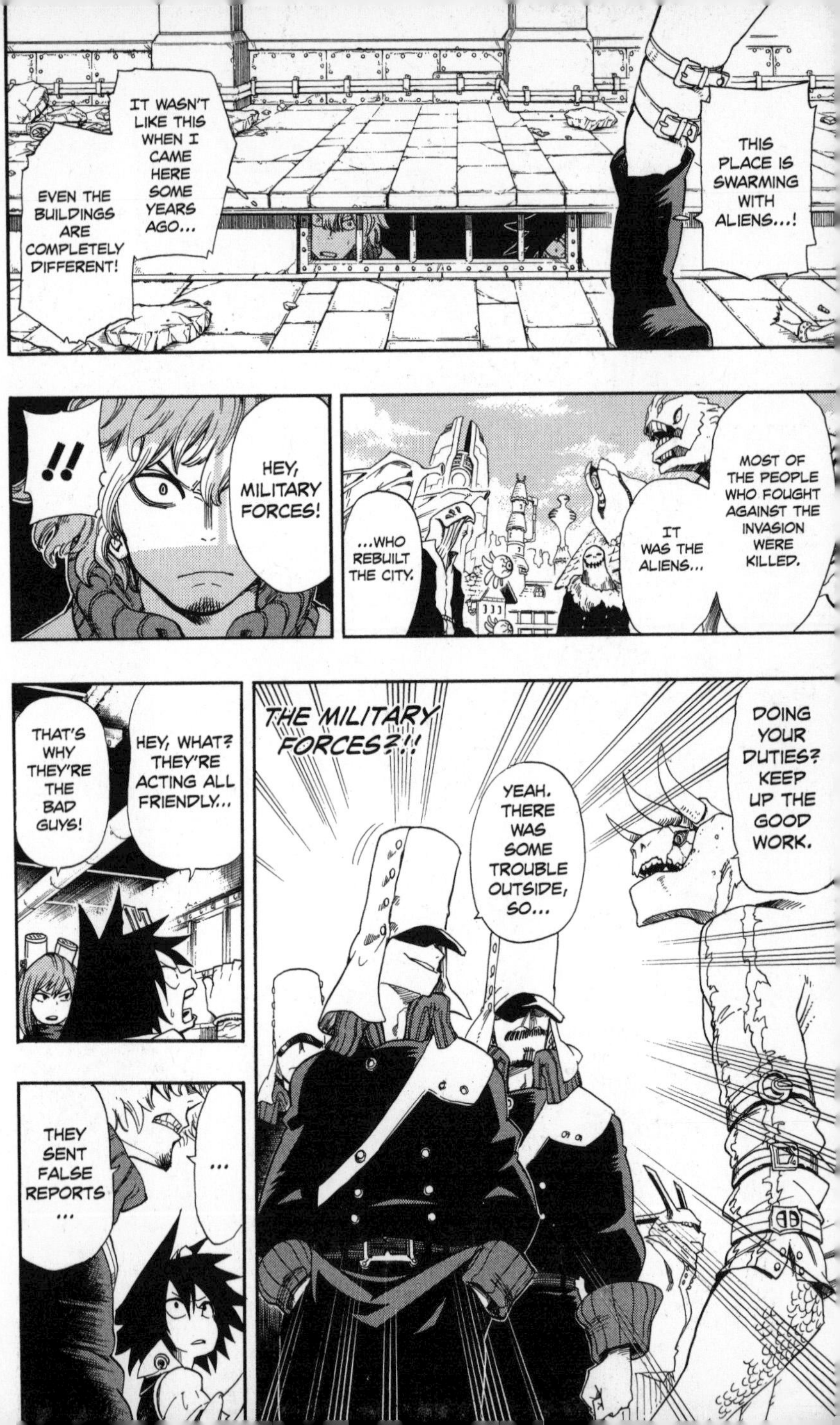
THIS PLACE IS SWARMING WITH ALIENS...!
IT WASN'T LIKE THIS WHEN I CAME HERE SOME YEARS AGO...
EVEN THE BUILDINGS ARE COMPLETELY DIFFERENT!
MOST OF THE PEOPLE WHO FOUGHT AGAINST THE INVASION WERE KILLED.
IT WAS THE ALIENS...
...WHO REBUILT THE CITY.
HEY, MILITARY FORCES!
!!
DOING YOUR DUTIES? KEEP UP THE GOOD WORK.
YEAH. THERE WAS SOME TROUBLE OUTSIDE, SO...
THE MILITARY FORCES?!!
HEY, WHAT? THEY'RE ACTING ALL FRIENDLY...
THAT'S WHY THEY'RE THE BAD GUYS!
...
THEY SENT FALSE REPORTS...

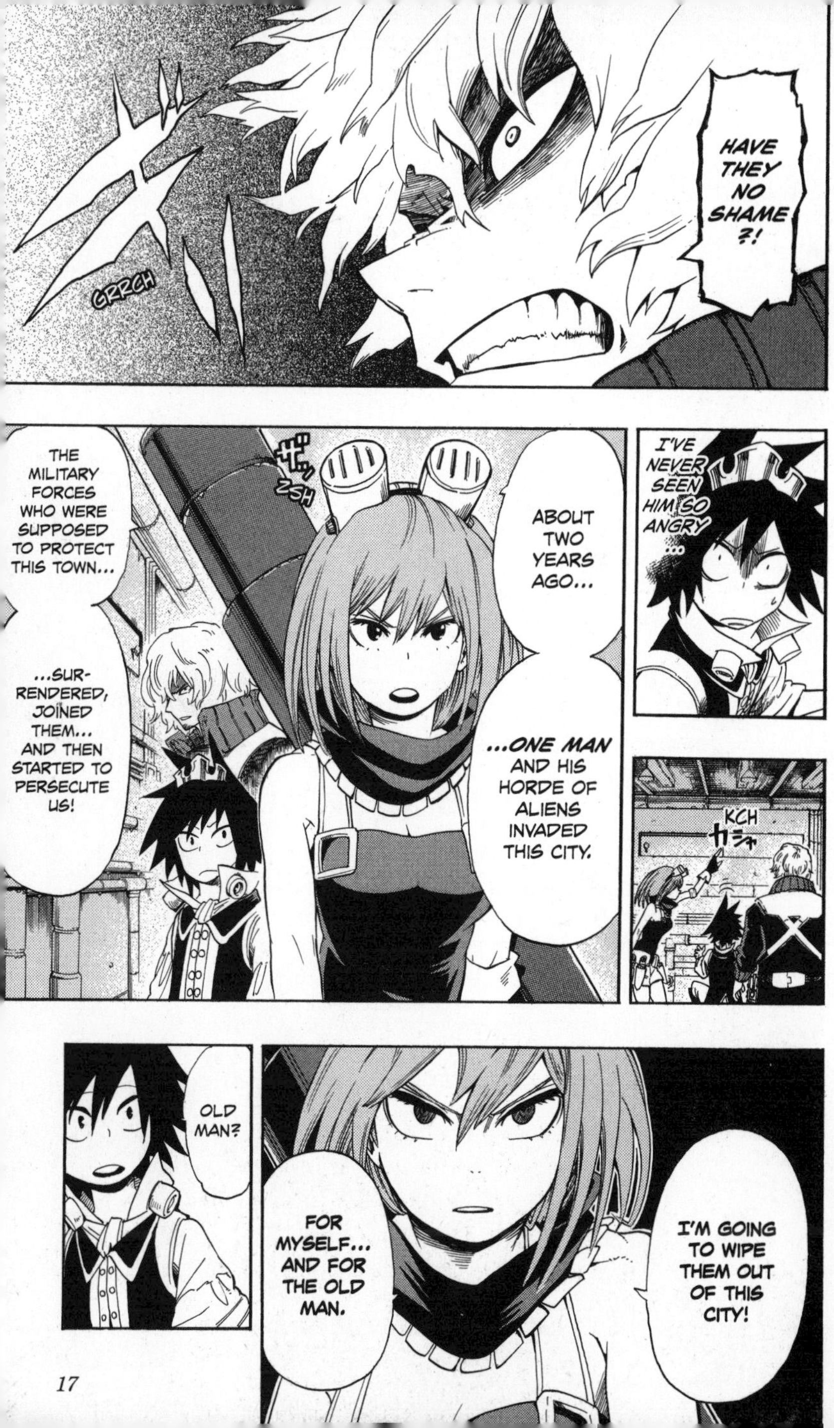
HAVE THEY NO SHAME ?!
GRRCH
I'VE NEVER SEEN HIM SO ANGRY...
KCH
ABOUT TWO YEARS AGO...
...ONE MAN AND HIS HORDE OF ALIENS INVADED THIS CITY.
ZSH
THE MILITARY FORCES WHO WERE SUPPOSED TO PROTECT THIS TOWN...
...SUR-RENDERED, JOINED THEM... AND THEN STARTED TO PERSECUTE US!
I'M GOING TO WIPE THEM OUT OF THIS CITY!
FOR MYSELF... AND FOR THE OLD MAN.
OLD MAN?

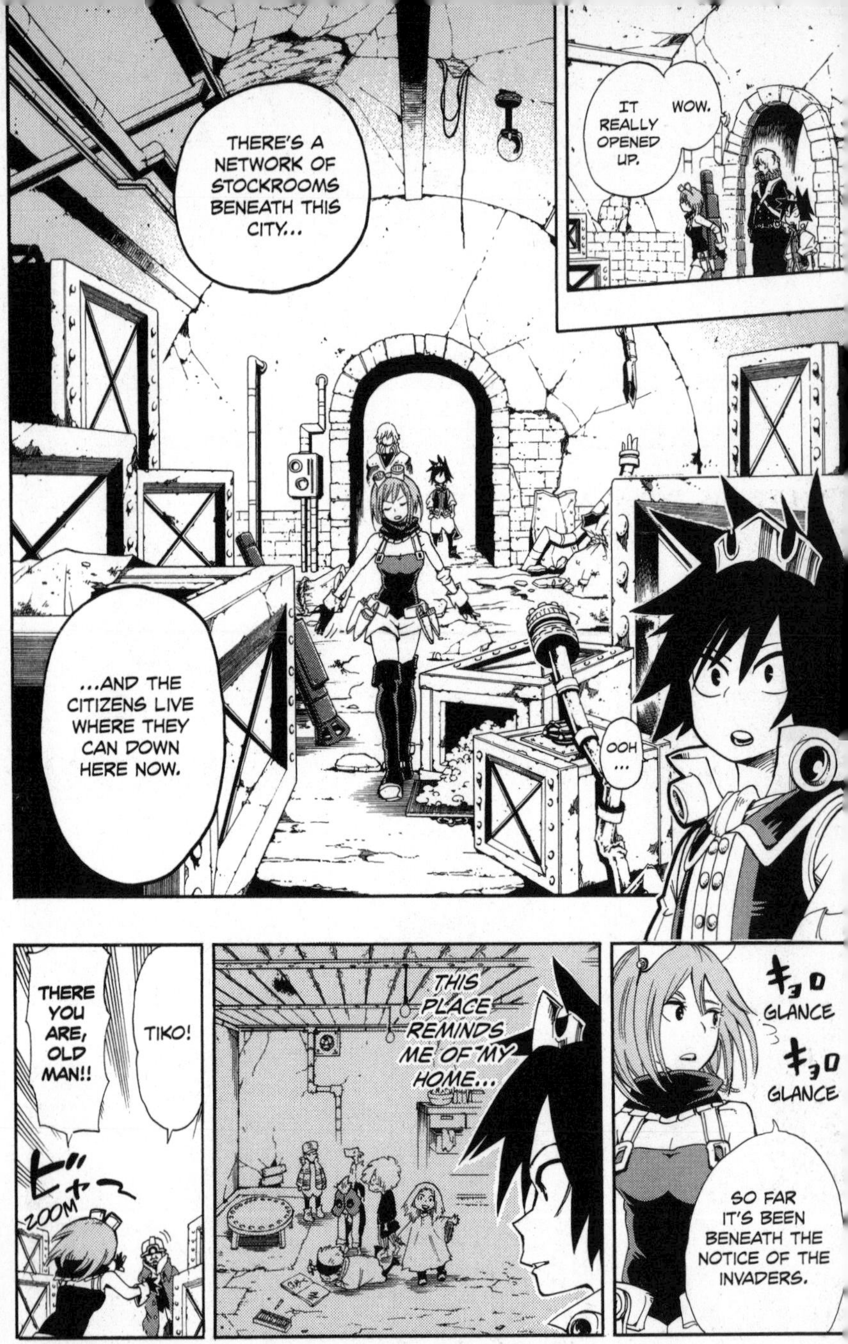
WOW.
IT REALLY OPENED UP.
THERE'S A NETWORK OF STOCKROOMS BENEATH THIS CITY...
...AND THE CITIZENS LIVE WHERE THEY CAN DOWN HERE NOW.
OOH...
GLANCE
GLANCE
SO FAR IT'S BEEN BENEATH THE NOTICE OF THE INVADERS.
THIS PLACE REMINDS ME OF MY HOME...
TIKO!
THERE YOU ARE, OLD MAN!!
ZOOM

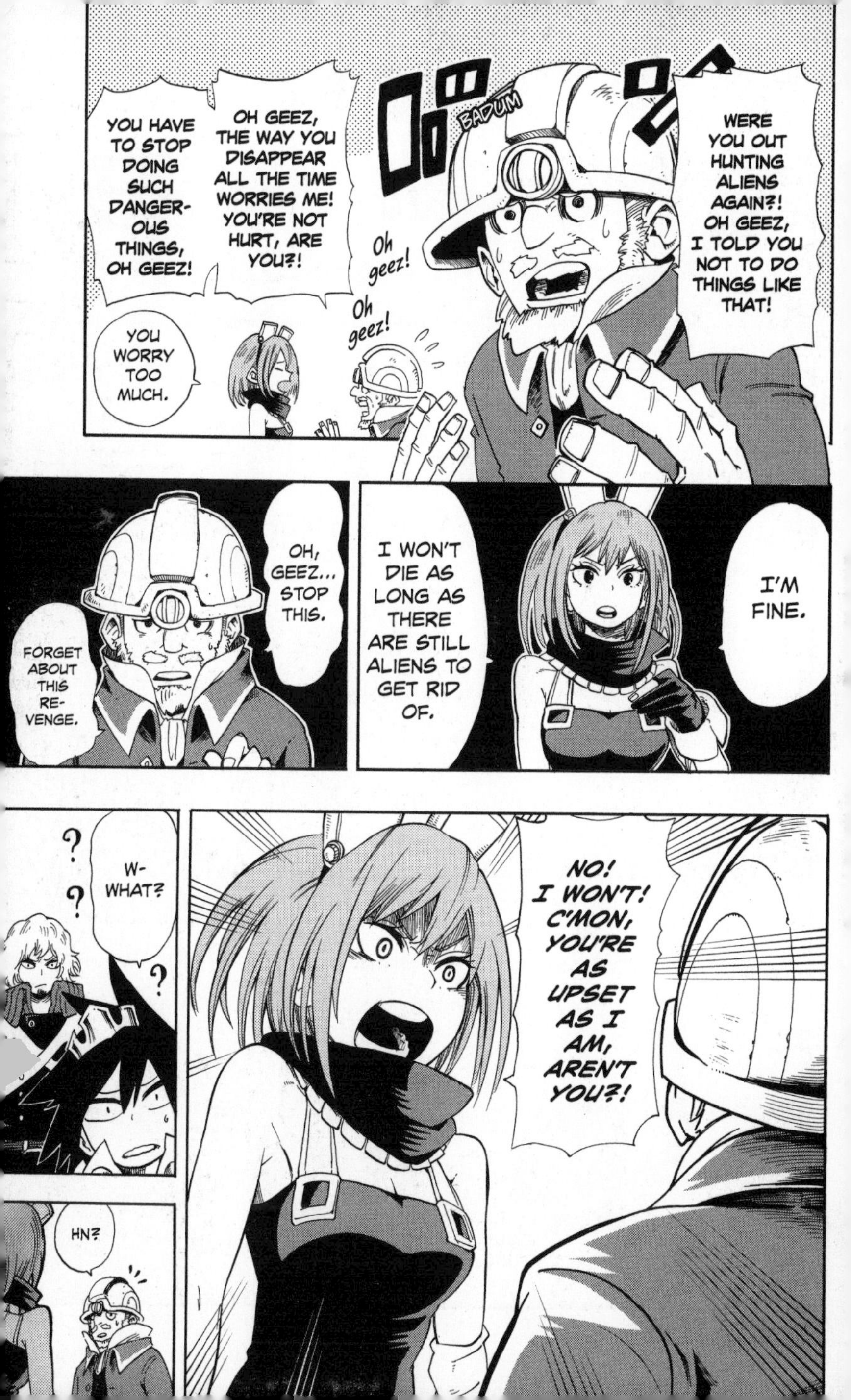
WERE YOU OUT HUNTING ALIENS AGAIN?! OH GEEZ, I TOLD YOU NOT TO DO THINGS LIKE THAT!
BADUM
OH GEEZ, THE WAY YOU DISAPPEAR ALL THE TIME WORRIES ME! YOU'RE NOT HURT, ARE YOU?!
YOU HAVE TO STOP DOING SUCH DANGER-OUS THINGS, OH GEEZ!
Oh geez!
Oh geez!
YOU WORRY TOO MUCH.
I'M FINE.
I WON'T DIE AS LONG AS THERE ARE STILL ALIENS TO GET RID OF.
OH, GEEZ... STOP THIS.
FORGET ABOUT THIS RE-VENGE.
NO! I WON'T! C'MON, YOU'RE AS UPSET AS I AM, AREN'T YOU?!
?
?
?
W-WHAT?
HN?

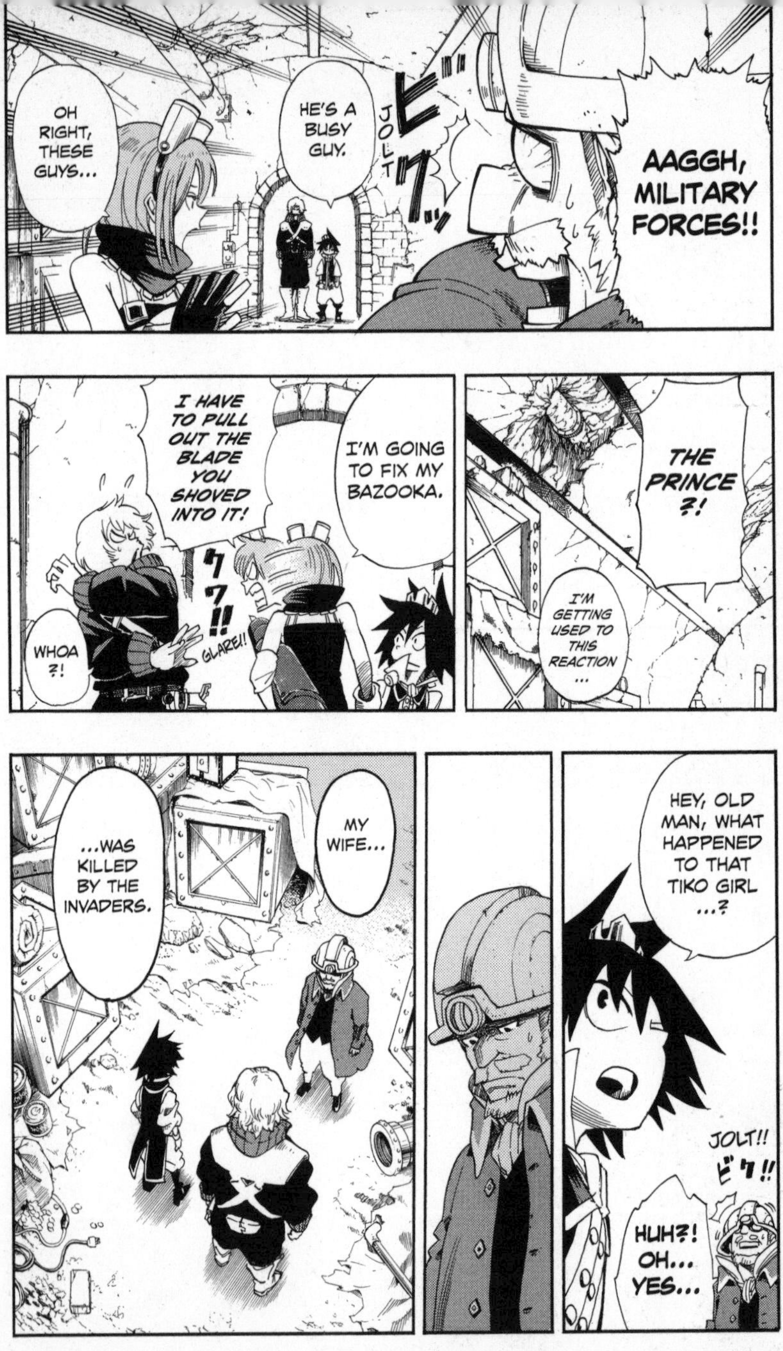
AAGGH, MILITARY FORCES!!
JOLT
ビクッ
HE'S A BUSY GUY.
OH RIGHT, THESE GUYS...
THE PRINCE ?!
I'M GETTING USED TO THIS REACTION...
I'M GOING TO FIX MY BAZOOKA.
I HAVE TO PULL OUT THE BLADE YOU SHOVED INTO IT!
クワッ!!
GLARE!!
WHOA ?!
HEY, OLD MAN, WHAT HAPPENED TO THAT TIKO GIRL...?
JOLT!!
ビク!!
HUH?! OH... YES...
MY WIFE...
...WAS KILLED BY THE INVADERS.

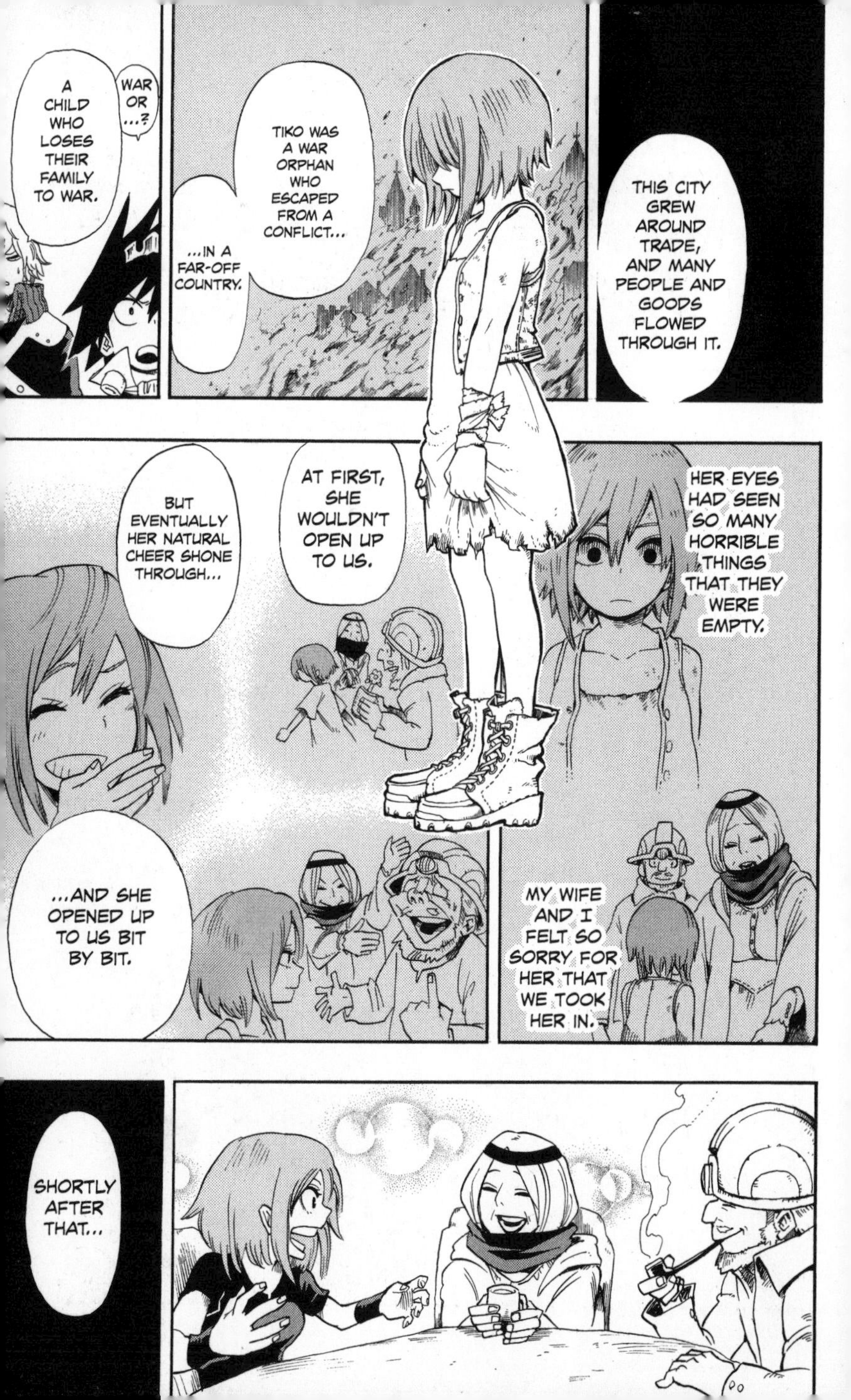
THIS CITY GREW AROUND TRADE, AND MANY PEOPLE AND GOODS FLOWED THROUGH IT.
TIKO WAS A WAR ORPHAN WHO ESCAPED FROM A CONFLICT...
...IN A FAR-OFF COUNTRY.
WAR OR ...?
A CHILD WHO LOSES THEIR FAMILY TO WAR.
HER EYES HAD SEEN SO MANY HORRIBLE THINGS THAT THEY WERE EMPTY.
MY WIFE AND I FELT SO SORRY FOR HER THAT WE TOOK HER IN.
AT FIRST, SHE WOULDN'T OPEN UP TO US.
BUT EVENTUALLY HER NATURAL CHEER SHONE THROUGH...
...AND SHE OPENED UP TO US BIT BY BIT.
SHORTLY AFTER THAT...

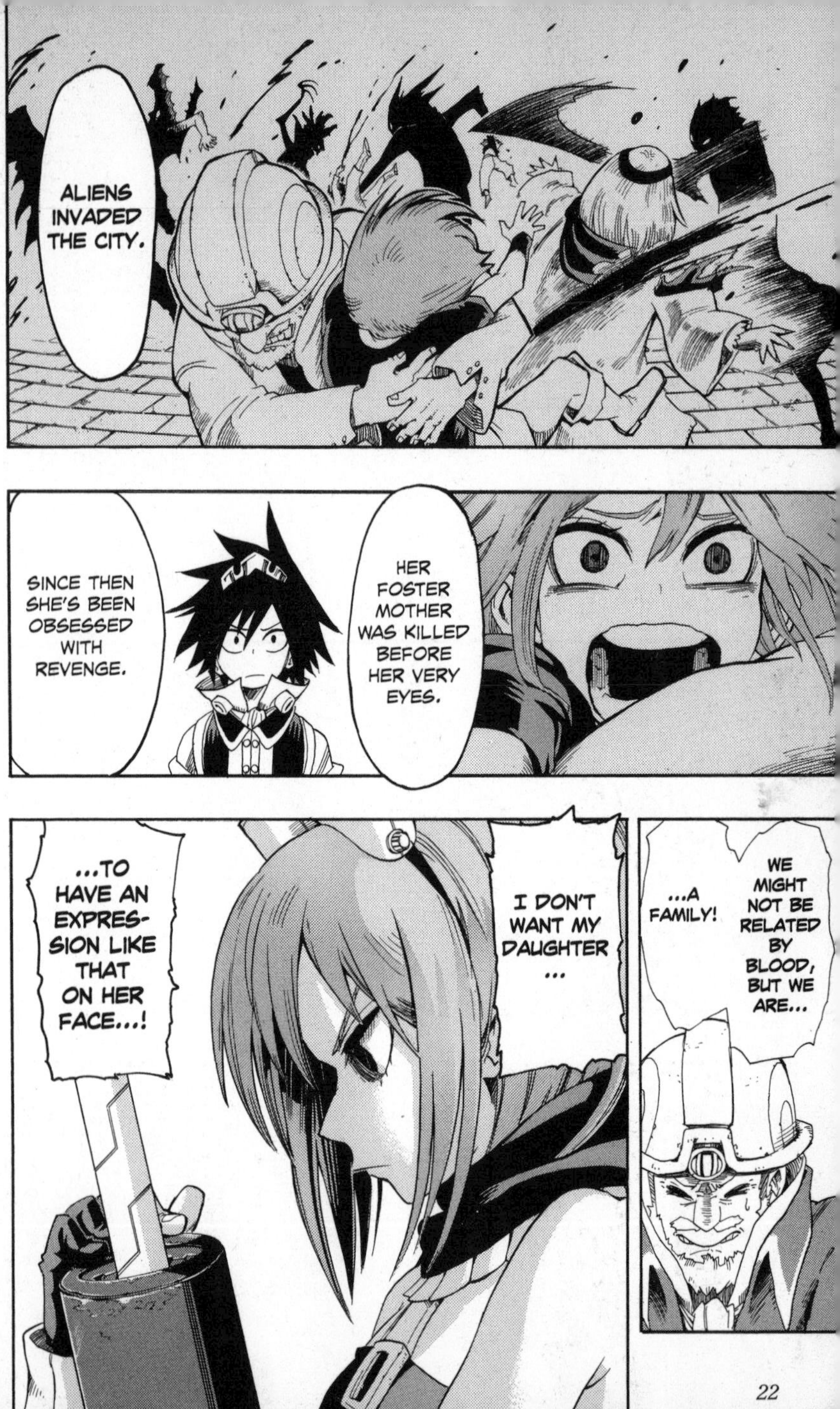
ALIENS INVADED THE CITY.
HER FOSTER MOTHER WAS KILLED BEFORE HER VERY EYES.
SINCE THEN SHE'S BEEN OBSESSED WITH REVENGE.
WE MIGHT NOT BE RELATED BY BLOOD, BUT WE ARE...
...A FAMILY!
I DON'T WANT MY DAUGHTER...
...TO HAVE AN EXPRESSION LIKE THAT ON HER FACE...!

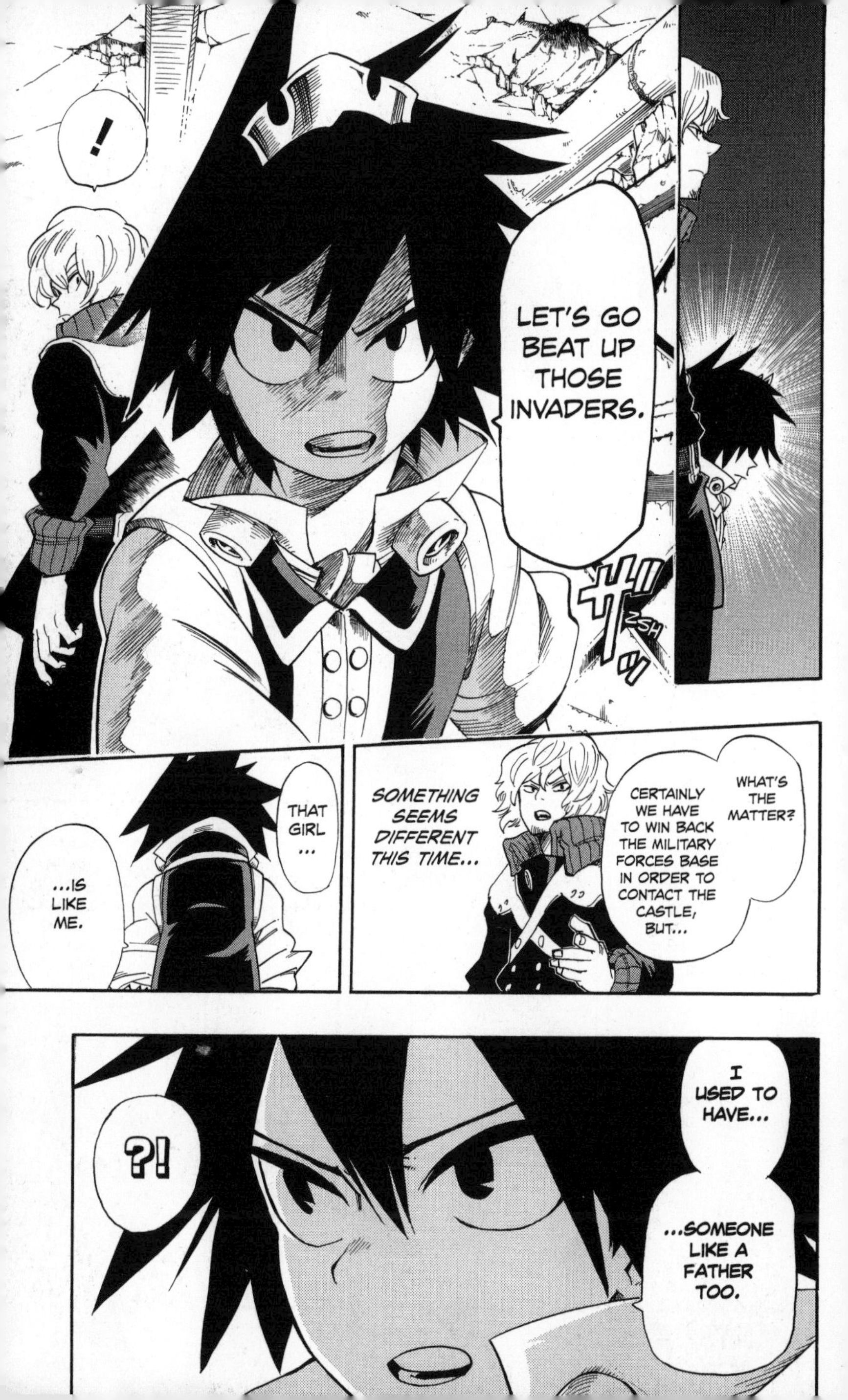
LET'S GO BEAT UP THOSE INVADERS.
ZSH
!
WHAT'S THE MATTER?
CERTAINLY WE HAVE TO WIN BACK THE MILITARY FORCES BASE IN ORDER TO CONTACT THE CASTLE, BUT...
SOMETHING SEEMS DIFFERENT THIS TIME...
THAT GIRL...
...IS LIKE ME.
I USED TO HAVE...
...SOMEONE LIKE A FATHER TOO.
?!

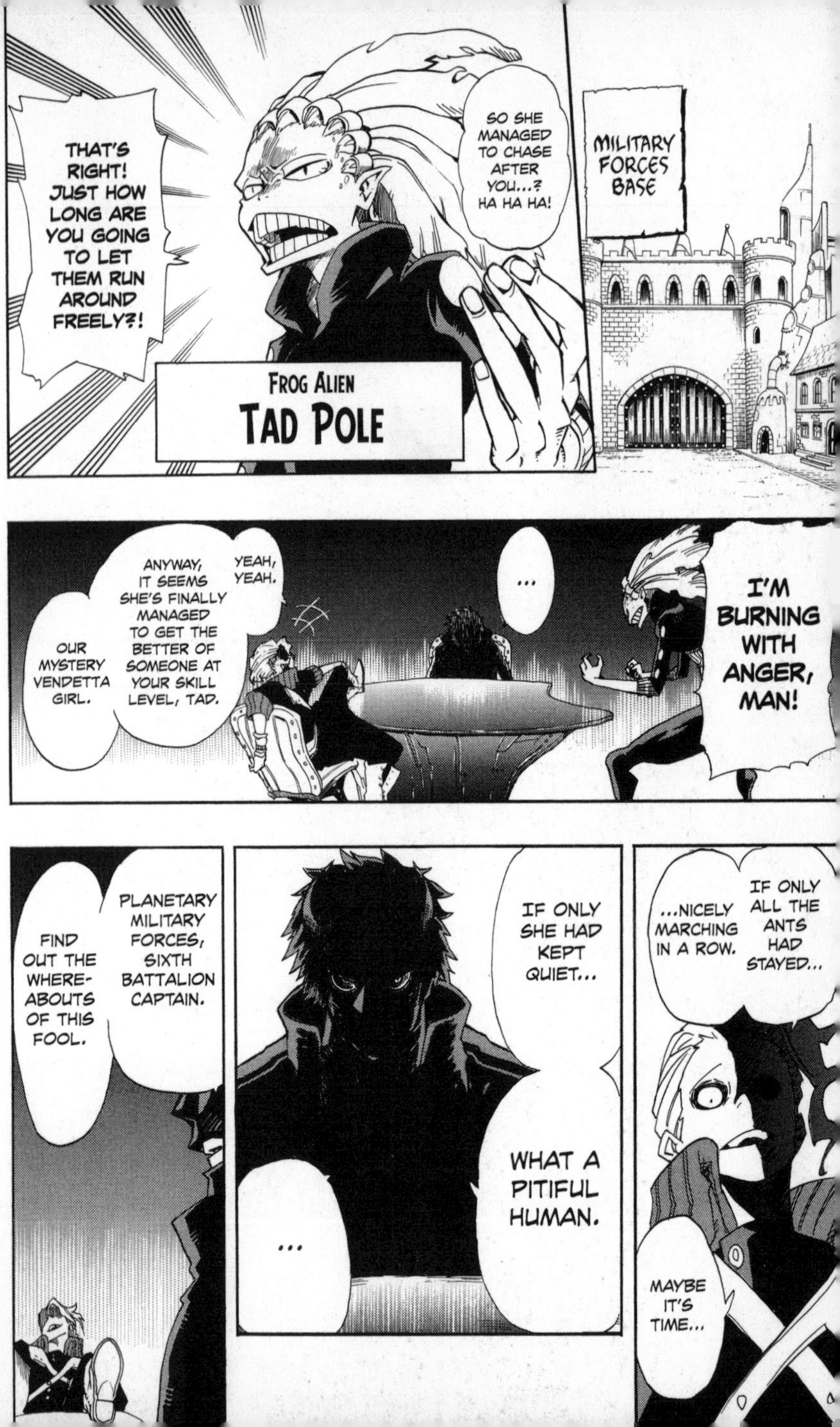
MILITARY FORCES BASE
SO SHE MANAGED TO CHASE AFTER YOU...? HA HA HA!
THAT'S RIGHT! JUST HOW LONG ARE YOU GOING TO LET THEM RUN AROUND FREELY?!
FROG ALIEN
TAD POLE
I'M BURNING WITH ANGER, MAN!
...
YEAH, YEAH.
ANYWAY, IT SEEMS SHE'S FINALLY MANAGED TO GET THE BETTER OF SOMEONE AT YOUR SKILL LEVEL, TAD.
OUR MYSTERY VENDETTA GIRL.
IF ONLY ALL THE ANTS HAD STAYED...
...NICELY MARCHING IN A ROW.
MAYBE IT'S TIME...
IF ONLY SHE HAD KEPT QUIET...
WHAT A PITIFUL HUMAN.
...
PLANETARY MILITARY FORCES, SIXTH BATTALION CAPTAIN.
FIND OUT THE WHERE-ABOUTS OF THIS FOOL.

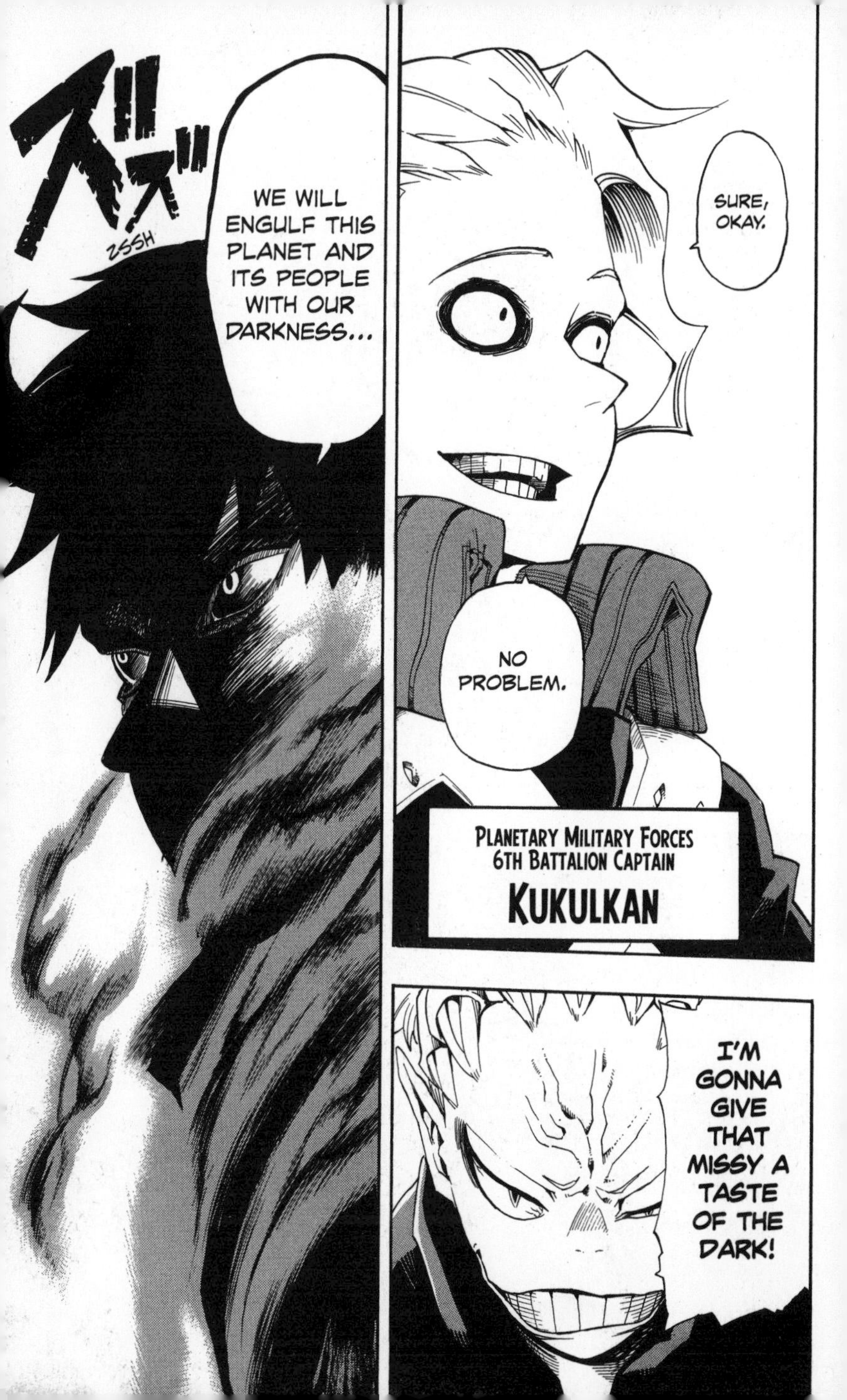

SURE, OKAY.
NO PROBLEM.
PLANETARY MILITARY FORCES 6TH BATTALION CAPTAIN
KUKULKAN
I'M GONNA GIVE THAT MISSY A TASTE OF THE DARK!
ズ!!ズ!!
ZSSH
WE WILL ENGULF THIS PLANET AND ITS PEOPLE WITH OUR DARKNESS...

TIKO

Age: 17

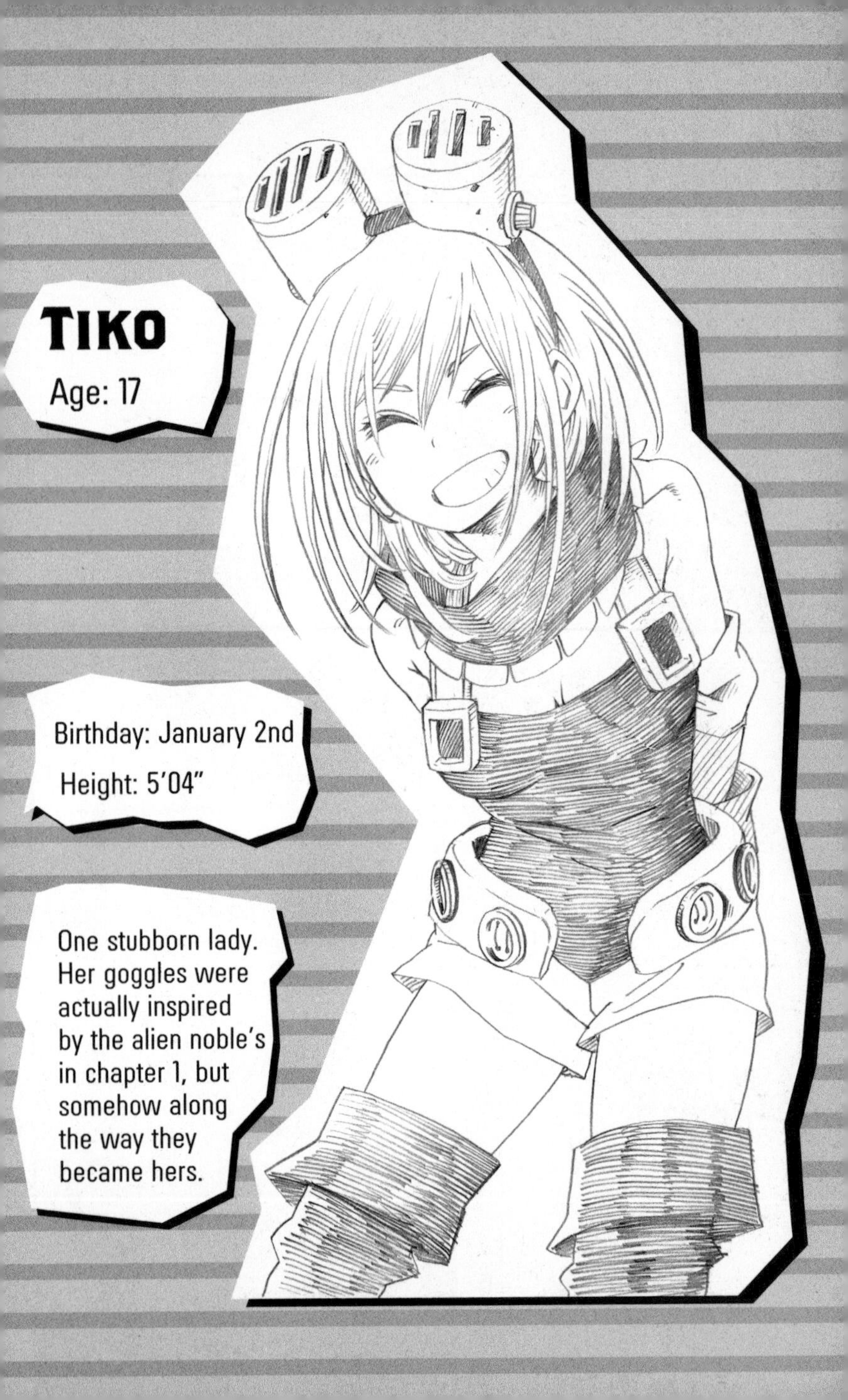

Birthday: January 2nd

Height: 5’04”

One stubborn lady. Her goggles were actually inspired by the alien noble’s in chapter 1, but somehow along the way they became hers.

Chapter 9: Astro's Past

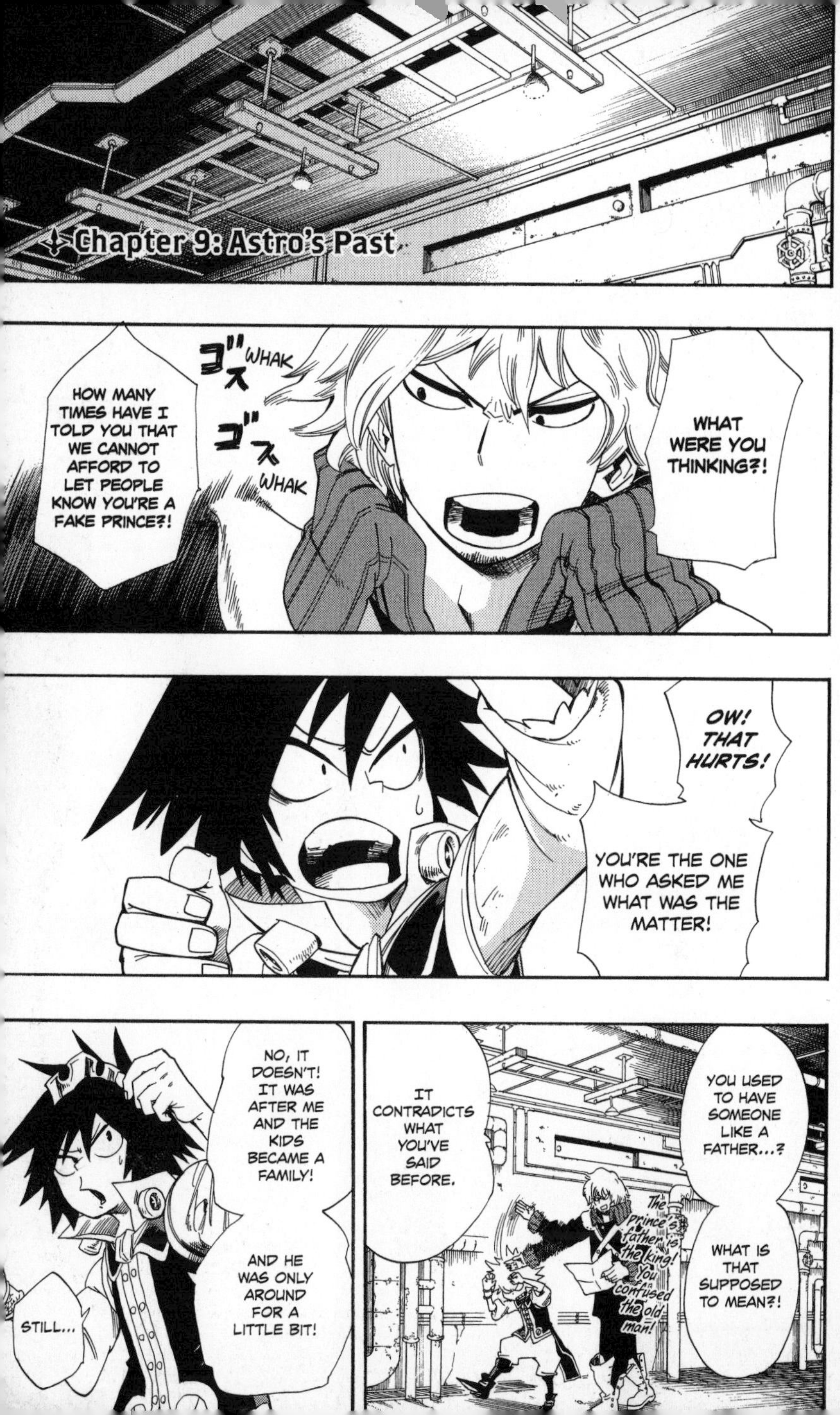
WHAT WERE YOU THINKING?!
ゴス WHAK
ゴス WHAK
HOW MANY TIMES HAVE I TOLD YOU THAT WE CANNOT AFFORD TO LET PEOPLE KNOW YOU'RE A FAKE PRINCE?!
OW! THAT HURTS!
YOU'RE THE ONE WHO ASKED ME WHAT WAS THE MATTER!
YOU USED TO HAVE SOMEONE LIKE A FATHER...?
IT CONTRADICTS WHAT YOU'VE SAID BEFORE.
WHAT IS THAT SUPPOSED TO MEAN?!
The prince's father is the king! You confused the old man!
NO, IT DOESN'T! IT WAS AFTER ME AND THE KIDS BECAME A FAMILY!
AND HE WAS ONLY AROUND FOR A LITTLE BIT!
STILL...

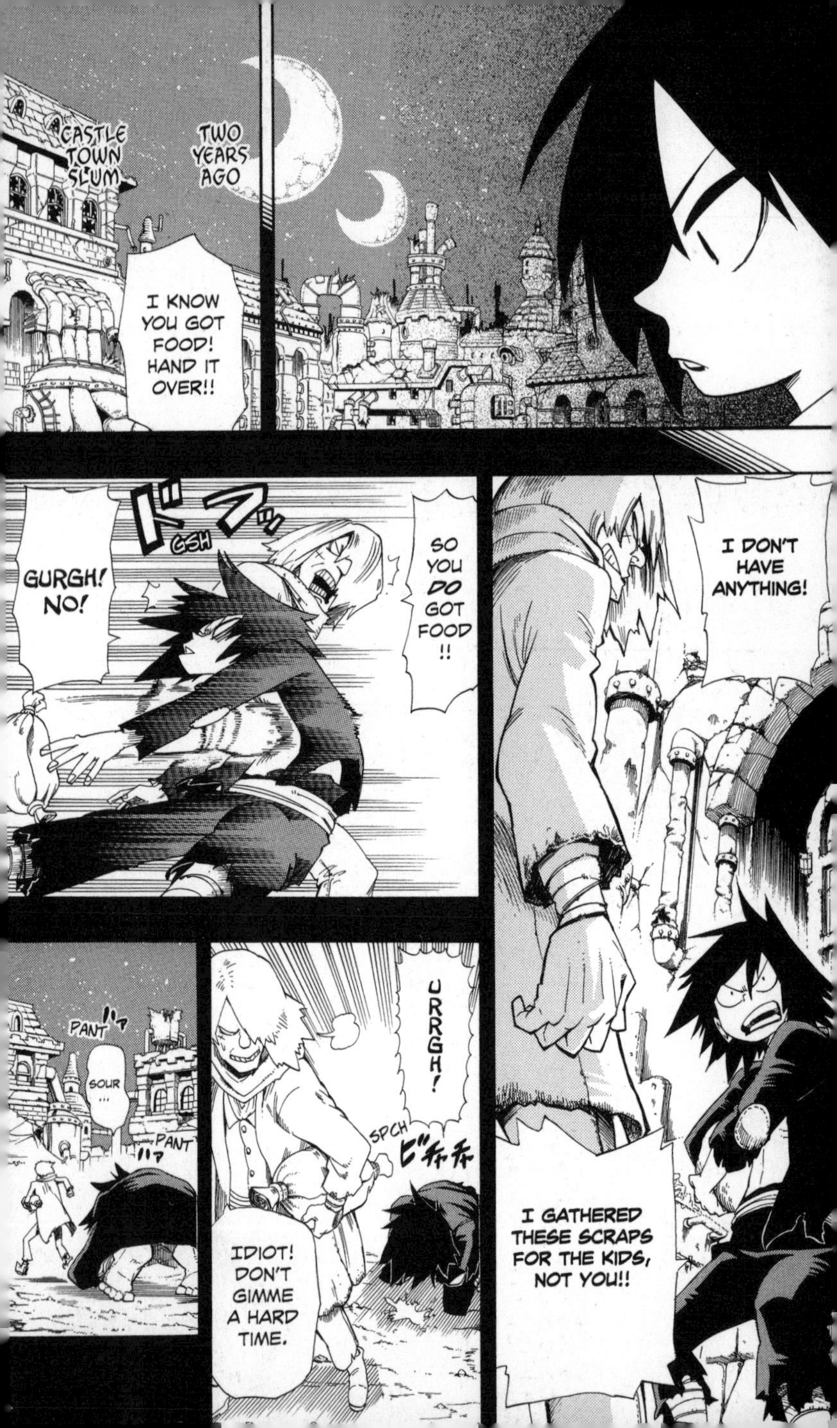
TWO YEARS AGO
CASTLE TOWN SLUM
I KNOW YOU GOT FOOD! HAND IT OVER!!
I DON'T HAVE ANYTHING!
I GATHERED THESE SCRAPS FOR THE KIDS, NOT YOU!!
SO YOU DO GOT FOOD!!
GSH
GURGH! NO!
URRGH!
SPCH
IDIOT! DON'T GIMME A HARD TIME.
PANT
SOUR ...
PANT

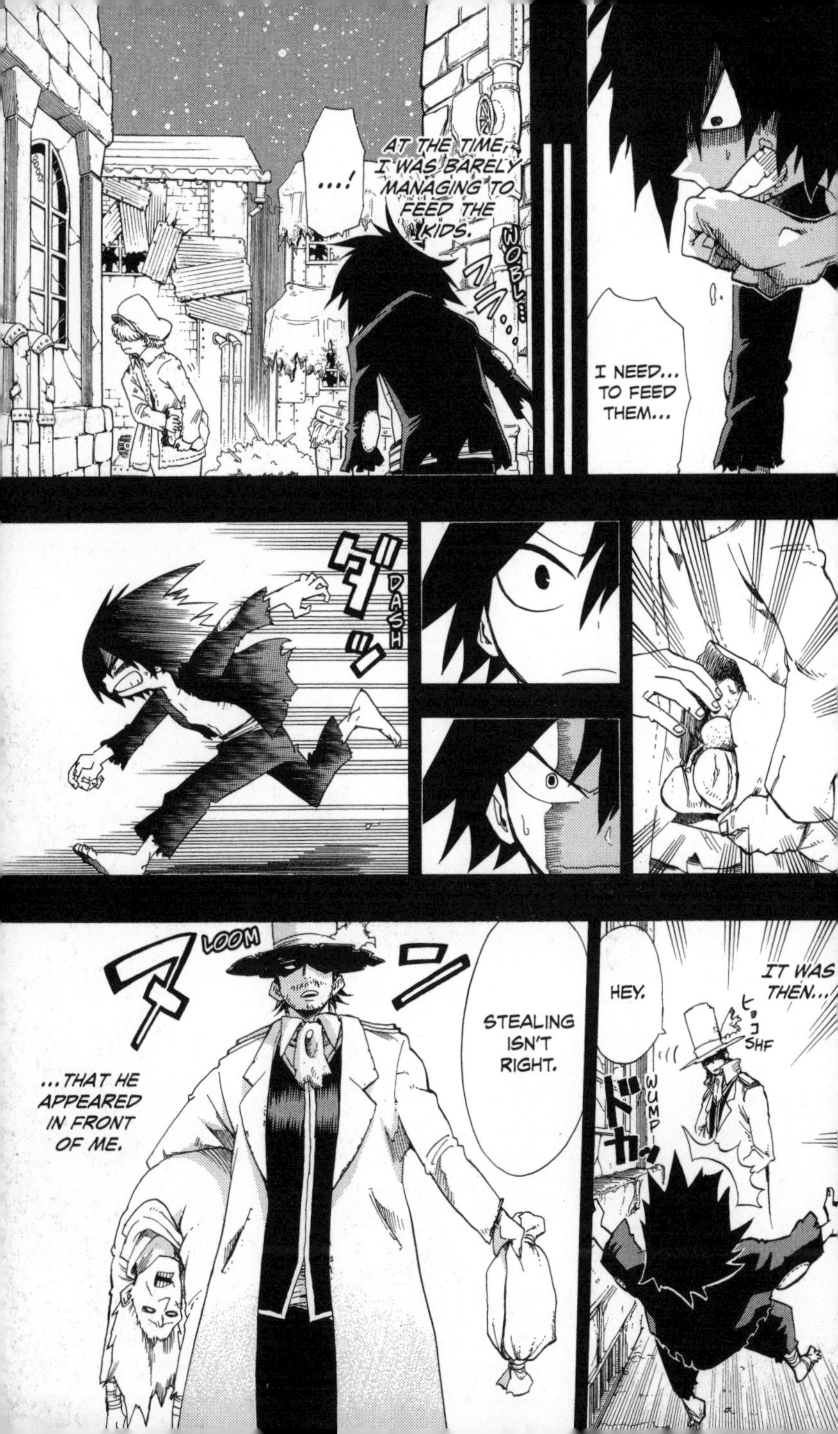

I NEED... TO FEED THEM...
AT THE TIME, I WAS BARELY MANAGING TO FEED THE KIDS.
...!
WOBL...
DASH
IT WAS THEN...
HEY.
SHF
WUMP
STEALING ISN'T RIGHT.
LOOM
...THAT HE APPEARED IN FRONT OF ME.

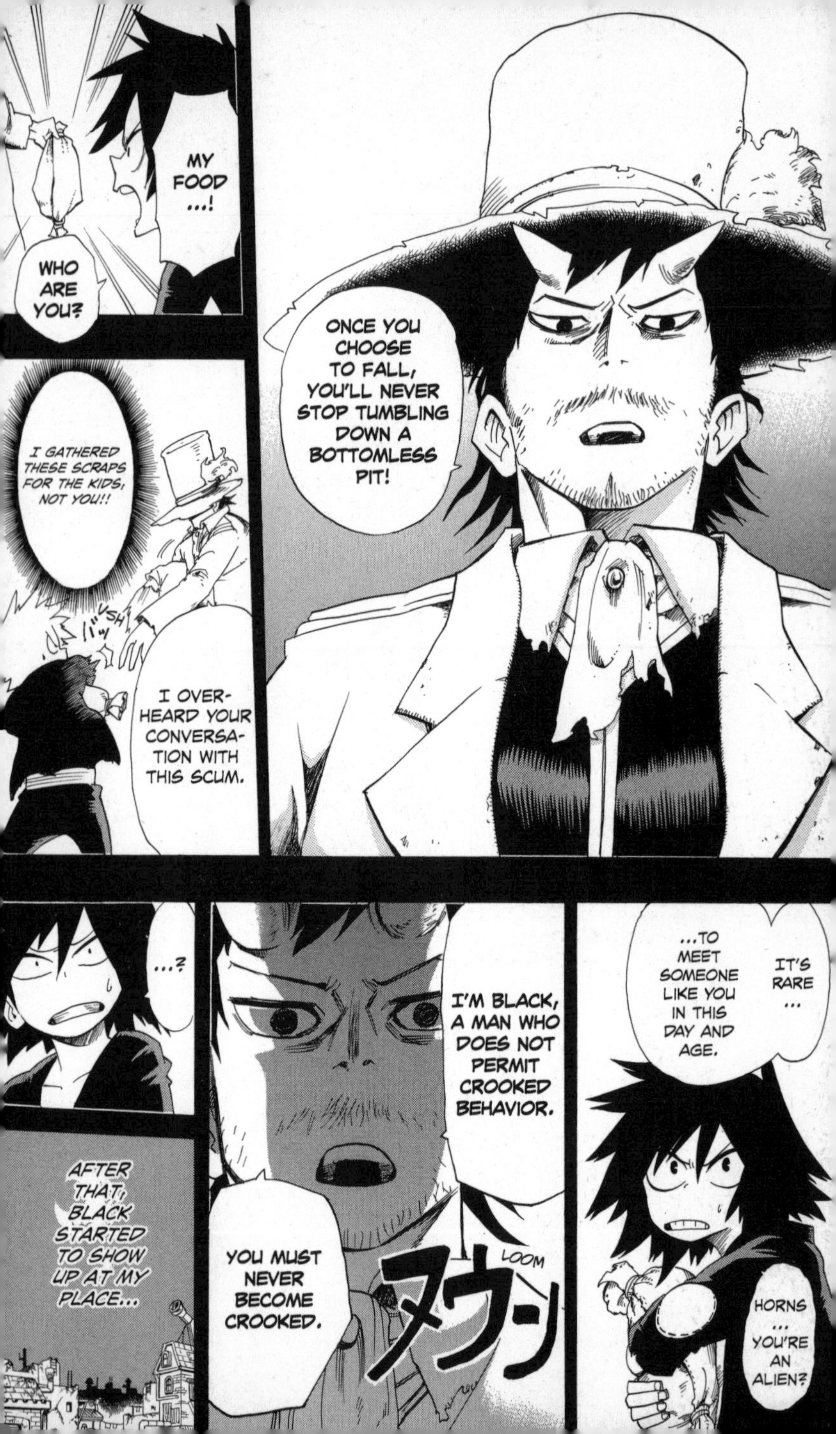

ONCE YOU CHOOSE TO FALL, YOU'LL NEVER STOP TUMBLING DOWN A BOTTOMLESS PIT!
MY FOOD ...!
WHO ARE YOU?
I GATHERED THESE SCRAPS FOR THE KIDS, NOT YOU!!
バッ VSH
I OVER-HEARD YOUR CONVERSA-TION WITH THIS SCUM.
IT'S RARE ...
...TO MEET SOMEONE LIKE YOU IN THIS DAY AND AGE.
HORNS ... YOU'RE AN ALIEN?
I'M BLACK, A MAN WHO DOES NOT PERMIT CROOKED BEHAVIOR.
YOU MUST NEVER BECOME CROOKED.
ヌウーッ LOOM
...?
AFTER THAT, BLACK STARTED TO SHOW UP AT MY PLACE...

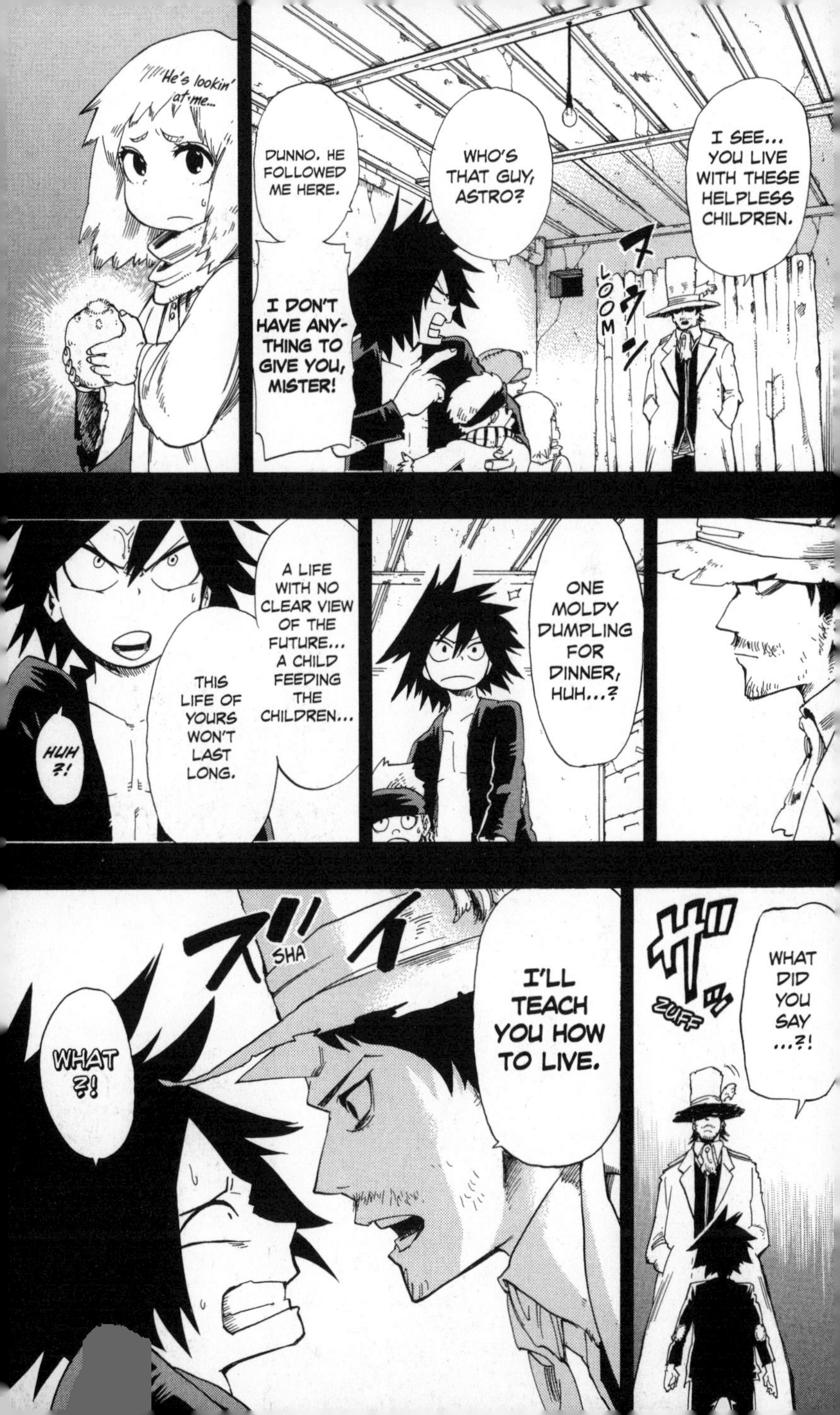
I SEE... YOU LIVE WITH THESE HELPLESS CHILDREN.
LOOM
WHO'S THAT GUY, ASTRO?
DUNNO. HE FOLLOWED ME HERE.
I DON'T HAVE ANY-THING TO GIVE YOU, MISTER!
He's lookin' at me...
ONE MOLDY DUMPLING FOR DINNER, HUH...?
A LIFE WITH NO CLEAR VIEW OF THE FUTURE... A CHILD FEEDING THE CHILDREN...
THIS LIFE OF YOURS WON'T LAST LONG.
HUH?!
ZUFF
WHAT DID YOU SAY...?!
SHA
I'LL TEACH YOU HOW TO LIVE.
WHAT?!

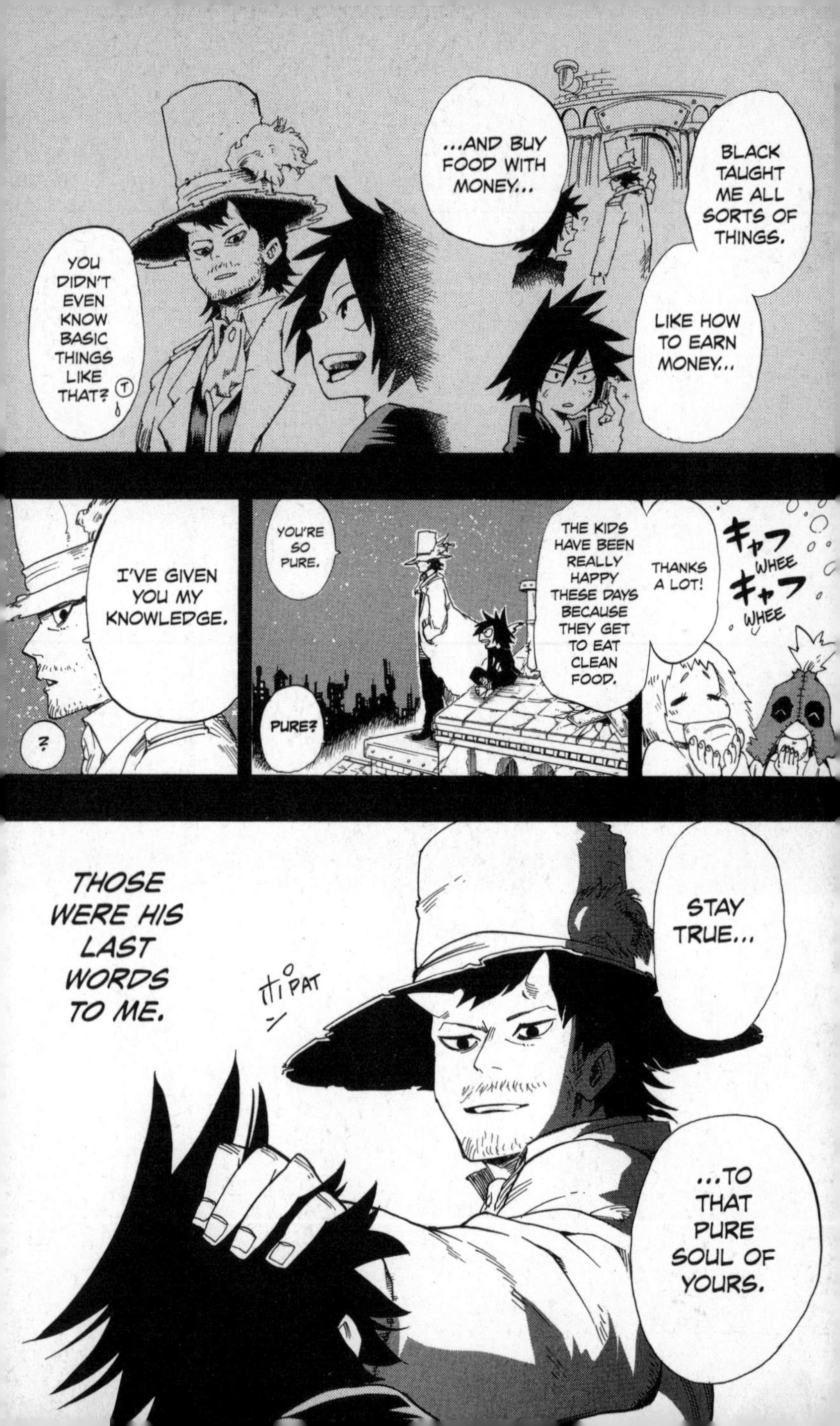
BLACK TAUGHT ME ALL SORTS OF THINGS.
LIKE HOW TO EARN MONEY...
...AND BUY FOOD WITH MONEY...
YOU DIDN'T EVEN KNOW BASIC THINGS LIKE THAT?
キャフ WHEE キャフ WHEE
THANKS A LOT!
THE KIDS HAVE BEEN REALLY HAPPY THESE DAYS BECAUSE THEY GET TO EAT CLEAN FOOD.
YOU'RE SO PURE.
PURE?
I'VE GIVEN YOU MY KNOWLEDGE.
?
STAY TRUE...
...TO THAT PURE SOUL OF YOURS.
PAT
THOSE WERE HIS LAST WORDS TO ME.

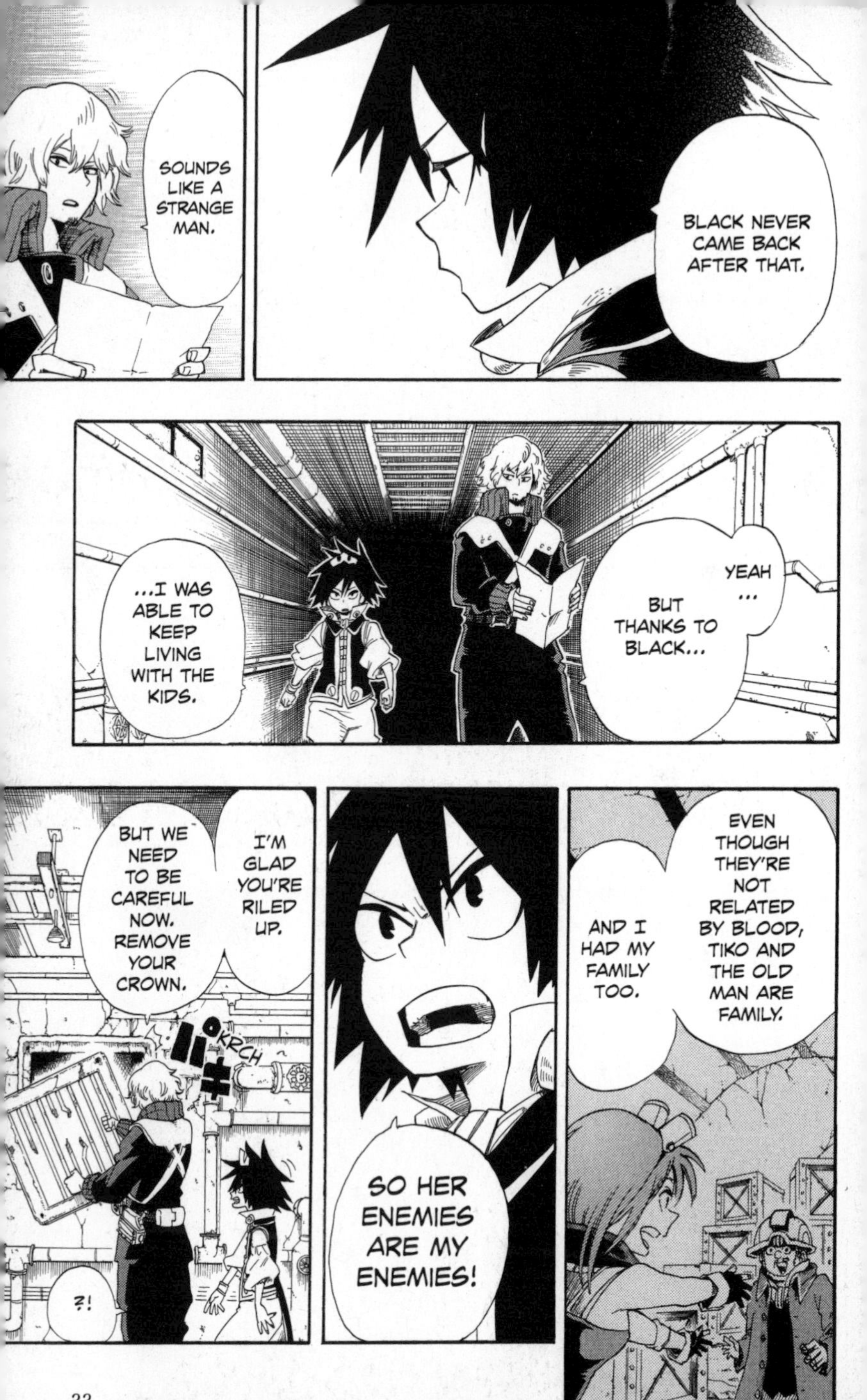
BLACK NEVER CAME BACK AFTER THAT.
SOUNDS LIKE A STRANGE MAN.
YEAH...
BUT THANKS TO BLACK...
...I WAS ABLE TO KEEP LIVING WITH THE KIDS.
EVEN THOUGH THEY'RE NOT RELATED BY BLOOD, TIKO AND THE OLD MAN ARE FAMILY.
AND I HAD MY FAMILY TOO.
SO HER ENEMIES ARE MY ENEMIES!
I'M GLAD YOU'RE RILED UP.
BUT WE NEED TO BE CAREFUL NOW. REMOVE YOUR CROWN.
KRCH
?!

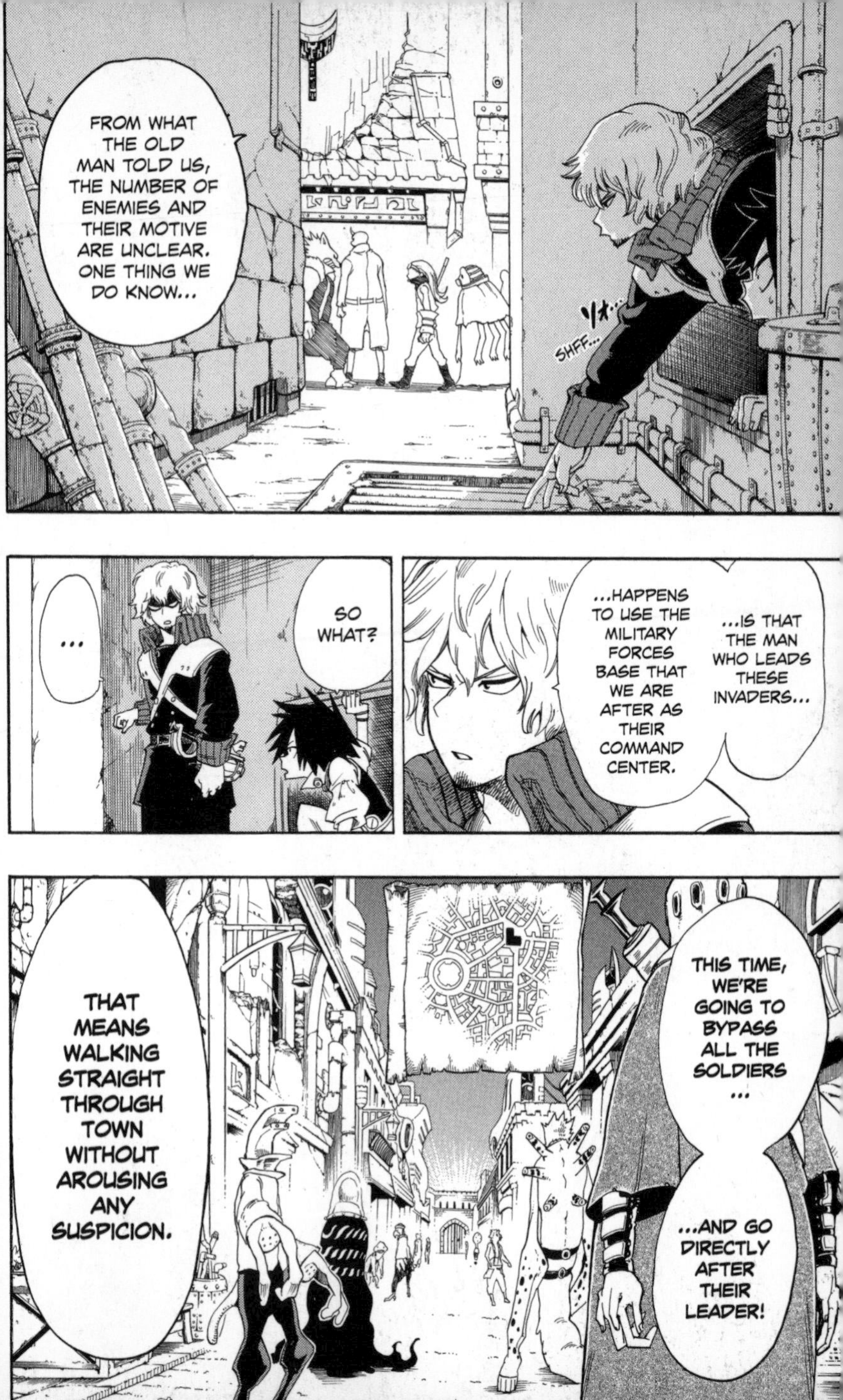
FROM WHAT THE OLD MAN TOLD US, THE NUMBER OF ENEMIES AND THEIR MOTIVE ARE UNCLEAR. ONE THING WE DO KNOW...
ソォ…
SHFF...
...IS THAT THE MAN WHO LEADS THESE INVADERS...
...HAPPENS TO USE THE MILITARY FORCES BASE THAT WE ARE AFTER AS THEIR COMMAND CENTER.
SO WHAT?
...
THIS TIME, WE'RE GOING TO BYPASS ALL THE SOLDIERS ...
...AND GO DIRECTLY AFTER THEIR LEADER!
THAT MEANS WALKING STRAIGHT THROUGH TOWN WITHOUT AROUSING ANY SUSPICION.

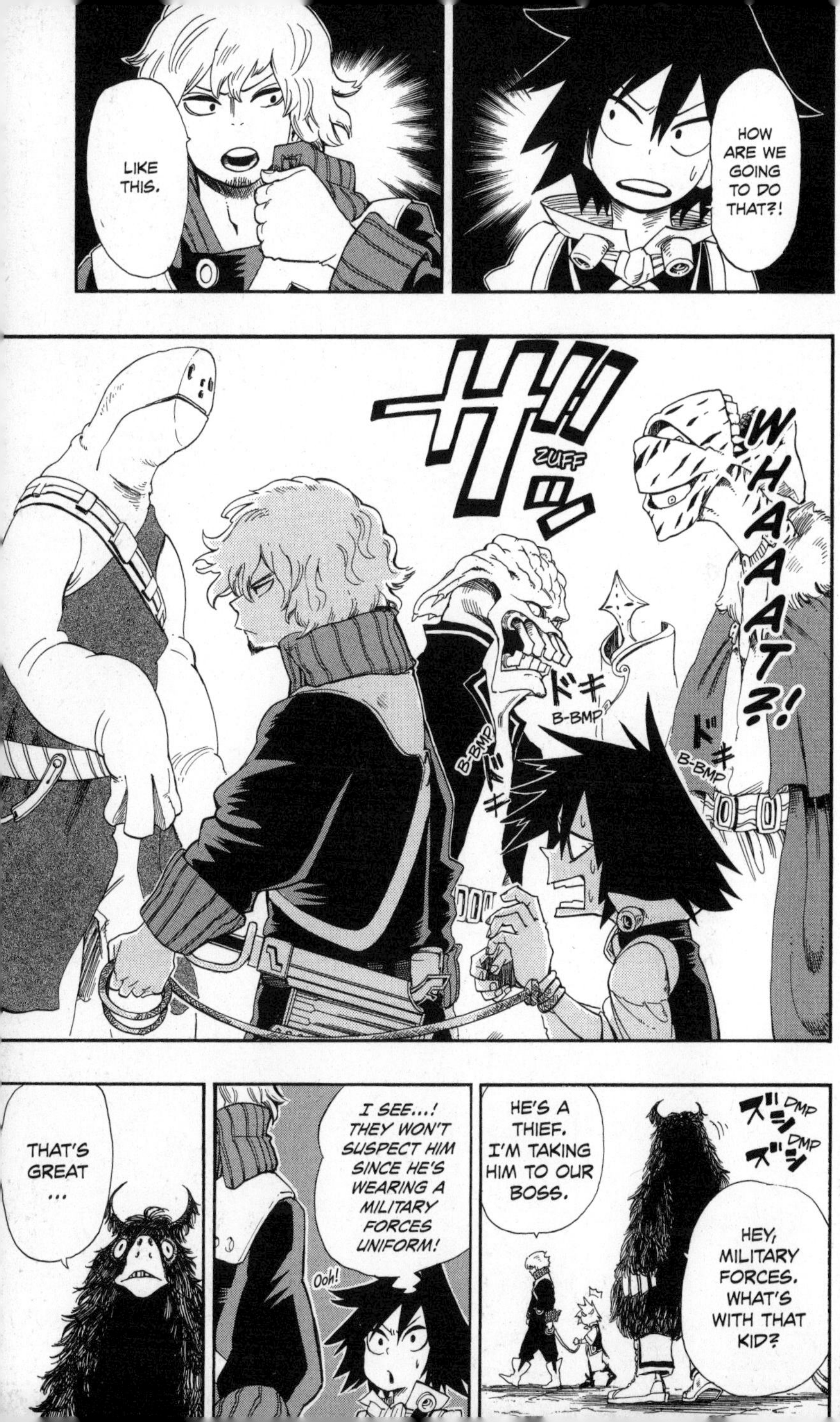
HOW ARE WE GOING TO DO THAT?!
LIKE THIS.
ザッ
ZUFF
WHAAAAT?!
ドキ
B-BMP
ドキ
B-BMP
ドキ
B-BMP
ズシ
DMP
ズシ
DMP
HEY, MILITARY FORCES. WHAT'S WITH THAT KID?
HE'S A THIEF. I'M TAKING HIM TO OUR BOSS.
I SEE...! THEY WON'T SUSPECT HIM SINCE HE'S WEARING A MILITARY FORCES UNIFORM!
Ooh!
THAT'S GREAT ...

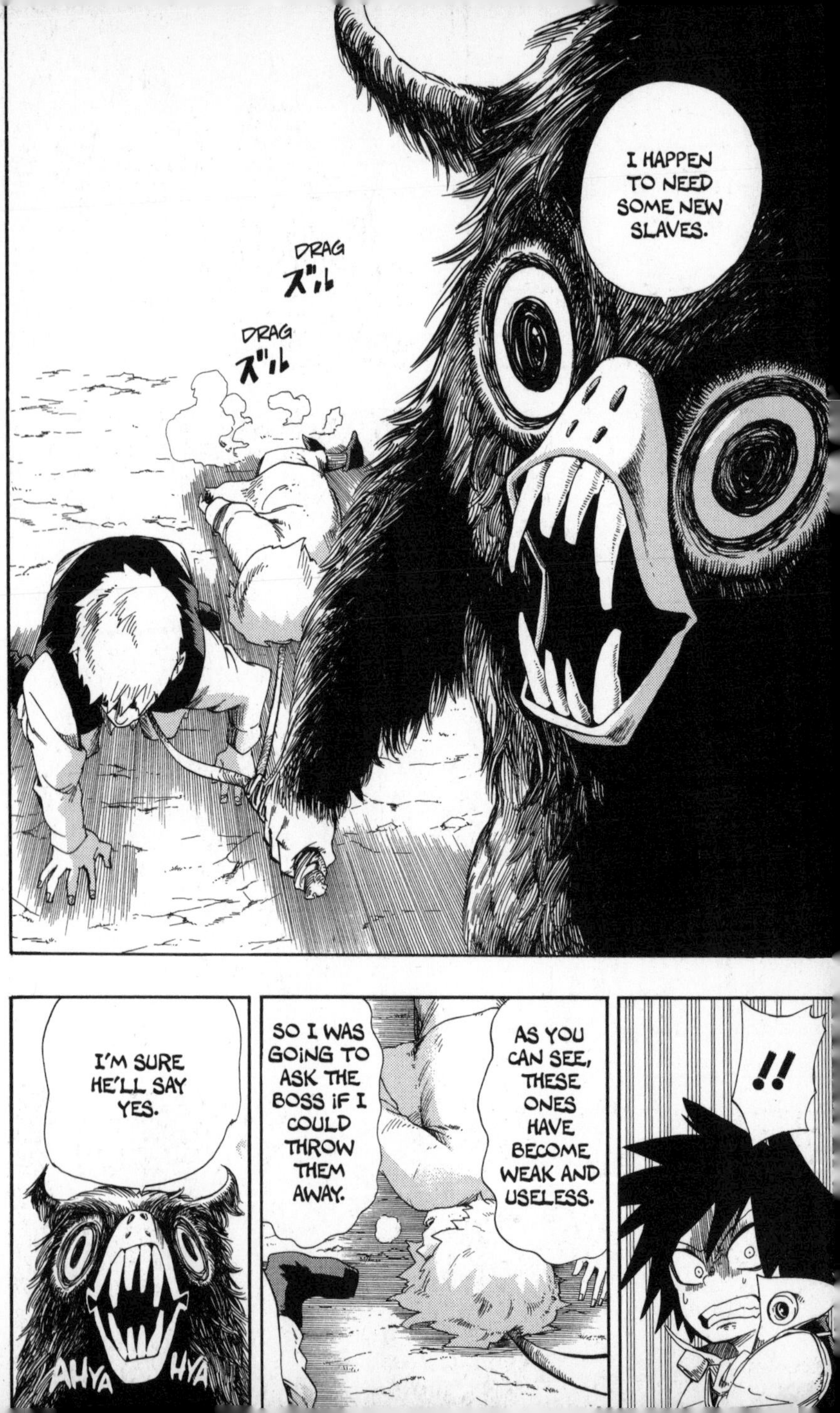
I HAPPEN TO NEED SOME NEW SLAVES.
DRAG ズル
DRAG ズル
!!
AS YOU CAN SEE, THESE ONES HAVE BECOME WEAK AND USELESS.
SO I WAS GOING TO ASK THE BOSS IF I COULD THROW THEM AWAY.
I'M SURE HE'LL SAY YES.
AHYA HYA

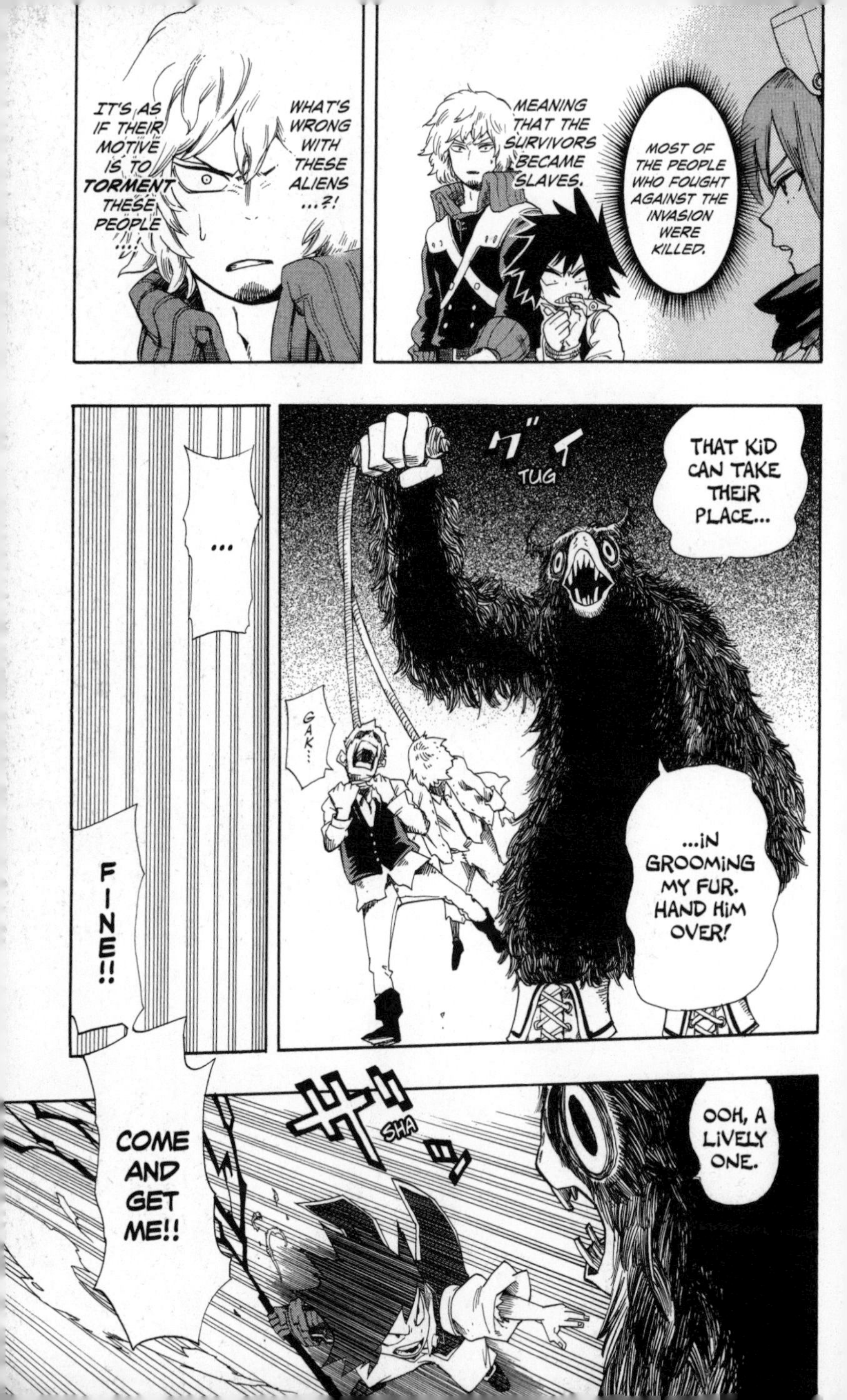
MOST OF THE PEOPLE WHO FOUGHT AGAINST THE INVASION WERE KILLED.
MEANING THAT THE SURVIVORS BECAME SLAVES.
WHAT'S WRONG WITH THESE ALIENS ...?!
IT'S AS IF THEIR MOTIVE IS TO TORMENT THESE PEOPLE ...!
グイ
TUG
THAT KID CAN TAKE THEIR PLACE...
GAK...
...IN GROOMING MY FUR. HAND HIM OVER!
...
FINE!!
OOH, A LIVELY ONE.
シャッ
SHA
COME AND GET ME!!

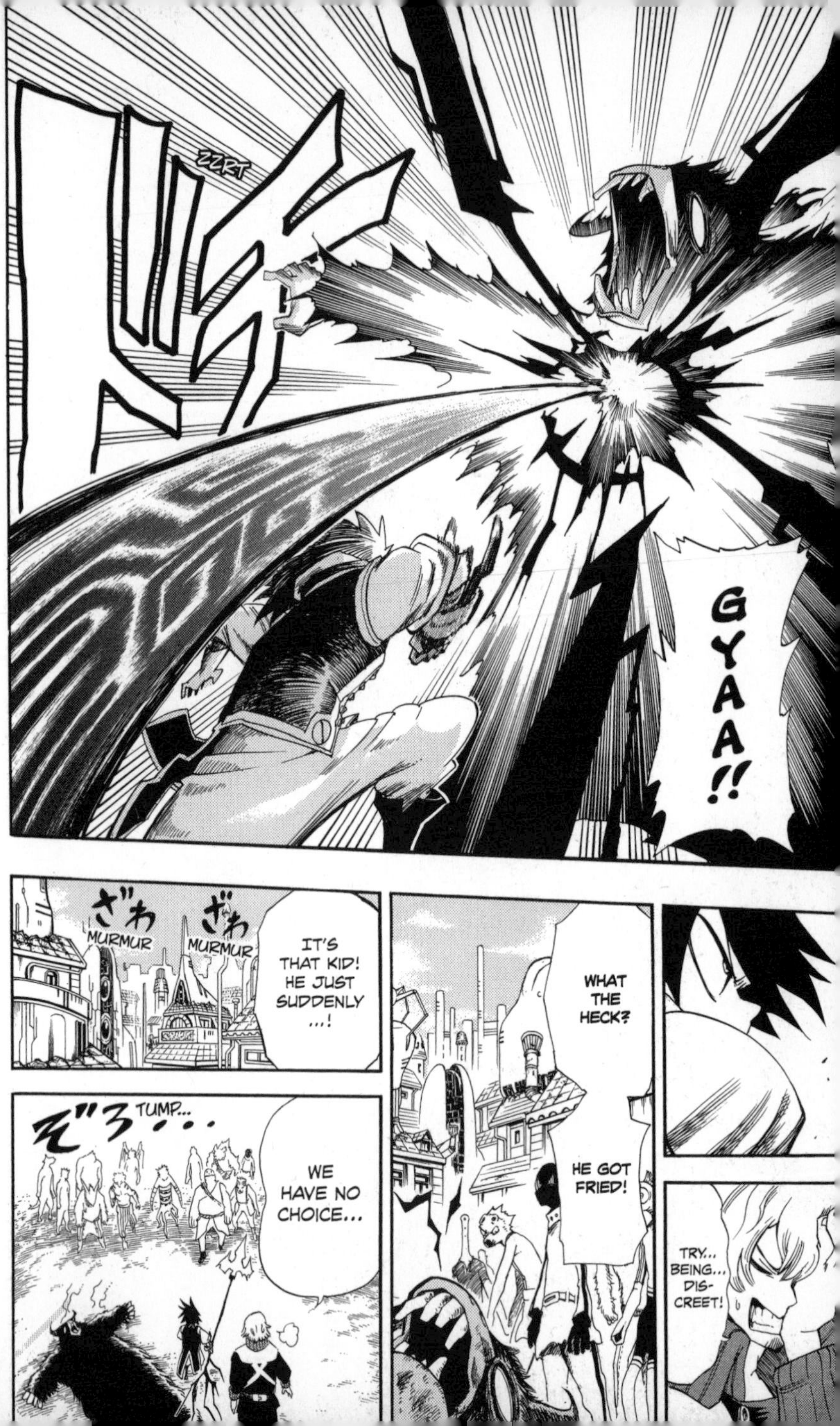
ZZRT
GYAA!!
TRY... BEING... DIS-CREET!
WHAT THE HECK?
HE GOT FRIED!
ざわ MURMUR
ざわ MURMUR
IT'S THAT KID! HE JUST SUDDENLY ...!
ぞろ TUMP...
WE HAVE NO CHOICE...

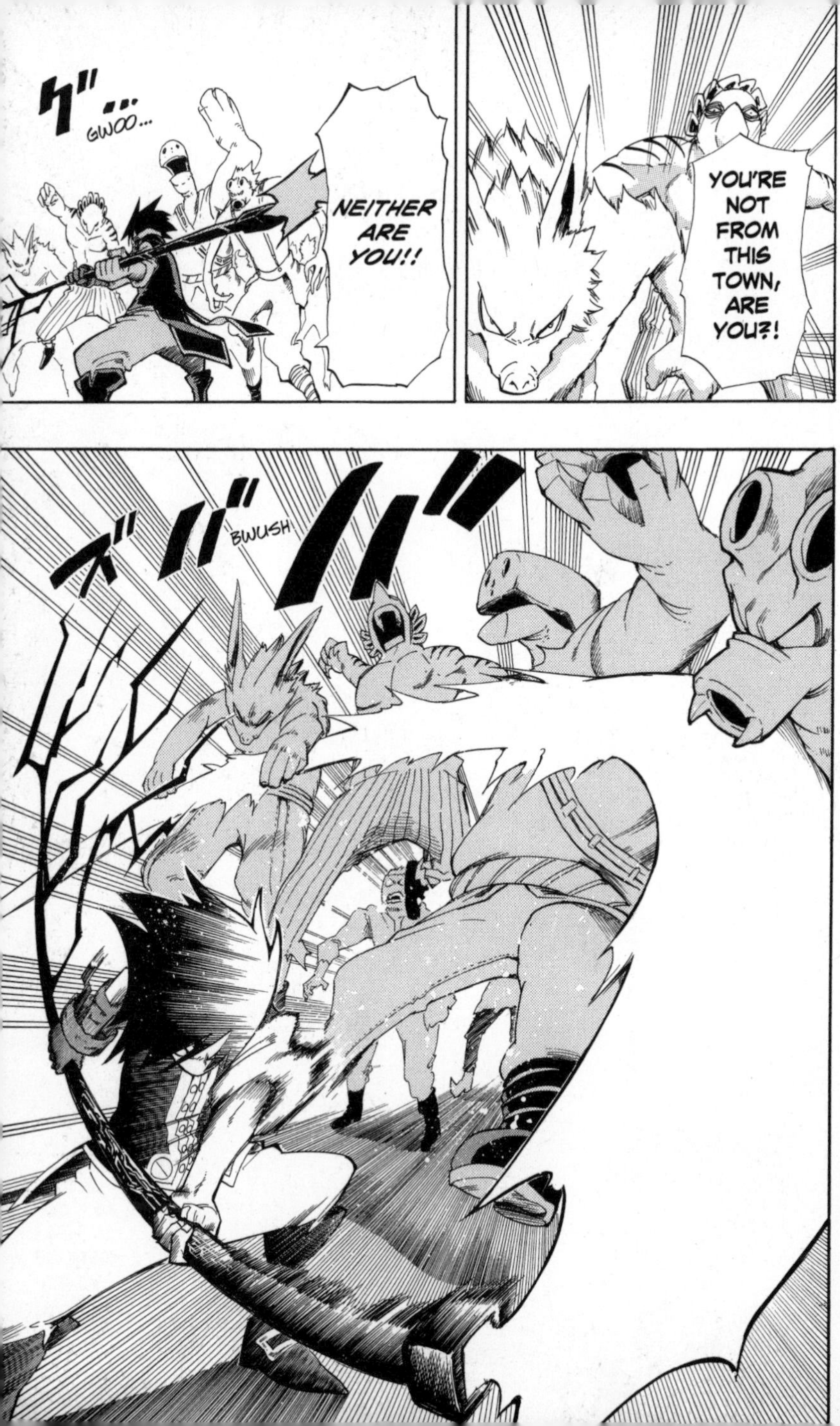
YOU'RE NOT FROM THIS TOWN, ARE YOU?!
グ…
GWOO...
NEITHER ARE YOU!!
ズバ
BWUSH

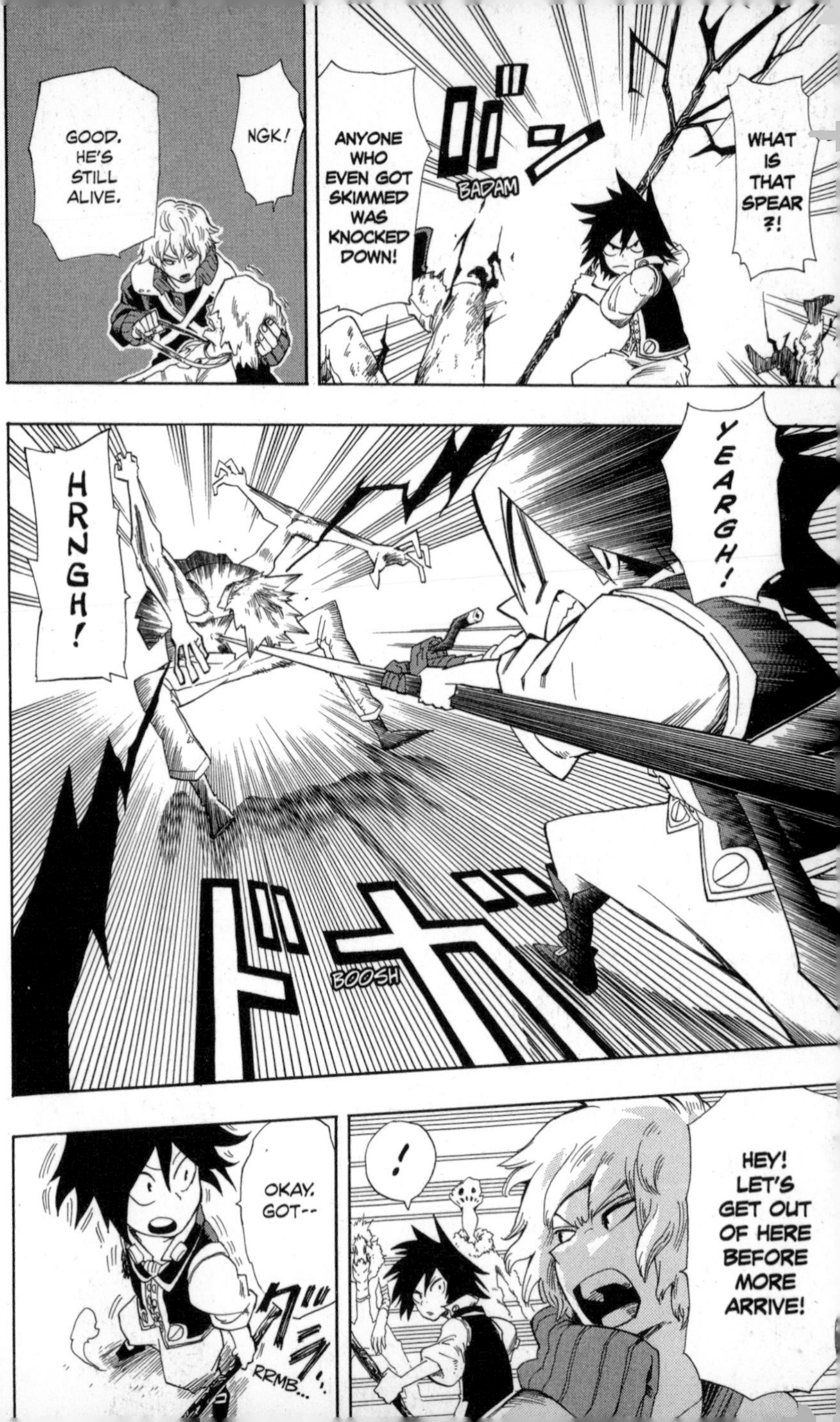
WHAT IS THAT SPEAR?!
ANYONE WHO EVEN GOT SKIMMED WAS KNOCKED DOWN!
BADAM
NGK!
GOOD. HE'S STILL ALIVE.
YEARGH!
HRNGH!
BOOSH
HEY! LET'S GET OUT OF HERE BEFORE MORE ARRIVE!
!
OKAY. GOT--
RRMB...

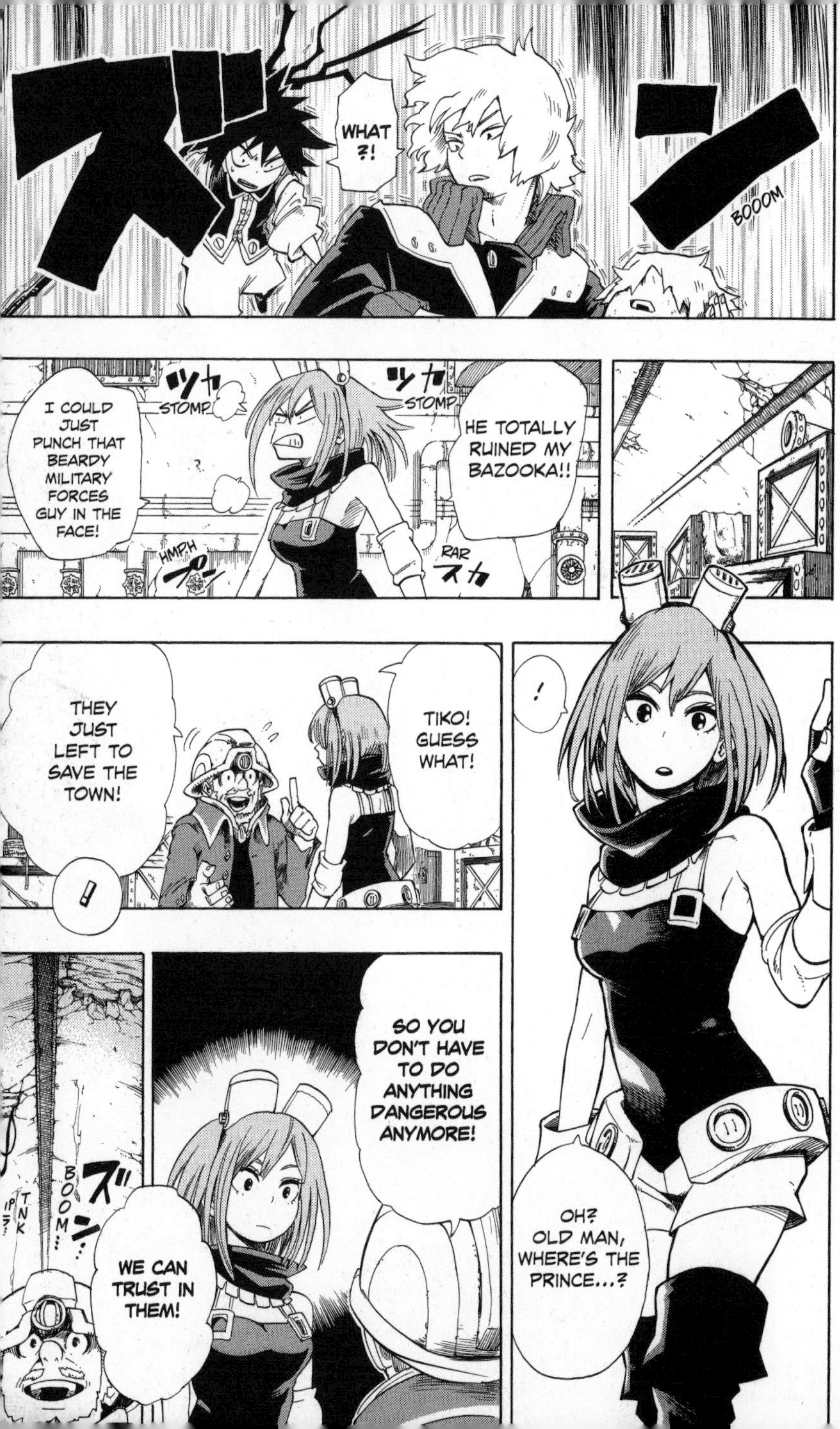
WHAT?!
BOOOM
HE TOTALLY RUINED MY BAZOOKA!!
STOMP
STOMP
I COULD JUST PUNCH THAT BEARDY MILITARY FORCES GUY IN THE FACE!
RAR
HMPH
!
OH? OLD MAN, WHERE'S THE PRINCE...?
TIKO! GUESS WHAT!
THEY JUST LEFT TO SAVE THE TOWN!
!
SO YOU DON'T HAVE TO DO ANYTHING DANGEROUS ANYMORE!
BOOOM...
TNK
WE CAN TRUST IN THEM!

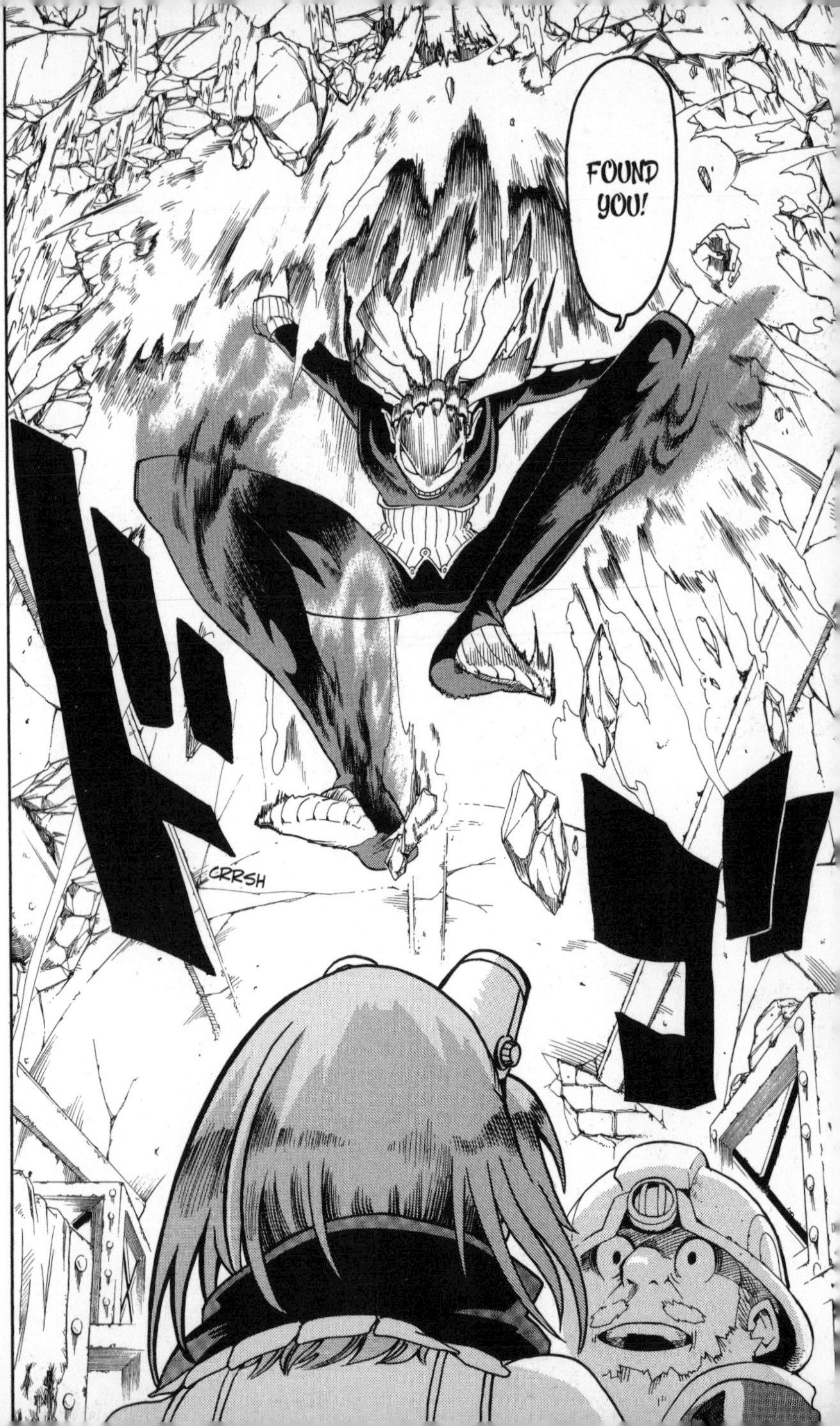
FOUND YOU!
CRRSH

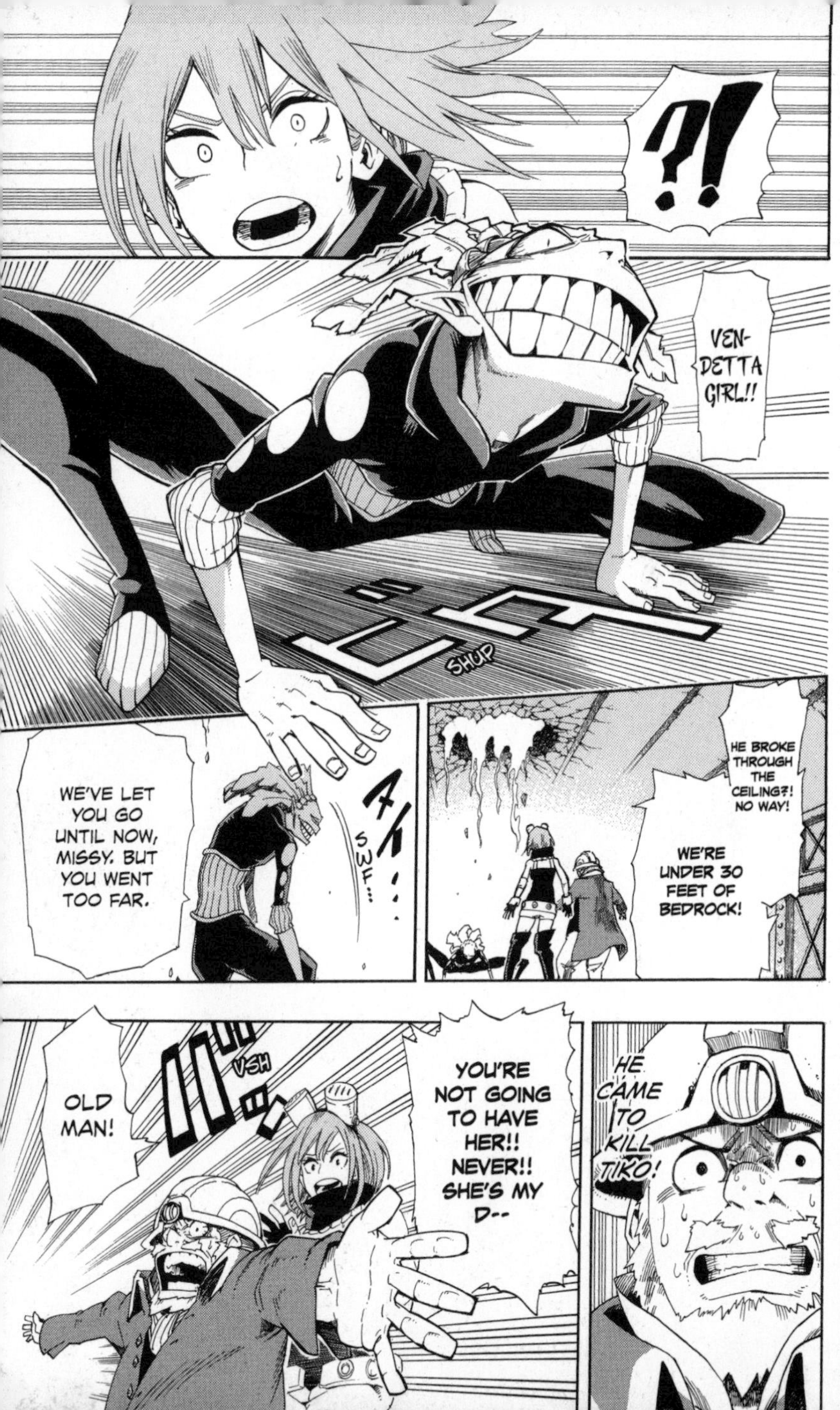
?!
VEN-DETTA GIRL!!
SHUP
HE BROKE THROUGH THE CEILING?! NO WAY!
WE'RE UNDER 30 FEET OF BEDROCK!
SWF...
WE'VE LET YOU GO UNTIL NOW, MISSY. BUT YOU WENT TOO FAR.
HE CAME TO KILL TIKO!
YOU'RE NOT GOING TO HAVE HER!! NEVER!! SHE'S MY D--
VSH
OLD MAN!

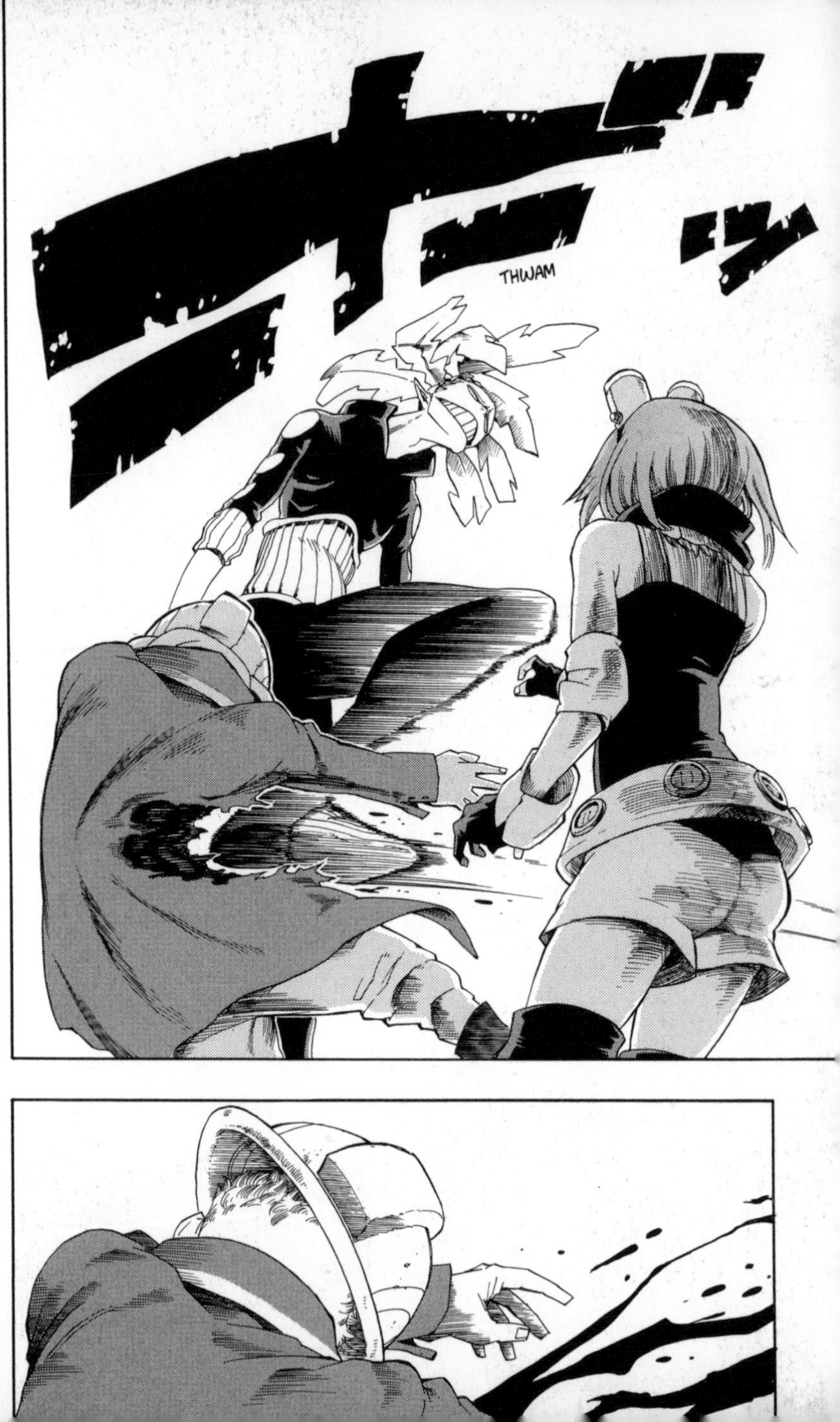
THWAM

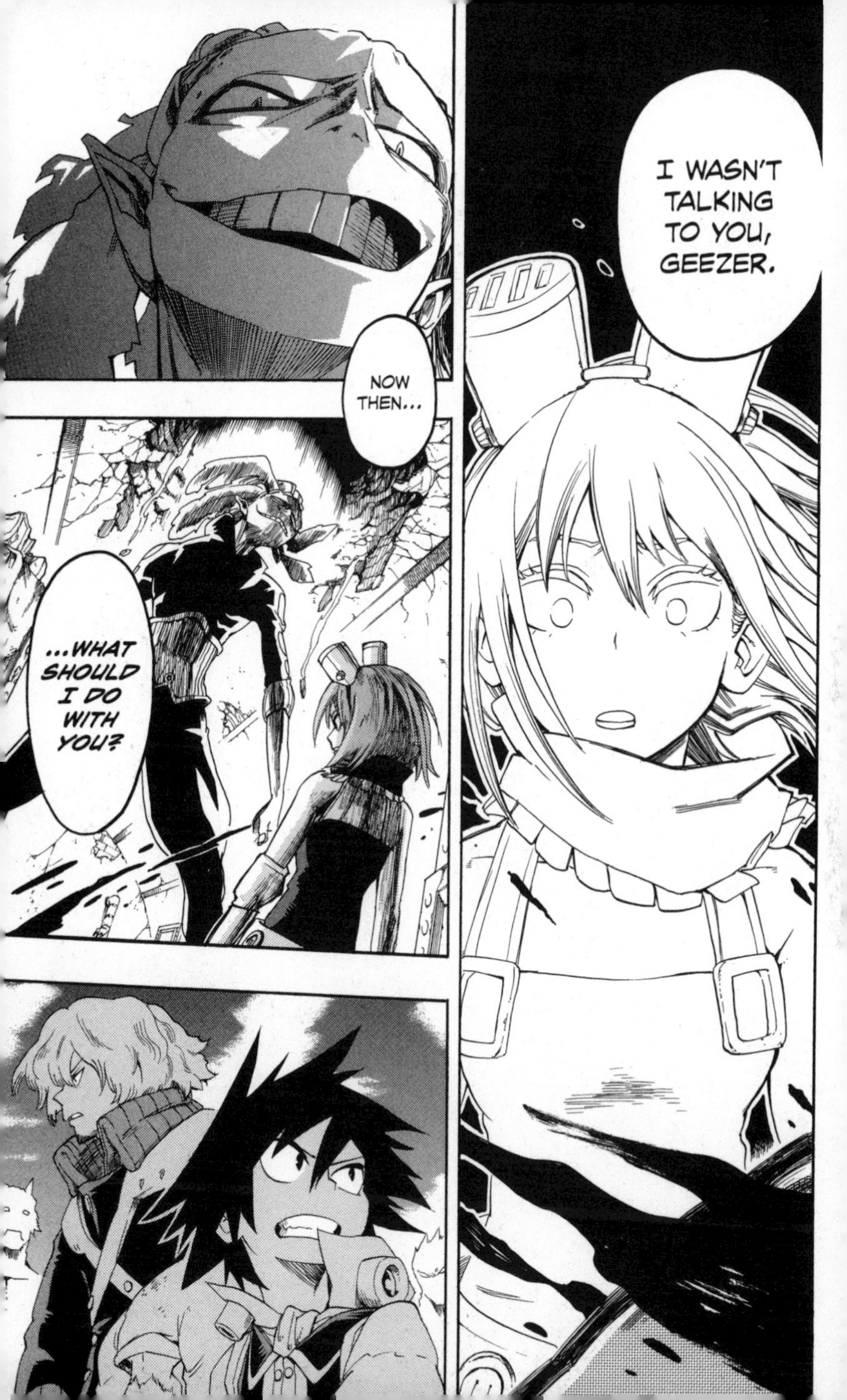
I WASN'T TALKING TO YOU, GEEZER.
NOW THEN...
...WHAT SHOULD I DO WITH YOU?

Totally Unrelated Illustration Corner

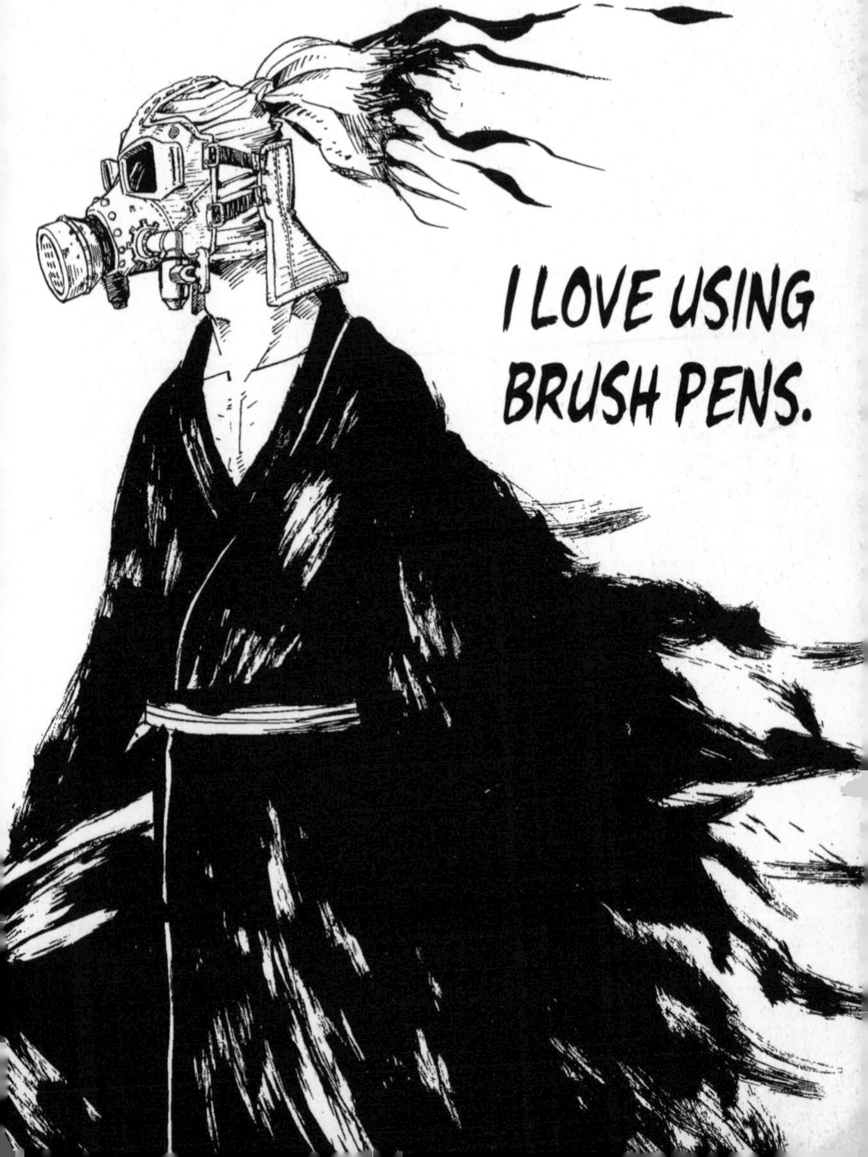
I LOVE USING BRUSH PENS.

Chapter 10: Dark Energy

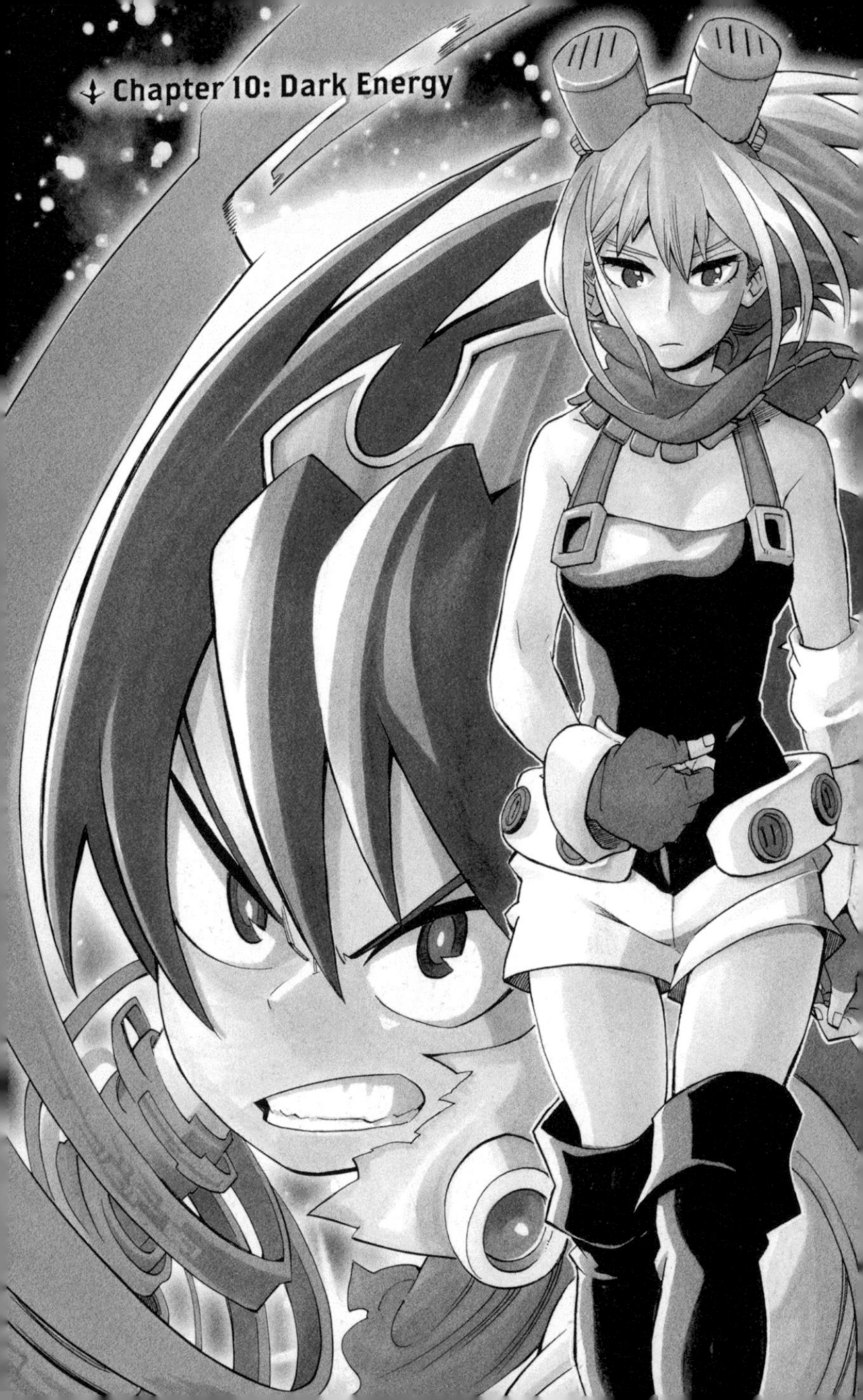

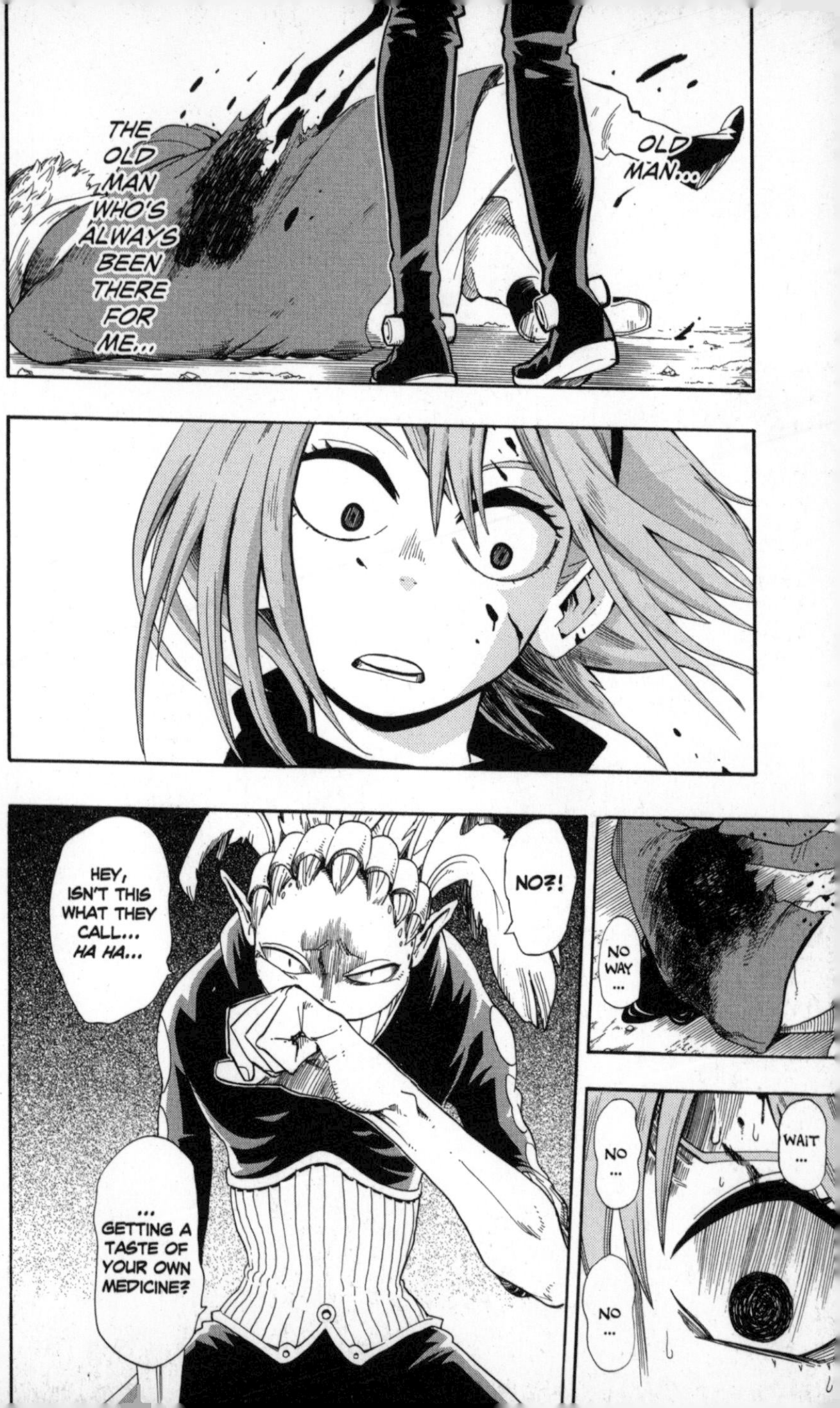
OLD MAN...
THE OLD MAN WHO'S ALWAYS BEEN THERE FOR ME...
NO WAY ...
WAIT ...
NO ...
NO ...
NO?!
HEY, ISN'T THIS WHAT THEY CALL... HA HA...
... GETTING A TASTE OF YOUR OWN MEDICINE?

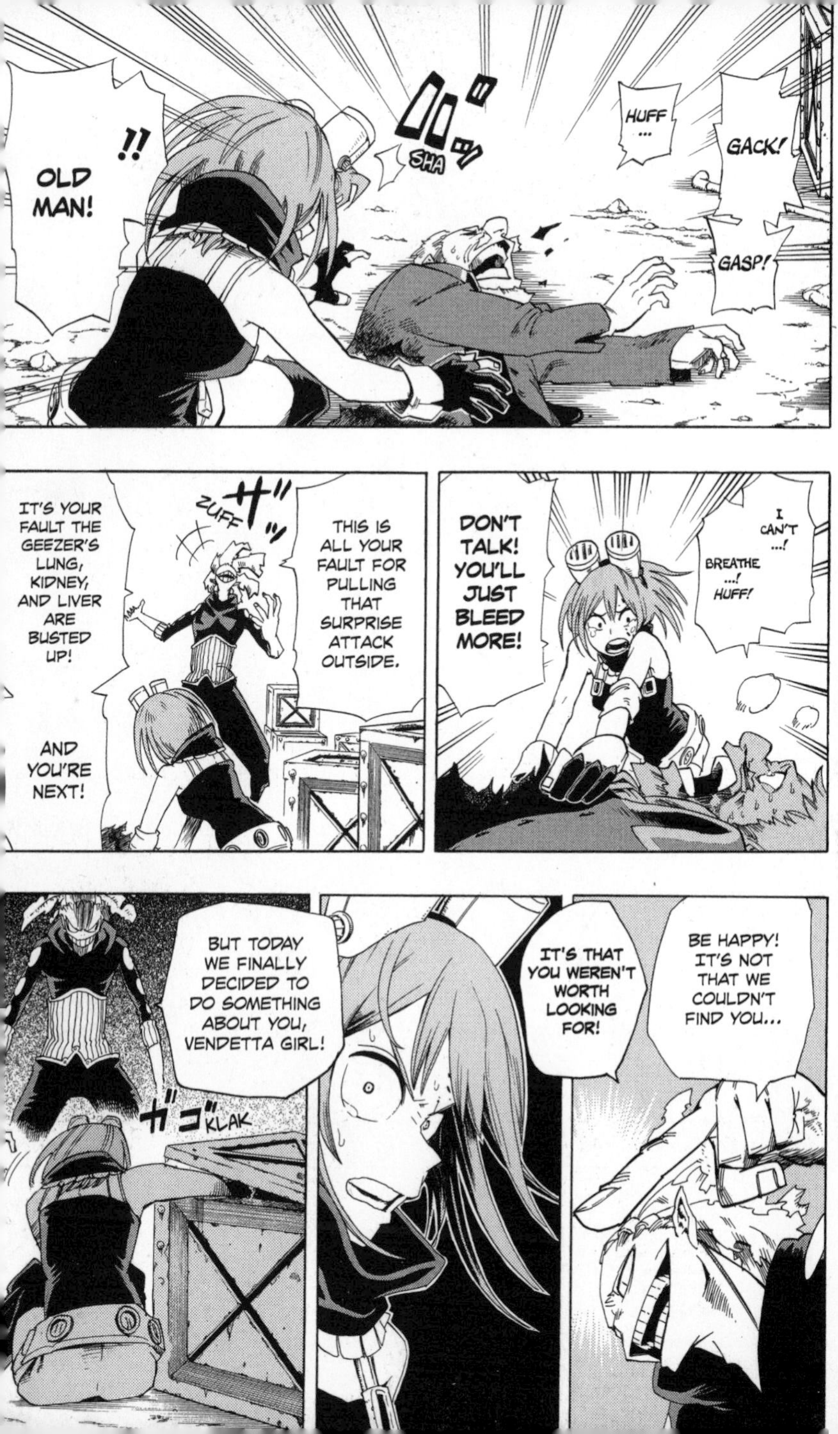
HUFF ...
GACK!
GASP!
SHA
!!
OLD MAN!
I CAN'T ...! BREATHE ...! HUFF!
DON'T TALK! YOU'LL JUST BLEED MORE!
THIS IS ALL YOUR FAULT FOR PULLING THAT SURPRISE ATTACK OUTSIDE.
ZUFF
IT'S YOUR FAULT THE GEEZER'S LUNG, KIDNEY, AND LIVER ARE BUSTED UP!
AND YOU'RE NEXT!
BE HAPPY! IT'S NOT THAT WE COULDN'T FIND YOU...
IT'S THAT YOU WEREN'T WORTH LOOKING FOR!
BUT TODAY WE FINALLY DECIDED TO DO SOMETHING ABOUT YOU, VENDETTA GIRL!
KLAK

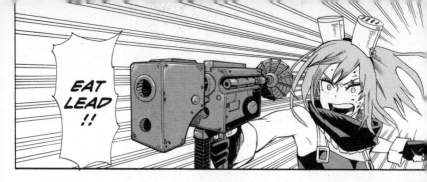

EAT LEAD !!

BOOSH **BLAM**

I'M STILL TALKIN' TO YOU!!

THE BULLET ....!!

FSSSH...

?!

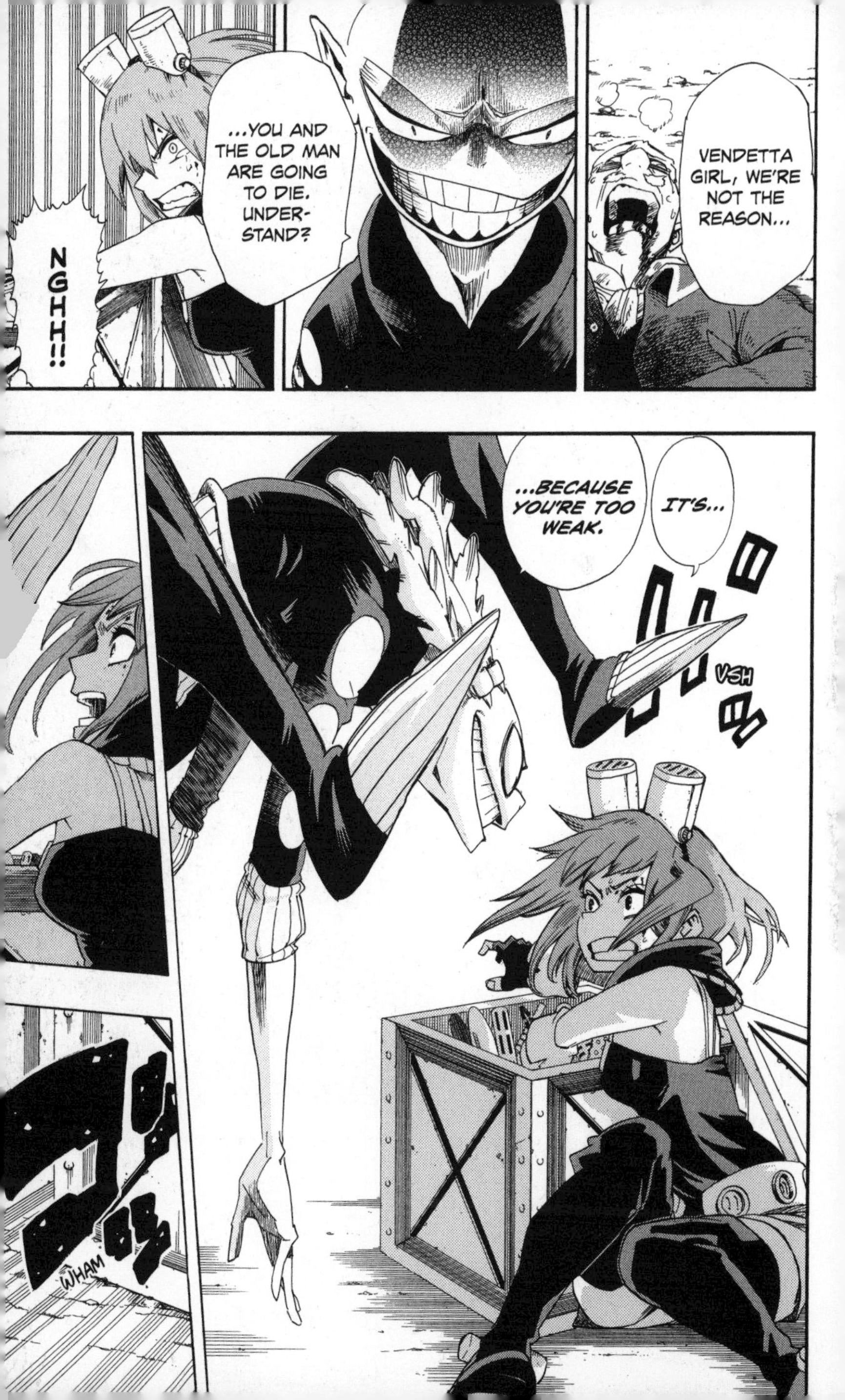
VENDETTA GIRL, WE'RE NOT THE REASON...
...YOU AND THE OLD MAN ARE GOING TO DIE. UNDER-STAND?
NGHH!!
IT'S...
...BECAUSE YOU'RE TOO WEAK.
VSH
WHAM

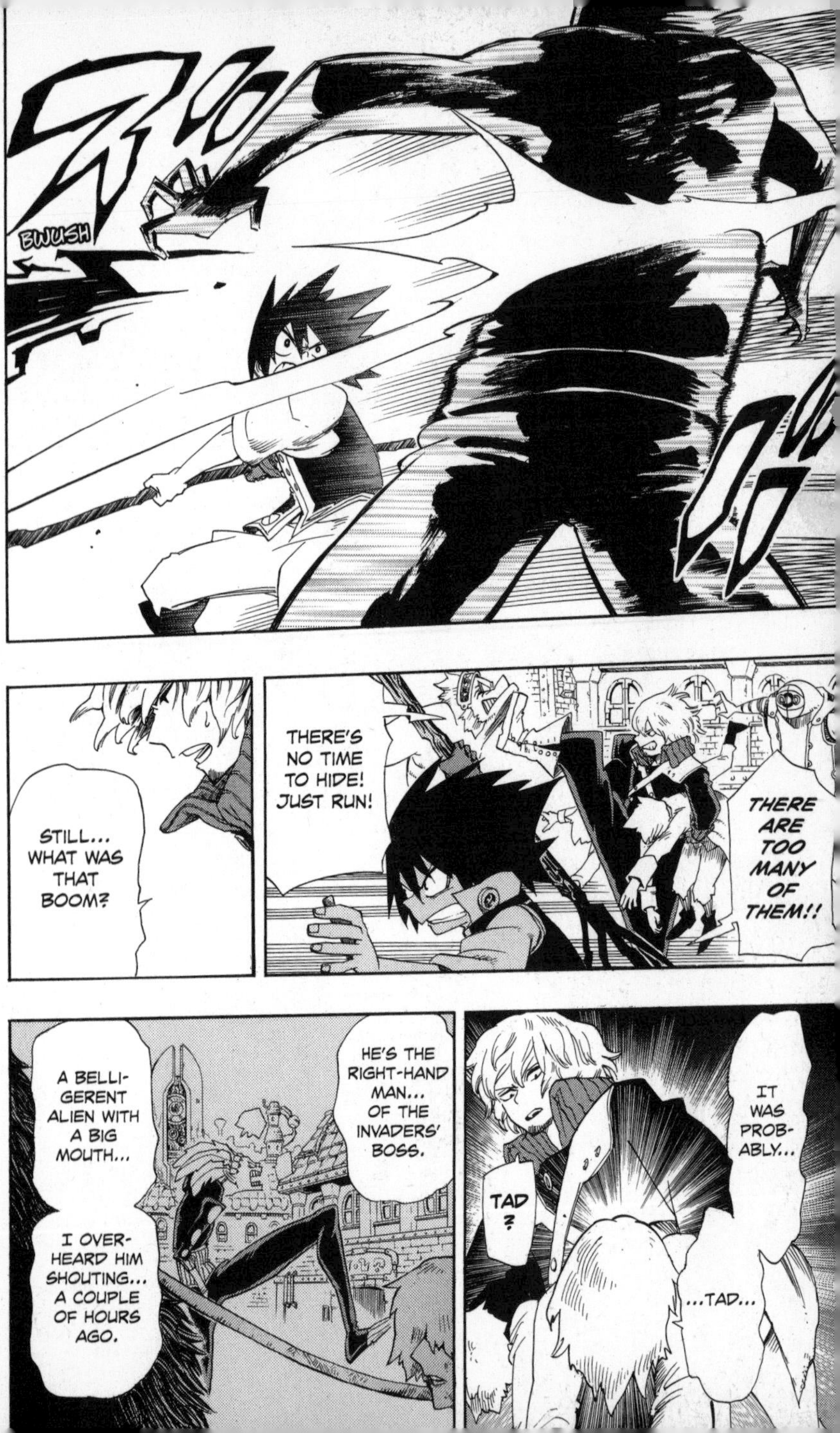
BWUSH
THERE ARE TOO MANY OF THEM!!
THERE'S NO TIME TO HIDE! JUST RUN!
STILL... WHAT WAS THAT BOOM?
IT WAS PROB-ABLY...
TAD?
...TAD...
HE'S THE RIGHT-HAND MAN... OF THE INVADERS' BOSS.
A BELLI-GERENT ALIEN WITH A BIG MOUTH...
I OVER-HEARD HIM SHOUTING... A COUPLE OF HOURS AGO.

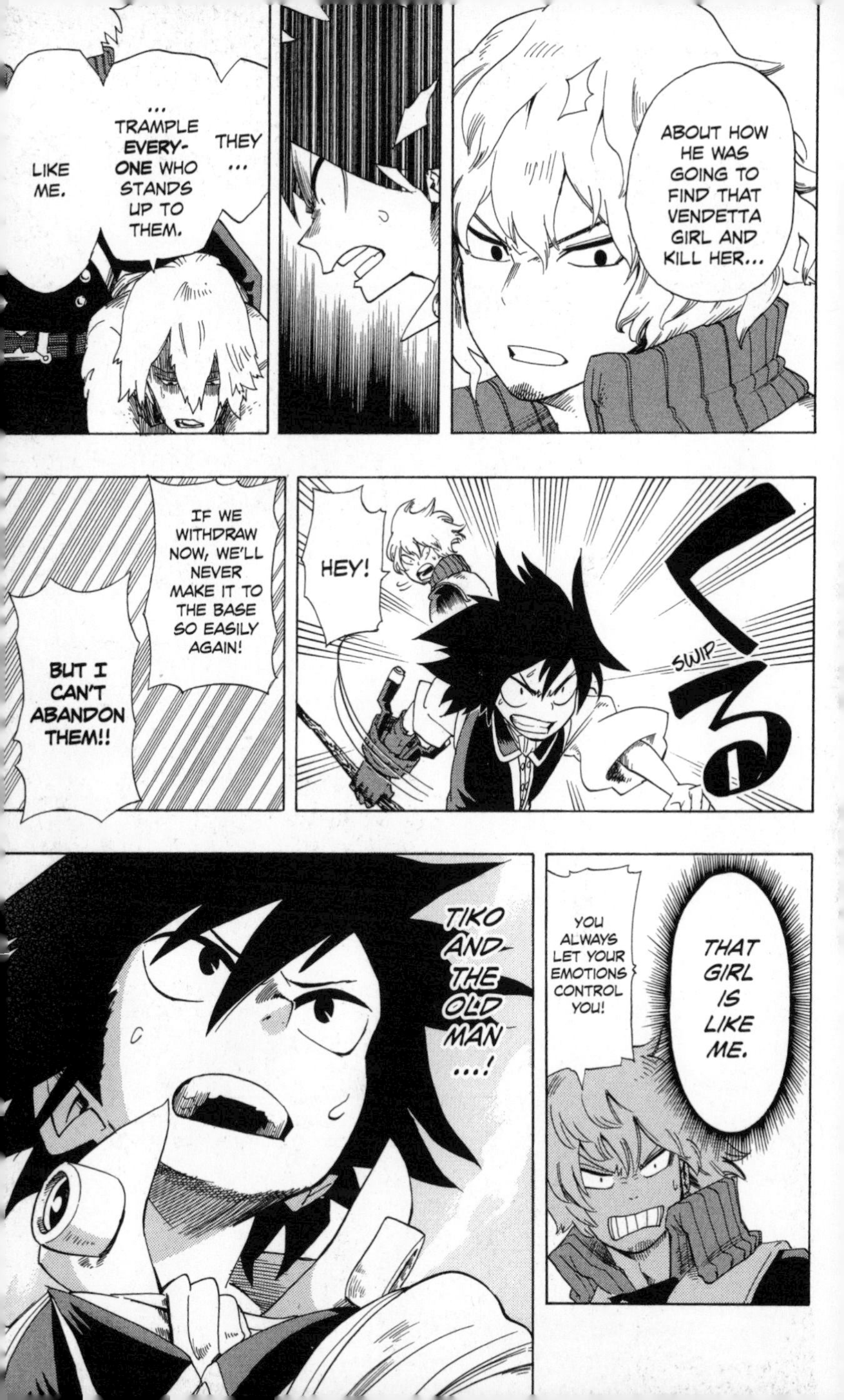
ABOUT HOW HE WAS GOING TO FIND THAT VENDETTA GIRL AND KILL HER...
THEY ...
... TRAMPLE EVERY-ONE WHO STANDS UP TO THEM.
LIKE ME.
HEY!
SWIP
IF WE WITHDRAW NOW, WE'LL NEVER MAKE IT TO THE BASE SO EASILY AGAIN!
BUT I CAN'T ABANDON THEM!!
THAT GIRL IS LIKE ME.
YOU ALWAYS LET YOUR EMOTIONS CONTROL YOU!
TIKO AND THE OLD MAN ...!

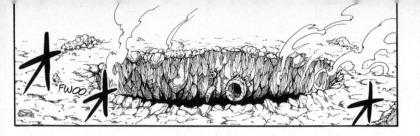

C'MON, YOU CAN DO BETTER THAN THIS, VENDETTA GIRL.

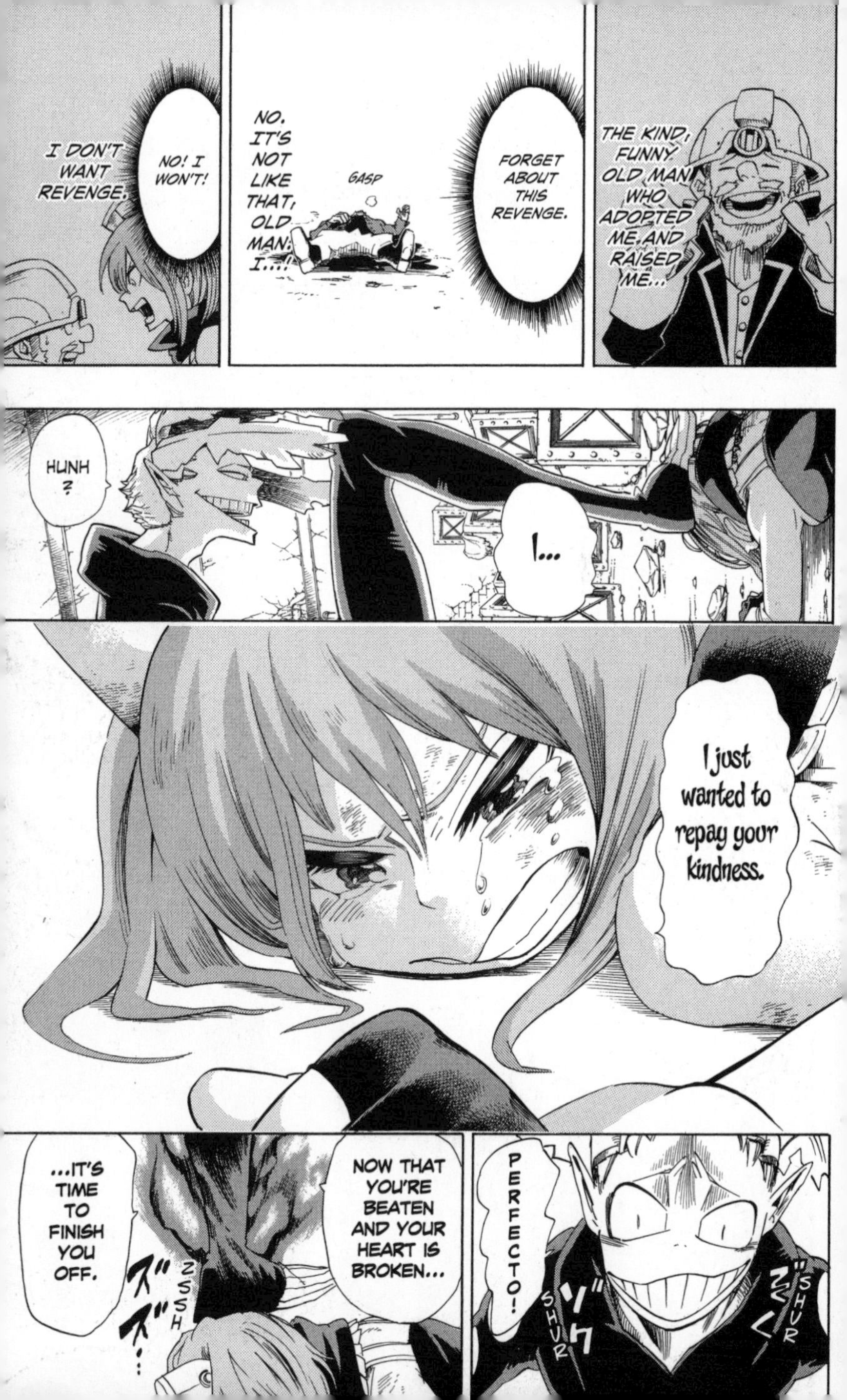
THE KIND, FUNNY OLD MAN WHO ADOPTED ME AND RAISED ME...
FORGET ABOUT THIS REVENGE.
GASP
NO. IT'S NOT LIKE THAT, OLD MAN. I...!!
NO! I WON'T!
I DON'T WANT REVENGE.
I...
HUNH?
I just wanted to repay your kindness.
PERFECTO!
SHUR
SHUR
NOW THAT YOU'RE BEATEN AND YOUR HEART IS BROKEN...
...IT'S TIME TO FINISH YOU OFF.
ZSSH

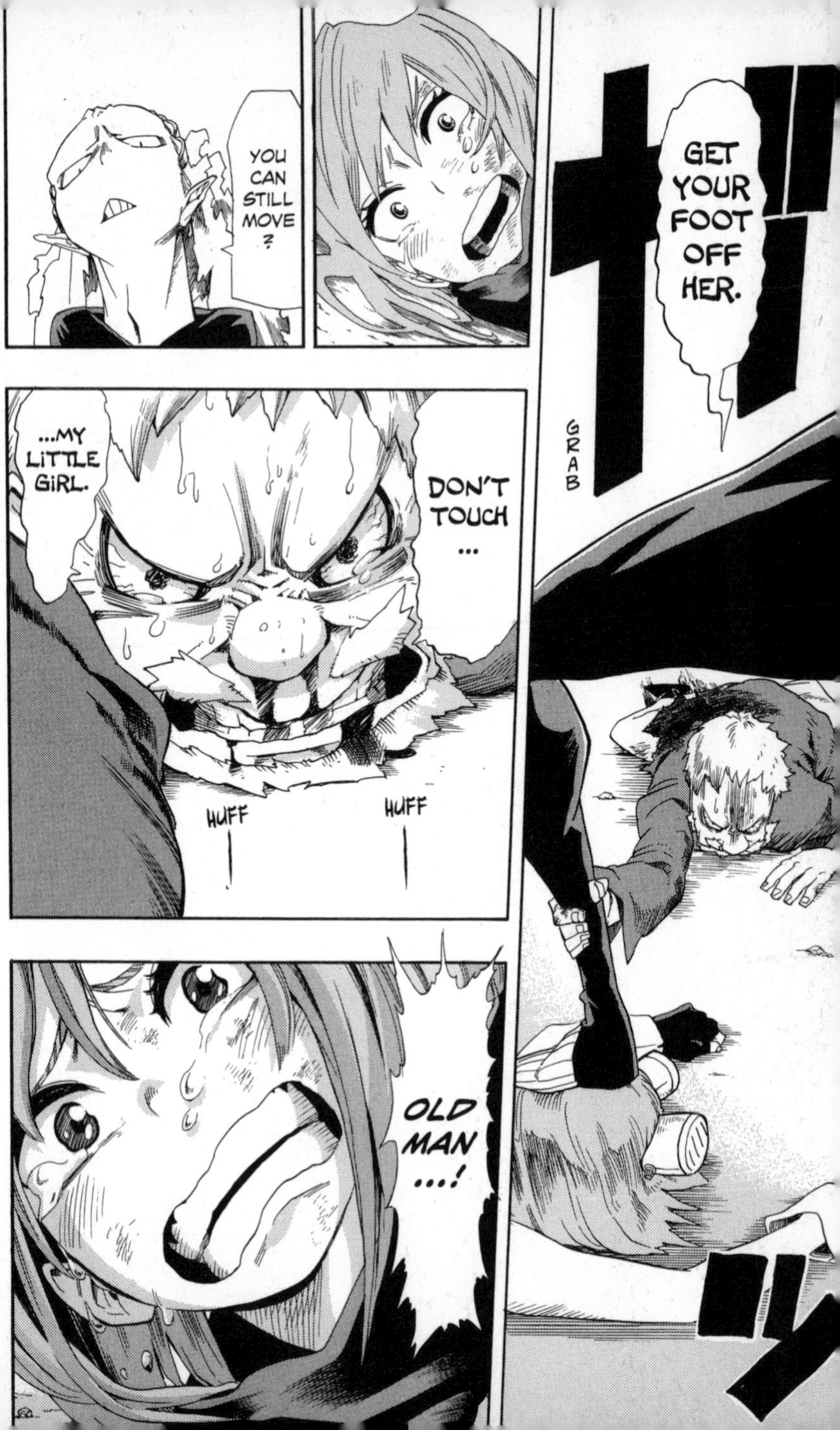
GET YOUR FOOT OFF HER.
GRAB
YOU CAN STILL MOVE?
DON'T TOUCH...
...MY LITTLE GIRL.
HUFF
HUFF
OLD MAN...!

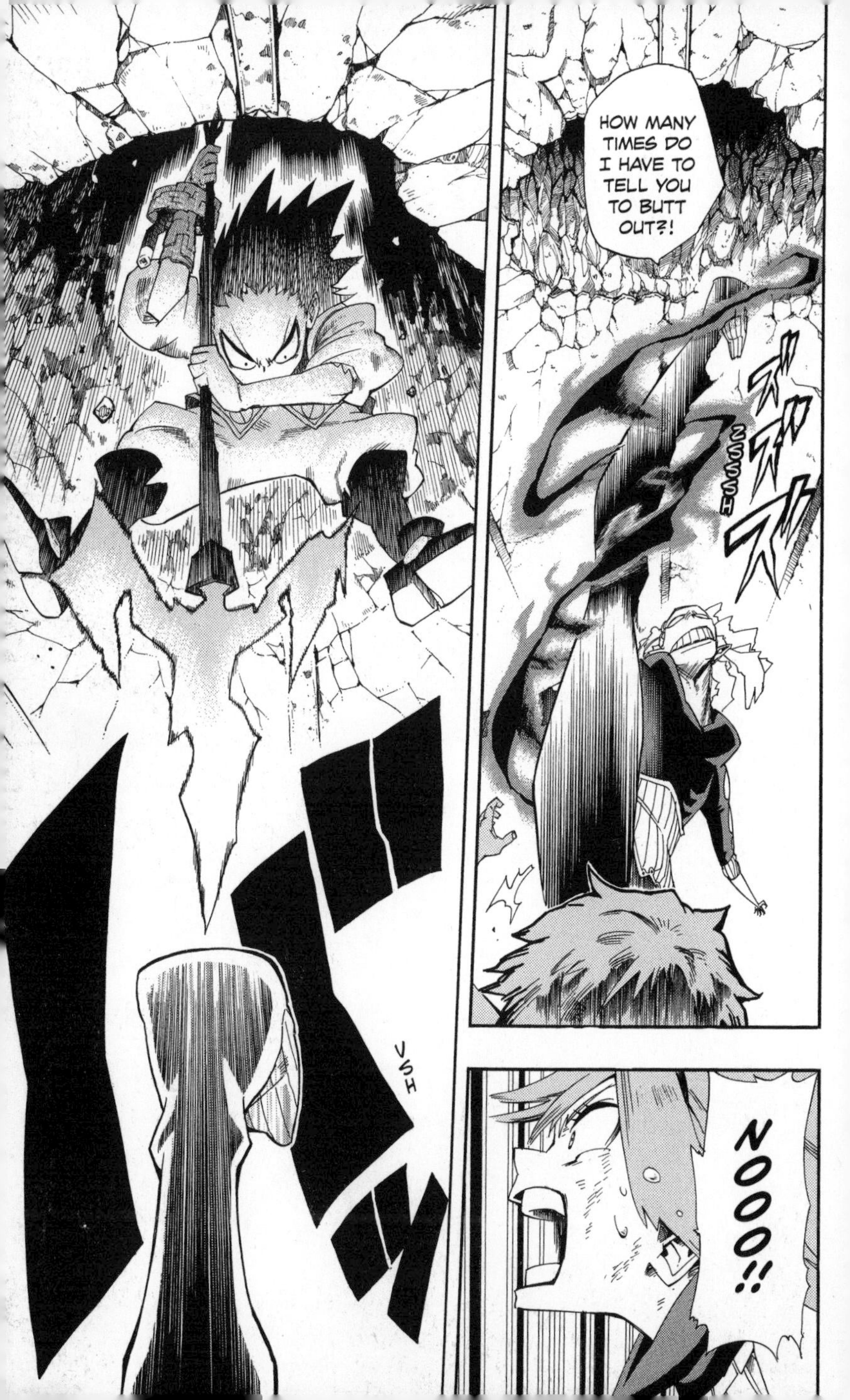
HOW MANY TIMES DO I HAVE TO TELL YOU TO BUTT OUT?!
ZSSSH
NOOOO!!
VSH

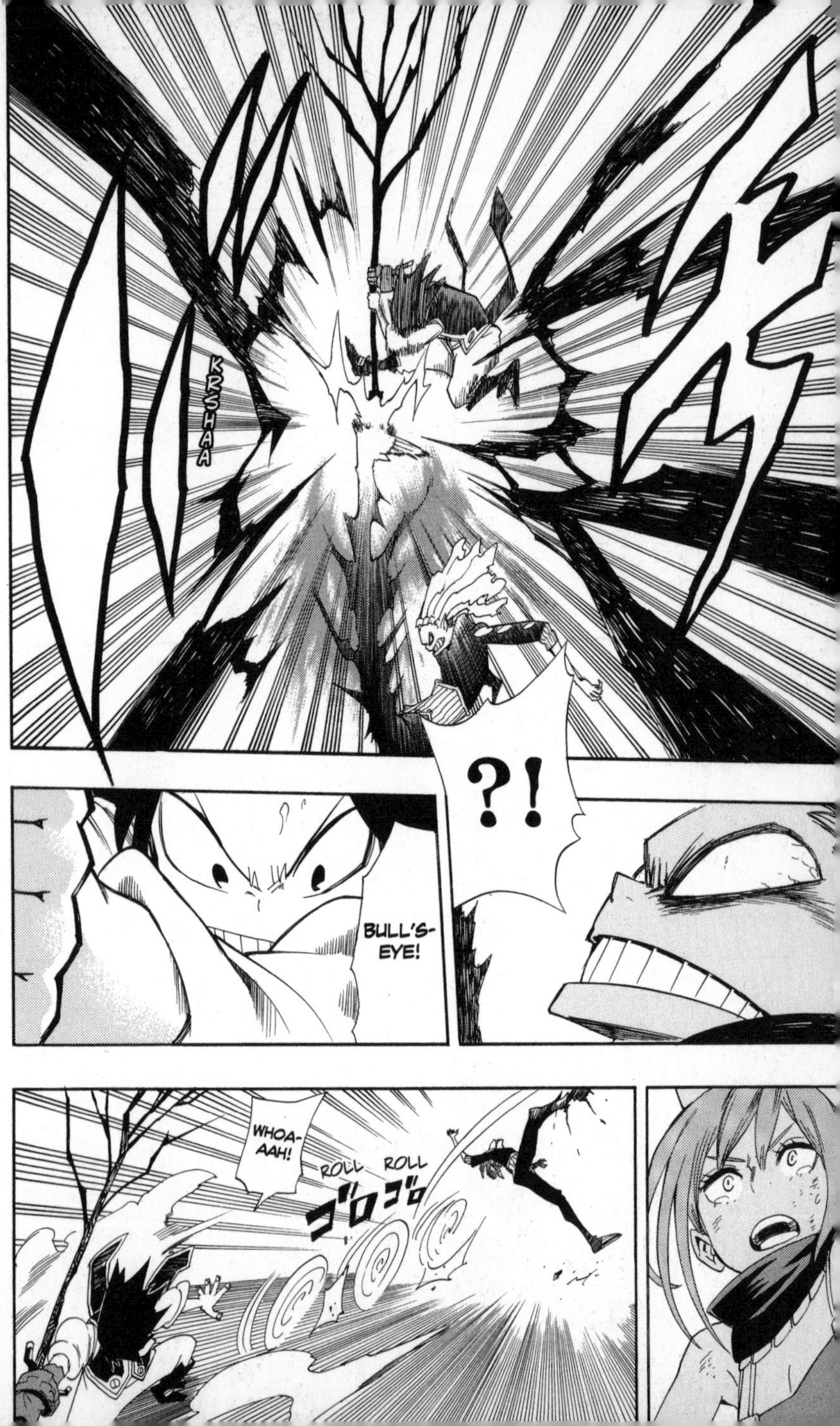
KRSHAA
?!
BULL'S-EYE!
WHOA-AAH!
ROLL ROLL
ゴロゴロ

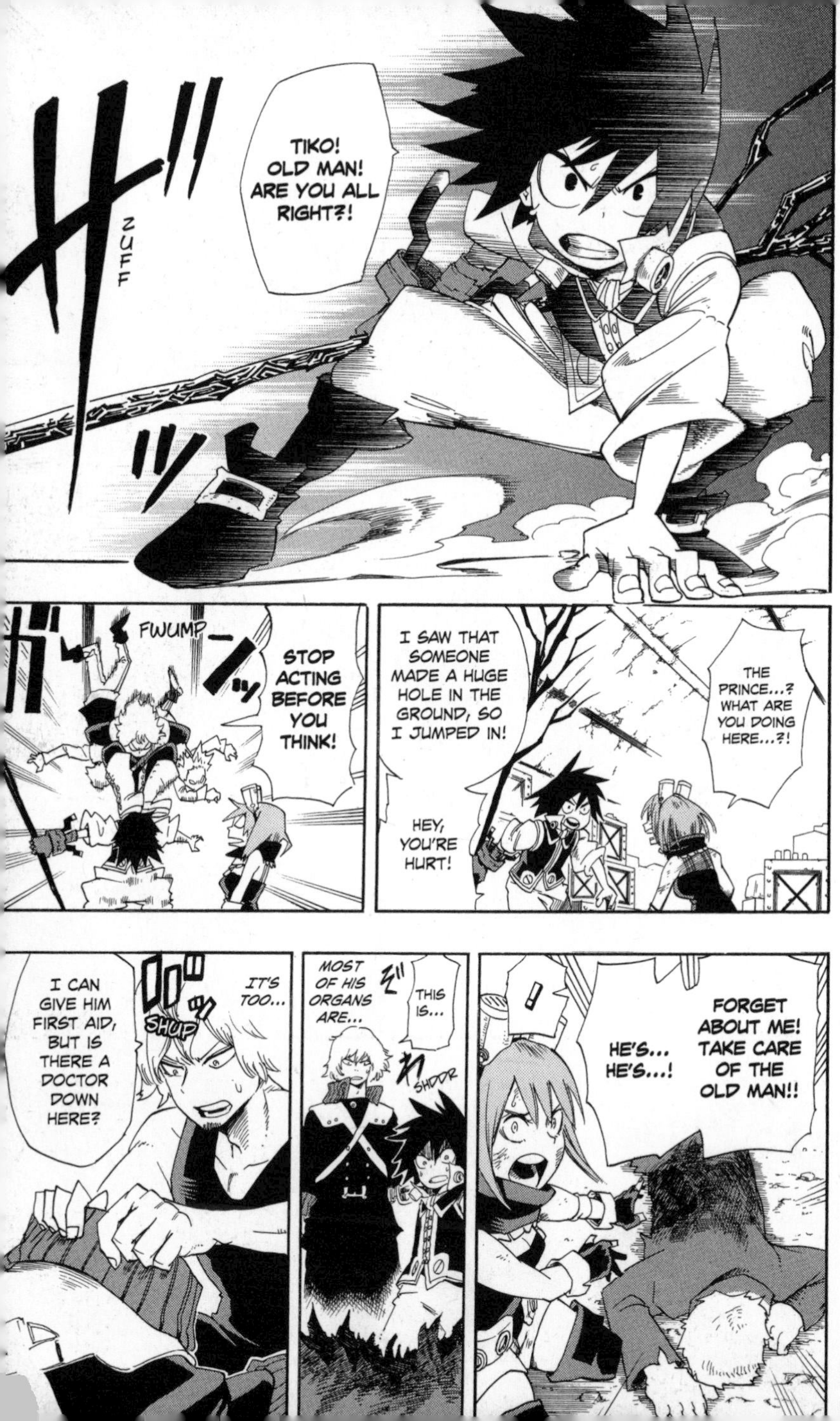
ZUFF
TIKO! OLD MAN! ARE YOU ALL RIGHT?!
THE PRINCE...? WHAT ARE YOU DOING HERE...?!
I SAW THAT SOMEONE MADE A HUGE HOLE IN THE GROUND, SO I JUMPED IN!
HEY, YOU'RE HURT!
FWUMP
STOP ACTING BEFORE YOU THINK!
!
FORGET ABOUT ME! TAKE CARE OF THE OLD MAN!!
HE'S... HE'S...!
THIS IS...
MOST OF HIS ORGANS ARE...
SHDDR
IT'S TOO...
SHUP
I CAN GIVE HIM FIRST AID, BUT IS THERE A DOCTOR DOWN HERE?

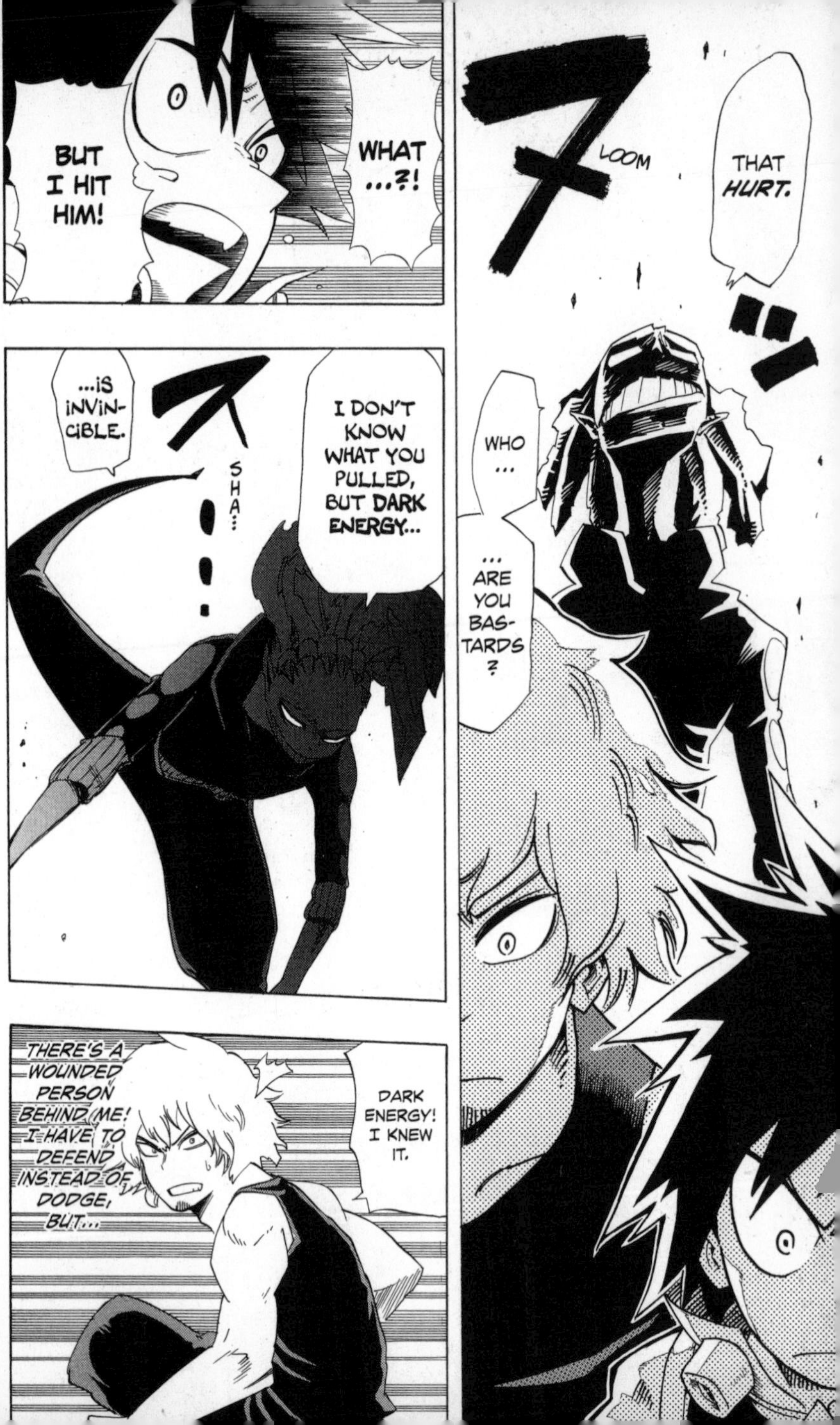
LOOM
THAT HURT.
WHO ...
... ARE YOU BASTARDS?
WHAT ...?!
BUT I HIT HIM!
I DON'T KNOW WHAT YOU PULLED, BUT DARK ENERGY...
...iS iNVINCIBLE.
SHA...
DARK ENERGY! I KNEW IT.
THERE'S A WOUNDED PERSON BEHIND ME! I HAVE TO DEFEND INSTEAD OF DODGE, BUT...

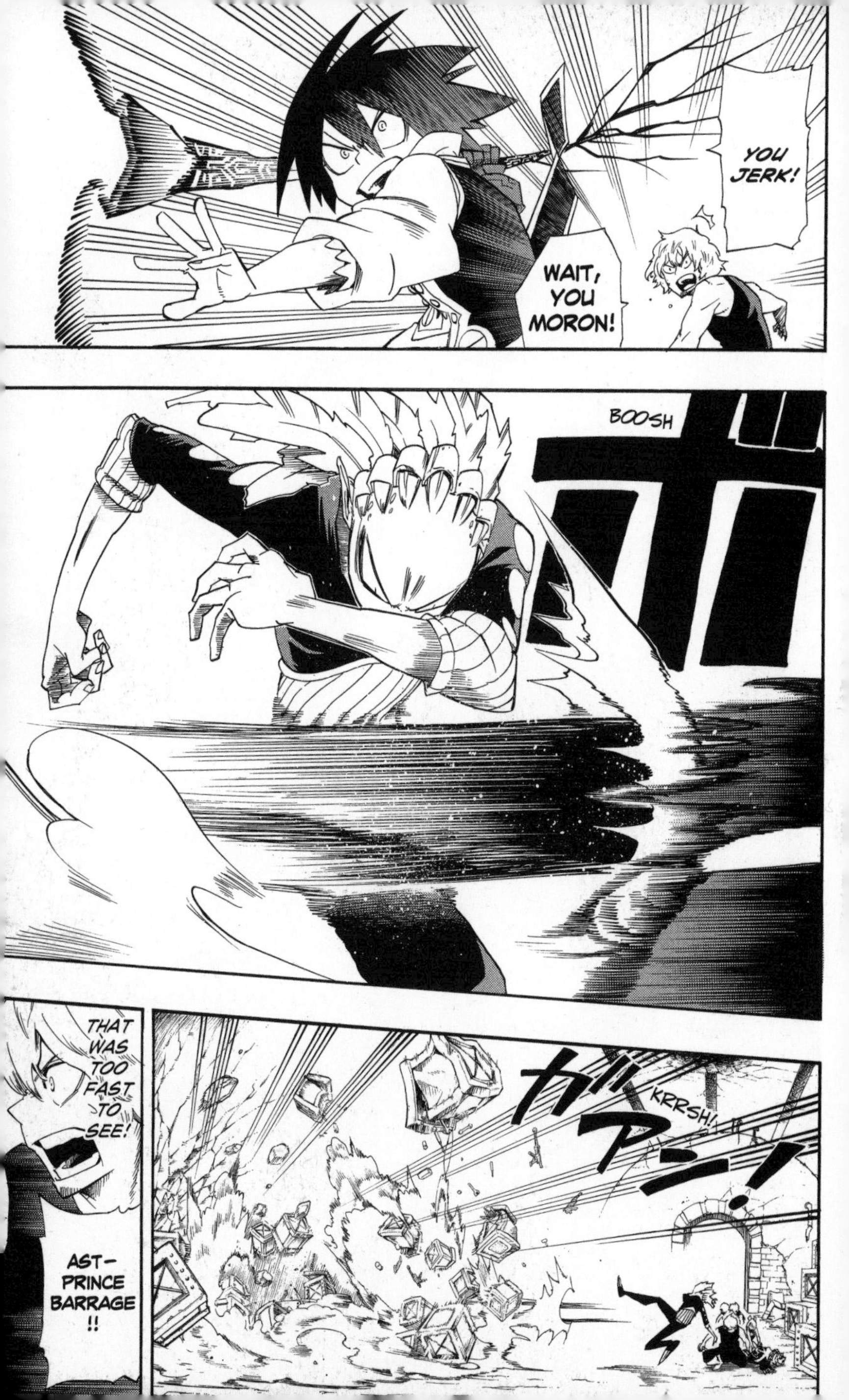
YOU JERK!
WAIT, YOU MORON!
BOOSH
KRRSH!
THAT WAS TOO FAST TO SEE!
AST-PRINCE BARRAGE!!

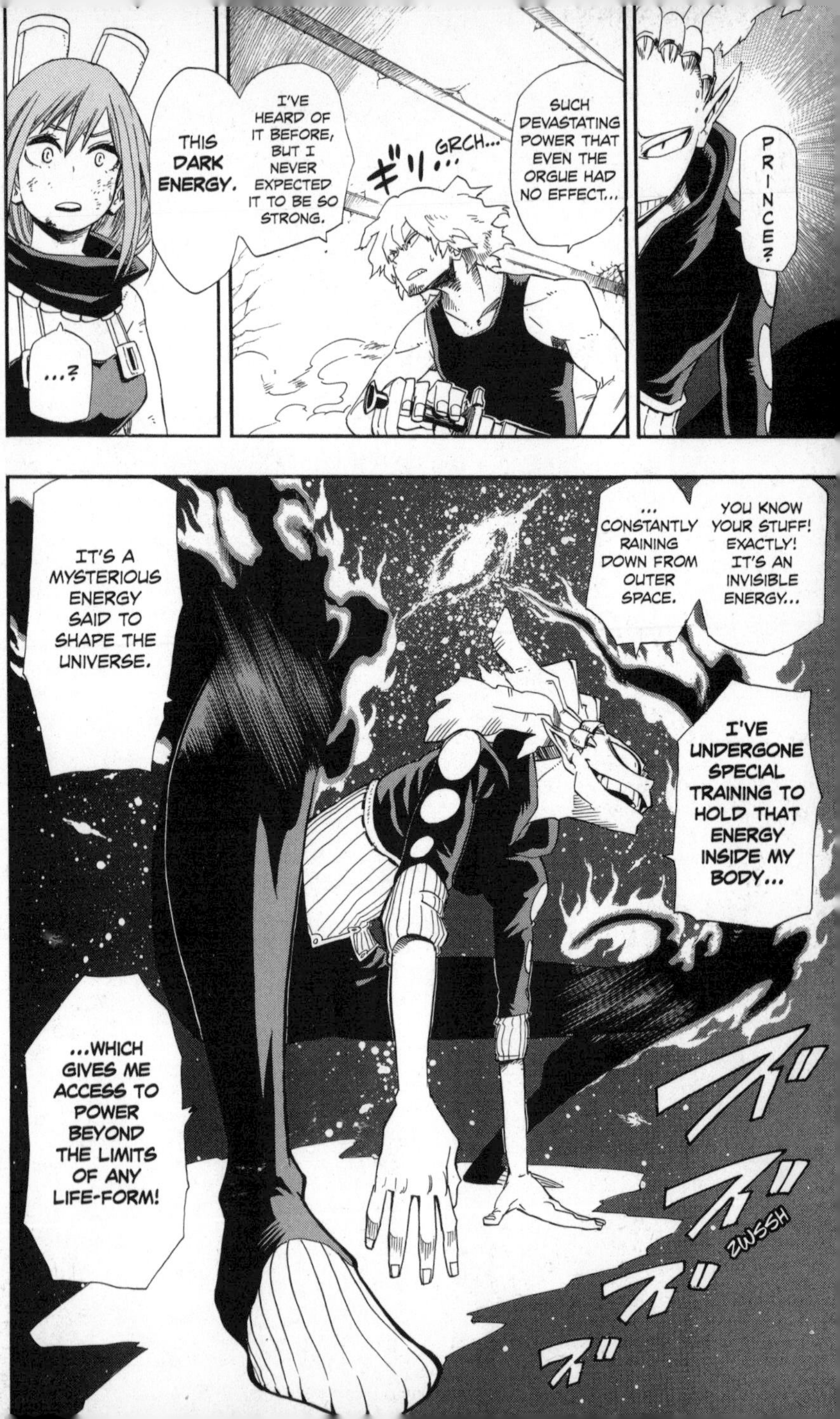
PRINCE?
SUCH DEVASTATING POWER THAT EVEN THE ORGUE HAD NO EFFECT...
GRCH...
I'VE HEARD OF IT BEFORE, BUT I NEVER EXPECTED IT TO BE SO STRONG.
THIS **DARK ENERGY.**
...?
YOU KNOW YOUR STUFF! EXACTLY! IT'S AN INVISIBLE ENERGY...
...CONSTANTLY RAINING DOWN FROM OUTER SPACE.
IT'S A MYSTERIOUS ENERGY SAID TO SHAPE THE UNIVERSE.
I'VE UNDERGONE SPECIAL TRAINING TO HOLD THAT ENERGY INSIDE MY BODY...
...WHICH GIVES ME ACCESS TO POWER BEYOND THE LIMITS OF ANY LIFE-FORM!
ZWSSH

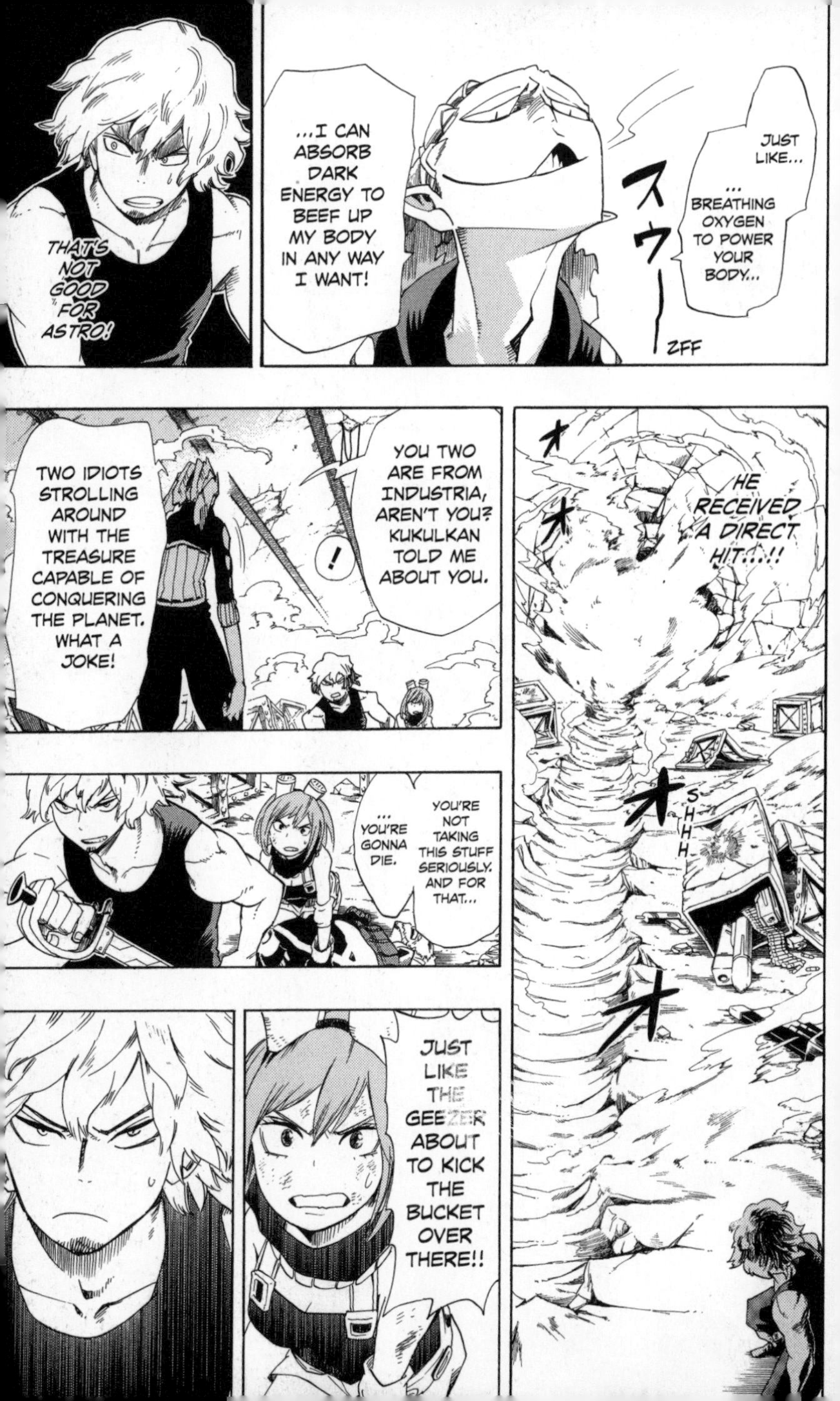
JUST LIKE...
...BREATHING OXYGEN TO POWER YOUR BODY...
スウー
ZFF
...I CAN ABSORB DARK ENERGY TO BEEF UP MY BODY IN ANY WAY I WANT!
THAT'S NOT GOOD FOR ASTRO!
オオオオ
HE RECEIVED A DIRECT HIT...!!
SHHH
YOU TWO ARE FROM INDUSTRIA, AREN'T YOU? KUKULKAN TOLD ME ABOUT YOU.
!
TWO IDIOTS STROLLING AROUND WITH THE TREASURE CAPABLE OF CONQUERING THE PLANET. WHAT A JOKE!
YOU'RE NOT TAKING THIS STUFF SERIOUSLY. AND FOR THAT...
...YOU'RE GONNA DIE.
JUST LIKE THE GEEZER ABOUT TO KICK THE BUCKET OVER THERE!!

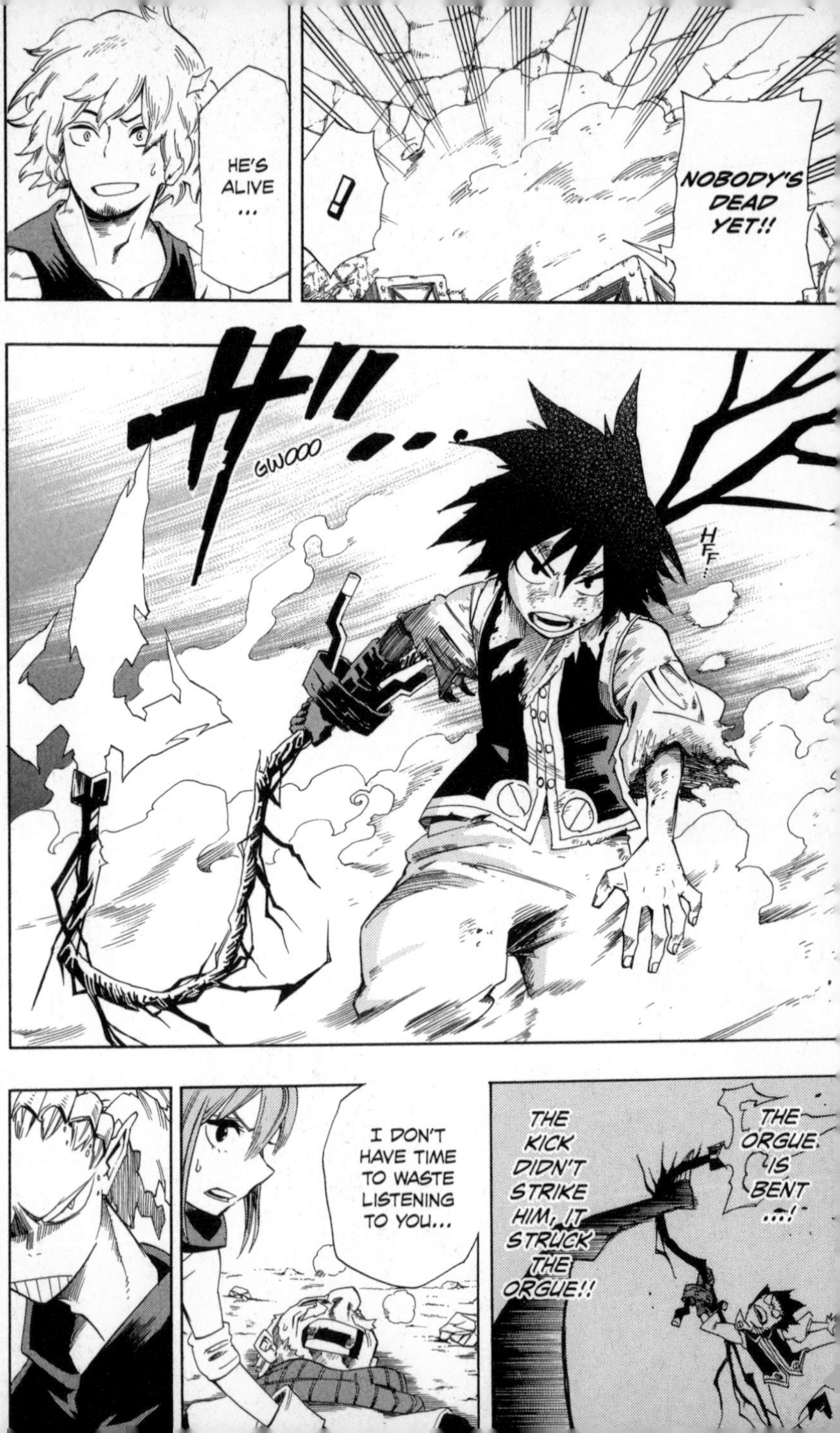
NOBODY'S DEAD YET!!
!
HE'S ALIVE ...
ザ…
GWOOO
HFF...
THE ORGUE IS BENT ...!
THE KICK DIDN'T STRIKE HIM, IT STRUCK THE ORGUE!!
I DON'T HAVE TIME TO WASTE LISTENING TO YOU...

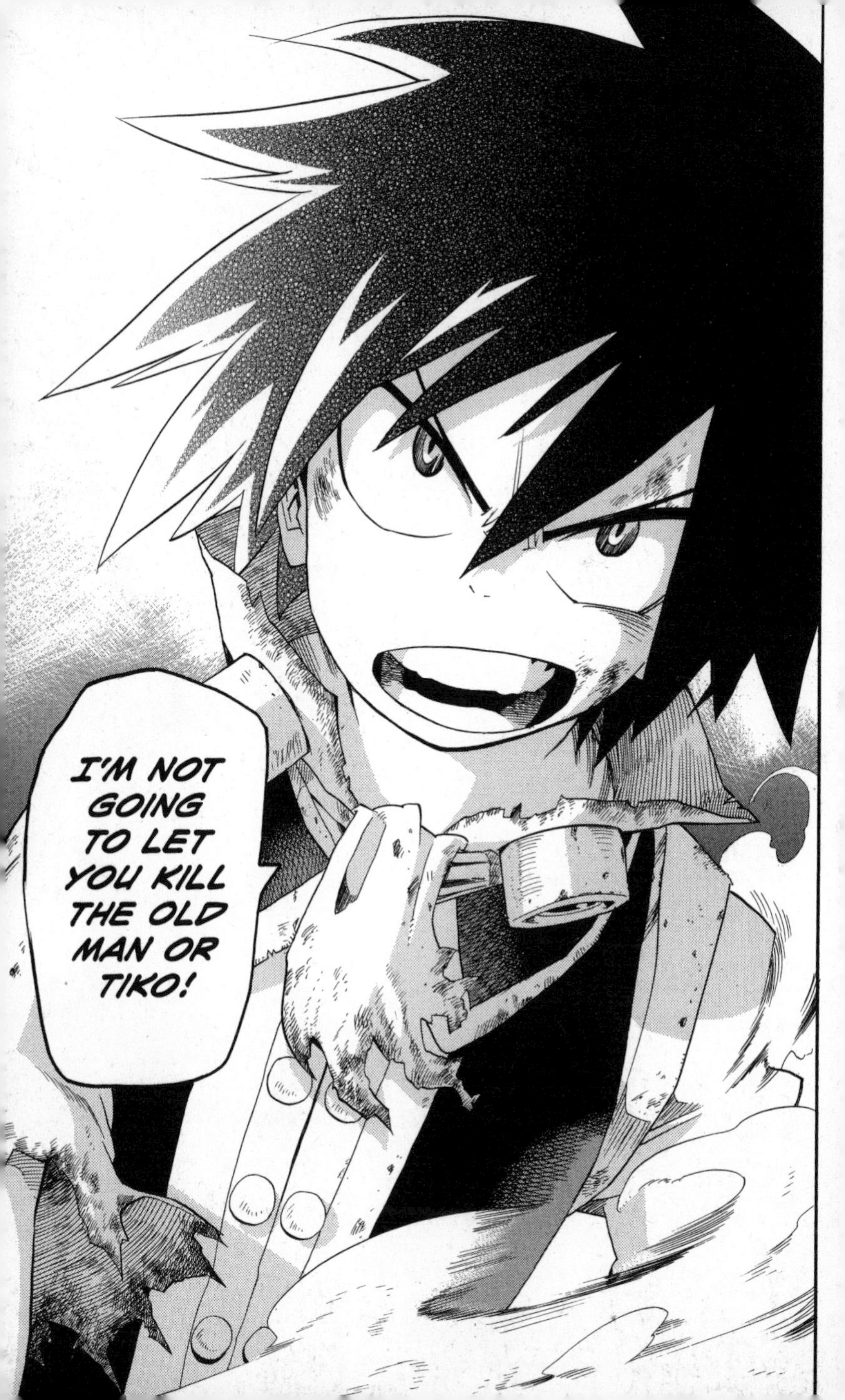
I'M NOT GOING TO LET YOU KILL THE OLD MAN OR TIKO!

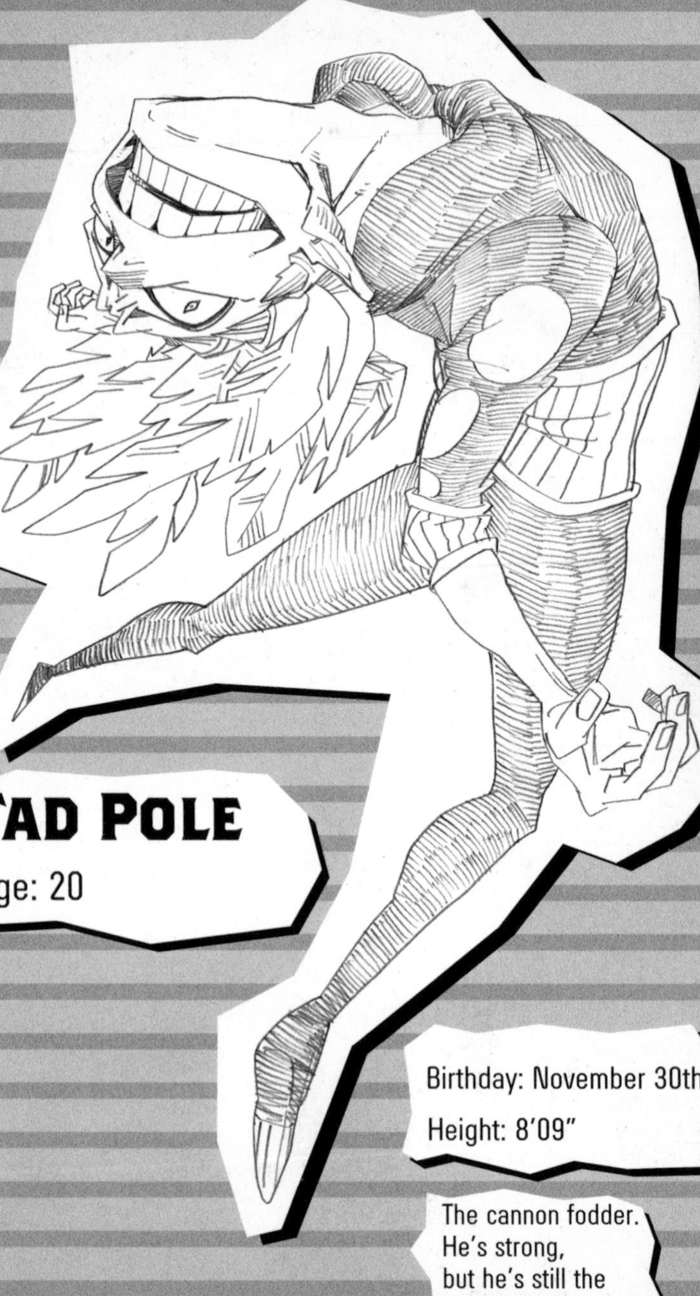

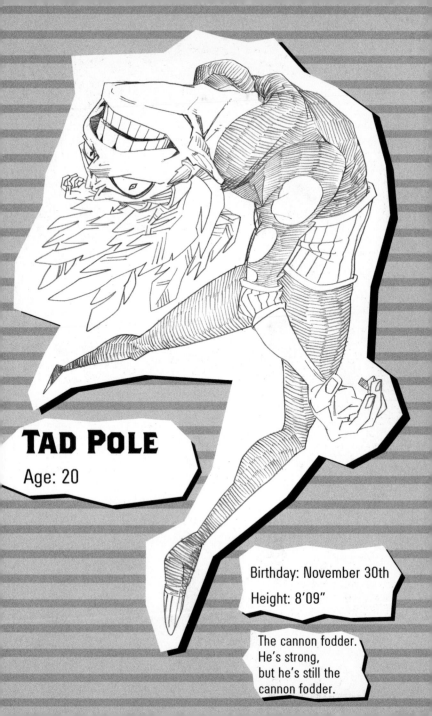

TAD POLE

Age: 20

Birthday: November 30th

Height: 8'09"

The cannon fodder.
He's strong,
but he's still the
cannon fodder.

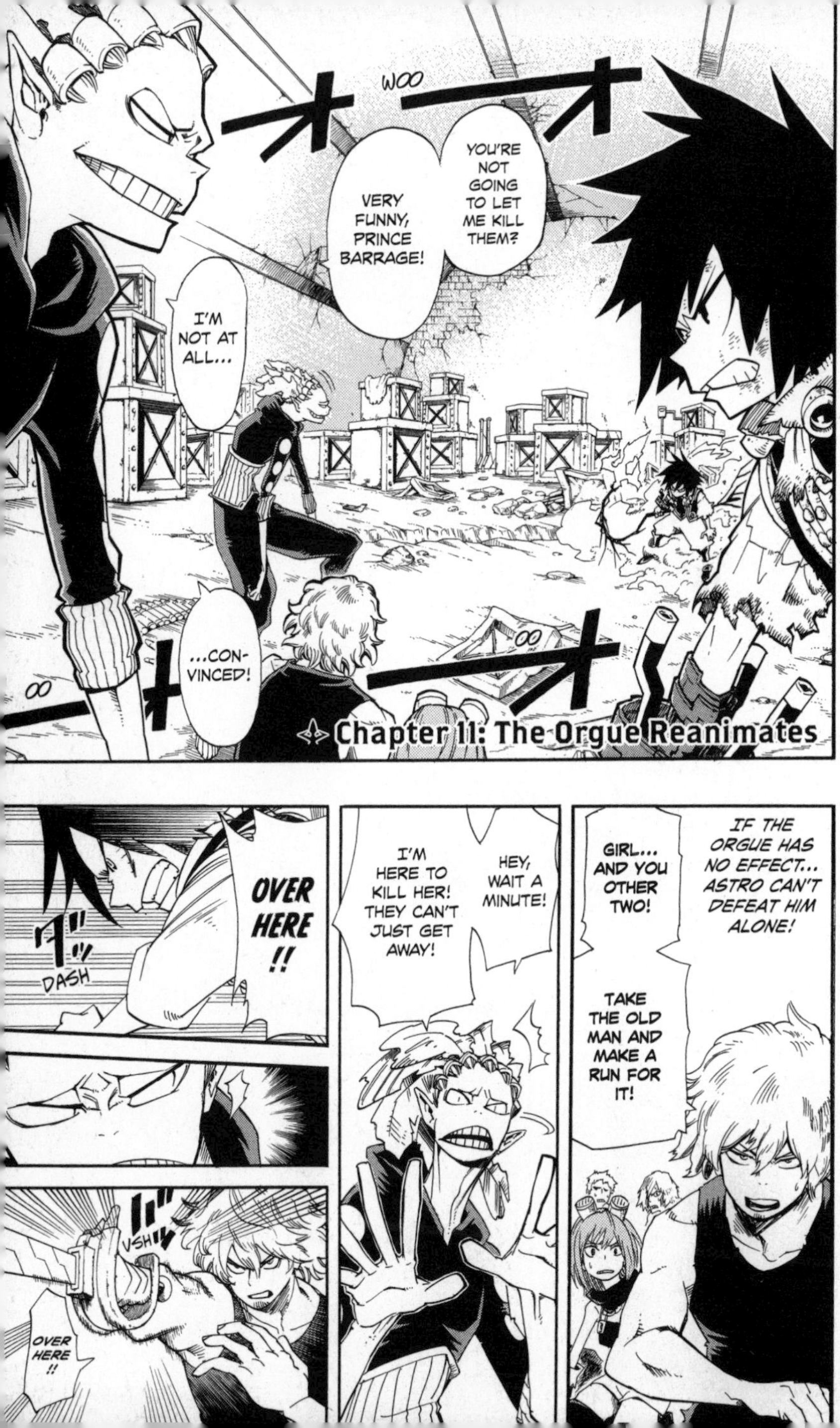
WOO
YOU'RE NOT GOING TO LET ME KILL THEM?
VERY FUNNY, PRINCE BARRAGE!
I'M NOT AT ALL...
...CON-VINCED!
OO
Chapter 11: The Orgue Reanimates
IF THE ORGUE HAS NO EFFECT... ASTRO CAN'T DEFEAT HIM ALONE!
GIRL... AND YOU OTHER TWO!
TAKE THE OLD MAN AND MAKE A RUN FOR IT!
HEY, WAIT A MINUTE!
I'M HERE TO KILL HER! THEY CAN'T JUST GET AWAY!
OVER HERE !!
DASH
VSH
OVER HERE !!

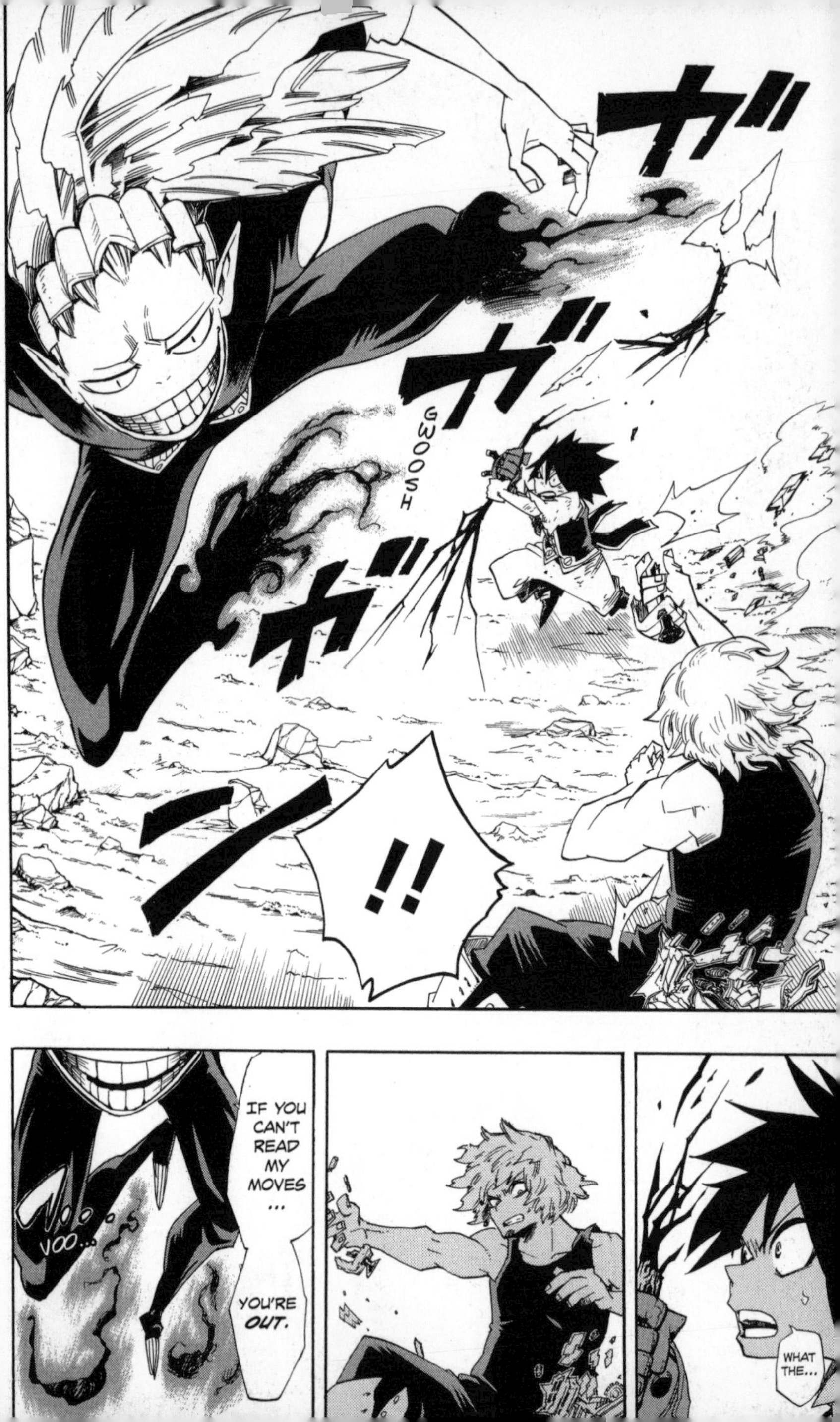
GWOOSH
!!
WHAT THE...
IF YOU CAN'T READ MY MOVES ...
YOU'RE *OUT*.
VOO...

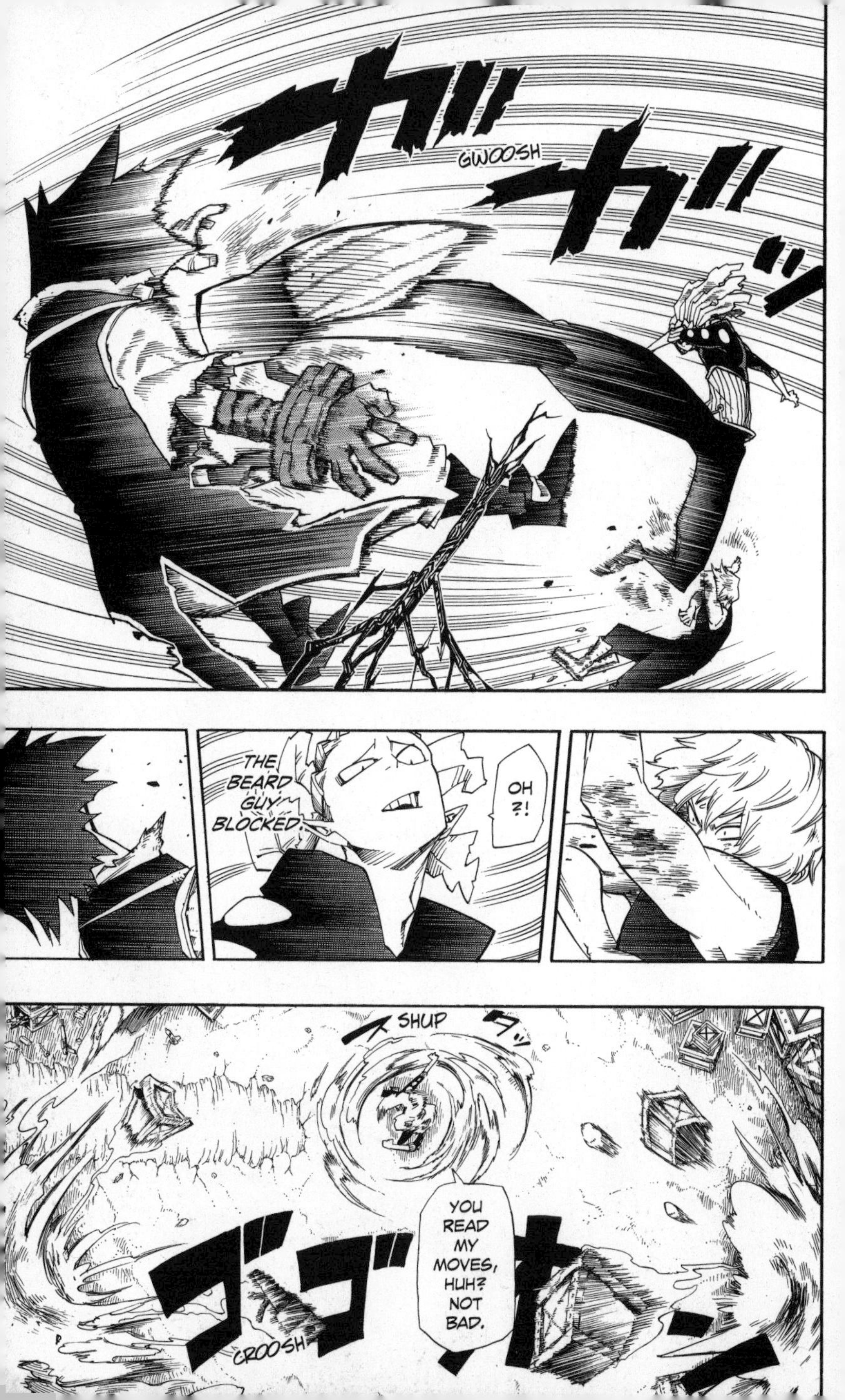
GWOOSH
OH ?!
THE BEARD GUY BLOCKED...
SHUP
YOU READ MY MOVES, HUH? NOT BAD.
CROOSH

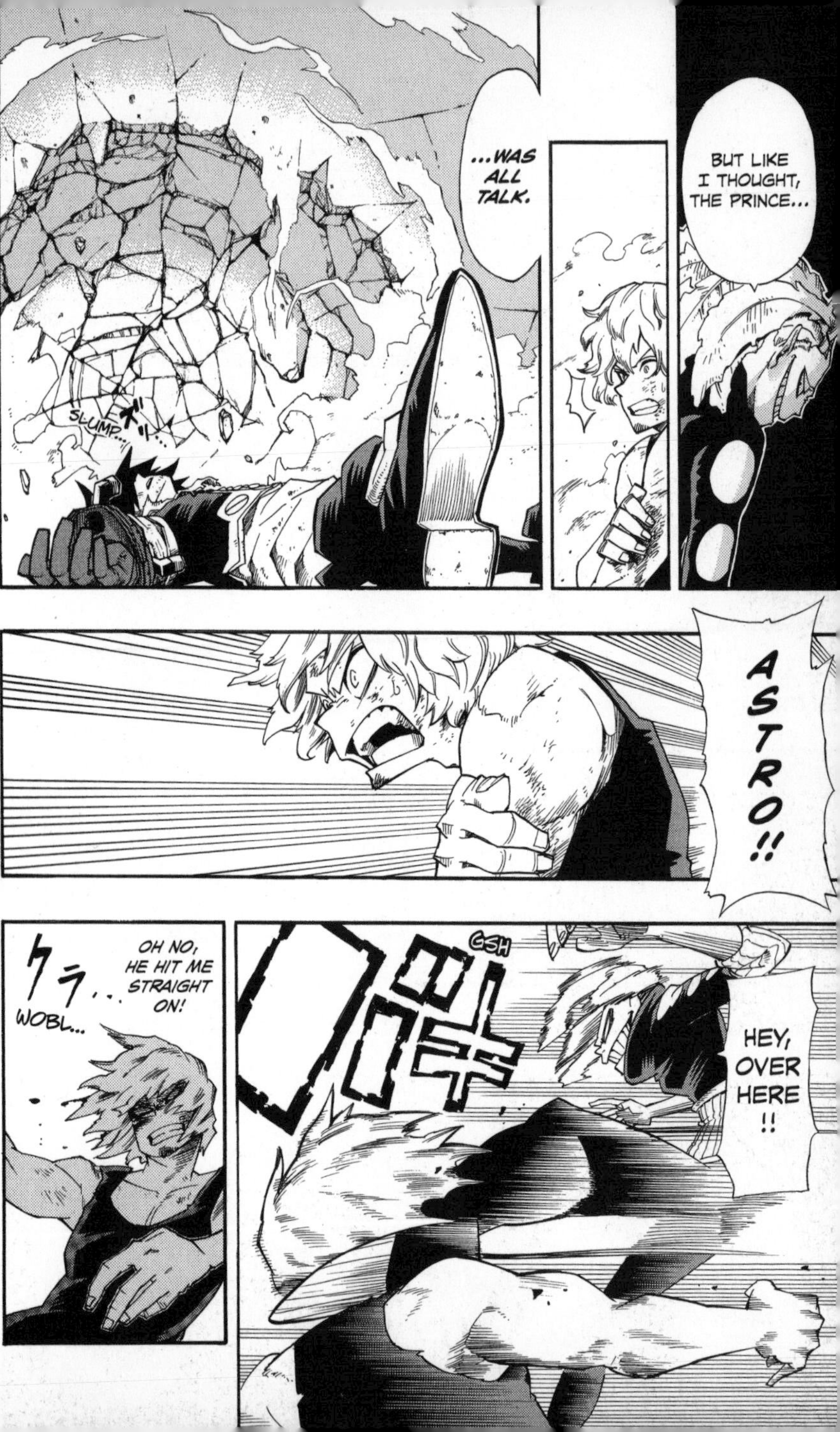
BUT LIKE I THOUGHT, THE PRINCE...
...WAS ALL TALK.
SLUMP...
ASTRO!!
HEY, OVER HERE !!
GSH
OH NO, HE HIT ME STRAIGHT ON!
WOBL...

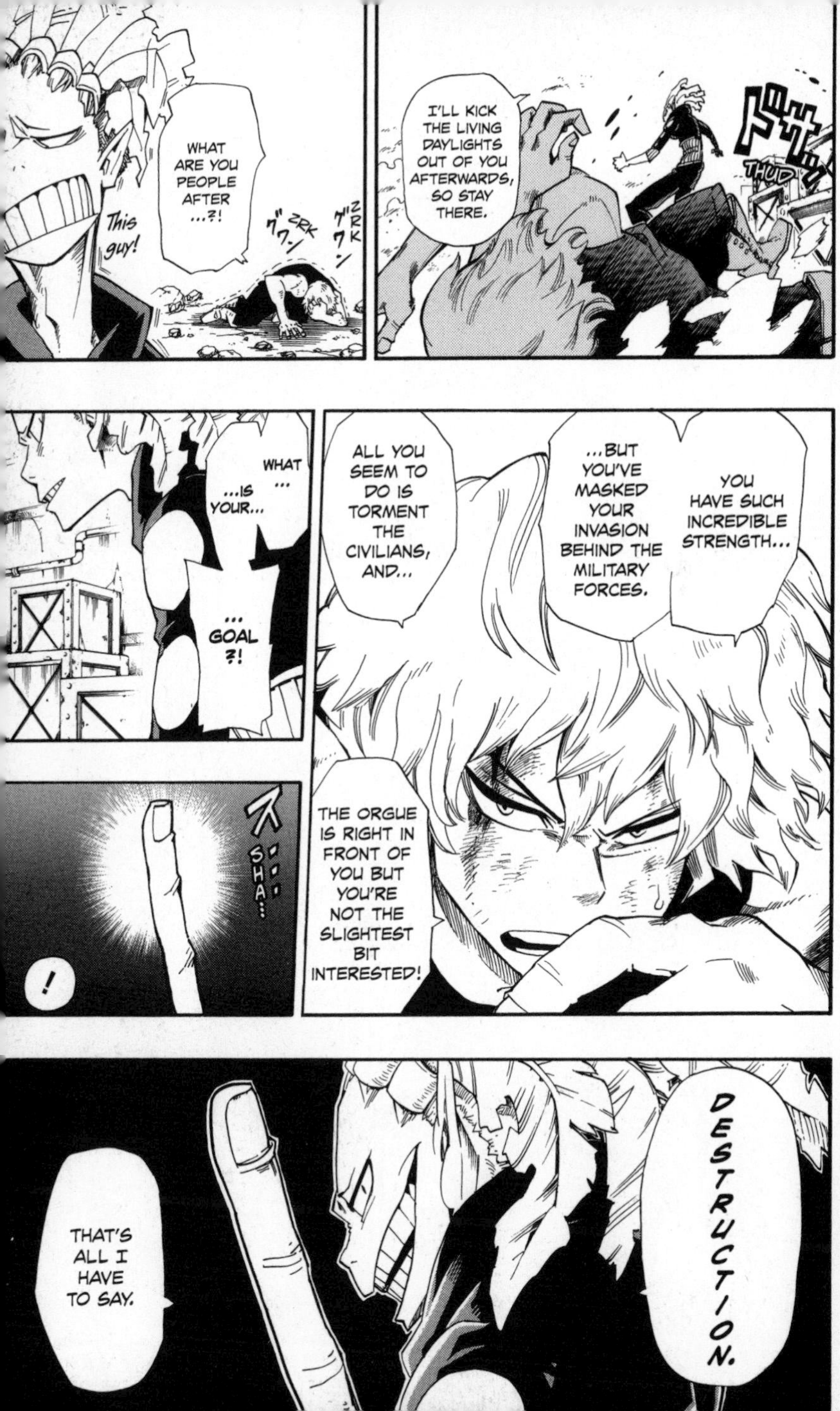
I'LL KICK THE LIVING DAYLIGHTS OUT OF YOU AFTERWARDS, SO STAY THERE.
THUD
ZRK
ZRK
WHAT ARE YOU PEOPLE AFTER ...?!
This guy!
YOU HAVE SUCH INCREDIBLE STRENGTH...
...BUT YOU'VE MASKED YOUR INVASION BEHIND THE MILITARY FORCES.
ALL YOU SEEM TO DO IS TORMENT THE CIVILIANS, AND...
THE ORGUE IS RIGHT IN FRONT OF YOU BUT YOU'RE NOT THE SLIGHTEST BIT INTERESTED!
WHAT ...
...IS YOUR...
... GOAL ?!
SHA...
!
DESTRUCTION.
THAT'S ALL I HAVE TO SAY.

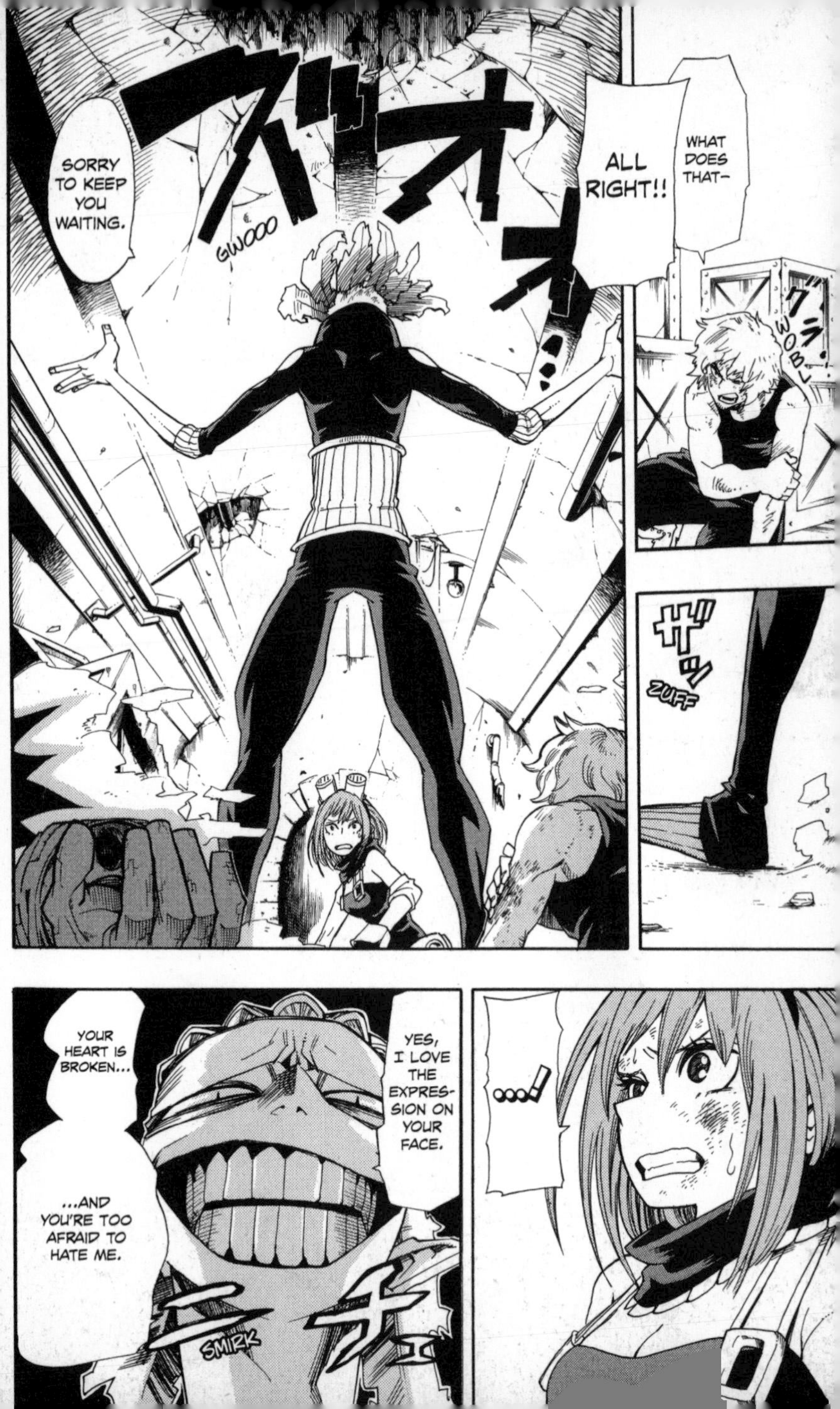
WHAT DOES THAT—
WOBBL
ZUFF
ALL RIGHT!!
GWOOO
SORRY TO KEEP YOU WAITING.
...!
YES, I LOVE THE EXPRES-SION ON YOUR FACE.
YOUR HEART IS BROKEN...
...AND YOU'RE TOO AFRAID TO HATE ME.
SMIRK

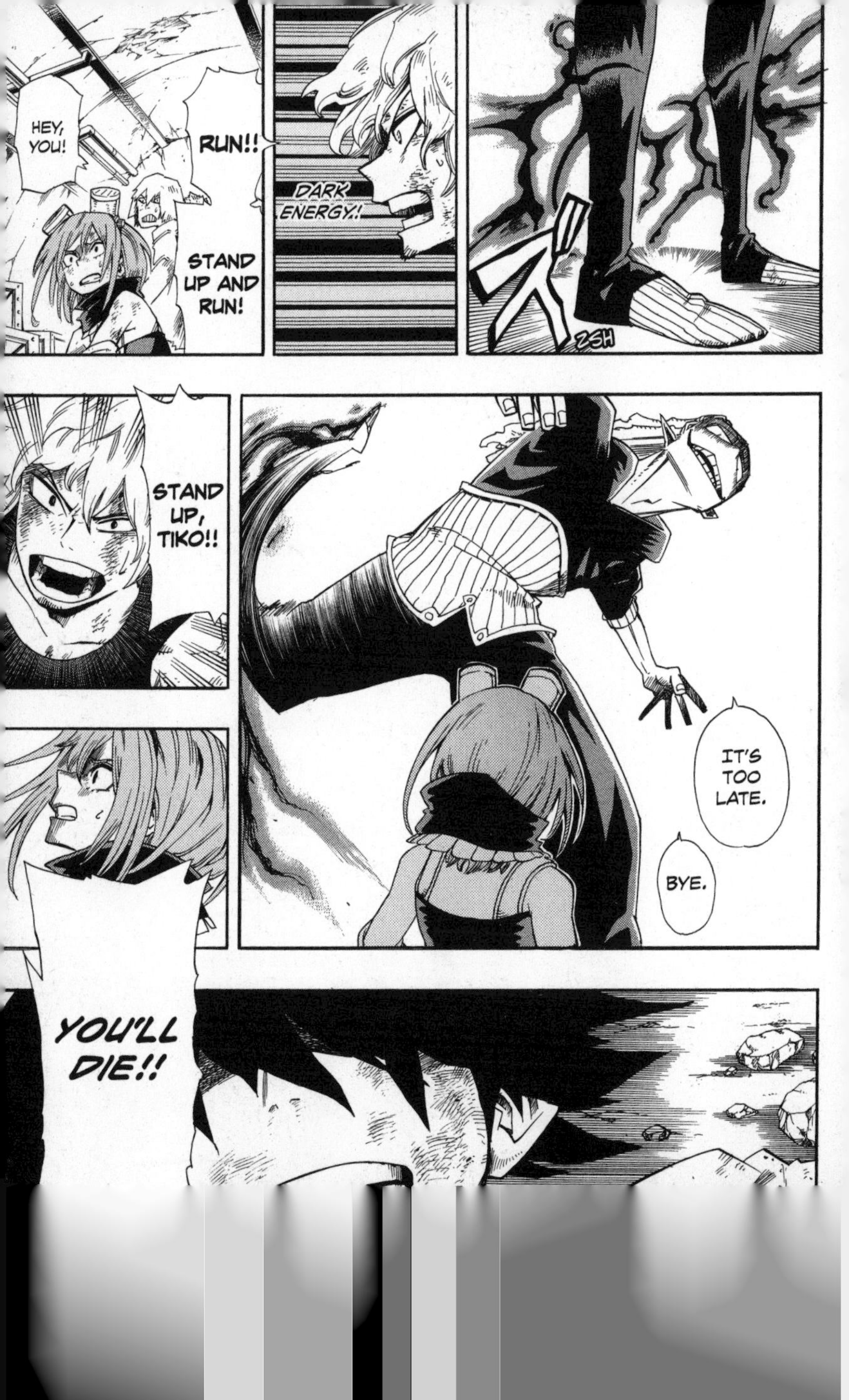
ZSH
RUN!!
DARK ENERGY!
HEY, YOU!
STAND UP AND RUN!
IT'S TOO LATE.
BYE.
STAND UP, TIKO!!
YOU'LL DIE!!

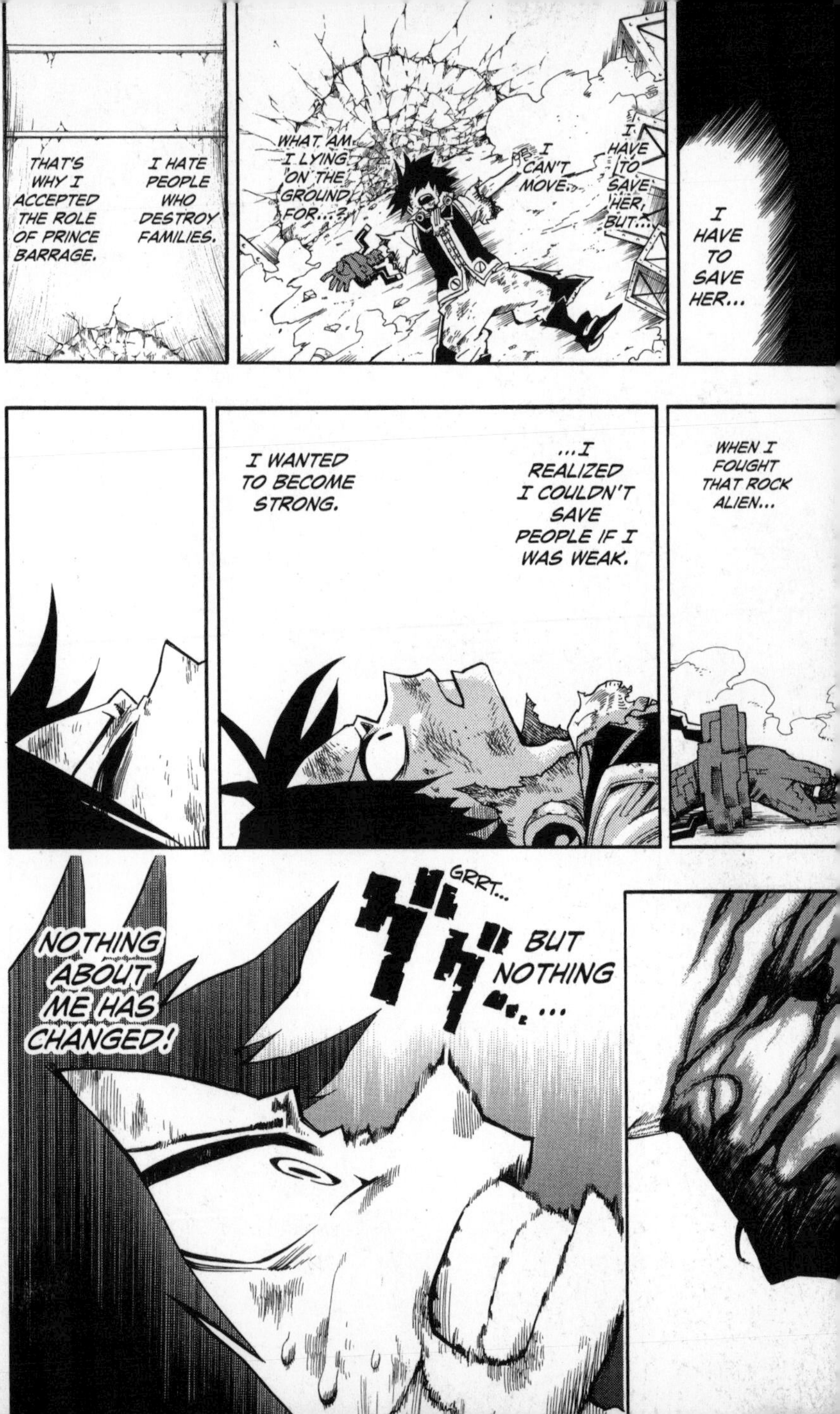
I HAVE TO SAVE HER...
I HAVE TO SAVE HER, BUT...
I CAN'T MOVE.
WHAT AM I LYING ON THE GROUND FOR...?
I HATE PEOPLE WHO DESTROY FAMILIES.
THAT'S WHY I ACCEPTED THE ROLE OF PRINCE BARRAGE.
WHEN I FOUGHT THAT ROCK ALIEN...
...I REALIZED I COULDN'T SAVE PEOPLE IF I WAS WEAK.
I WANTED TO BECOME STRONG.
GRRT...
BUT NOTHING...
NOTHING ABOUT ME HAS CHANGED!

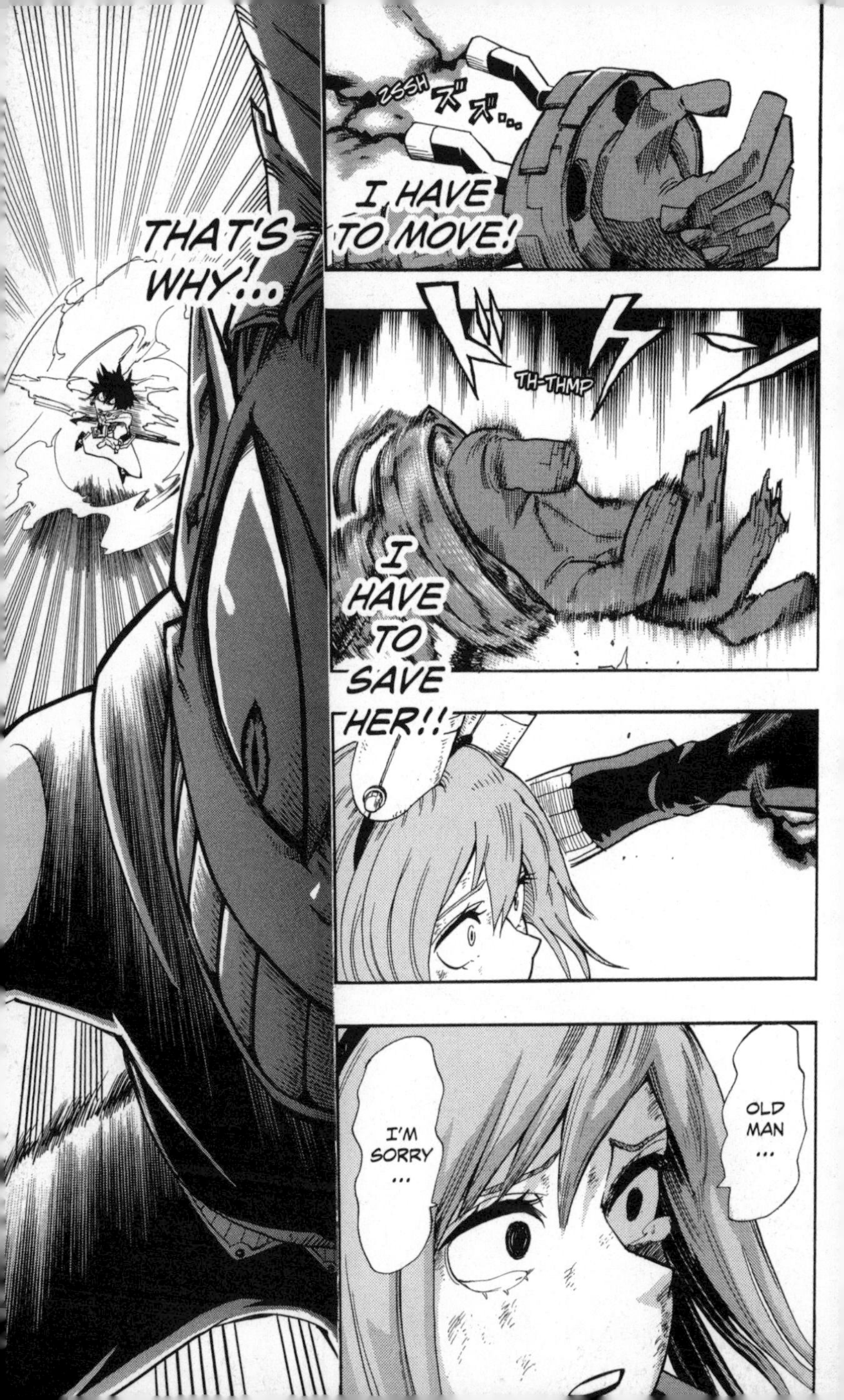
ZSSH ズズ...
I HAVE TO MOVE!
TH-THMP
I HAVE TO SAVE HER!!
OLD MAN...
I'M SORRY...
THAT'S WHY...

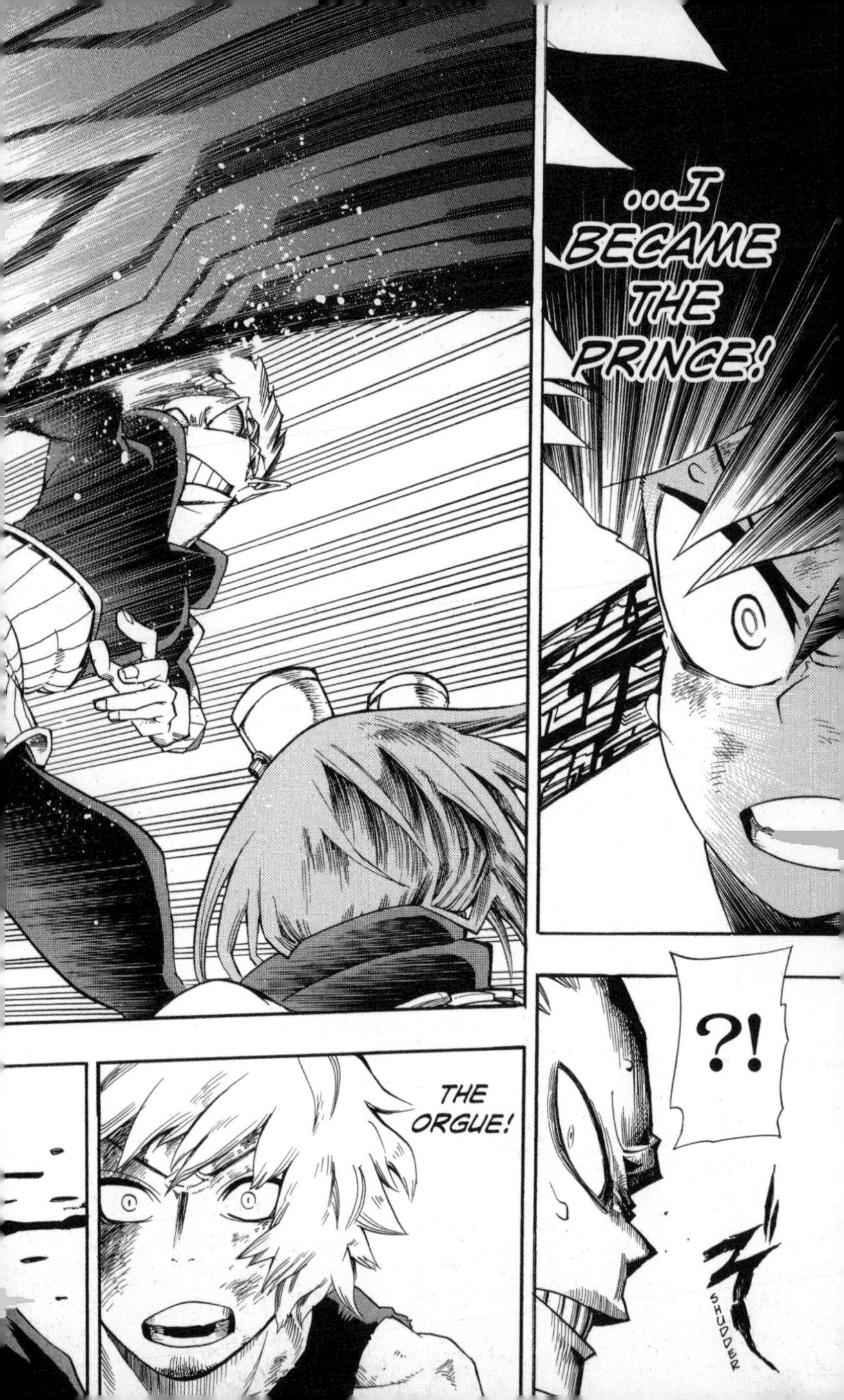
...I BECAME THE PRINCE!
?!
SHUDDER
THE ORGUE!

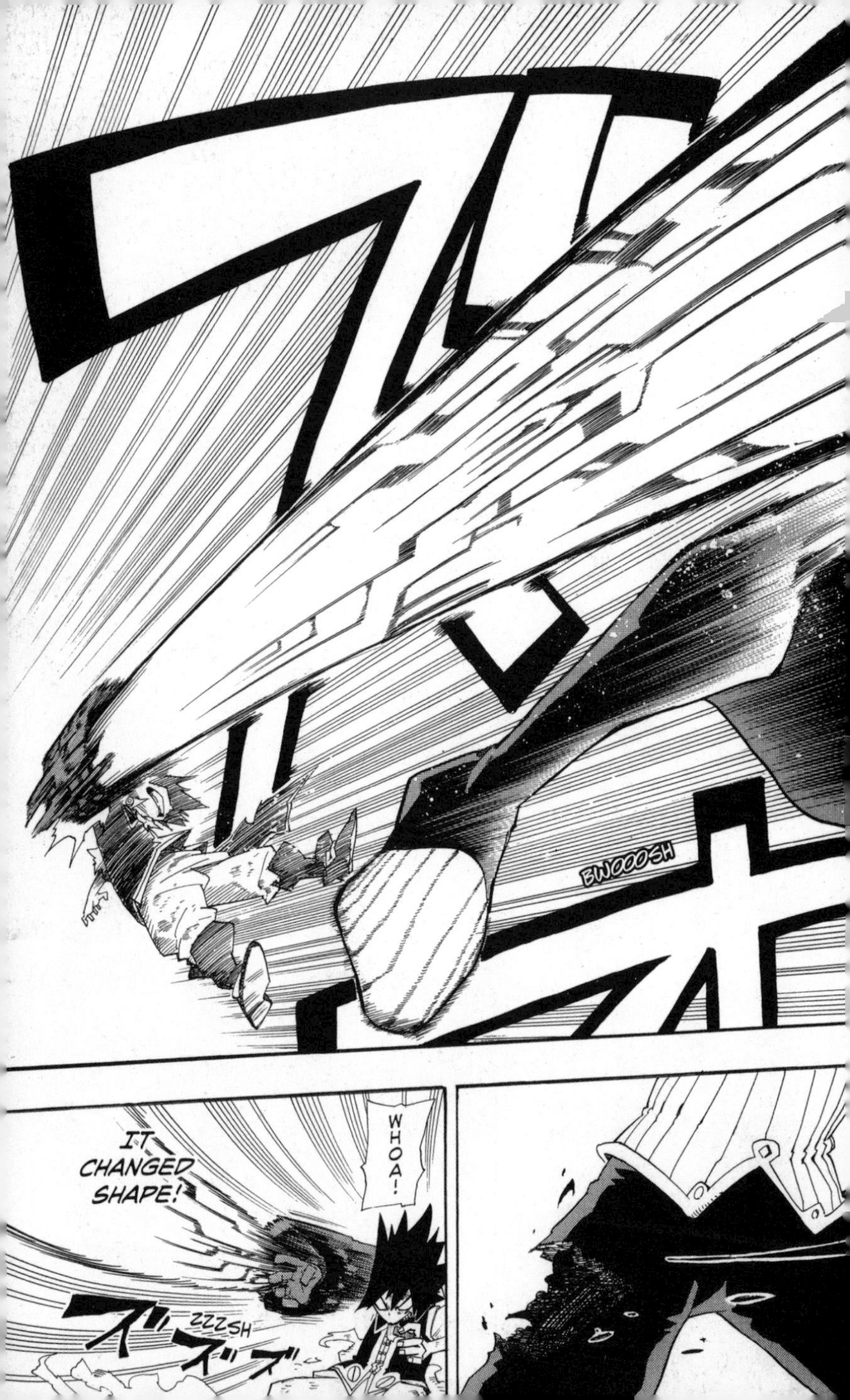
BWOOOSH
WHOA!
IT CHANGED SHAPE!
ZZZSH

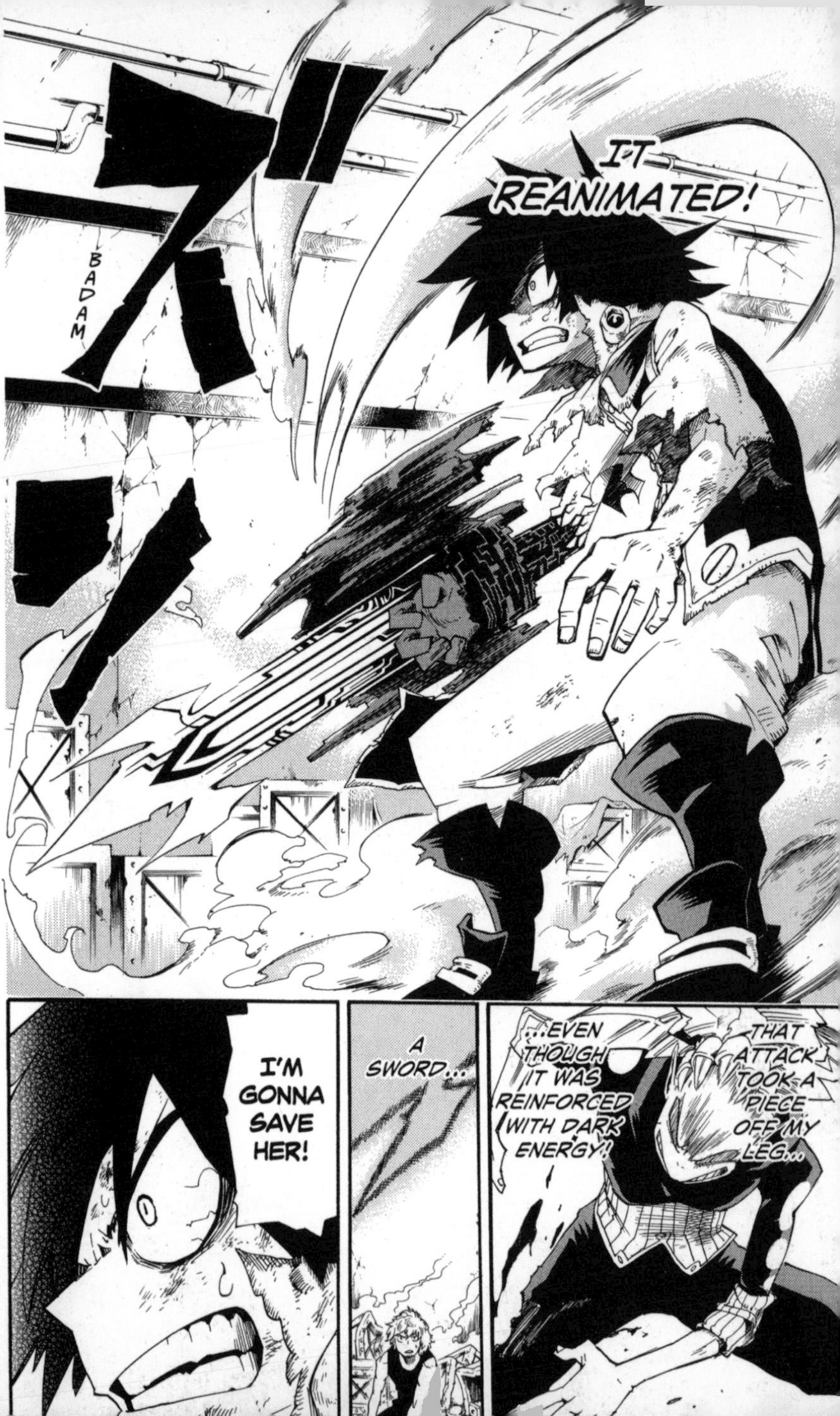
IT REANIMATED!
BADAM
THAT ATTACK TOOK A PIECE OFF MY LEG...
...EVEN THOUGH IT WAS REINFORCED WITH DARK ENERGY!
A SWORD...
I'M GONNA SAVE HER!

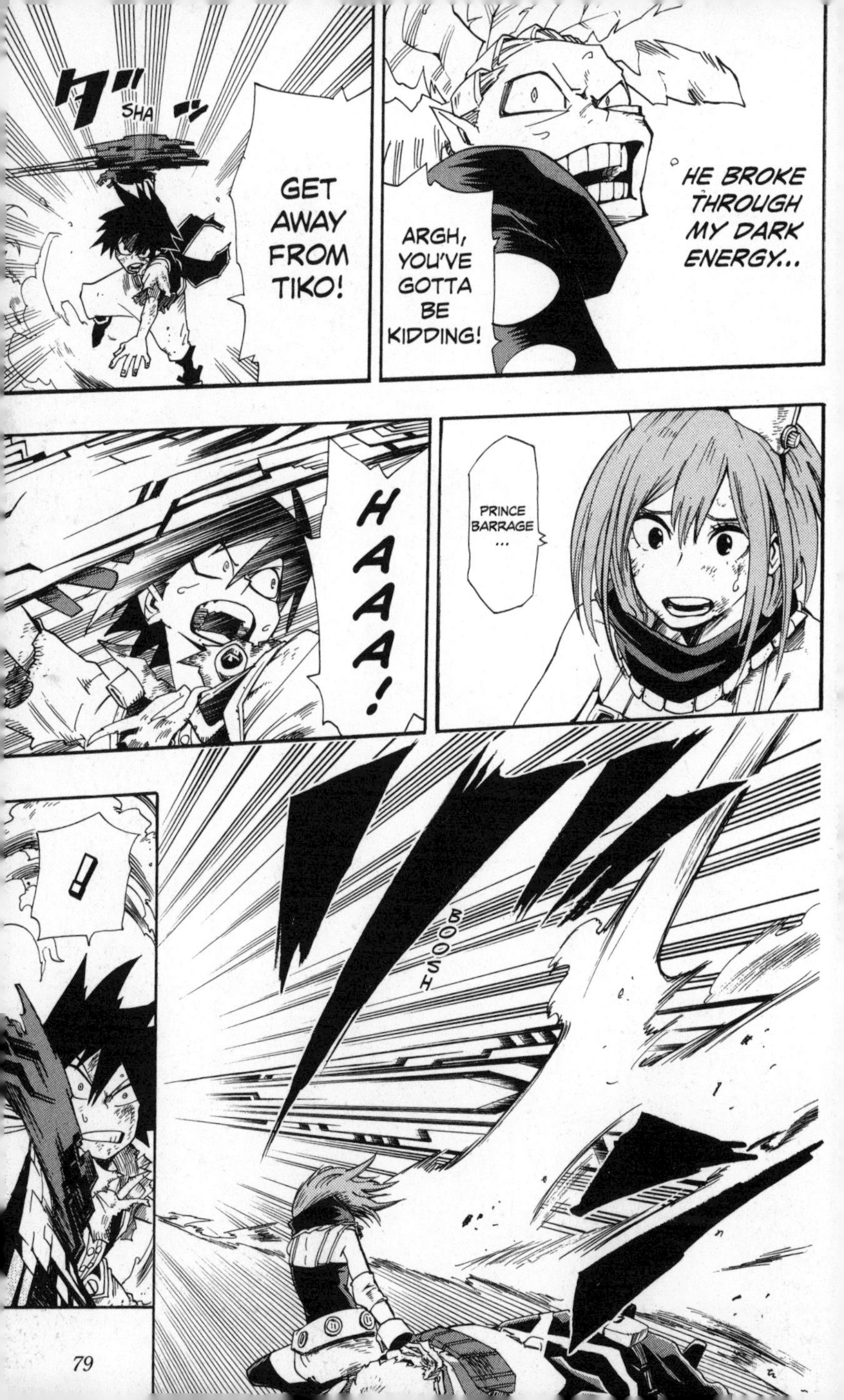
HE BROKE THROUGH MY DARK ENERGY...
ARGH, YOU'VE GOTTA BE KIDDING!
GET AWAY FROM TIKO!
SHA
PRINCE BARRAGE ...
HAAAA!
BOOOSH
!

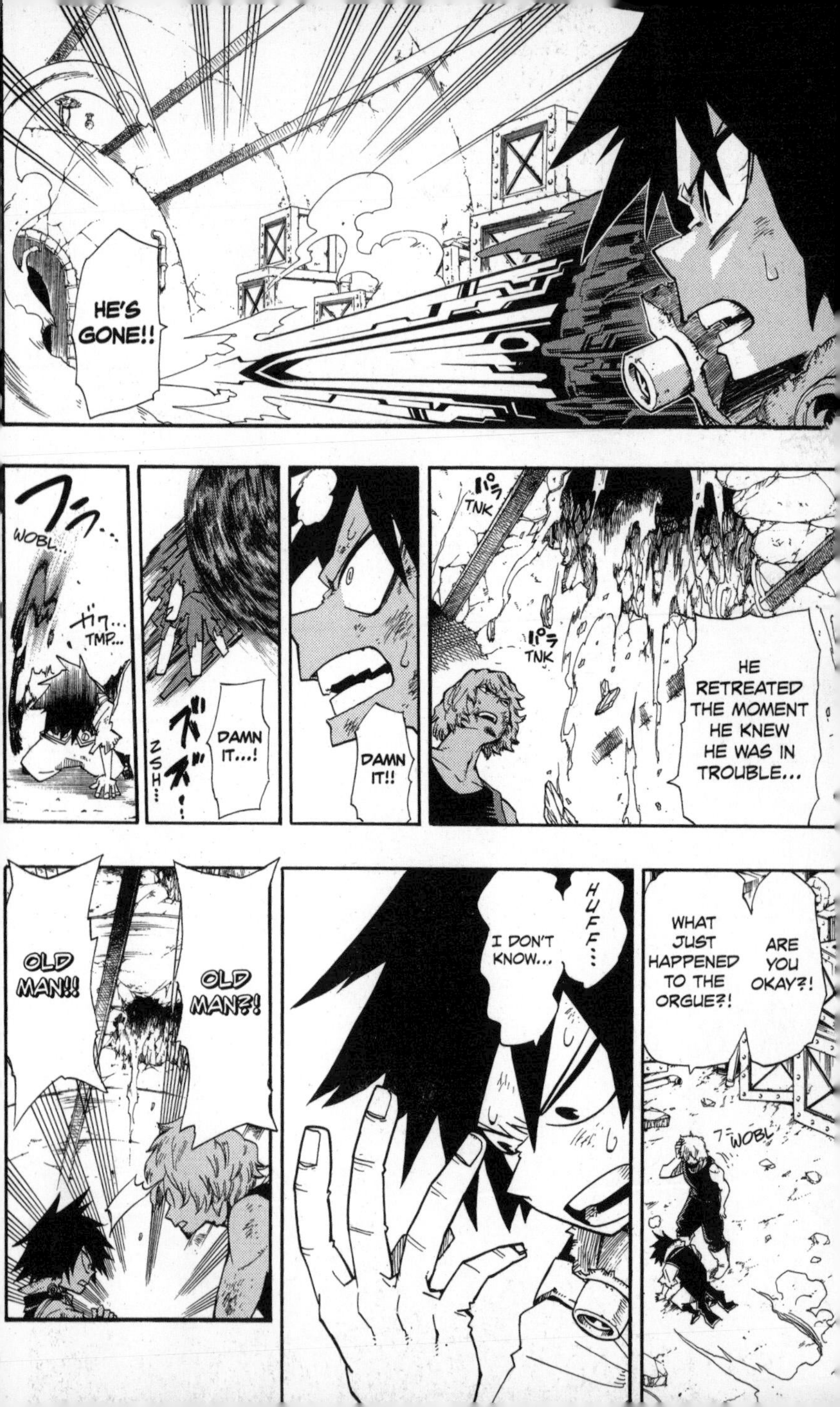
HE'S GONE!!
パラ
TNK
パラ
TNK
HE RETREATED THE MOMENT HE KNEW HE WAS IN TROUBLE...
DAMN IT!!
DAMN IT...!
ズズ
ZSH...
フラ...
WOBL...
ガク...
TMP...
ARE YOU OKAY?!
WHAT JUST HAPPENED TO THE ORGUE?!
WOBL
HUFF...
I DON'T KNOW...
OLD MAN?!
OLD MAN!!

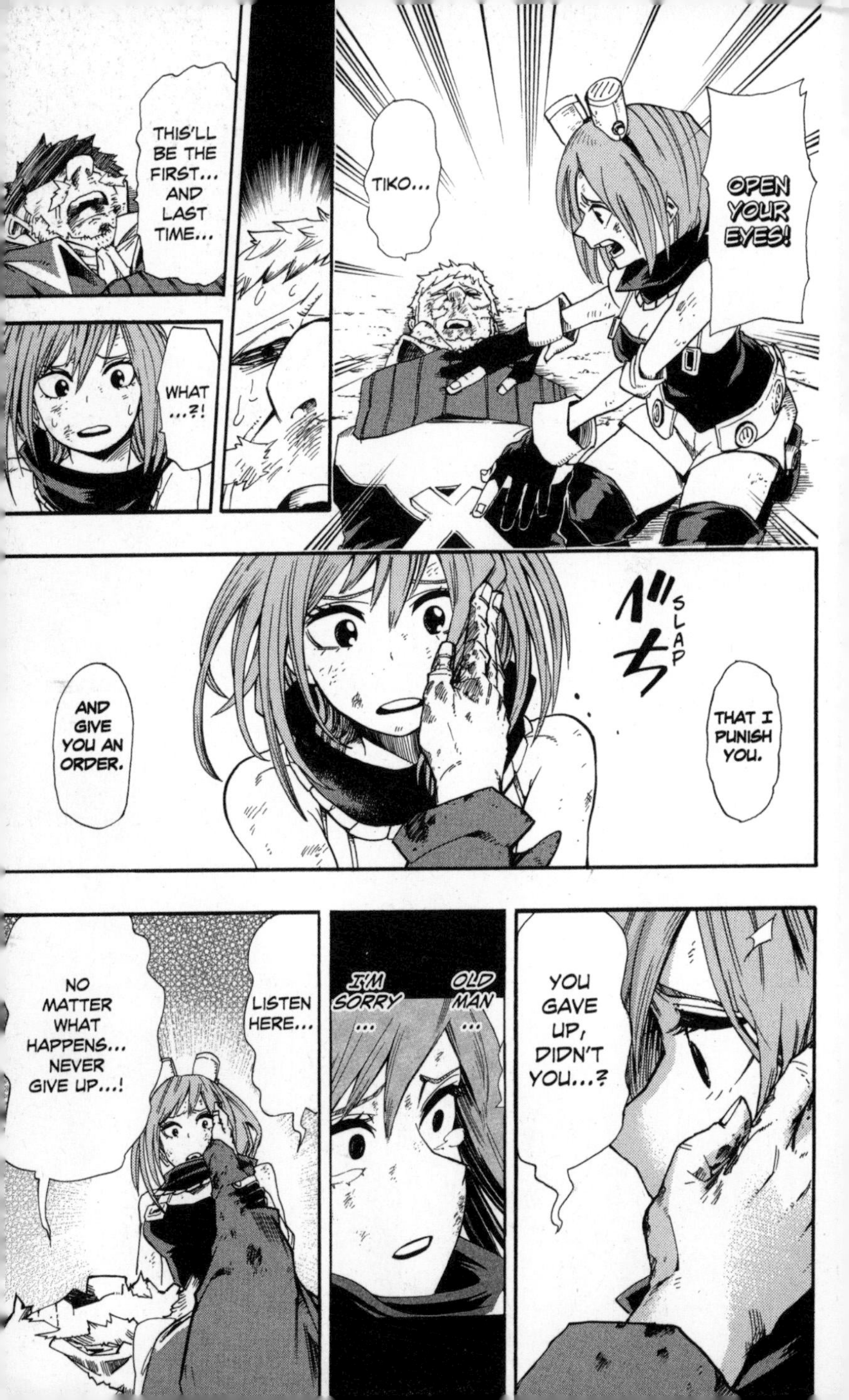
OPEN YOUR EYES!
TIKO...
THIS'LL BE THE FIRST... AND LAST TIME...
WHAT ...?!
THAT I PUNISH YOU.
SLAP
AND GIVE YOU AN ORDER.
YOU GAVE UP, DIDN'T YOU...?
OLD MAN ...
I'M SORRY ...
LISTEN HERE...
NO MATTER WHAT HAPPENS... NEVER GIVE UP...!

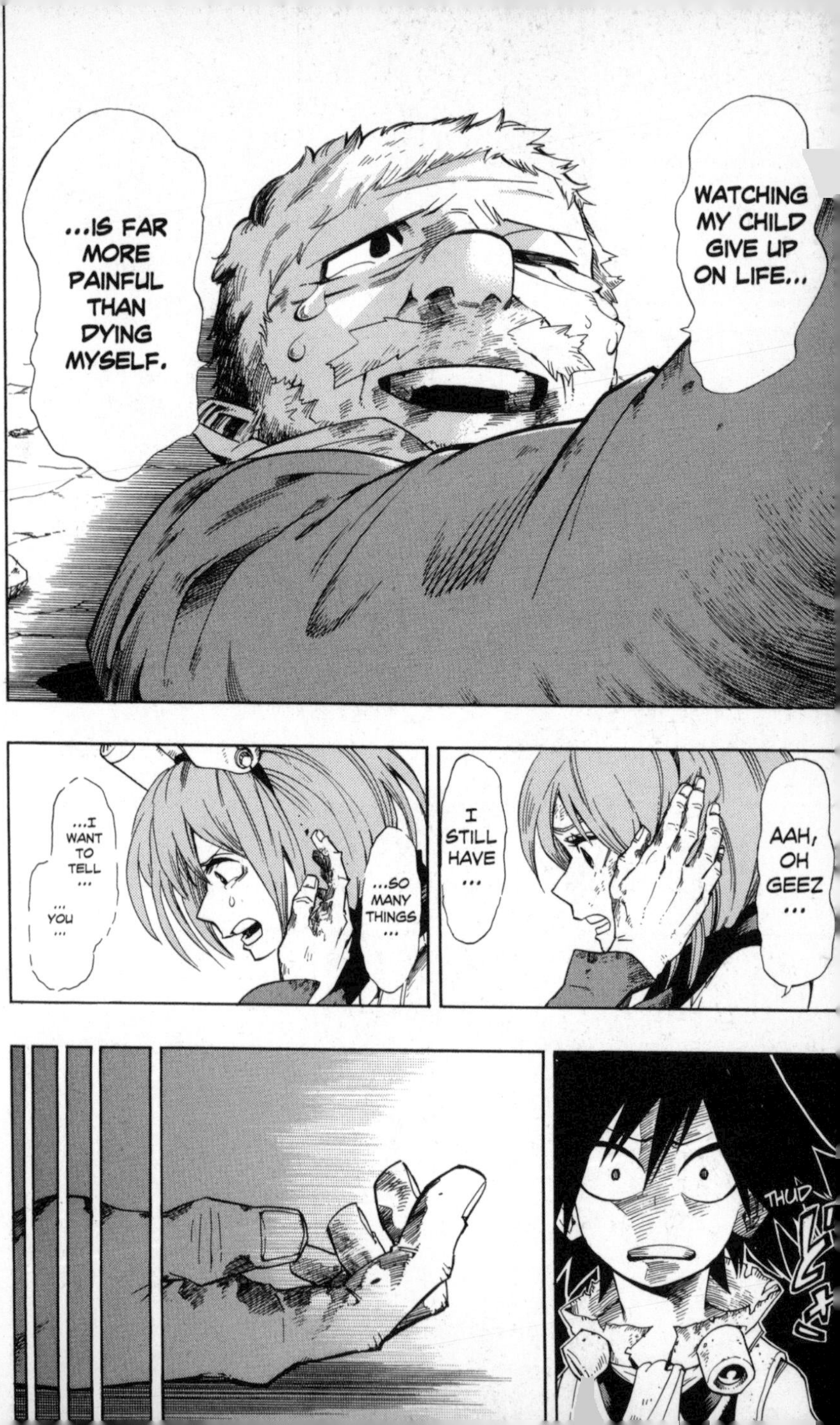
WATCHING MY CHILD GIVE UP ON LIFE...
...IS FAR MORE PAINFUL THAN DYING MYSELF.
AAH, OH GEEZ ...
I STILL HAVE ...
...SO MANY THINGS ...
...I WANT TO TELL ... ... YOU ...
THUD

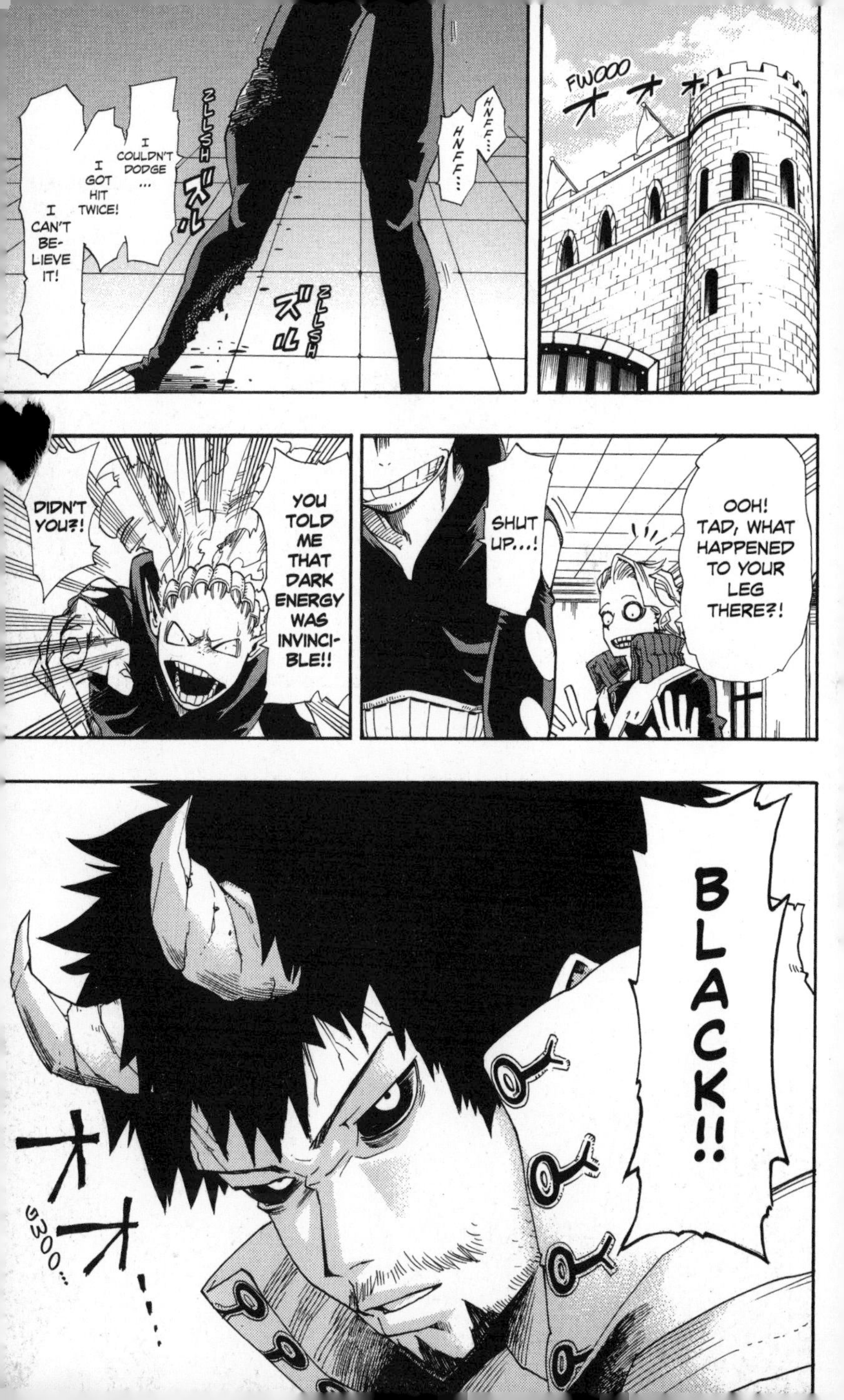
FWOOO
HNFF... HNFF...
ZLLSH
I COULDN'T DODGE...
I GOT HIT TWICE!
I CAN'T BELIEVE IT!
ZLLSH
OOH! TAD, WHAT HAPPENED TO YOUR LEG THERE?!
SHUT UP...!
YOU TOLD ME THAT DARK ENERGY WAS INVINCIBLE!!
DIDN'T YOU?!
BLACK!!
GWOO...

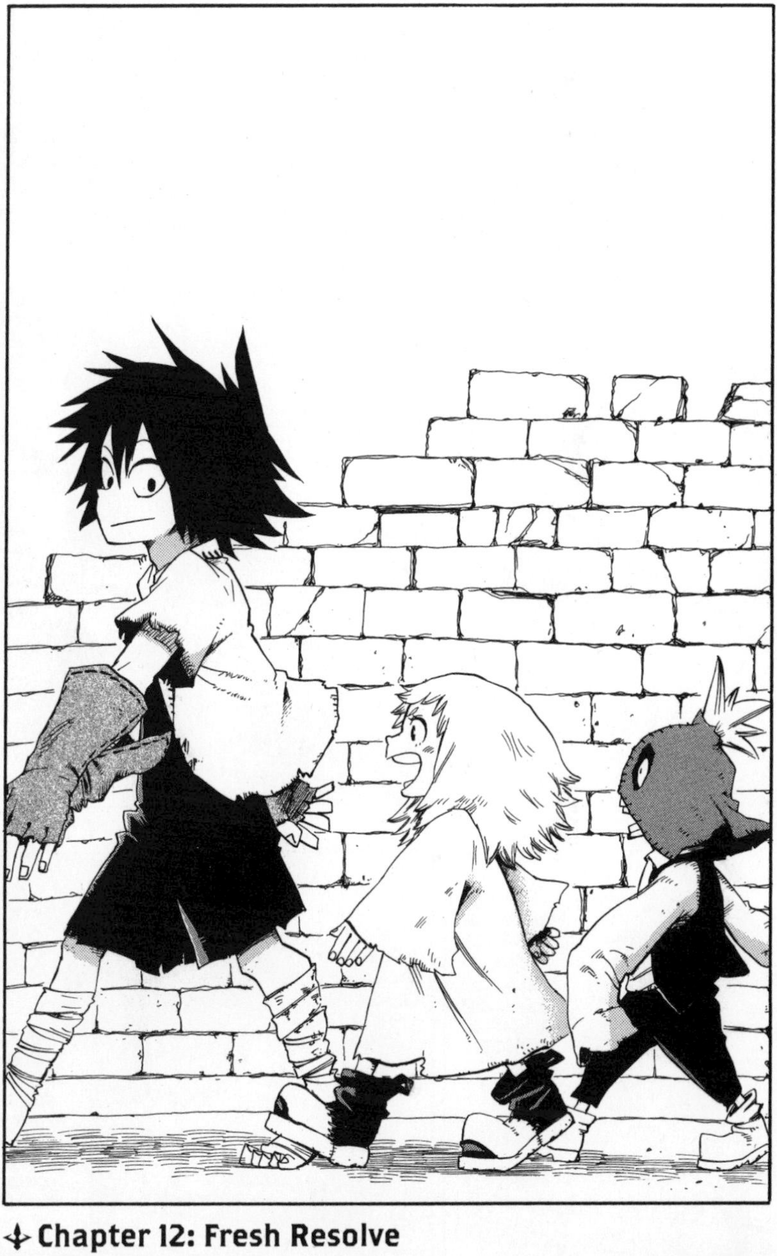

Chapter 12: Fresh Resolve

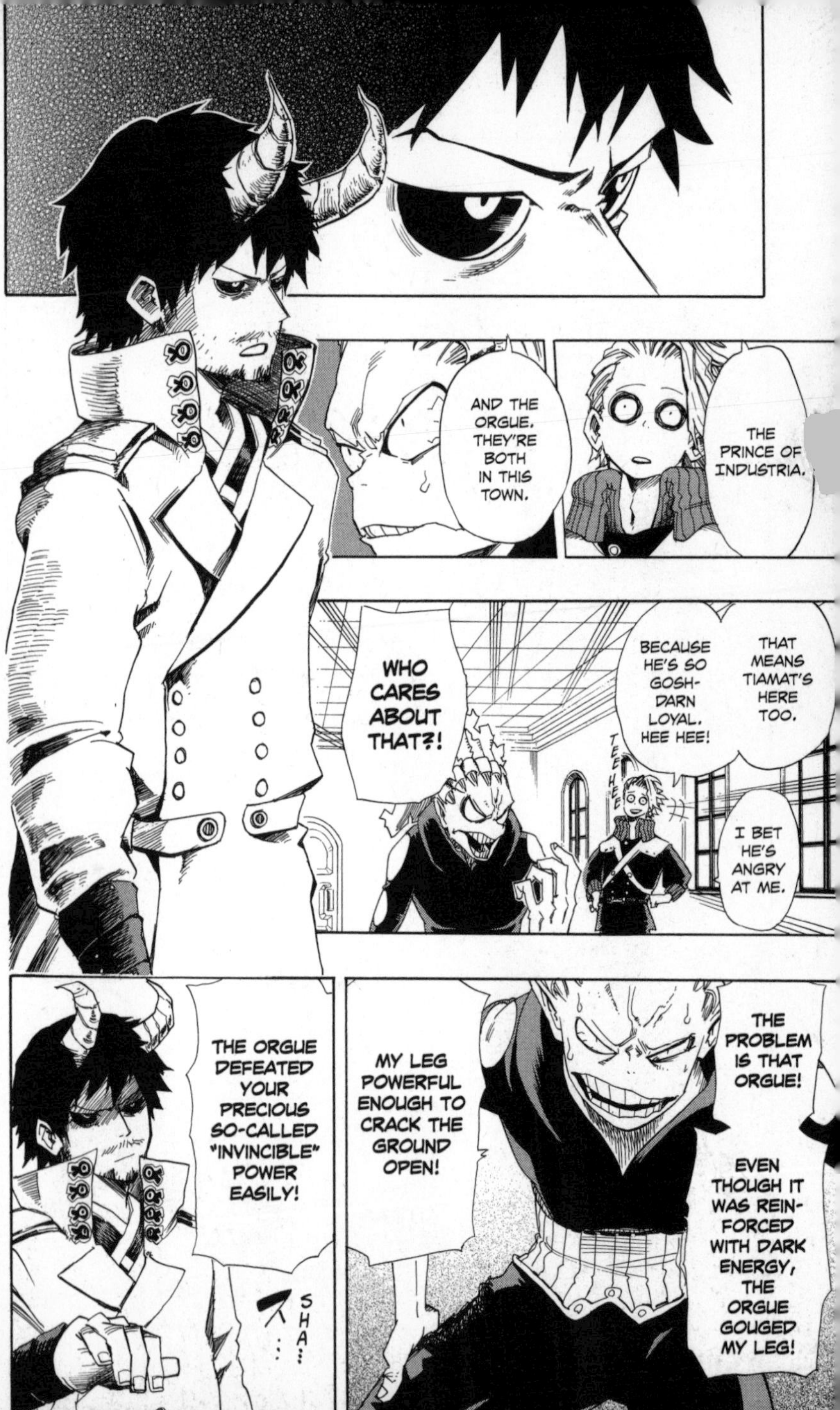
THE PRINCE OF INDUSTRIA.
AND THE ORGUE. THEY'RE BOTH IN THIS TOWN.
THAT MEANS TIAMAT'S HERE TOO.
BECAUSE HE'S SO GOSH-DARN LOYAL. HEE HEE!
TEE HEE
I BET HE'S ANGRY AT ME.
WHO CARES ABOUT THAT?!
THE PROBLEM IS THAT ORGUE!
EVEN THOUGH IT WAS REIN-FORCED WITH DARK ENERGY, THE ORGUE GOUGED MY LEG!
MY LEG POWERFUL ENOUGH TO CRACK THE GROUND OPEN!
THE ORGUE DEFEATED YOUR PRECIOUS SO-CALLED "INVINCIBLE" POWER EASILY!
SHA...

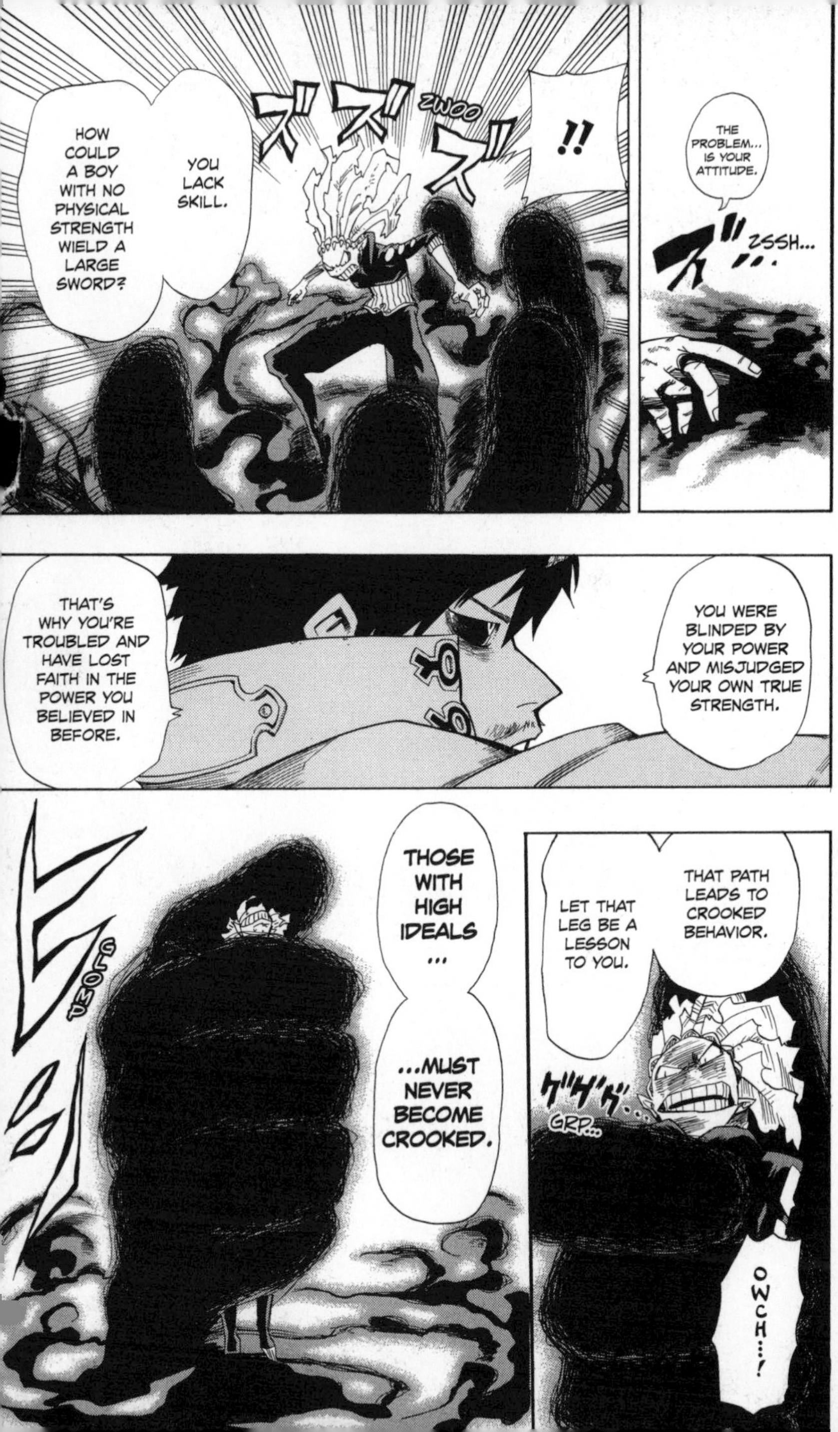
THE PROBLEM... IS YOUR ATTITUDE.
ZSSH...
!!
ZWOO
YOU LACK SKILL.
HOW COULD A BOY WITH NO PHYSICAL STRENGTH WIELD A LARGE SWORD?
YOU WERE BLINDED BY YOUR POWER AND MISJUDGED YOUR OWN TRUE STRENGTH.
THAT'S WHY YOU'RE TROUBLED AND HAVE LOST FAITH IN THE POWER YOU BELIEVED IN BEFORE.
THAT PATH LEADS TO CROOKED BEHAVIOR.
LET THAT LEG BE A LESSON TO YOU.
GRP...
OWCH...!
THOSE WITH HIGH IDEALS...
...MUST NEVER BECOME CROOKED.
GLOMP

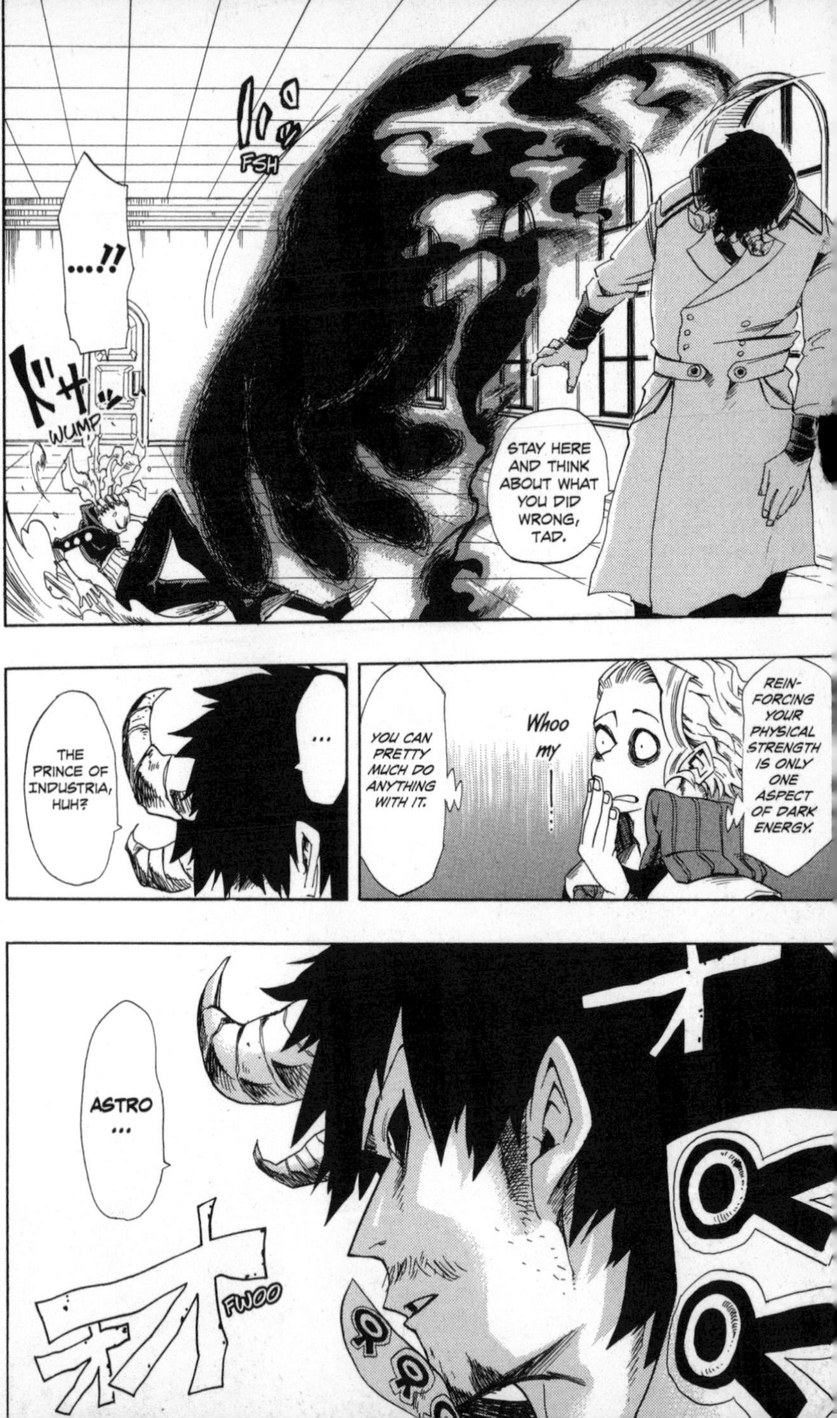
FSH
STAY HERE AND THINK ABOUT WHAT YOU DID WRONG, TAD.
...!!
WUMP
REIN-FORCING YOUR PHYSICAL STRENGTH IS ONLY ONE ASPECT OF DARK ENERGY.
Whoo my
YOU CAN PRETTY MUCH DO ANYTHING WITH IT.
...
THE PRINCE OF INDUSTRIA, HUH?
ASTRO ...
FWOO

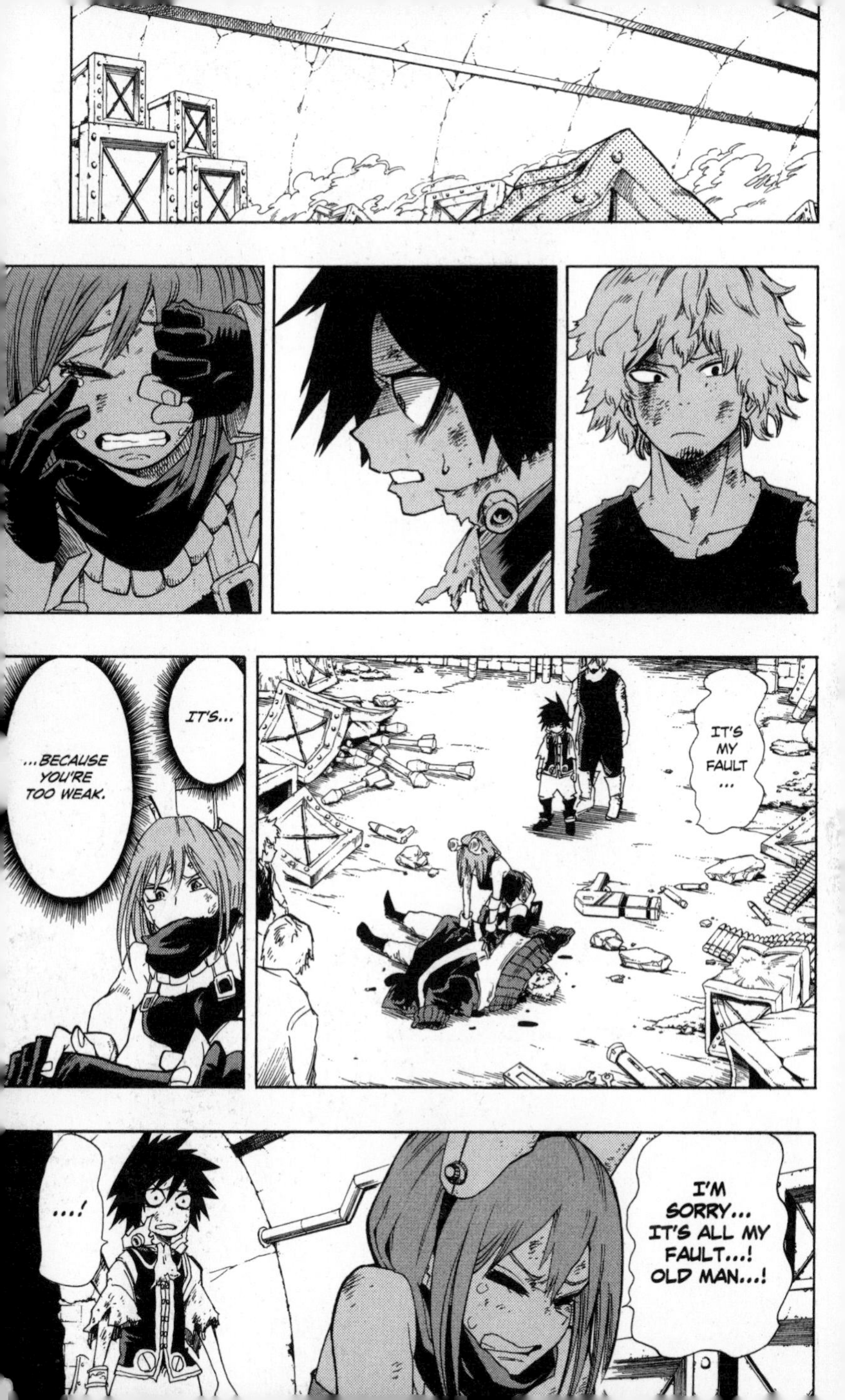
IT'S MY FAULT ...
IT'S...
...BECAUSE YOU'RE TOO WEAK.
I'M SORRY... IT'S ALL MY FAULT...! OLD MAN...!
...!

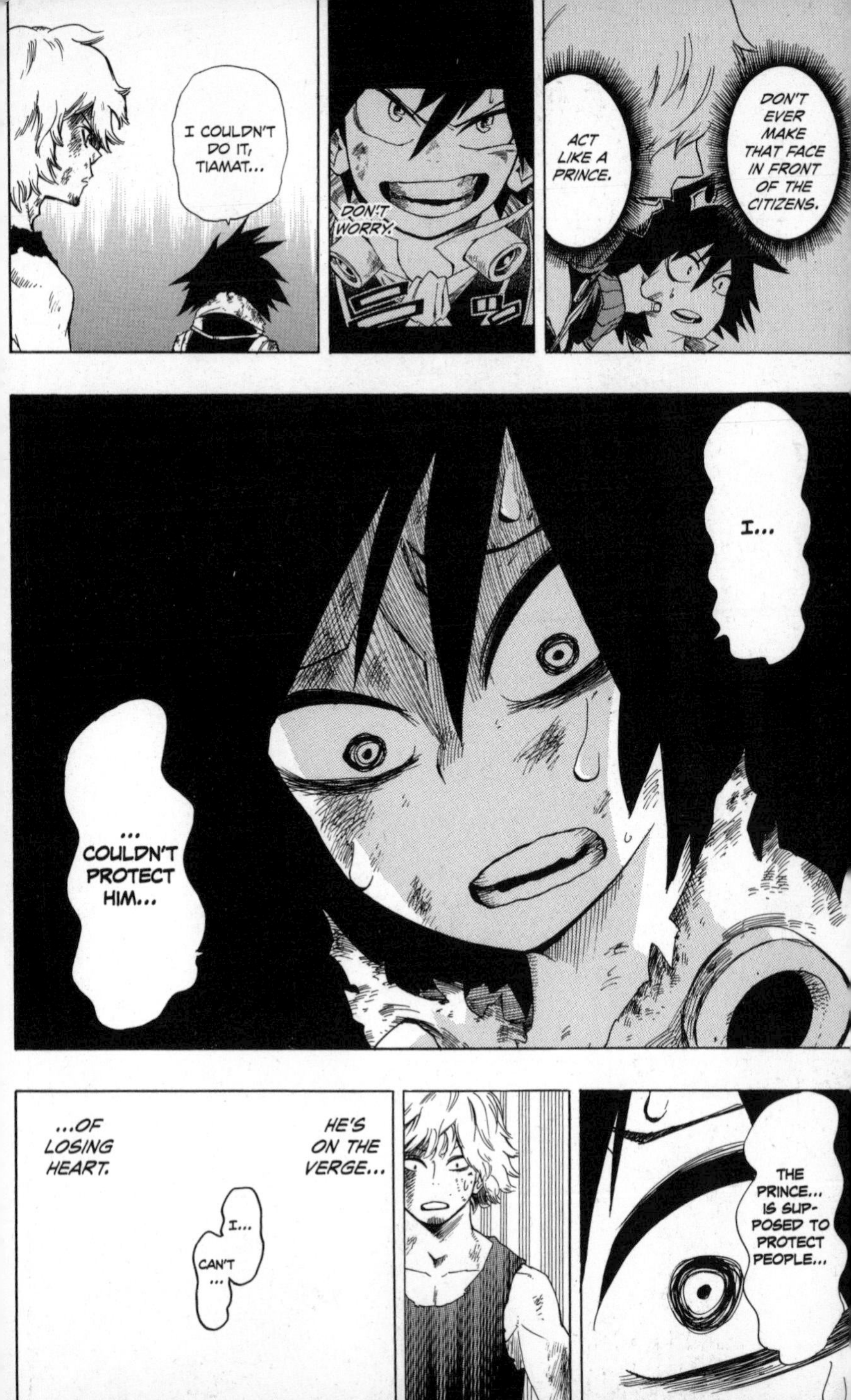
DON'T EVER MAKE THAT FACE IN FRONT OF THE CITIZENS.
ACT LIKE A PRINCE.
DON'T WORRY.
I COULDN'T DO IT, TIAMAT...
I...
...COULDN'T PROTECT HIM...
THE PRINCE... IS SUP-POSED TO PROTECT PEOPLE...
HE'S ON THE VERGE...
...OF LOSING HEART.
I...
CAN'T...

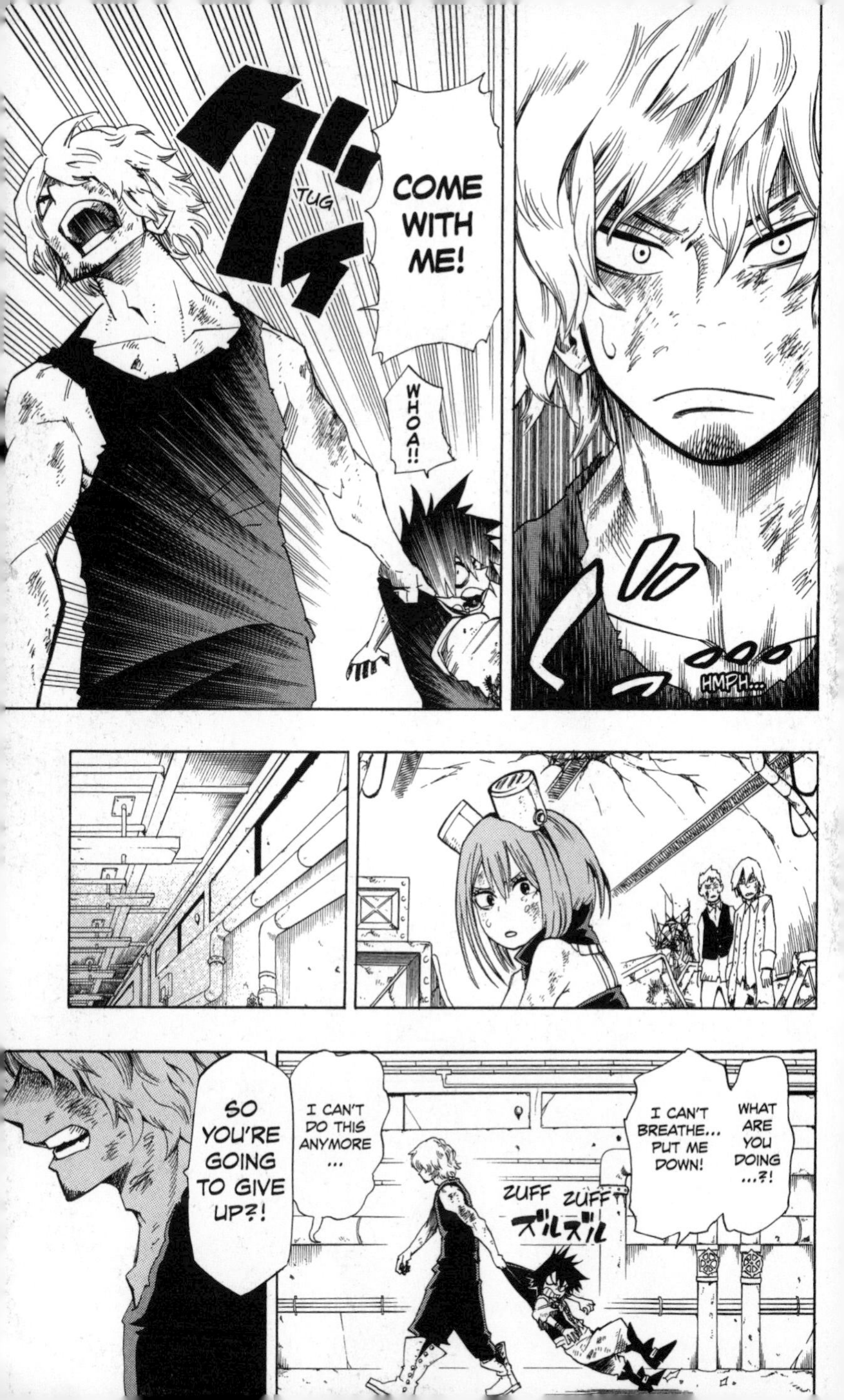
HMPH...
COME WITH ME!
TUG
WHOA!!
WHAT ARE YOU DOING...?!
I CAN'T BREATHE... PUT ME DOWN!
ZUFF ZUFF
ズルズル
I CAN'T DO THIS ANYMORE...
SO YOU'RE GOING TO GIVE UP?!

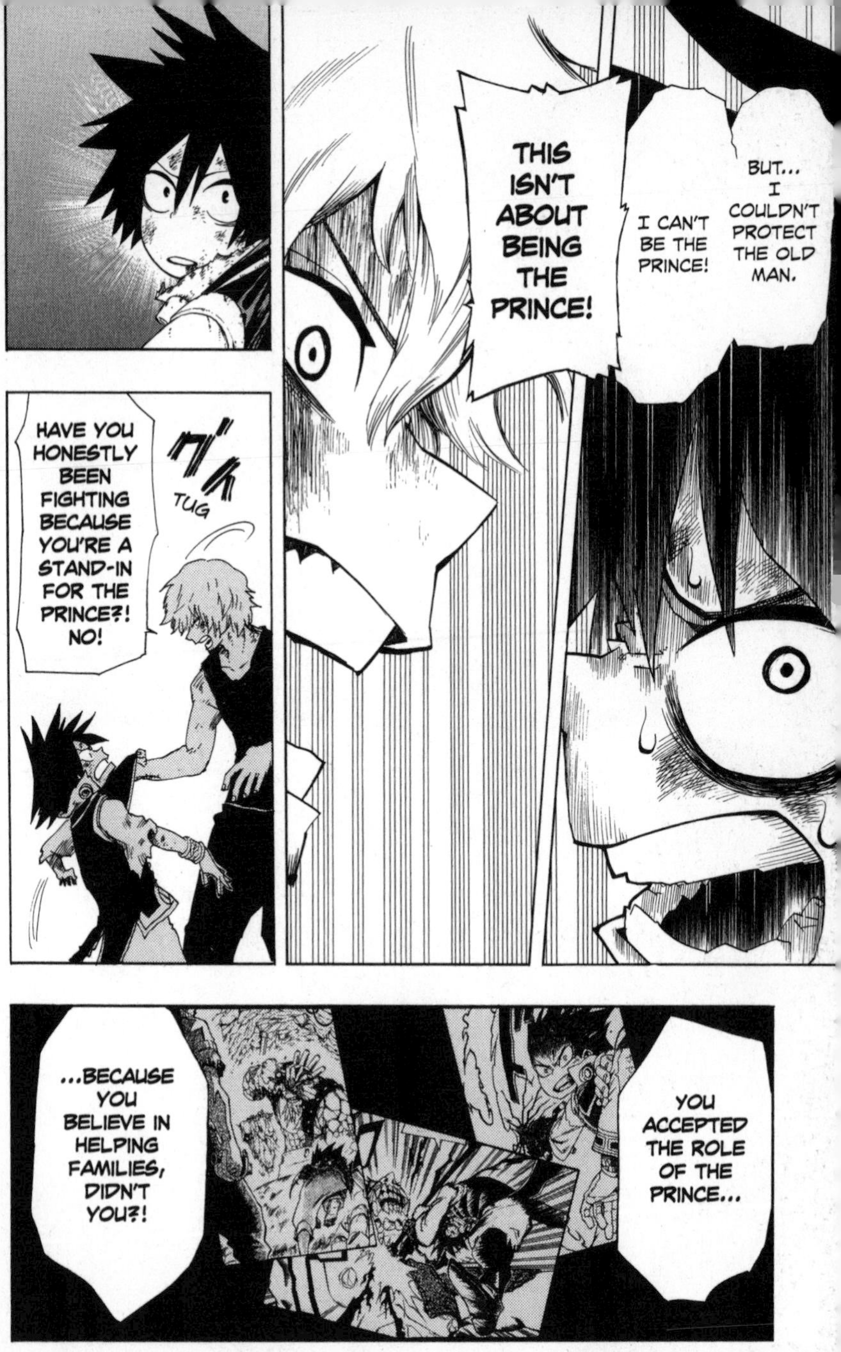
BUT... I COULDN'T PROTECT THE OLD MAN.
I CAN'T BE THE PRINCE!
THIS ISN'T ABOUT BEING THE PRINCE!
HAVE YOU HONESTLY BEEN FIGHTING BECAUSE YOU'RE A STAND-IN FOR THE PRINCE?! NO!
TUG
YOU ACCEPTED THE ROLE OF THE PRINCE...
...BECAUSE YOU BELIEVE IN HELPING FAMILIES, DIDN'T YOU?!

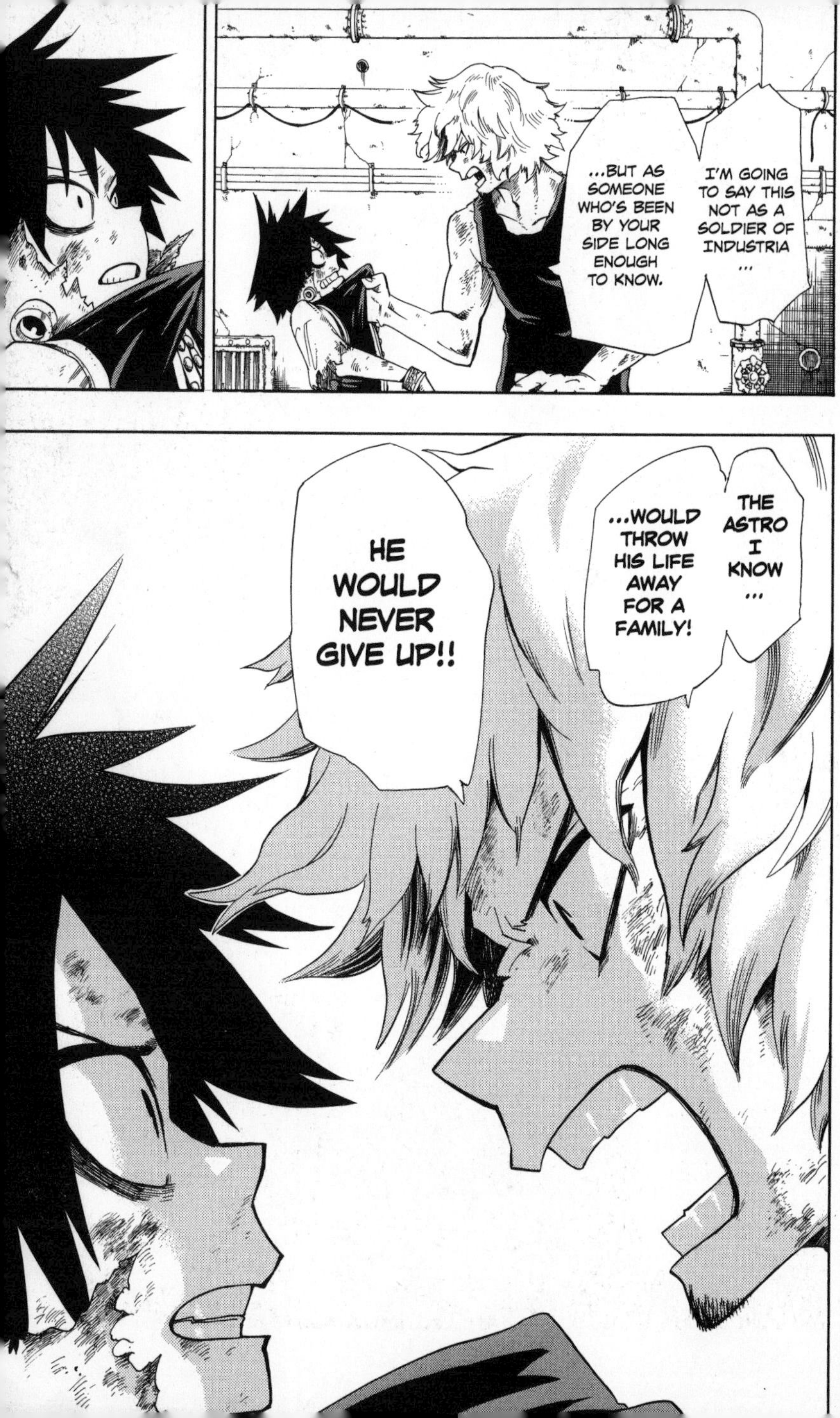
I'M GOING TO SAY THIS NOT AS A SOLDIER OF INDUSTRIA ...
...BUT AS SOMEONE WHO'S BEEN BY YOUR SIDE LONG ENOUGH TO KNOW.
THE ASTRO I KNOW ...
...WOULD THROW HIS LIFE AWAY FOR A FAMILY!
HE WOULD NEVER GIVE UP!!

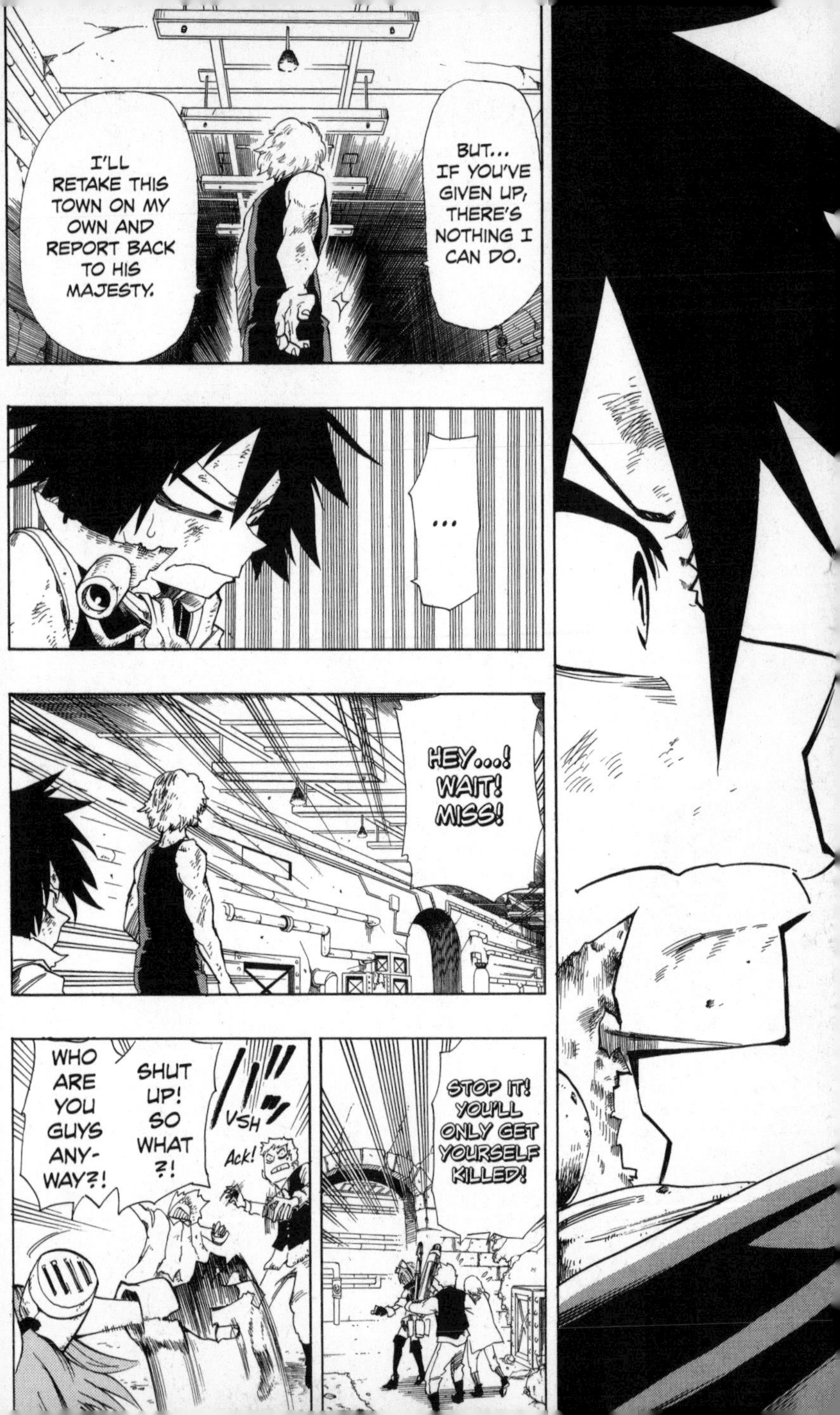
BUT... IF YOU'VE GIVEN UP, THERE'S NOTHING I CAN DO.
I'LL RETAKE THIS TOWN ON MY OWN AND REPORT BACK TO HIS MAJESTY.
...
HEY...! WAIT! MISS!
STOP IT! YOU'LL ONLY GET YOURSELF KILLED!
SHUT UP! SO WHAT?!
WHO ARE YOU GUYS ANY-WAY?!
VSH
Ack!

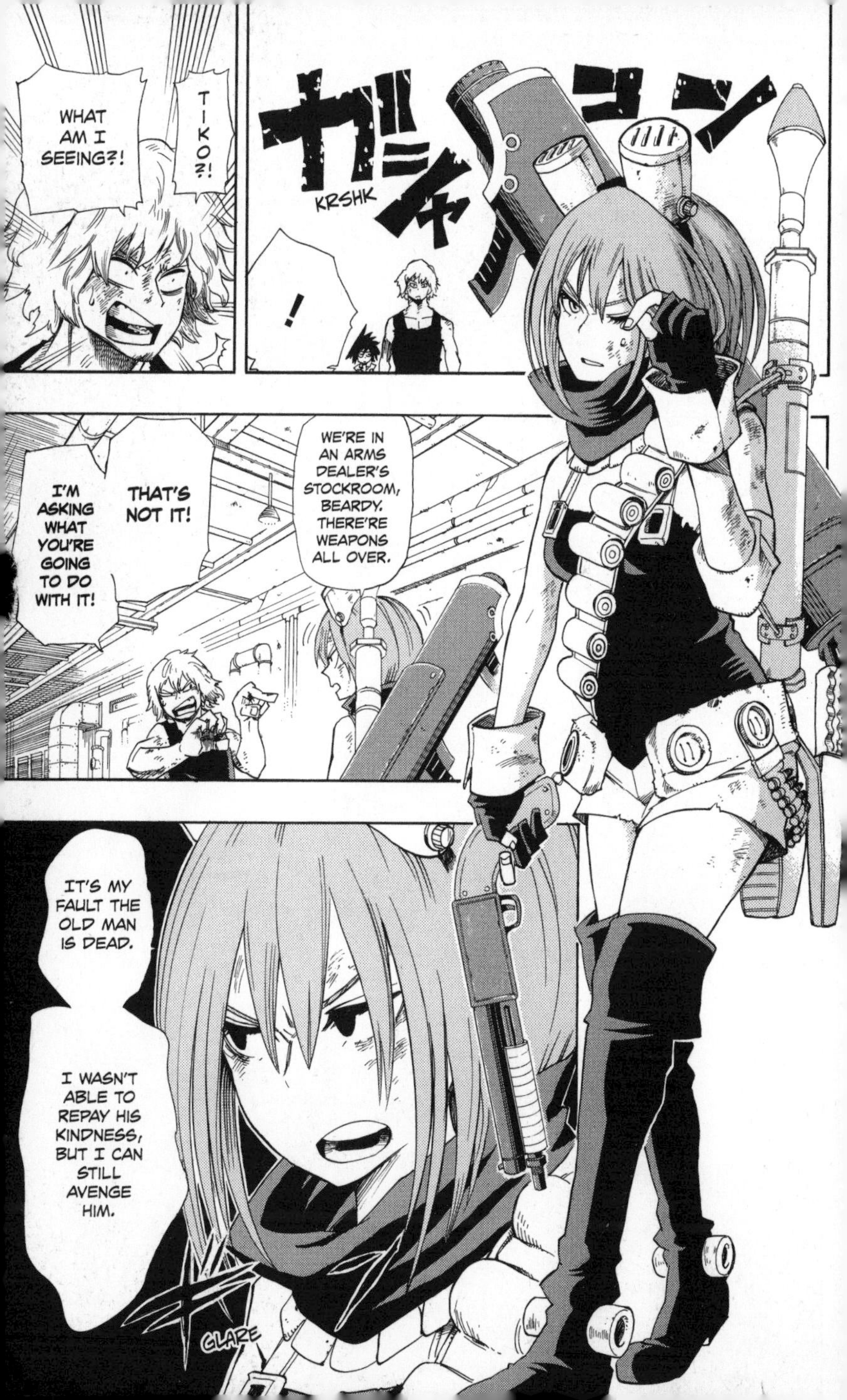

ガシャコン
KRSHK
!
TIKO?!
WHAT AM I SEEING?!
WE'RE IN AN ARMS DEALER'S STOCKROOM, BEARDY. THERE'RE WEAPONS ALL OVER.
THAT'S NOT IT!
I'M ASKING WHAT YOU'RE GOING TO DO WITH IT!
IT'S MY FAULT THE OLD MAN IS DEAD.
I WASN'T ABLE TO REPAY HIS KINDNESS, BUT I CAN STILL AVENGE HIM.
GLARE

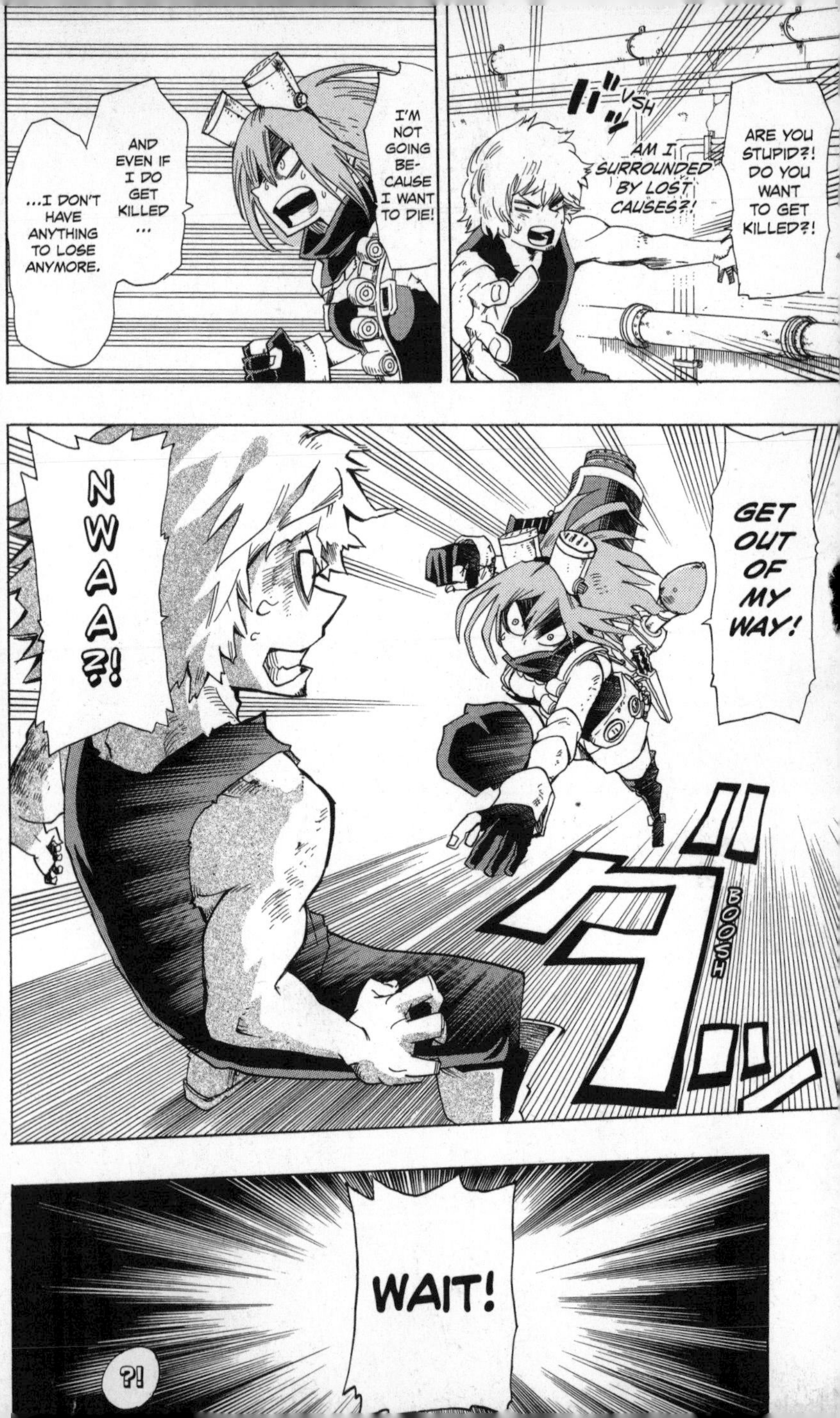
ARE YOU STUPID?! DO YOU WANT TO GET KILLED?!
VSH
AM I SURROUNDED BY LOST CAUSES?!
I'M NOT GOING BE-CAUSE I WANT TO DIE!
AND EVEN IF I DO GET KILLED...
...I DON'T HAVE ANYTHING TO LOSE ANYMORE.
GET OUT OF MY WAY!
NWAAA?!
BOOSH
WAIT!
?!

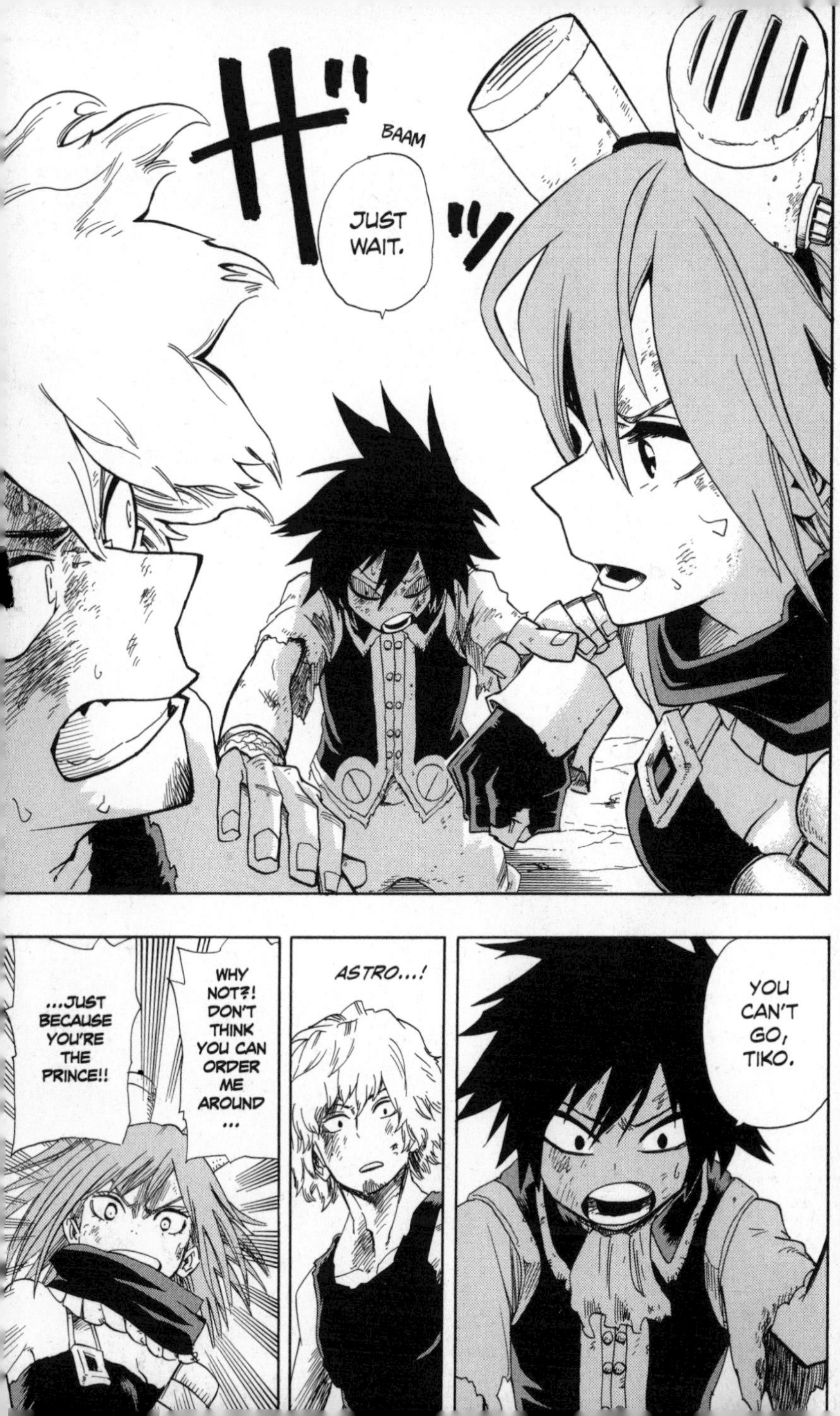
BAAM
JUST WAIT.
YOU CAN'T GO, TIKO.
ASTRO...!
WHY NOT?! DON'T THINK YOU CAN ORDER ME AROUND ...
...JUST BECAUSE YOU'RE THE PRINCE!!

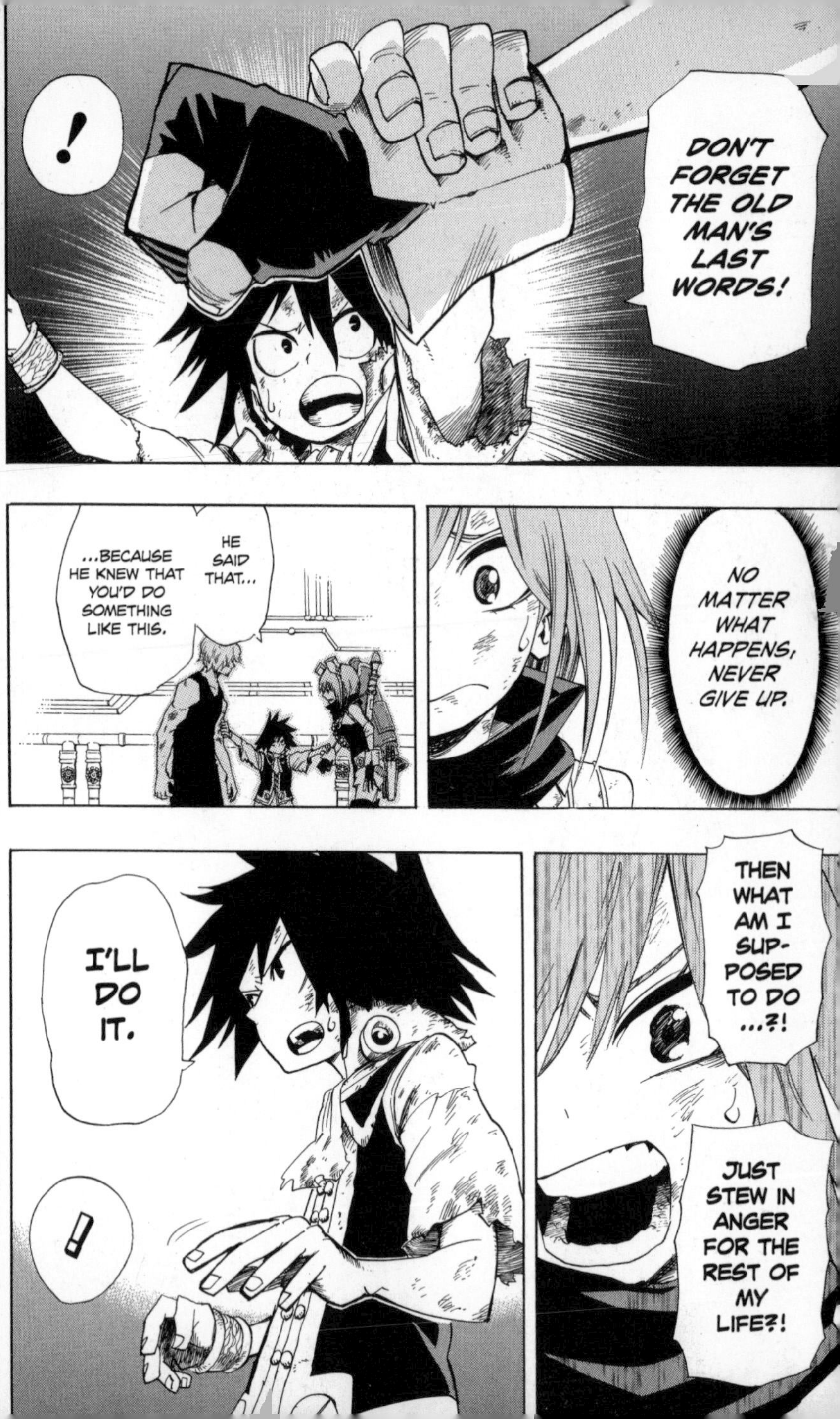
DON'T FORGET THE OLD MAN'S LAST WORDS!
!
NO MATTER WHAT HAPPENS, NEVER GIVE UP.
HE SAID THAT...
...BECAUSE HE KNEW THAT YOU'D DO SOMETHING LIKE THIS.
THEN WHAT AM I SUP-POSED TO DO ...?!
JUST STEW IN ANGER FOR THE REST OF MY LIFE?!
I'LL DO IT.
!

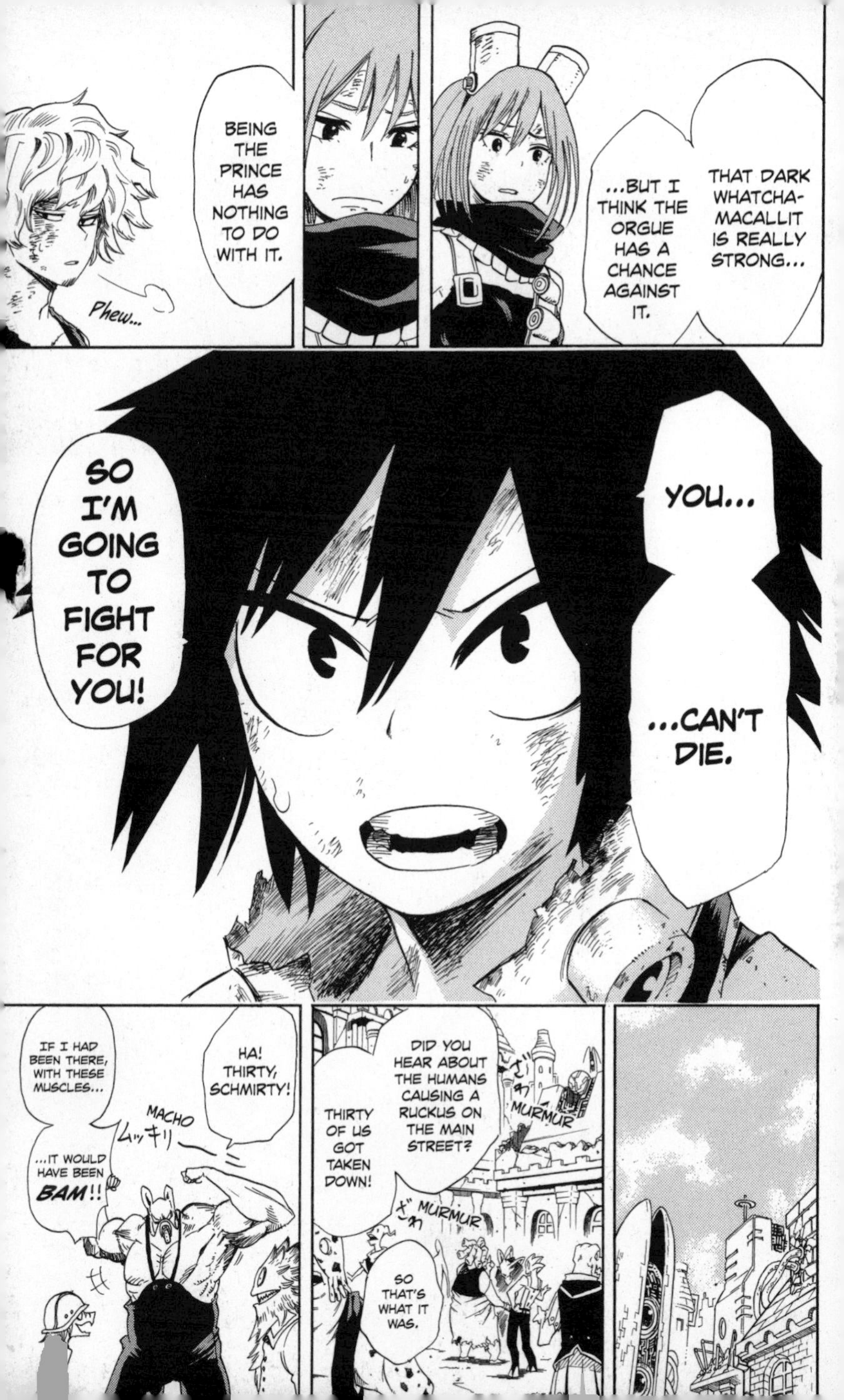
THAT DARK WHATCHA-MACALLIT IS REALLY STRONG...
...BUT I THINK THE ORGUE HAS A CHANCE AGAINST IT.
BEING THE PRINCE HAS NOTHING TO DO WITH IT.
Phew...
YOU...
...CAN'T DIE.
SO I'M GOING TO FIGHT FOR YOU!
DID YOU HEAR ABOUT THE HUMANS CAUSING A RUCKUS ON THE MAIN STREET?
MURMUR
THIRTY OF US GOT TAKEN DOWN!
MURMUR
SO THAT'S WHAT IT WAS.
HA! THIRTY, SCHMIRTY!
IF I HAD BEEN THERE, WITH THESE MUSCLES...
MACHO
...IT WOULD HAVE BEEN BAM!!

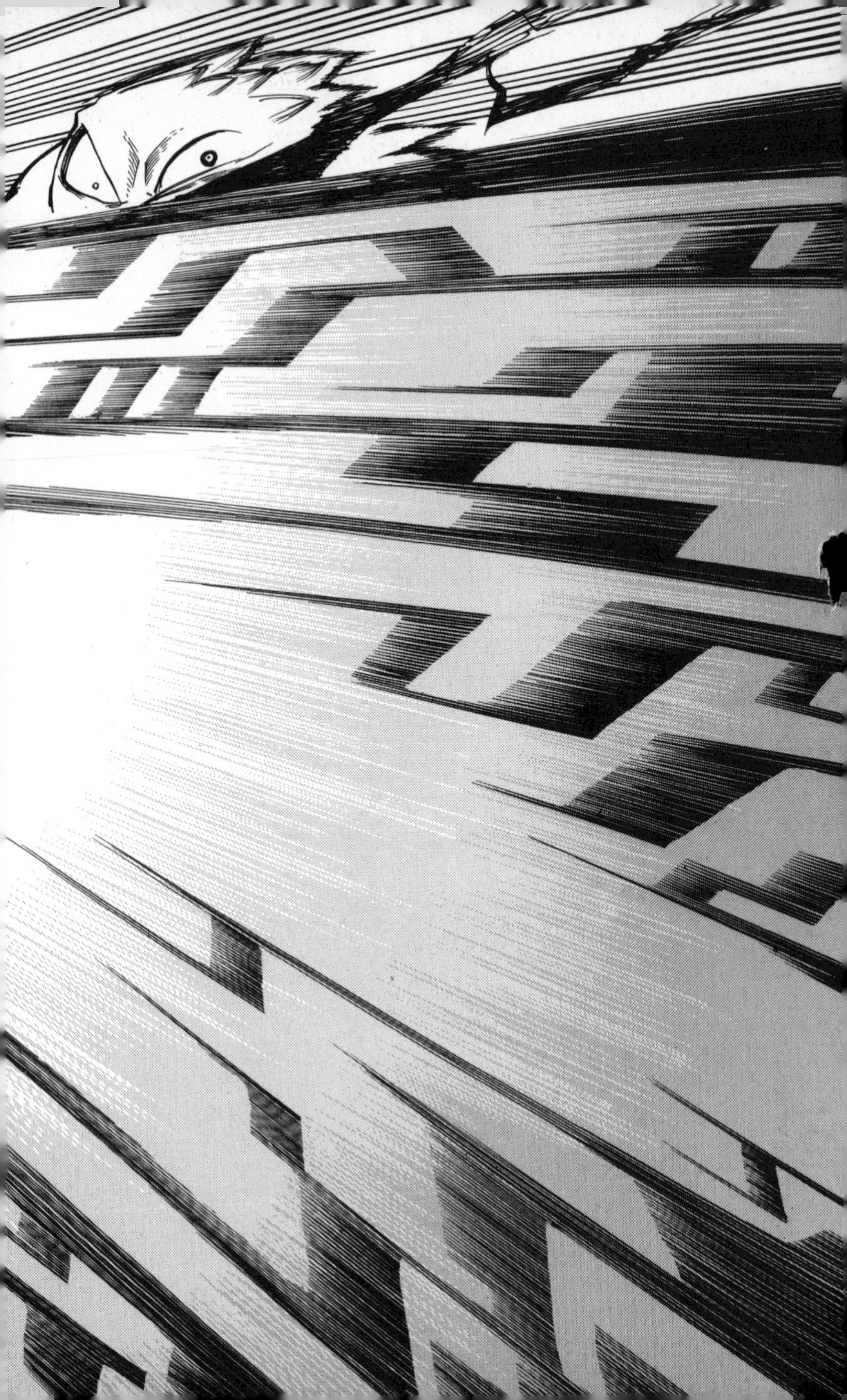

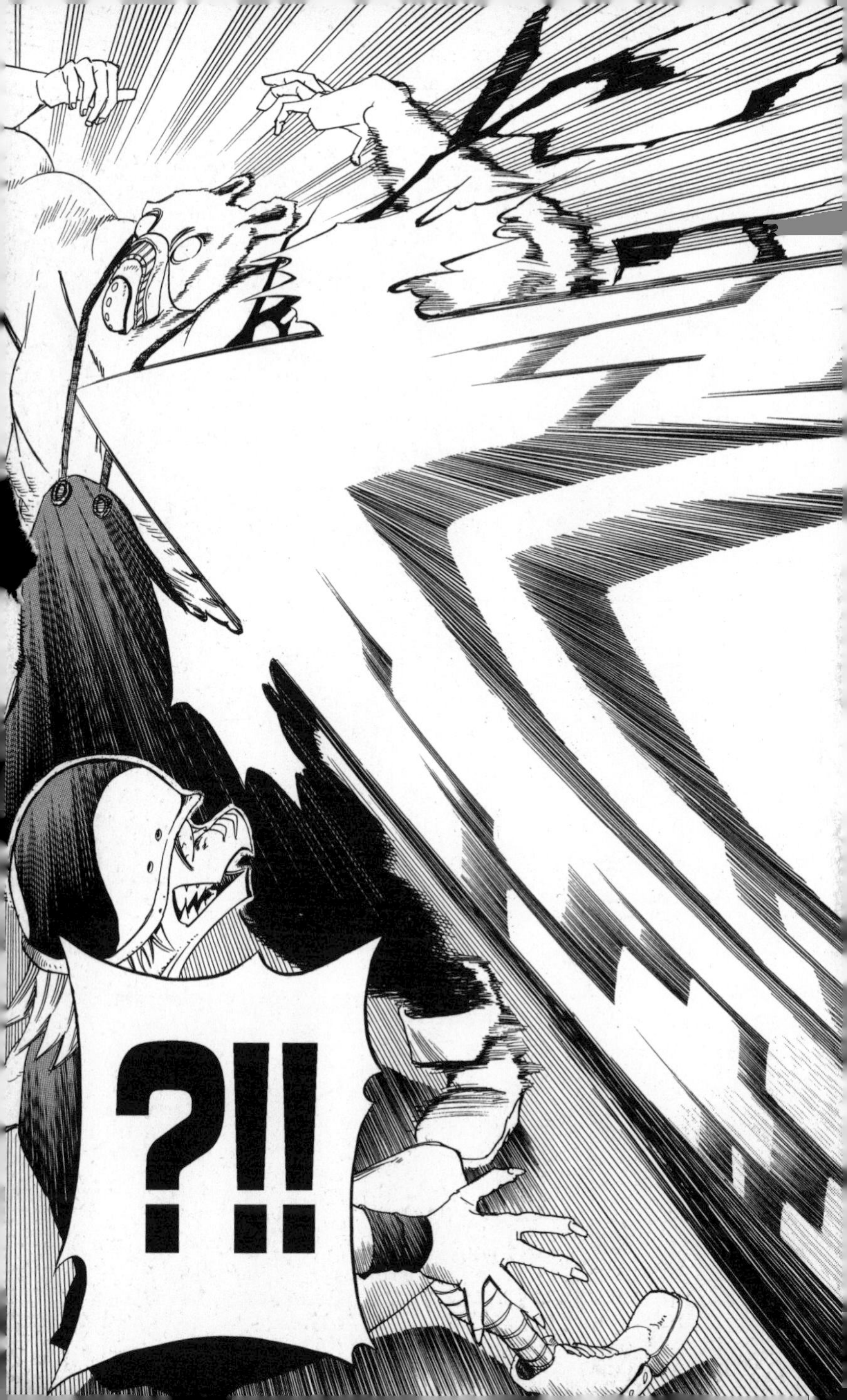
?!!

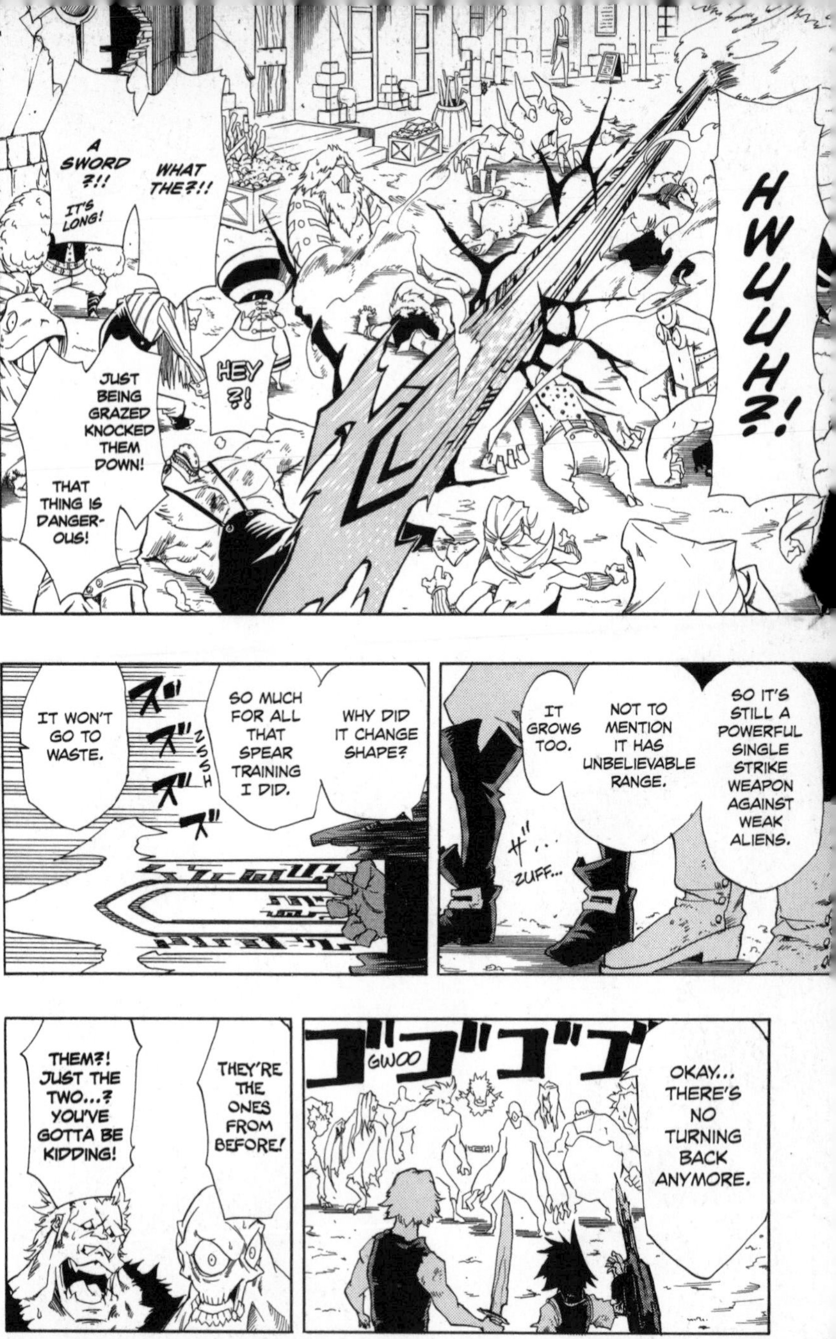
HWUUH?!
WHAT THE?!!
A SWORD?!!
IT'S LONG!
HEY?!
JUST BEING GRAZED KNOCKED THEM DOWN!
THAT THING IS DANGEROUS!
SO IT'S STILL A POWERFUL SINGLE STRIKE WEAPON AGAINST WEAK ALIENS.
NOT TO MENTION IT HAS UNBELIEVABLE RANGE.
IT GROWS TOO.
ZUFF...
WHY DID IT CHANGE SHAPE?
SO MUCH FOR ALL THAT SPEAR TRAINING I DID.
ZSSH
IT WON'T GO TO WASTE.
OKAY... THERE'S NO TURNING BACK ANYMORE.
GWOO
THEY'RE THE ONES FROM BEFORE!
THEM?! JUST THE TWO...? YOU'VE GOTTA BE KIDDING!

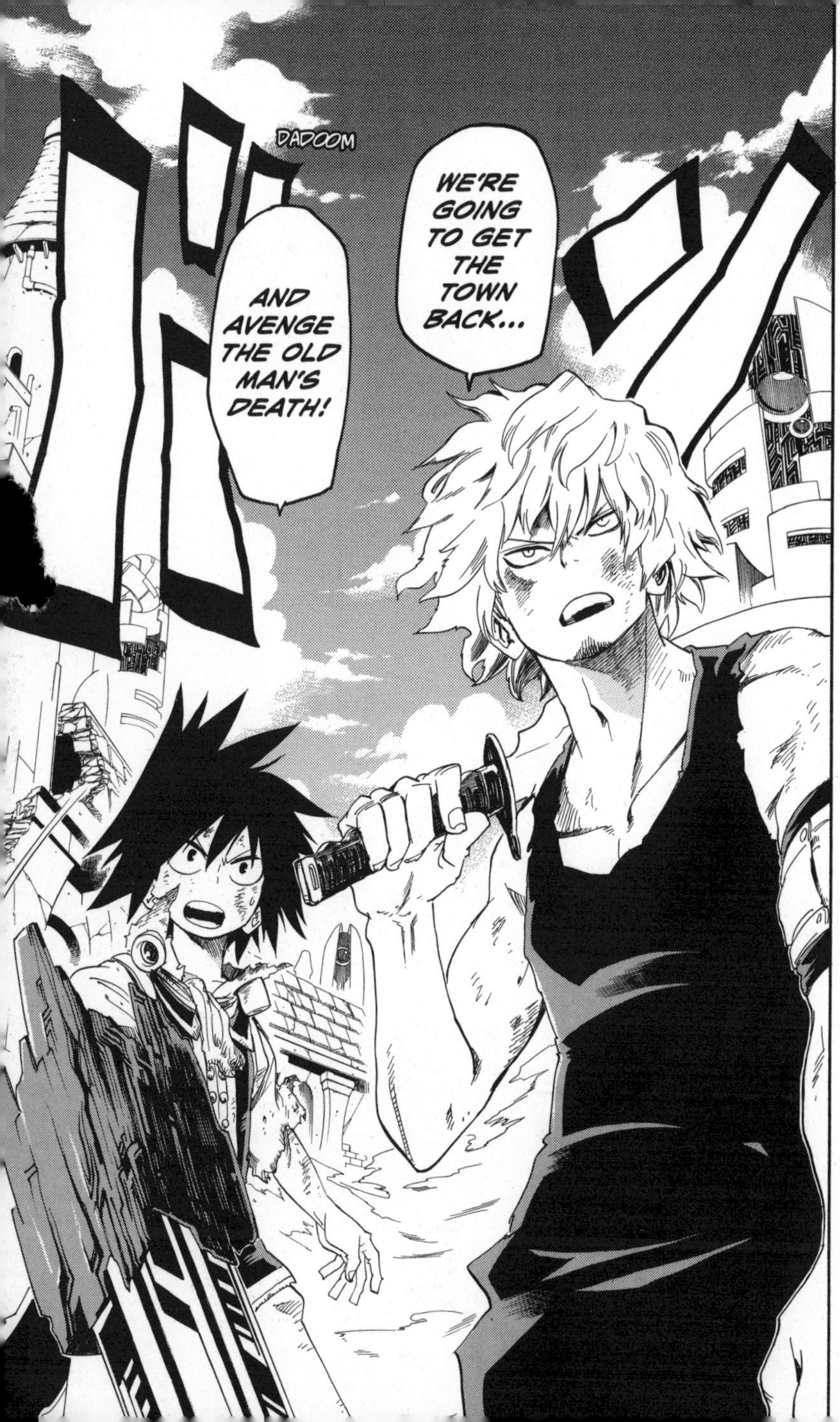
DADOOM
WE'RE GOING TO GET THE TOWN BACK...
AND AVENGE THE OLD MAN'S DEATH!

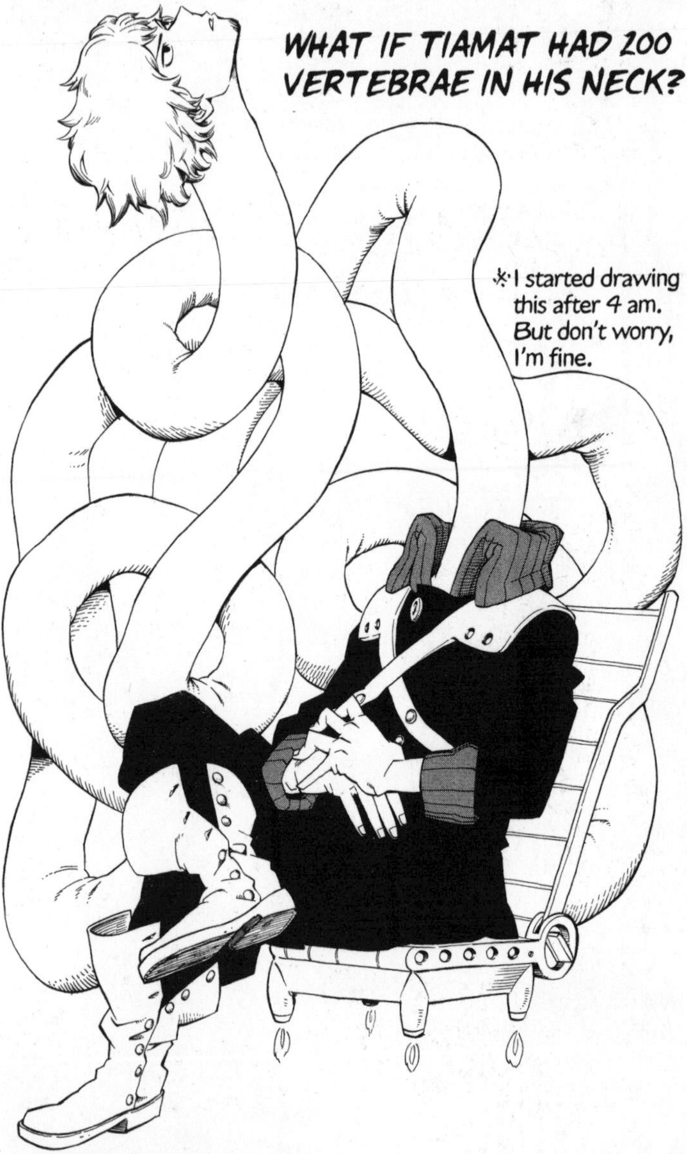
WHAT IF TIAMAT HAD 200 VERTEBRAE IN HIS NECK?
※I started drawing this after 4 am. But don't worry, I'm fine.

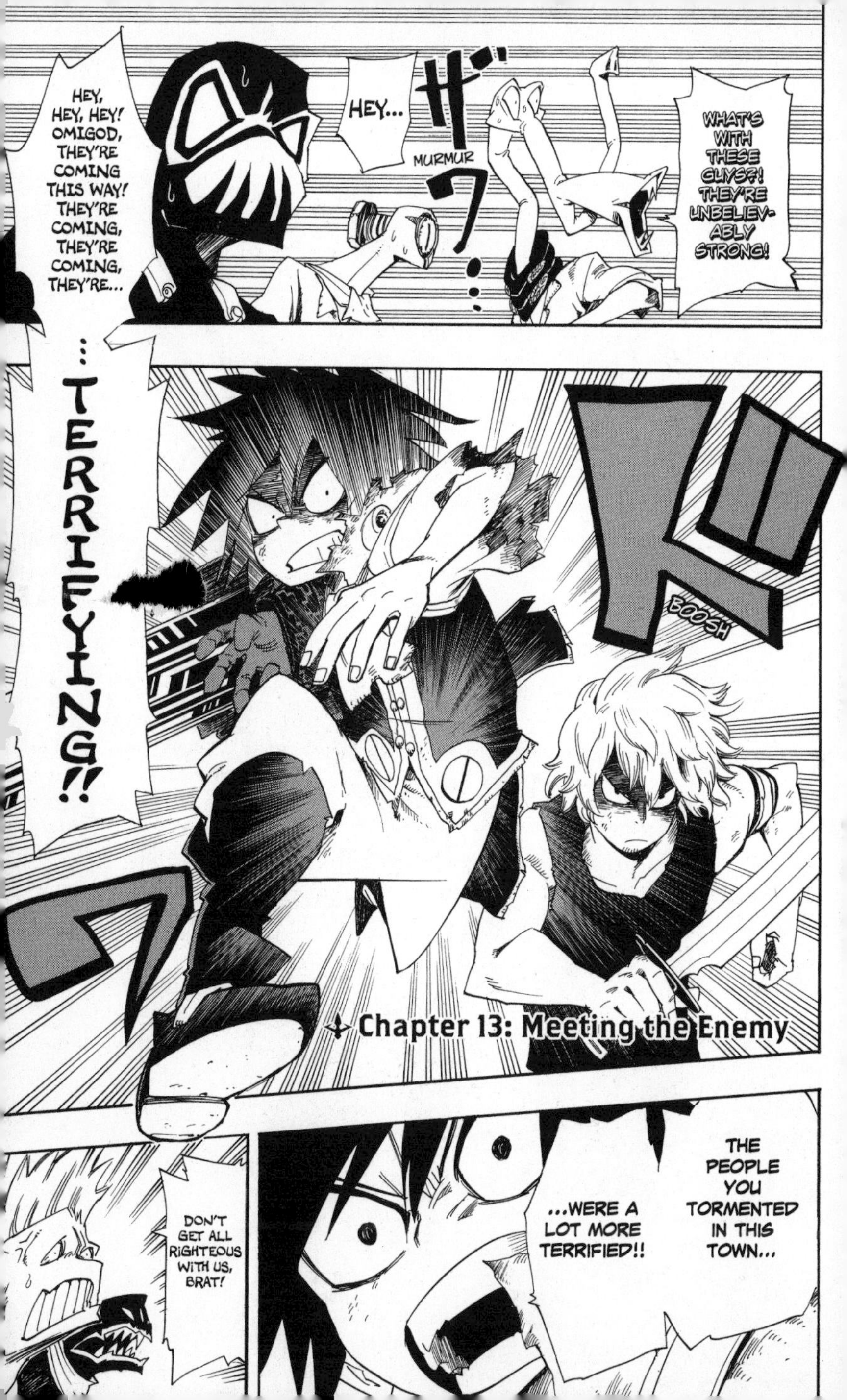
WHAT'S WITH THESE GUYS?! THEY'RE UNBELIEV-ABLY STRONG!
HEY...
MURMUR
HEY, HEY, HEY! OMIGOD, THEY'RE COMING THIS WAY! THEY'RE COMING, THEY'RE COMING, THEY'RE...
...TERRIFYING!!
BOOSH
Chapter 13: Meeting the Enemy
THE PEOPLE YOU TORMENTED IN THIS TOWN...
...WERE A LOT MORE TERRIFIED!!
DON'T GET ALL RIGHTEOUS WITH US, BRAT!

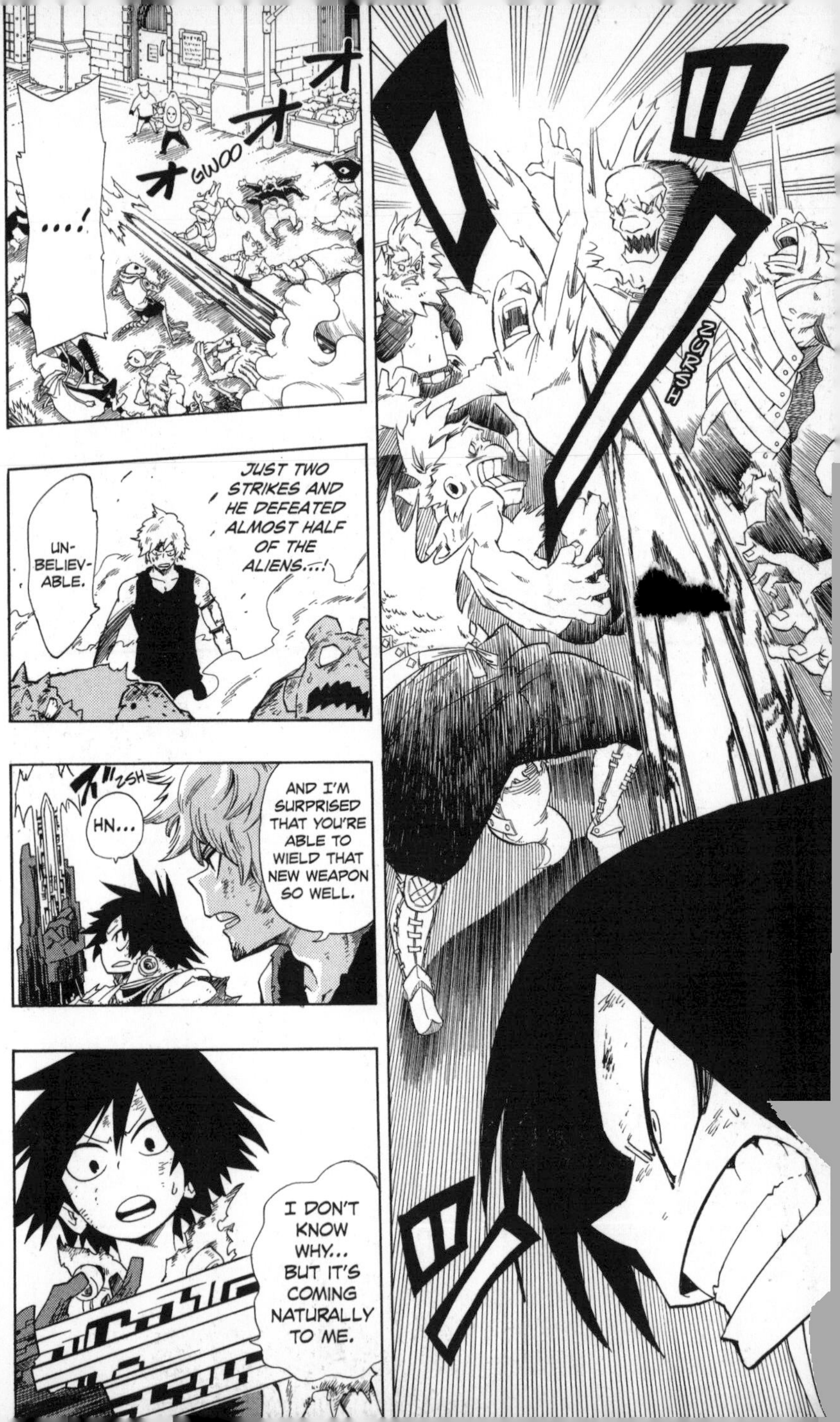
ZURSH
GWOO
...!
JUST TWO STRIKES AND HE DEFEATED ALMOST HALF OF THE ALIENS...!
UN-BELIEV-ABLE.
ZSH
AND I'M SURPRISED THAT YOU'RE ABLE TO WIELD THAT NEW WEAPON SO WELL.
HN...
I DON'T KNOW WHY... BUT IT'S COMING NATURALLY TO ME.

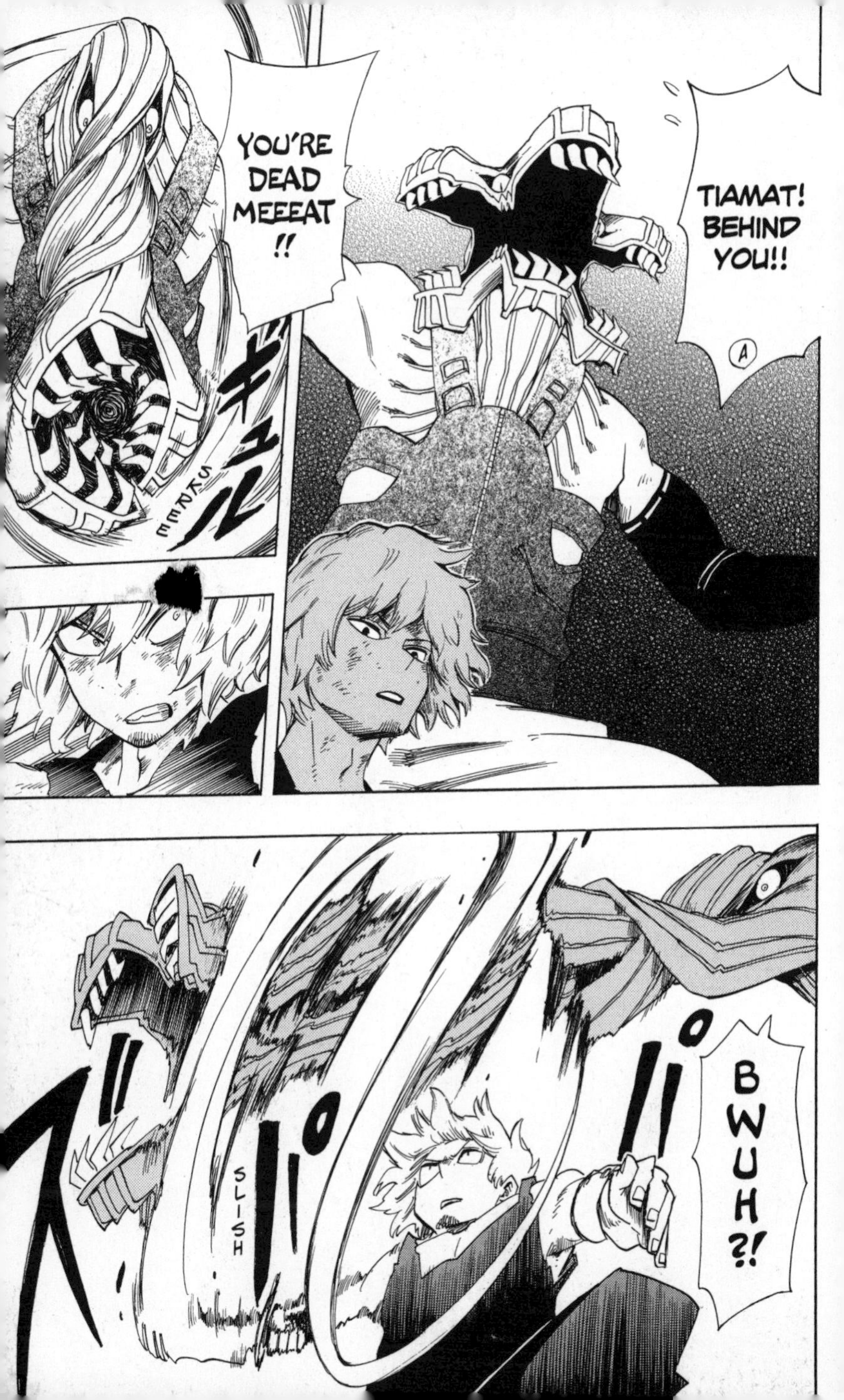
TIAMAT! BEHIND YOU!!
A
YOU'RE DEAD MEEEAT!!
キュル
SKREE
BWUH?!
SLISH

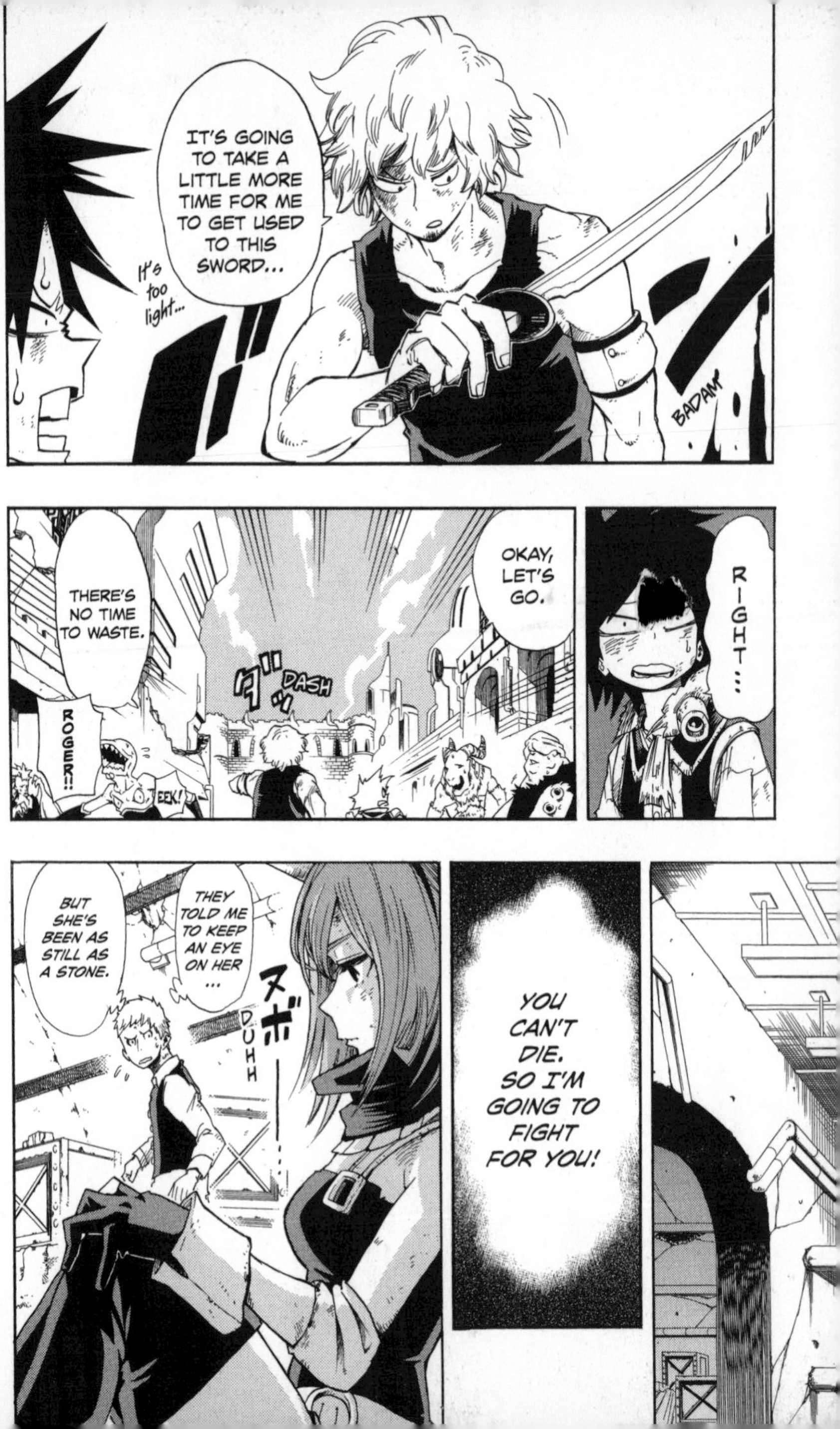
IT'S GOING TO TAKE A LITTLE MORE TIME FOR ME TO GET USED TO THIS SWORD...
It's too light...
BADAM
RIGHT...
OKAY, LET'S GO.
THERE'S NO TIME TO WASTE.
DASH
ROGER!!
EEK!
YOU CAN'T DIE. SO I'M GOING TO FIGHT FOR YOU!
THEY TOLD ME TO KEEP AN EYE ON HER...
BUT SHE'S BEEN AS STILL AS A STONE.
ヌボ
DUHH

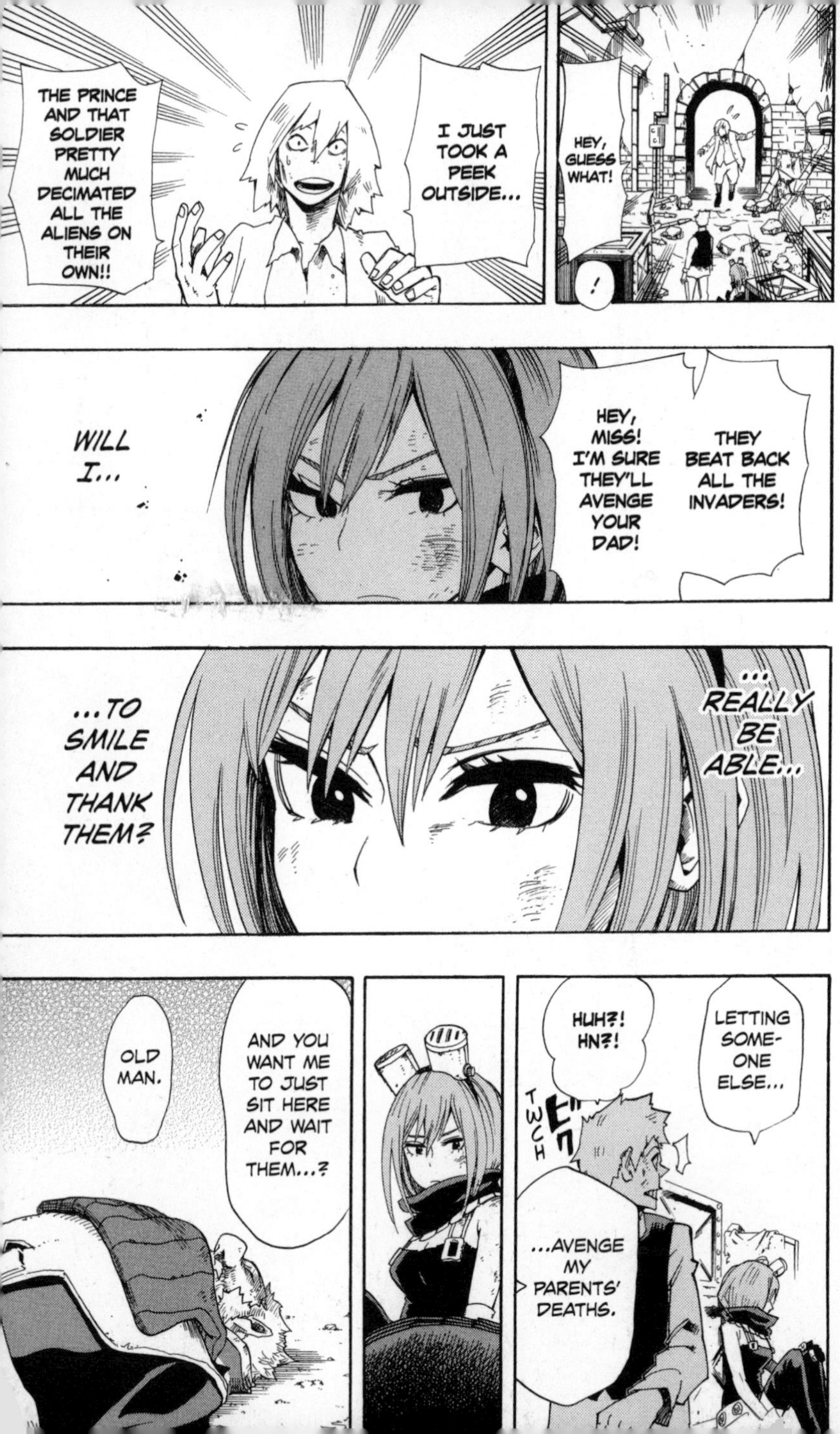
HEY, GUESS WHAT!
!
I JUST TOOK A PEEK OUTSIDE...
THE PRINCE AND THAT SOLDIER PRETTY MUCH DECIMATED ALL THE ALIENS ON THEIR OWN!!
THEY BEAT BACK ALL THE INVADERS!
HEY, MISS! I'M SURE THEY'LL AVENGE YOUR DAD!
WILL I...
...REALLY BE ABLE...
...TO SMILE AND THANK THEM?
LETTING SOME-ONE ELSE...
HUH?! HN?!
TWCH
...AVENGE MY PARENTS' DEATHS.
AND YOU WANT ME TO JUST SIT HERE AND WAIT FOR THEM...?
OLD MAN.

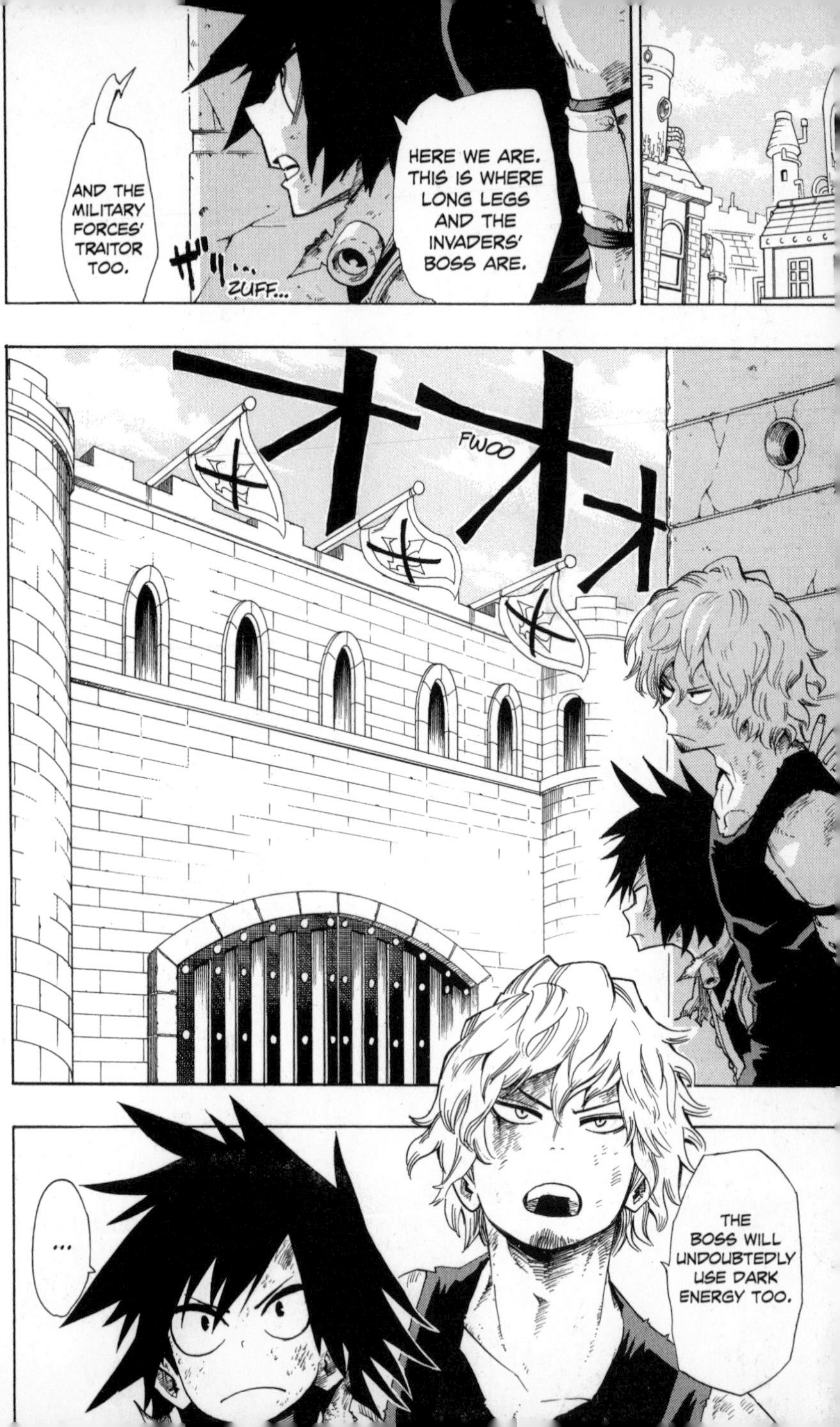
HERE WE ARE. THIS IS WHERE LONG LEGS AND THE INVADERS' BOSS ARE.
ザリ...
ZUFF...
AND THE MILITARY FORCES' TRAITOR TOO.
オオオ
FWOO
THE BOSS WILL UNDOUBTEDLY USE DARK ENERGY TOO.
...

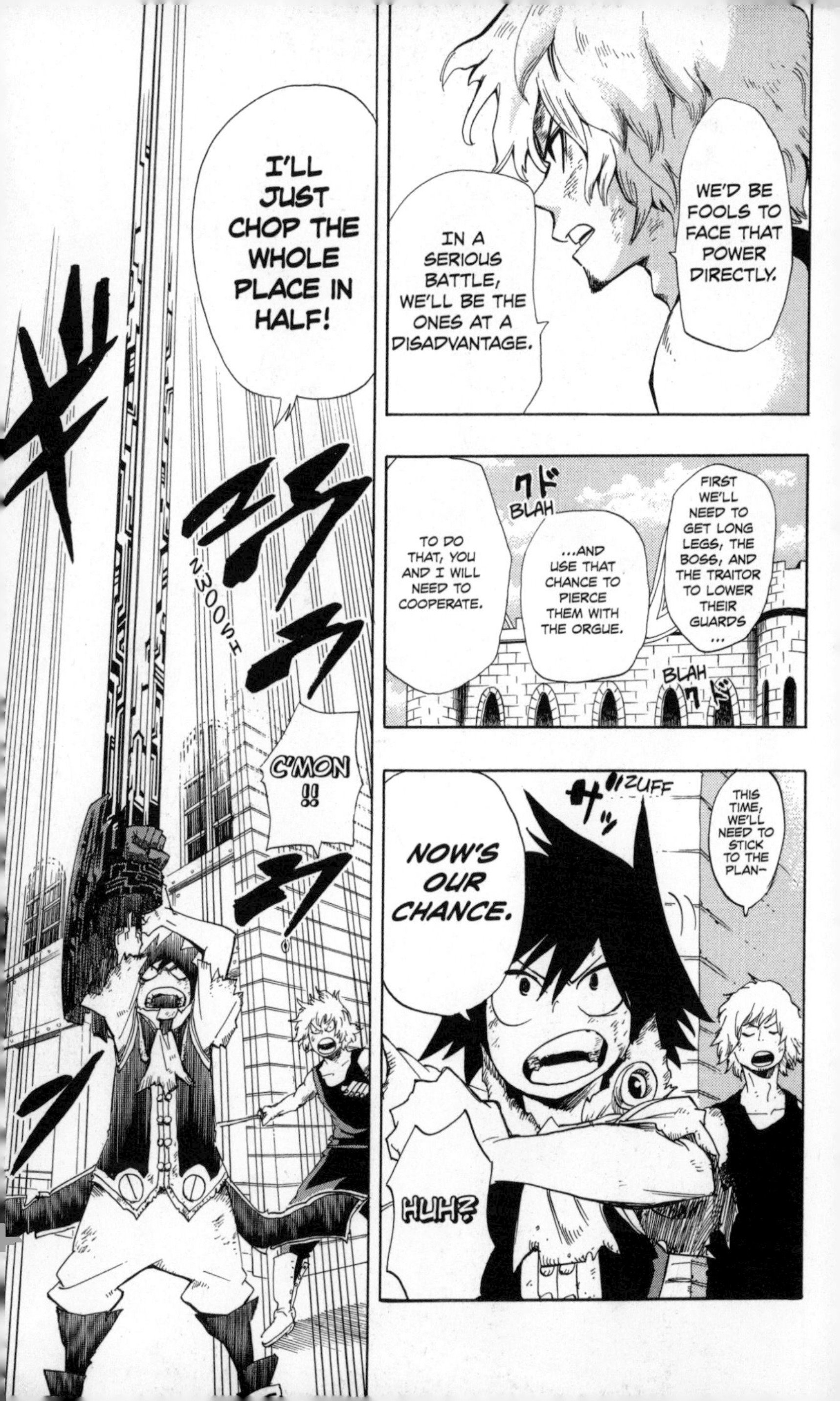
WE'D BE FOOLS TO FACE THAT POWER DIRECTLY.
IN A SERIOUS BATTLE, WE'LL BE THE ONES AT A DISADVANTAGE.
FIRST WE'LL NEED TO GET LONG LEGS, THE BOSS, AND THE TRAITOR TO LOWER THEIR GUARDS...
クド BLAH
...AND USE THAT CHANCE TO PIERCE THEM WITH THE ORGUE.
TO DO THAT, YOU AND I WILL NEED TO COOPERATE.
BLAH
THIS TIME, WE'LL NEED TO STICK TO THE PLAN-
ザッ ZUFF
NOW'S OUR CHANCE.
HUH?
I'LL JUST CHOP THE WHOLE PLACE IN HALF!
WHOOSH
C'MON!!

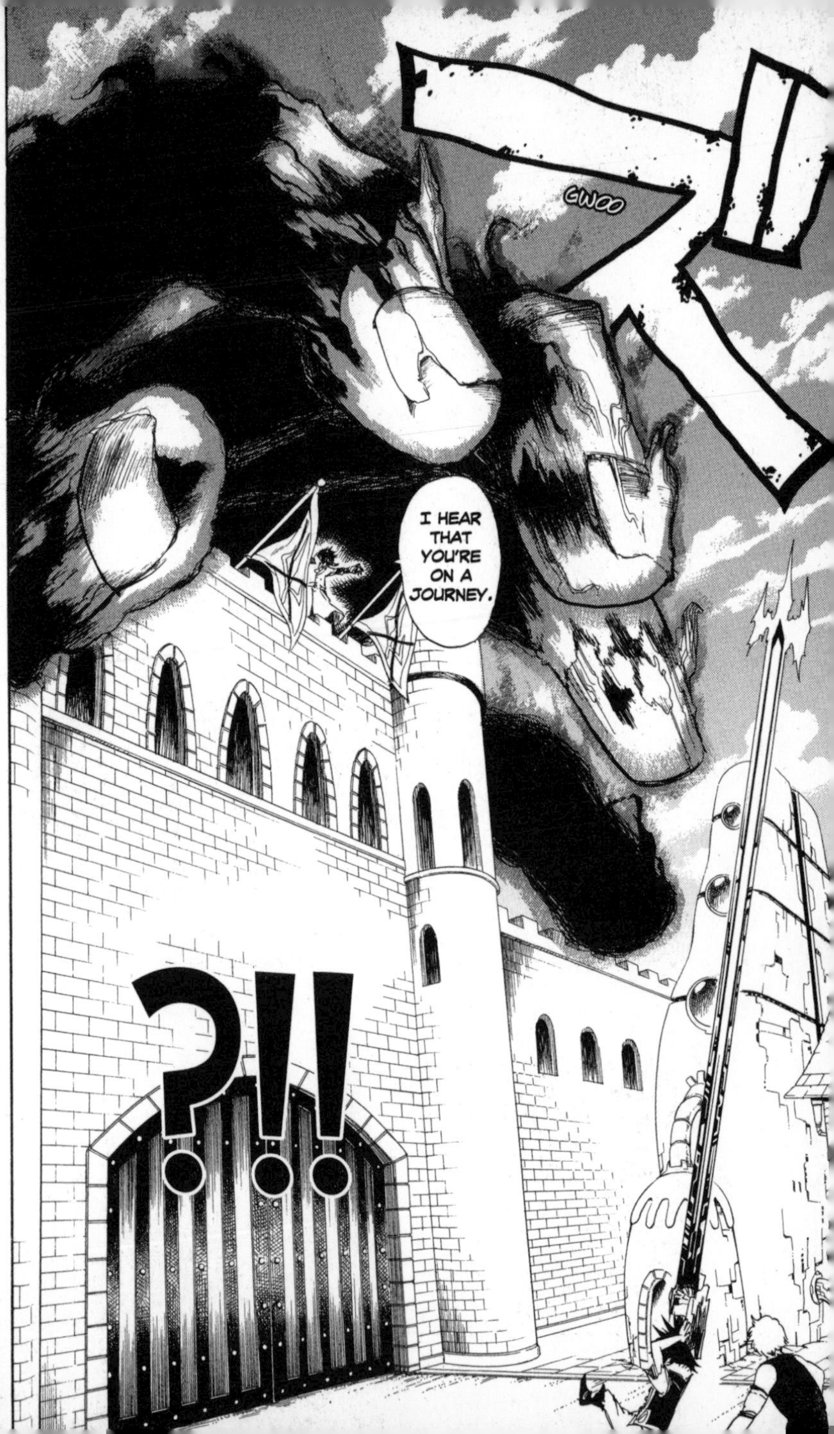
GWOO
I HEAR THAT YOU'RE ON A JOURNEY.
?!!

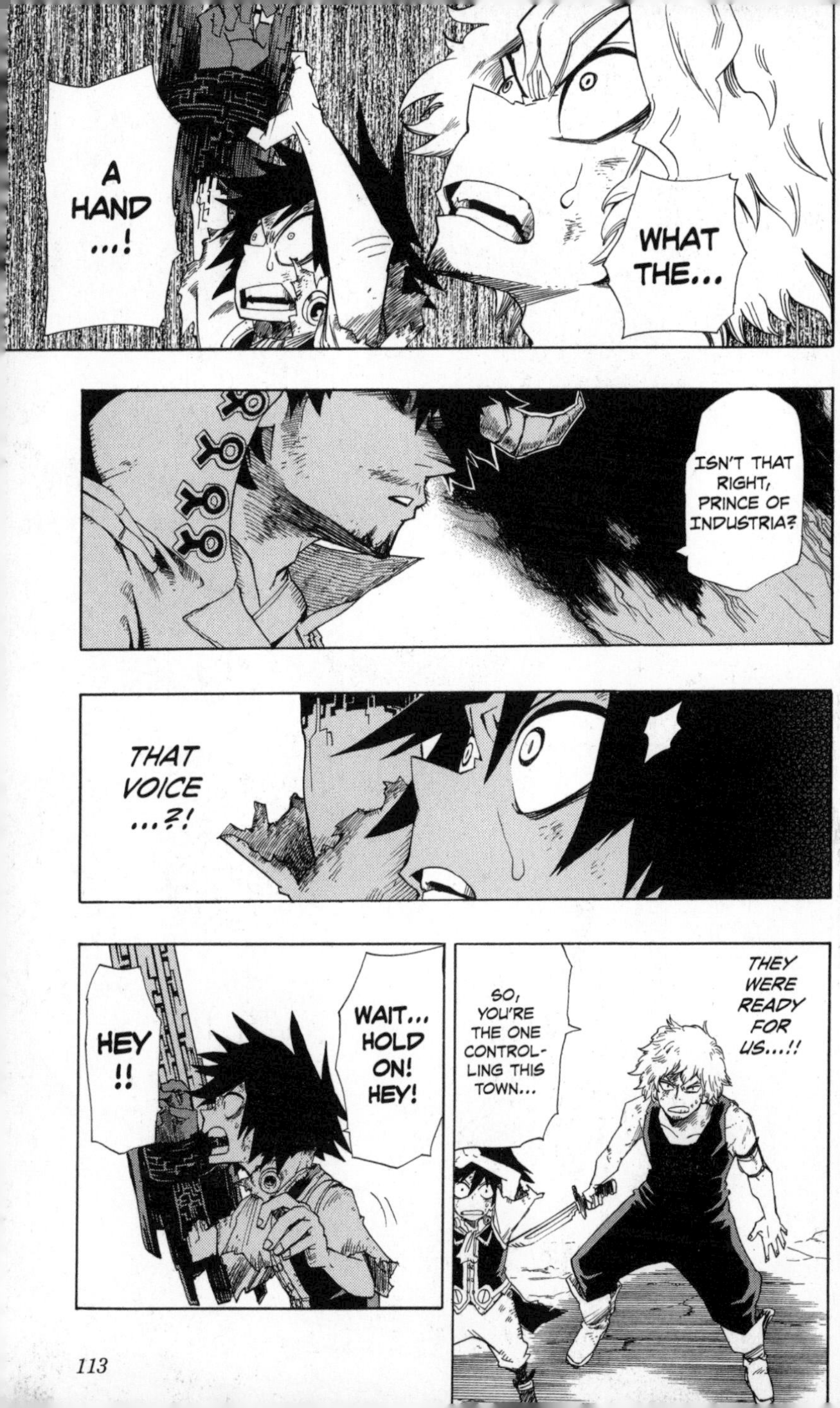
WHAT THE...
A HAND ...!
ISN'T THAT RIGHT, PRINCE OF INDUSTRIA?
THAT VOICE ...?!
THEY WERE READY FOR US...!!
SO, YOU'RE THE ONE CONTROL-LING THIS TOWN...
WAIT... HOLD ON! HEY!
HEY !!

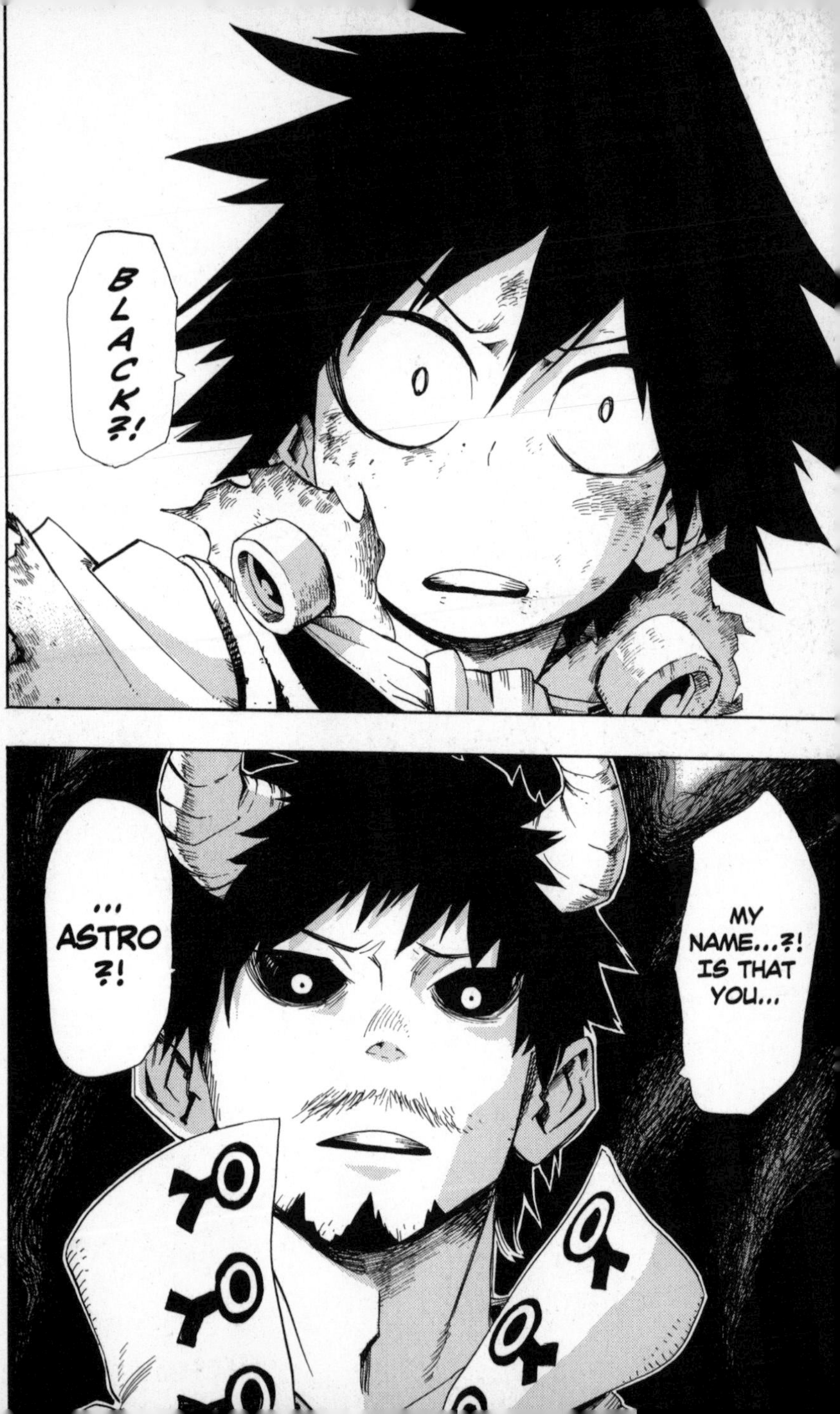
BLACK?!
MY NAME...?! IS THAT YOU...
...ASTRO?!

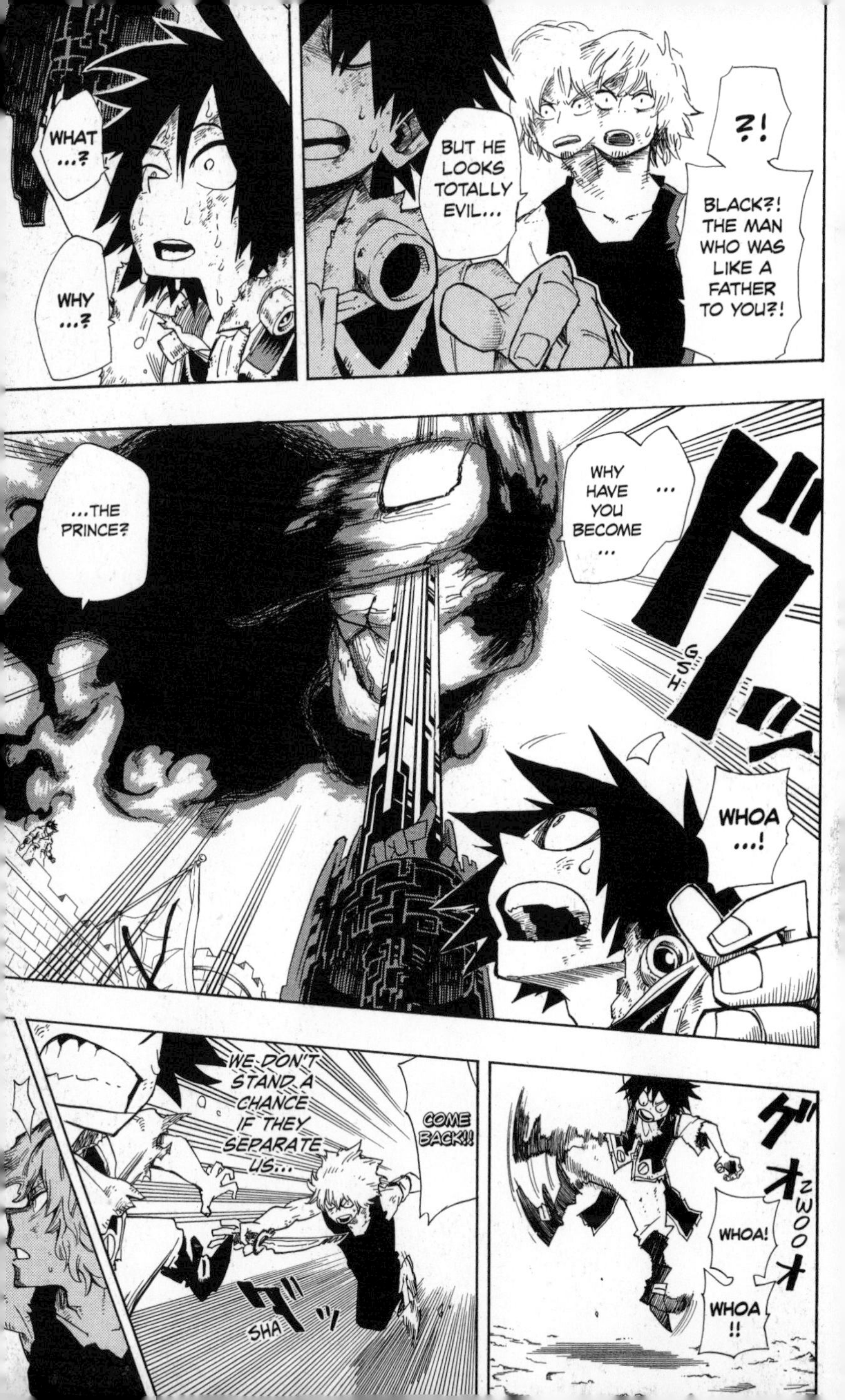
?!
BLACK?! THE MAN WHO WAS LIKE A FATHER TO YOU?!
BUT HE LOOKS TOTALLY EVIL...
WHAT ...?
WHY ...?
WHY HAVE YOU BECOME ... ...
...THE PRINCE?
GSH
WHOA ...!
ZWOOO
WHOA!
WHOA !!
COME BACK!!
WE DON'T STAND A CHANCE IF THEY SEPARATE US...
SHA

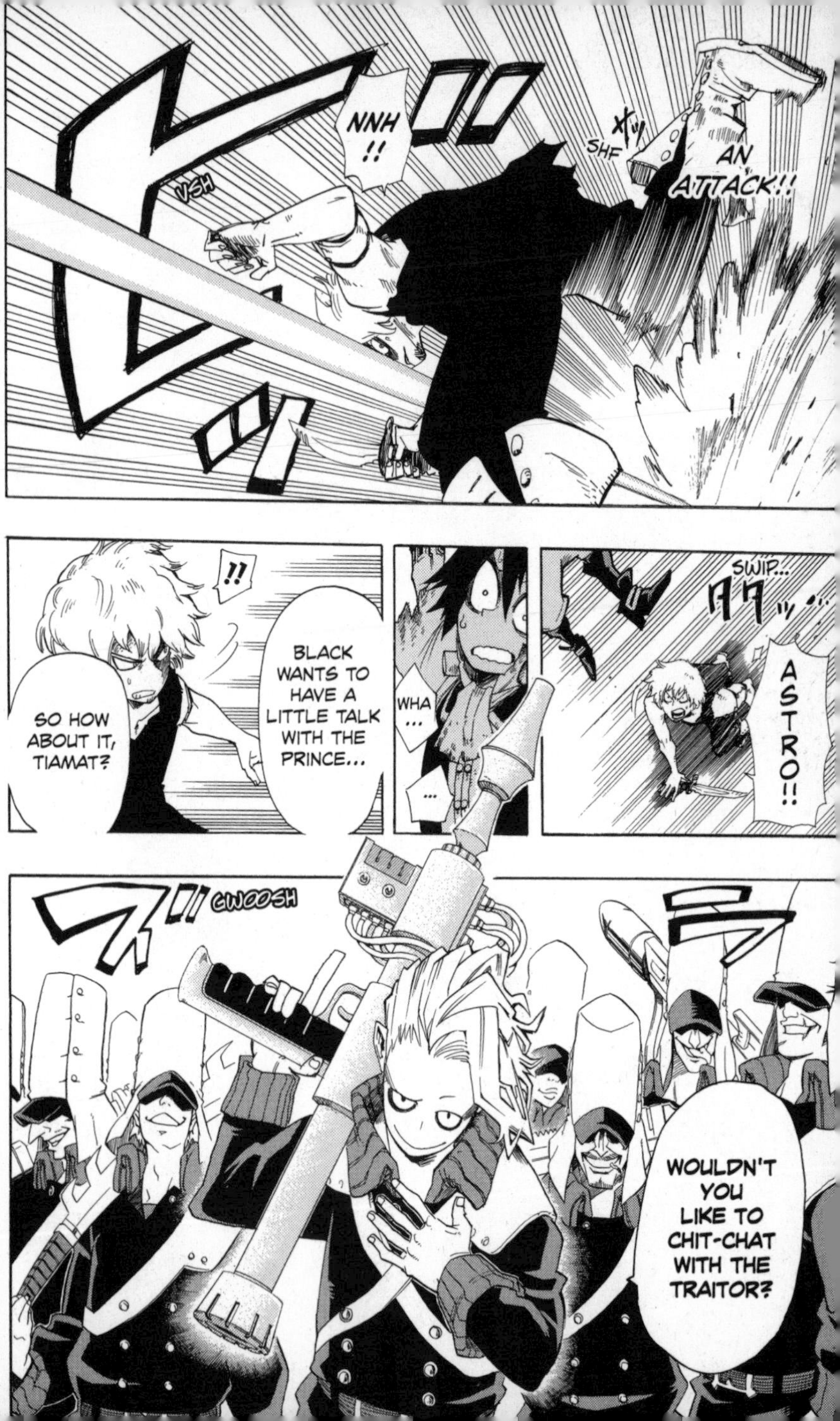
SHF
AN ATTACK!!
NNH!!
VSH
SWIP...
ASTRO!!
WHA...
...
!!
BLACK WANTS TO HAVE A LITTLE TALK WITH THE PRINCE...
SO HOW ABOUT IT, TIAMAT?
WOULDN'T YOU LIKE TO CHIT-CHAT WITH THE TRAITOR?
GWOOSH

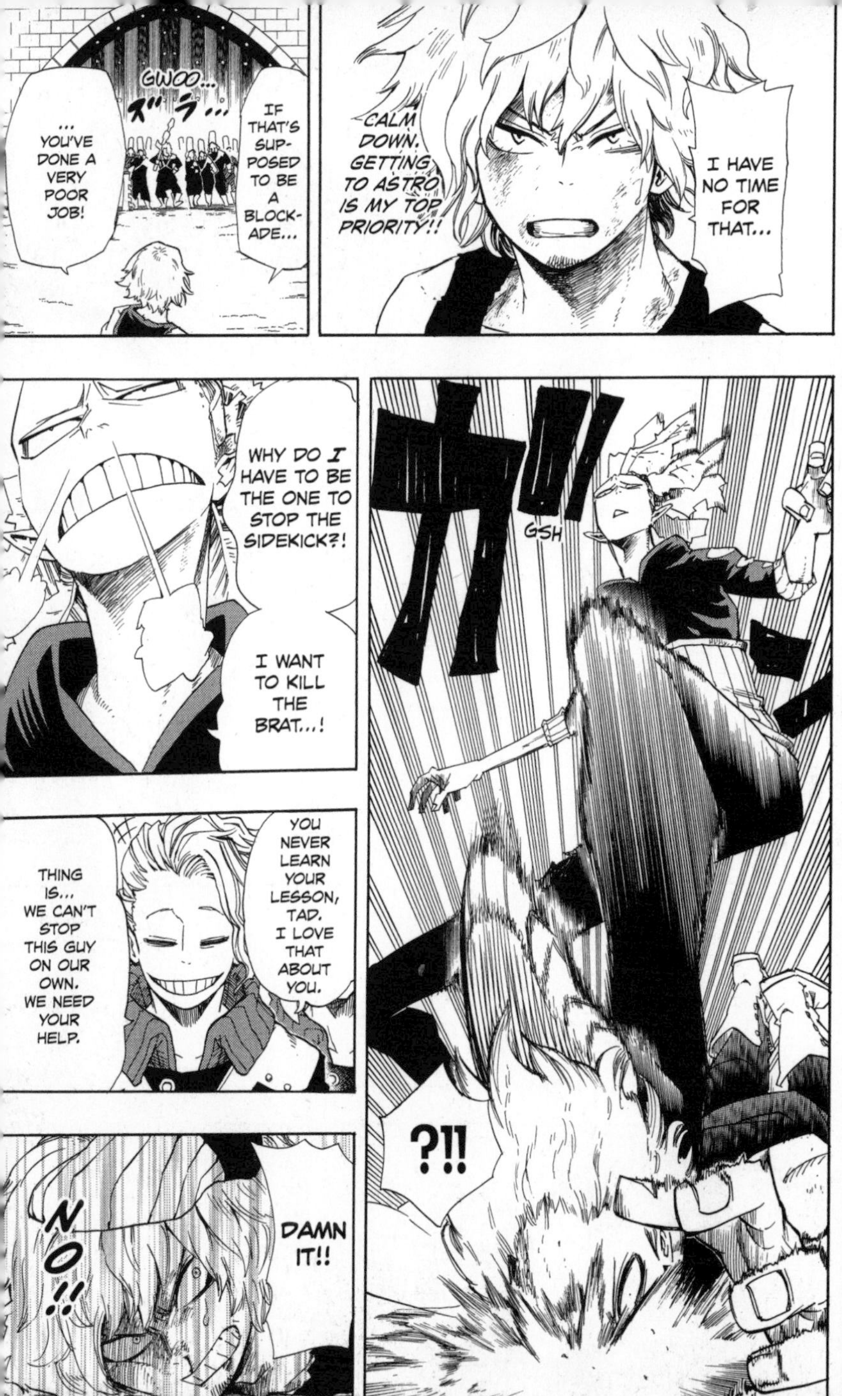
I HAVE NO TIME FOR THAT...
CALM DOWN. GETTING TO ASTRO IS MY TOP PRIORITY!!
GWOO...
IF THAT'S SUP-POSED TO BE A BLOCK-ADE...
... YOU'VE DONE A VERY POOR JOB!
GSH
?!!
WHY DO I HAVE TO BE THE ONE TO STOP THE SIDEKICK?!
I WANT TO KILL THE BRAT...!
YOU NEVER LEARN YOUR LESSON, TAD. I LOVE THAT ABOUT YOU.
THING IS... WE CAN'T STOP THIS GUY ON OUR OWN. WE NEED YOUR HELP.
DAMN IT!!
NO!!

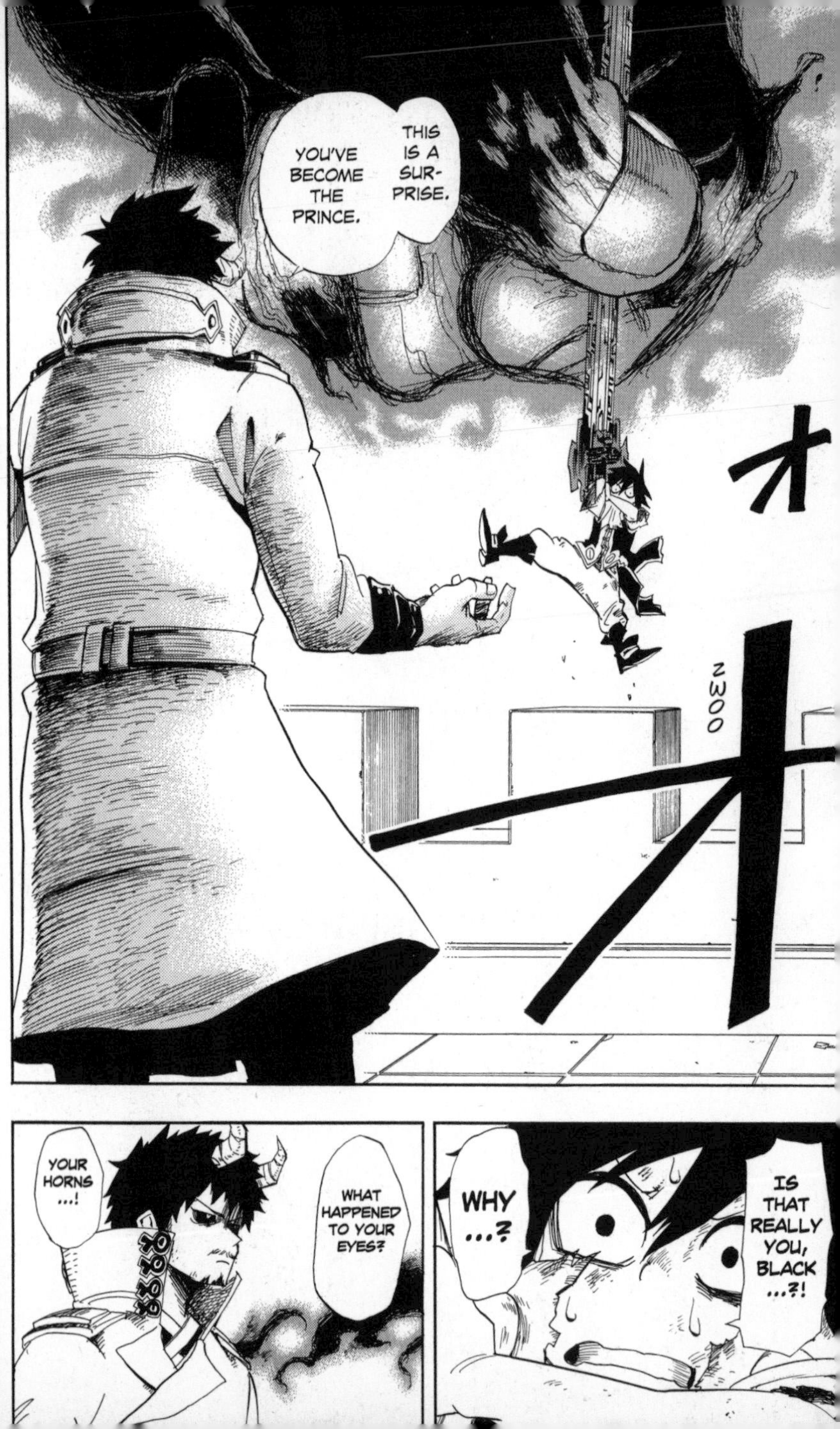
THIS IS A SURPRISE.
YOU'VE BECOME THE PRINCE.
IS THAT REALLY YOU, BLACK...?!
WHY...?
WHAT HAPPENED TO YOUR EYES?
YOUR HORNS...!

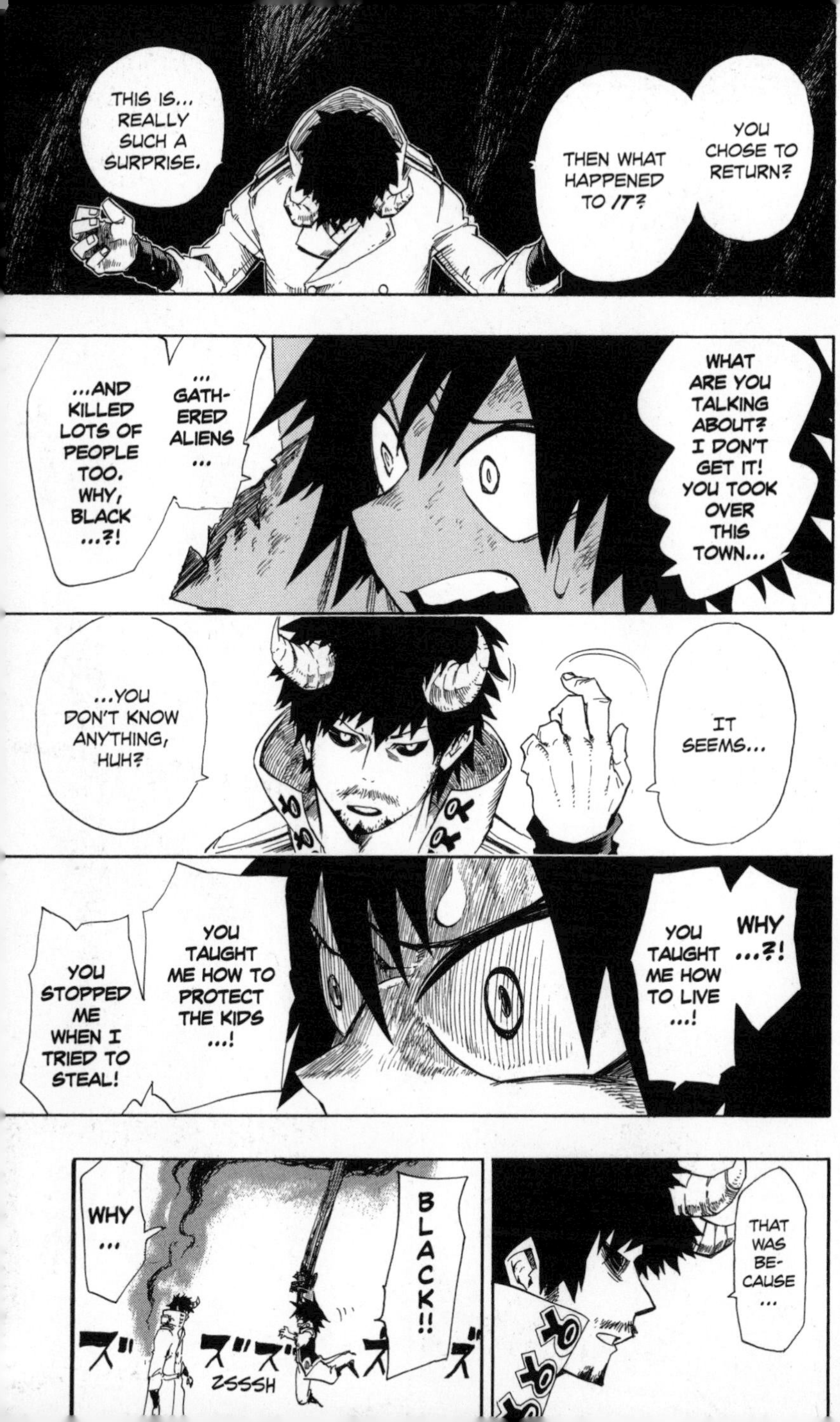
YOU CHOSE TO RETURN?
THEN WHAT HAPPENED TO *IT*?
THIS IS... REALLY SUCH A SURPRISE.
WHAT ARE YOU TALKING ABOUT? I DON'T GET IT! YOU TOOK OVER THIS TOWN...
...GATH-ERED ALIENS...
...AND KILLED LOTS OF PEOPLE TOO. WHY, BLACK...?!
IT SEEMS...
...YOU DON'T KNOW ANYTHING, HUH?
WHY...?!
YOU TAUGHT ME HOW TO LIVE...!
YOU TAUGHT ME HOW TO PROTECT THE KIDS...!
YOU STOPPED ME WHEN I TRIED TO STEAL!
THAT WAS BE-CAUSE...
BLACK!!
WHY...
ZSSSH

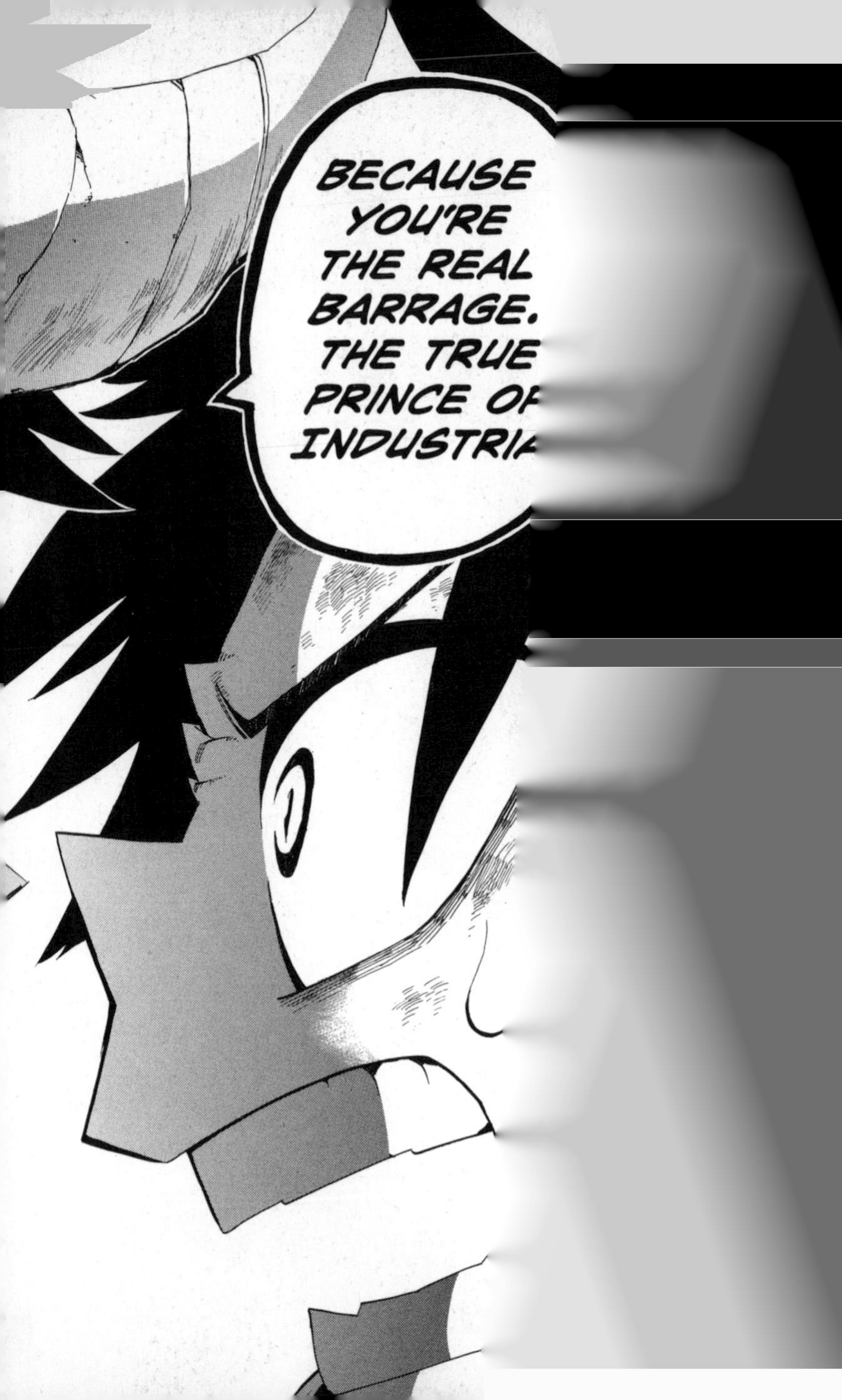
BECAUSE YOU'RE THE REAL BARRAGE. THE TRUE PRINCE OF INDUSTRI

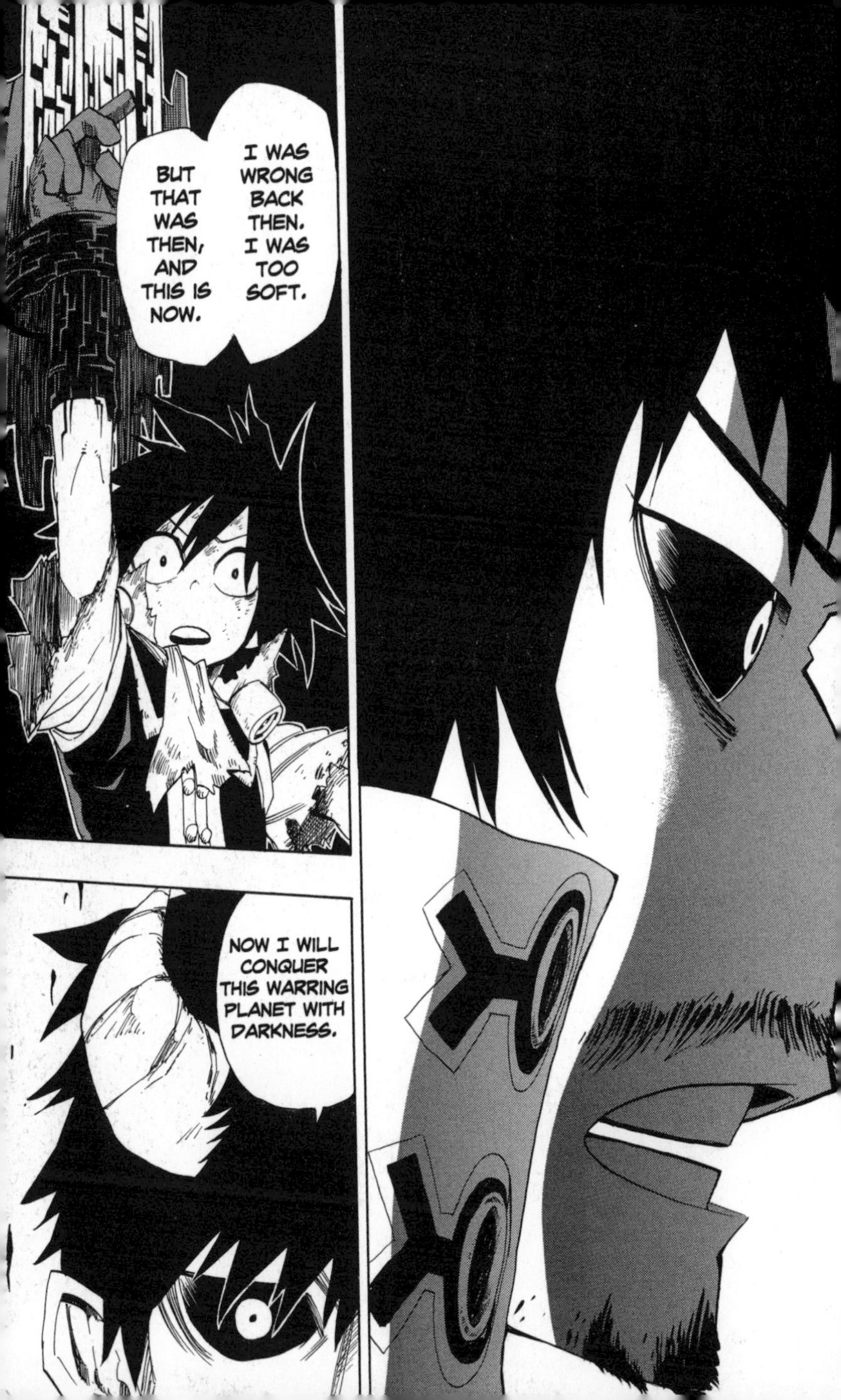
I WAS WRONG BACK THEN. I WAS TOO SOFT.
BUT THAT WAS THEN, AND THIS IS NOW.
NOW I WILL CONQUER THIS WARRING PLANET WITH DARKNESS.

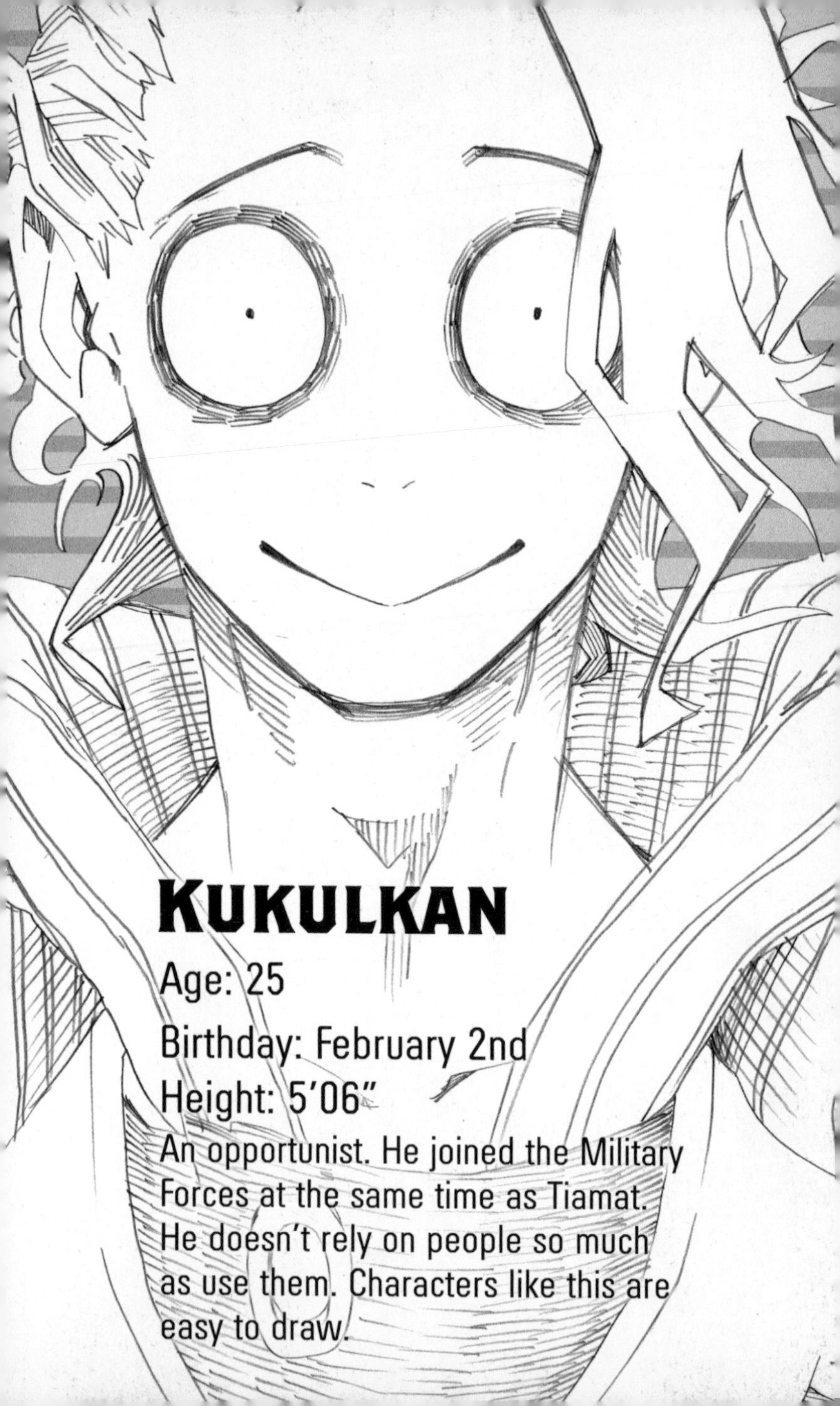

KUKULKAN

Age: 25

Birthday: February 2nd

Height: 5'06"

An opportunist. He joined the Military Forces at the same time as Tiamat. He doesn't rely on people so much as use them. Characters like this are easy to draw.

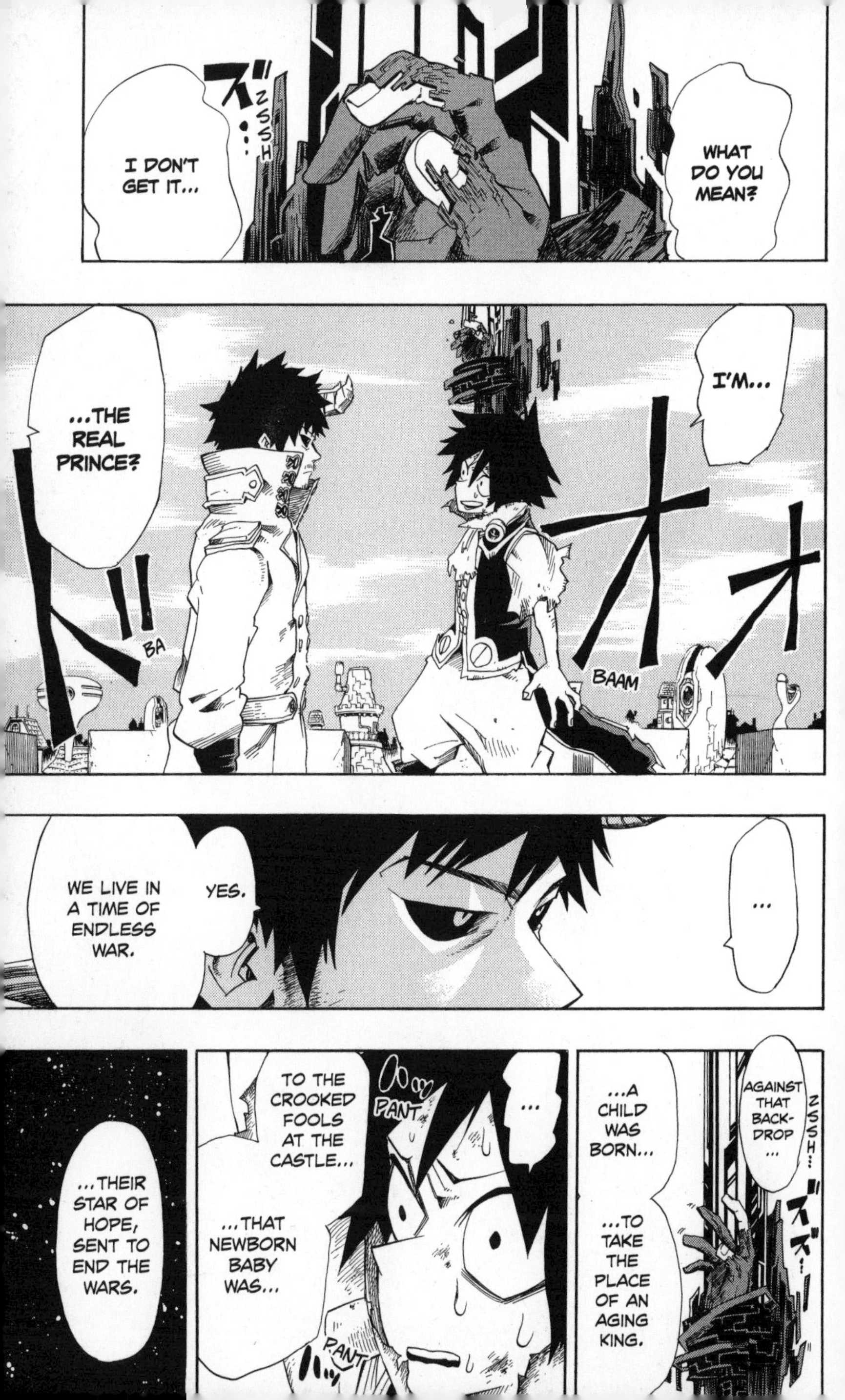
WHAT DO YOU MEAN?
ZSSH
I DON'T GET IT...
I'M...
BAAM
BA
...THE REAL PRINCE?
...
YES.
WE LIVE IN A TIME OF ENDLESS WAR.
AGAINST THAT BACKDROP...
ZSSH
...A CHILD WAS BORN...
...TO TAKE THE PLACE OF AN AGING KING.
...
TO THE CROOKED FOOLS AT THE CASTLE...
PANT
...THAT NEWBORN BABY WAS...
PANT
...THEIR STAR OF HOPE, SENT TO END THE WARS.

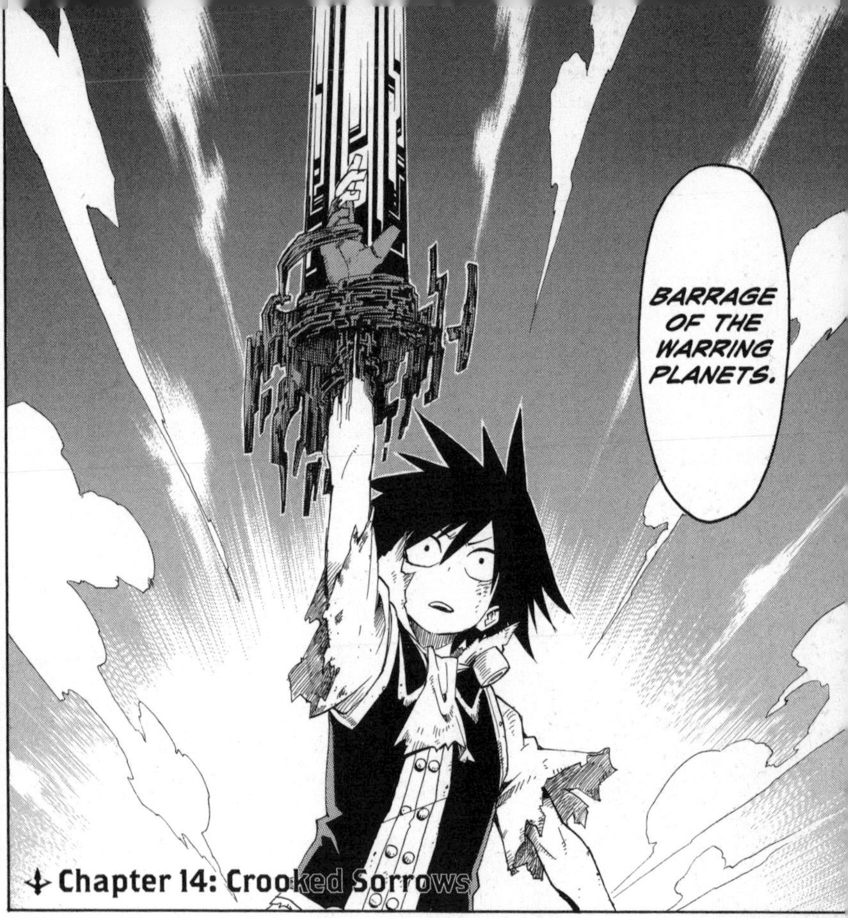
BARRAGE OF THE WARRING PLANETS.

Chapter 14: Crooked Sorrows

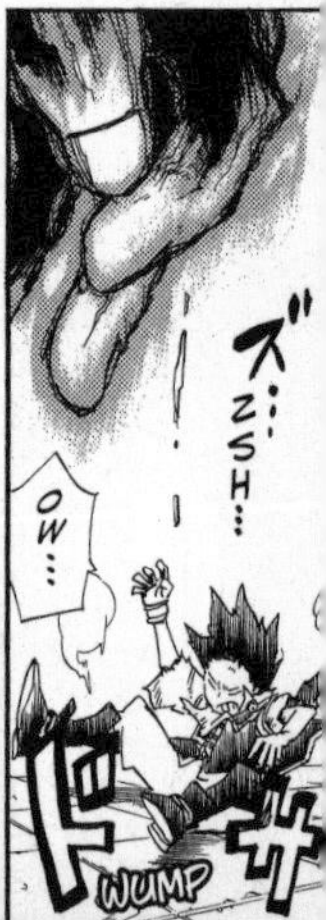
ZSH...
OW...
WUMP

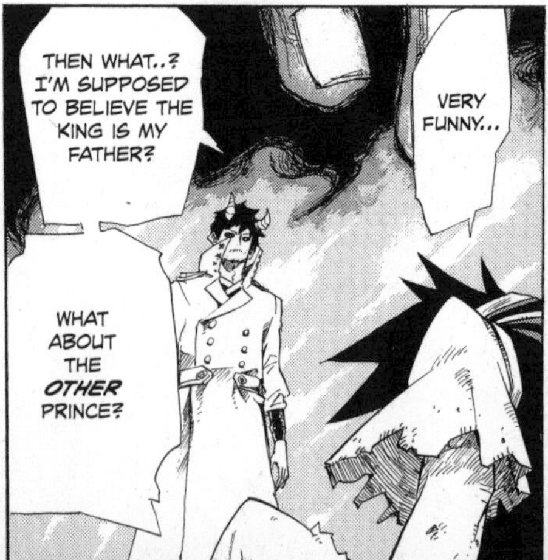
VERY FUNNY...
THEN WHAT..? I'M SUPPOSED TO BELIEVE THE KING IS MY FATHER?
WHAT ABOUT THE OTHER PRINCE?

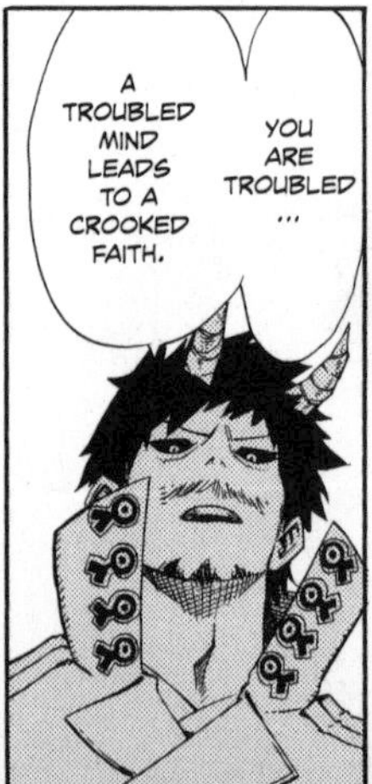
YOU ARE TROUBLED ...
A TROUBLED MIND LEADS TO A CROOKED FAITH.

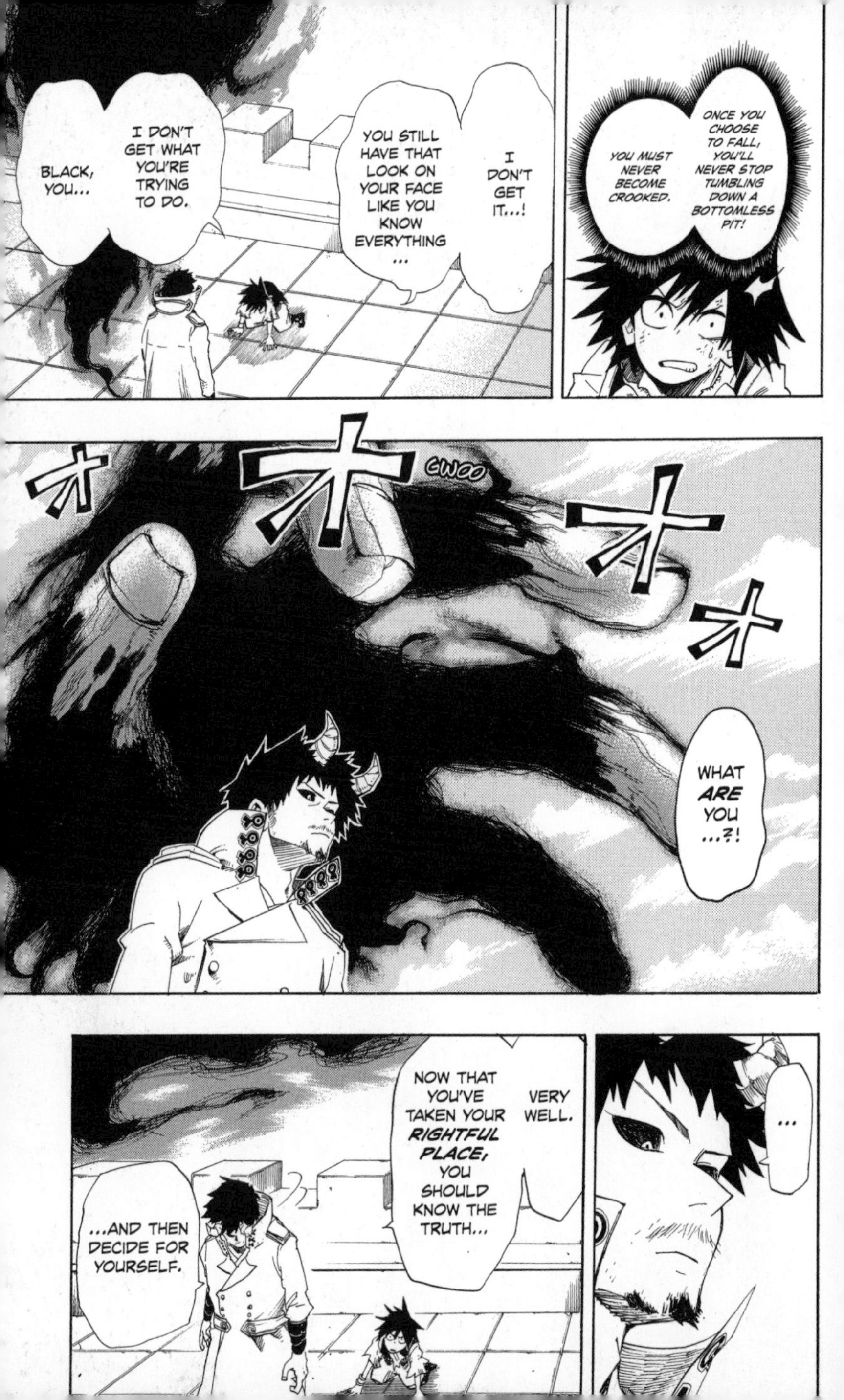
ONCE YOU CHOOSE TO FALL, YOU'LL NEVER STOP TUMBLING DOWN A BOTTOMLESS PIT!
YOU MUST NEVER BECOME CROOKED.
I DON'T GET IT...!
YOU STILL HAVE THAT LOOK ON YOUR FACE LIKE YOU KNOW EVERYTHING...
I DON'T GET WHAT YOU'RE TRYING TO DO.
BLACK, YOU...
オ
オ
オ
オ
GWOO
WHAT *ARE* YOU...?!
...
VERY WELL.
NOW THAT YOU'VE TAKEN YOUR ***RIGHTFUL PLACE,*** YOU SHOULD KNOW THE TRUTH...
...AND THEN DECIDE FOR YOURSELF.

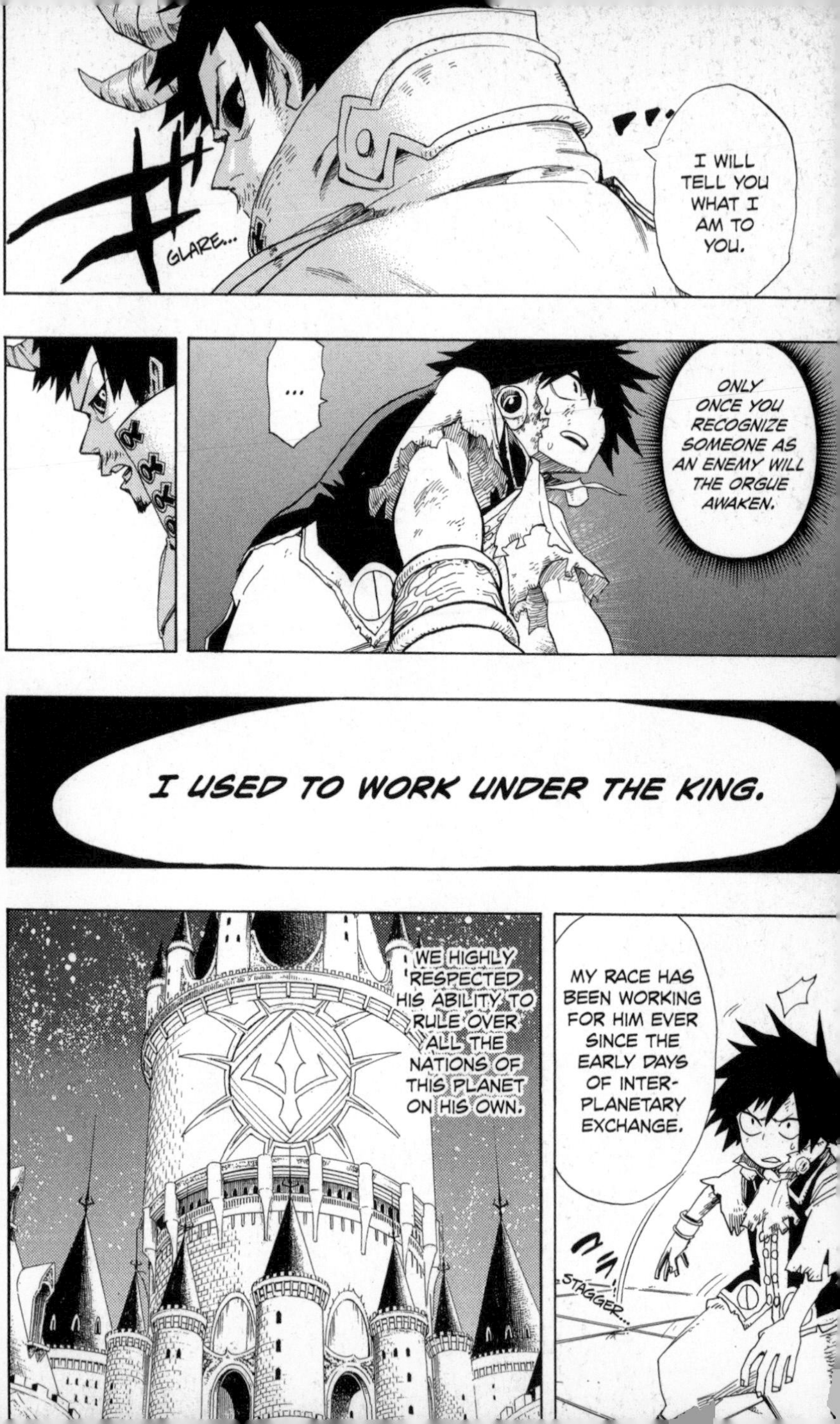
I WILL TELL YOU WHAT I AM TO YOU.
GLARE...
ONLY ONCE YOU RECOGNIZE SOMEONE AS AN ENEMY WILL THE ORGUE AWAKEN.
...
I USED TO WORK UNDER THE KING.
MY RACE HAS BEEN WORKING FOR HIM EVER SINCE THE EARLY DAYS OF INTER-PLANETARY EXCHANGE.
STAGGER...
WE HIGHLY RESPECTED HIS ABILITY TO RULE OVER ALL THE NATIONS OF THIS PLANET ON HIS OWN.

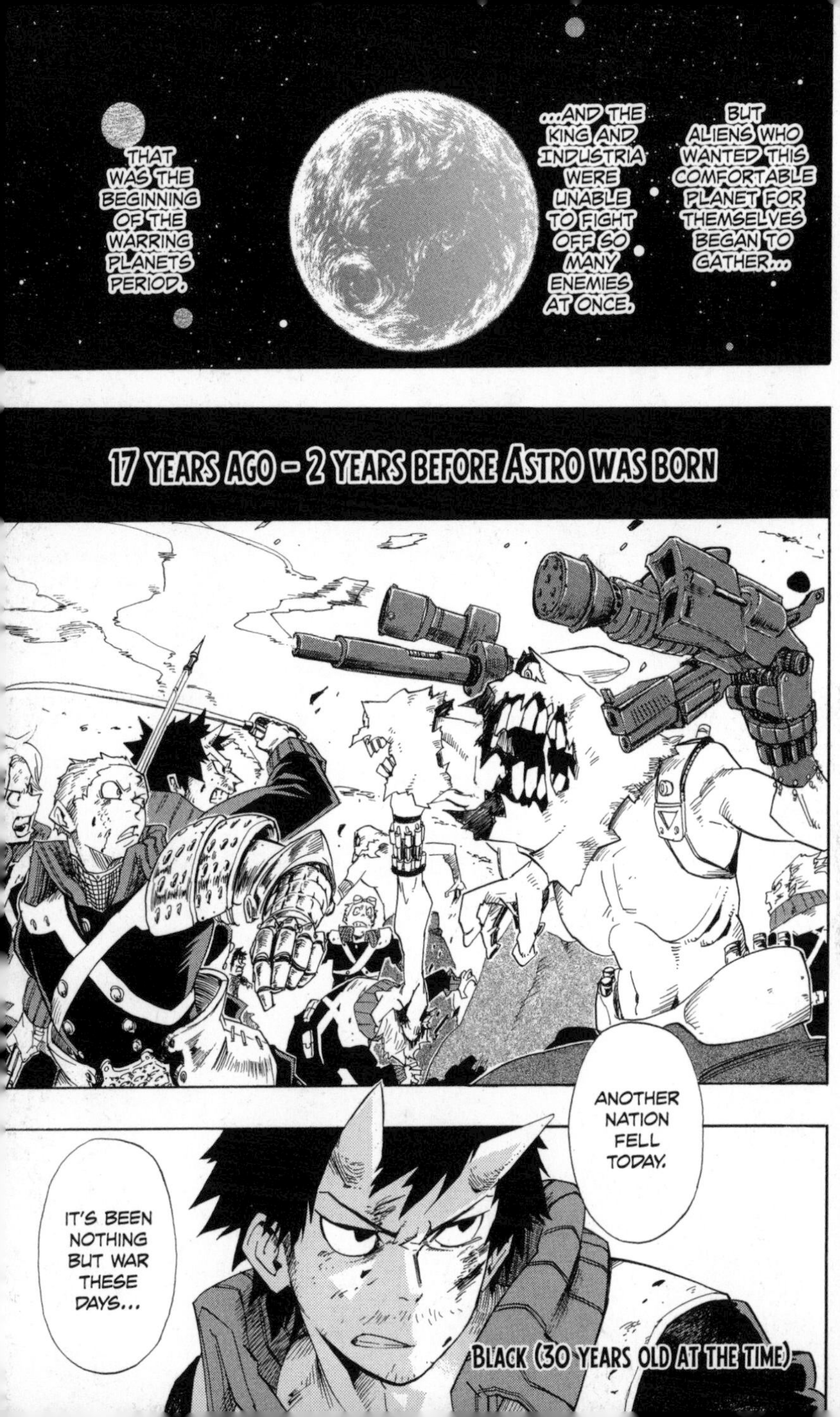
BUT ALIENS WHO WANTED THIS COMFORTABLE PLANET FOR THEMSELVES BEGAN TO GATHER...
...AND THE KING AND INDUSTRIA WERE UNABLE TO FIGHT OFF SO MANY ENEMIES AT ONCE.
THAT WAS THE BEGINNING OF THE WARRING PLANETS PERIOD.
17 YEARS AGO - 2 YEARS BEFORE ASTRO WAS BORN
ANOTHER NATION FELL TODAY.
IT'S BEEN NOTHING BUT WAR THESE DAYS...
BLACK (30 YEARS OLD AT THE TIME)

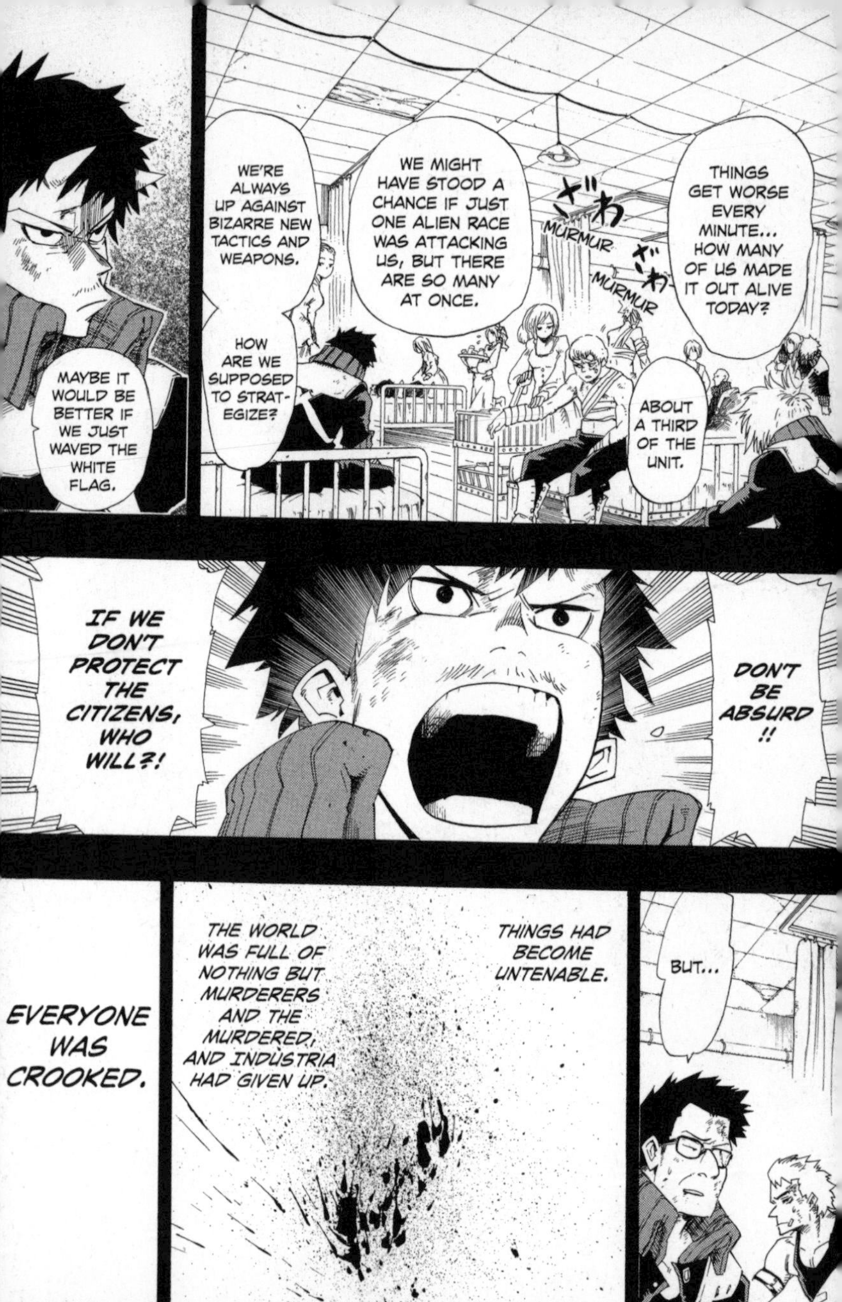
THINGS GET WORSE EVERY MINUTE... HOW MANY OF US MADE IT OUT ALIVE TODAY?
ざわ MURMUR
ざわ MURMUR
ABOUT A THIRD OF THE UNIT.
WE MIGHT HAVE STOOD A CHANCE IF JUST ONE ALIEN RACE WAS ATTACKING US, BUT THERE ARE SO MANY AT ONCE.
WE'RE ALWAYS UP AGAINST BIZARRE NEW TACTICS AND WEAPONS.
HOW ARE WE SUPPOSED TO STRATEGIZE?
MAYBE IT WOULD BE BETTER IF WE JUST WAVED THE WHITE FLAG.
DON'T BE ABSURD!!
IF WE DON'T PROTECT THE CITIZENS, WHO WILL?!
BUT...
THINGS HAD BECOME UNTENABLE.
THE WORLD WAS FULL OF NOTHING BUT MURDERERS AND THE MURDERED, AND INDUSTRIA HAD GIVEN UP.
EVERYONE WAS CROOKED.

2 years later... Barrage (Astro) is born

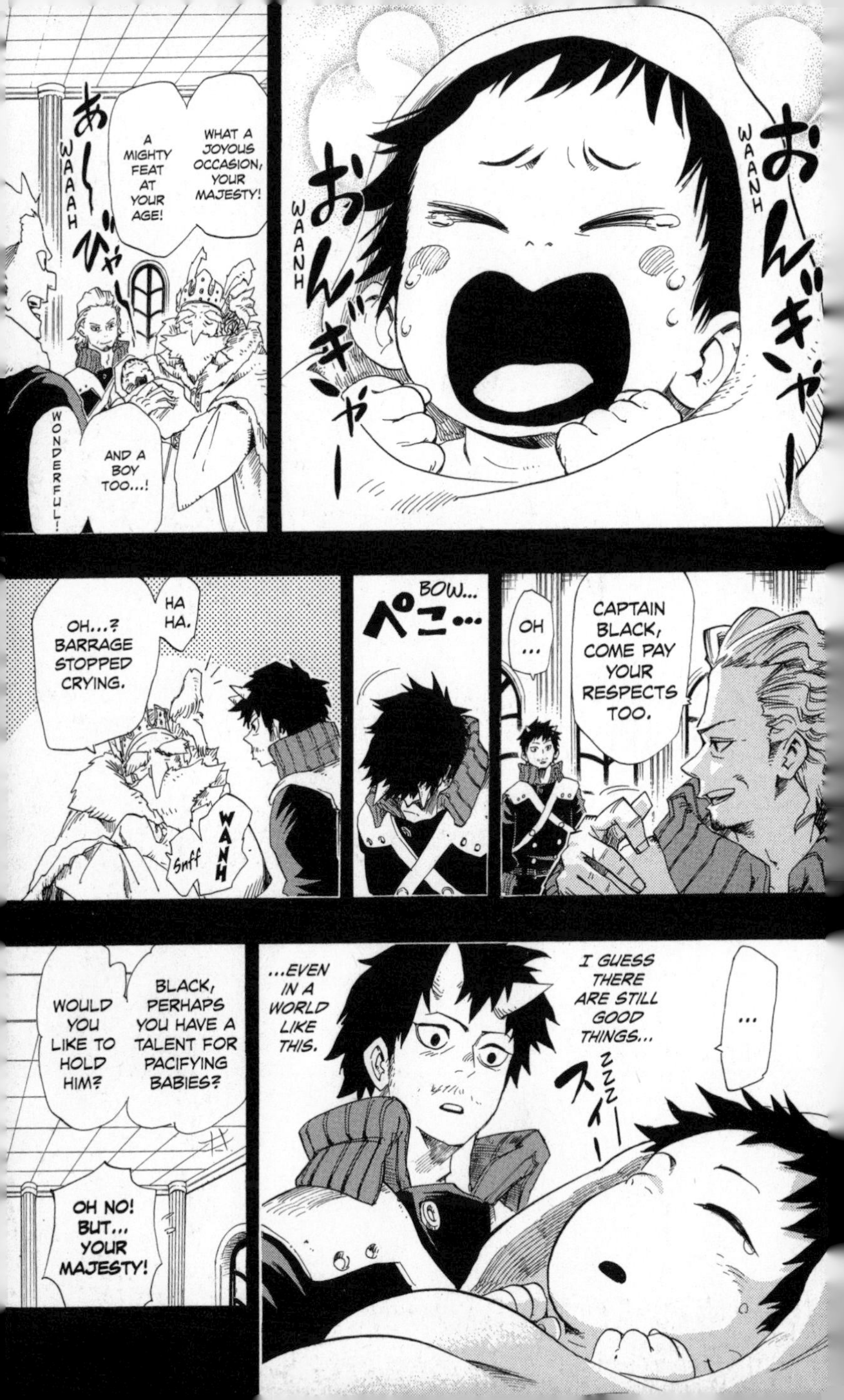
おんギャー
WAANH
おんギャー
WAANH
WHAT A JOYOUS OCCASION, YOUR MAJESTY!
A MIGHTY FEAT AT YOUR AGE!
あ〜
WAAAAH
びゃ〜
AND A BOY TOO...!
WONDERFUL!
CAPTAIN BLACK, COME PAY YOUR RESPECTS TOO.
OH...
ぺこ...
BOW...
HA HA.
OH...? BARRAGE STOPPED CRYING.
WANH
Snff
...
I GUESS THERE ARE STILL GOOD THINGS...
...EVEN IN A WORLD LIKE THIS.
スィー
ZZZ
BLACK, PERHAPS YOU HAVE A TALENT FOR PACIFYING BABIES?
WOULD YOU LIKE TO HOLD HIM?
OH NO! BUT... YOUR MAJESTY!

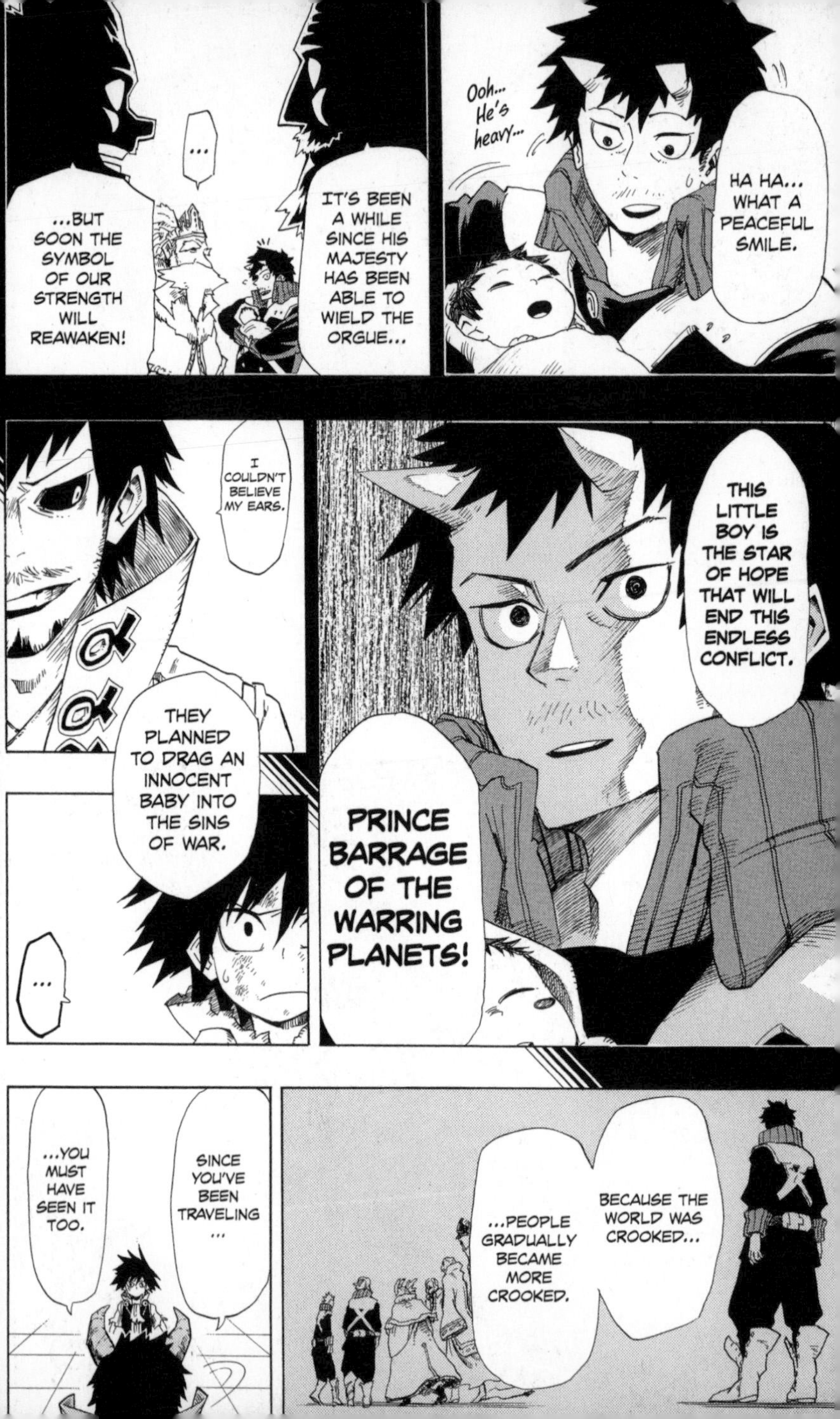

Ooh... He's heavy...
HA HA... WHAT A PEACEFUL SMILE.
...
IT'S BEEN A WHILE SINCE HIS MAJESTY HAS BEEN ABLE TO WIELD THE ORGUE...
...BUT SOON THE SYMBOL OF OUR STRENGTH WILL REAWAKEN!
THIS LITTLE BOY IS THE STAR OF HOPE THAT WILL END THIS ENDLESS CONFLICT.
PRINCE BARRAGE OF THE WARRING PLANETS!
I COULDN'T BELIEVE MY EARS.
THEY PLANNED TO DRAG AN INNOCENT BABY INTO THE SINS OF WAR.
...
BECAUSE THE WORLD WAS CROOKED...
...PEOPLE GRADUALLY BECAME MORE CROOKED.
SINCE YOU'VE BEEN TRAVELING...
...YOU MUST HAVE SEEN IT TOO.

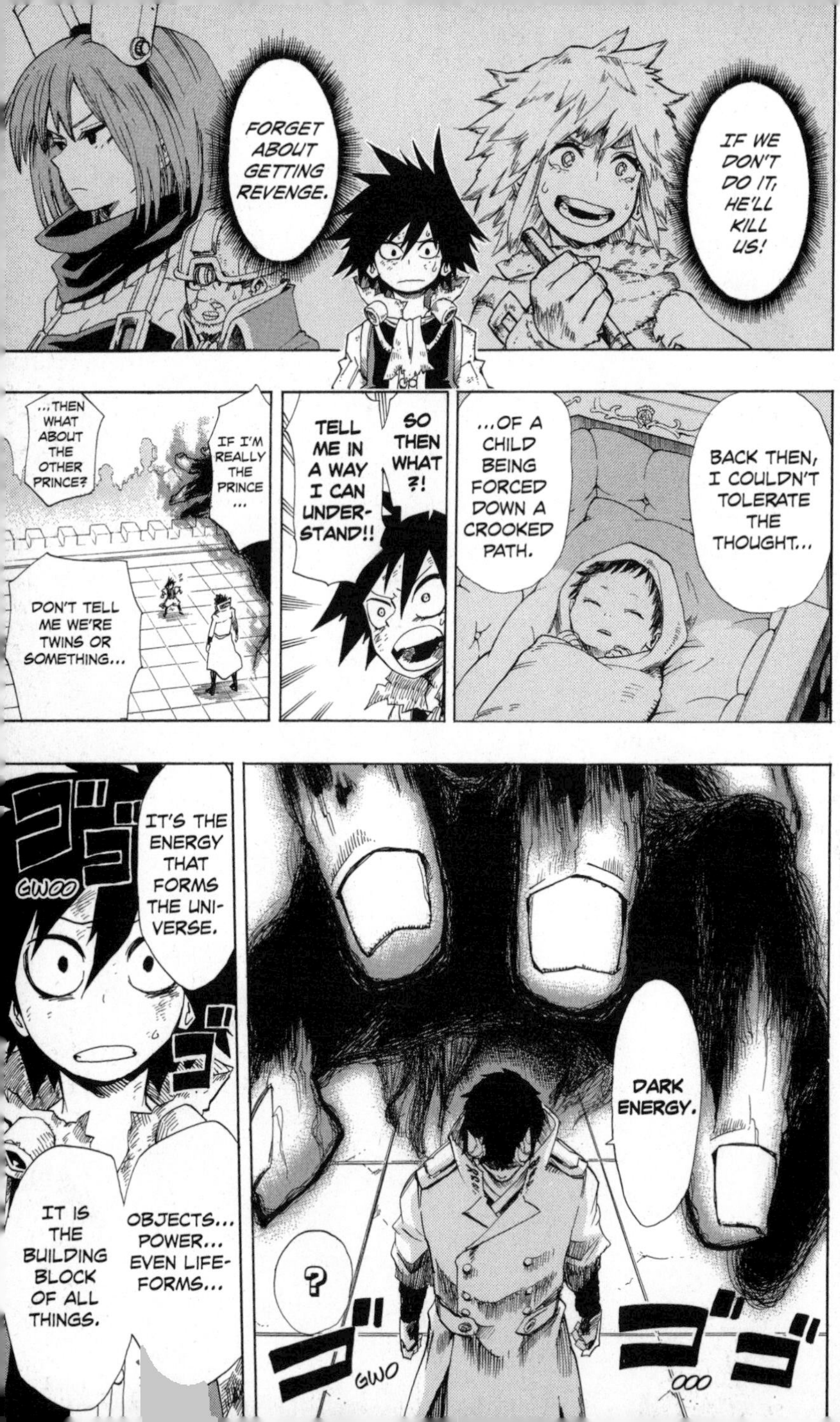
IF WE DON'T DO IT, HE'LL KILL US!
FORGET ABOUT GETTING REVENGE.
BACK THEN, I COULDN'T TOLERATE THE THOUGHT...
...OF A CHILD BEING FORCED DOWN A CROOKED PATH.
SO THEN WHAT?!
TELL ME IN A WAY I CAN UNDER-STAND!!
IF I'M REALLY THE PRINCE...
...THEN WHAT ABOUT THE OTHER PRINCE?
DON'T TELL ME WE'RE TWINS OR SOMETHING...
DARK ENERGY.
?
GWO
OOO
IT'S THE ENERGY THAT FORMS THE UNI-VERSE.
GWOO
OBJECTS... POWER... EVEN LIFE-FORMS...
IT IS THE BUILDING BLOCK OF ALL THINGS.

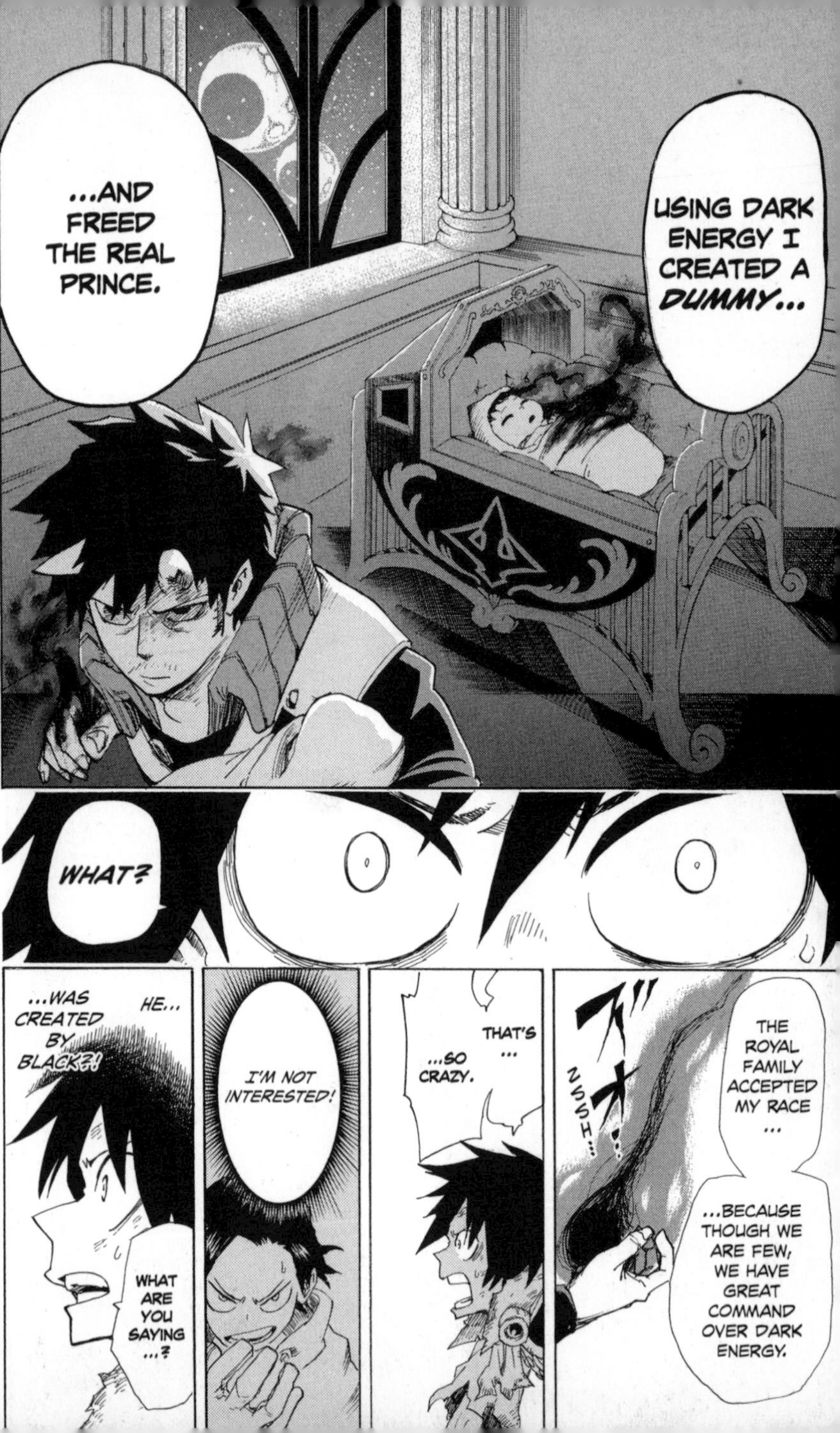
USING DARK ENERGY I CREATED A *DUMMY*...
...AND FREED THE REAL PRINCE.
WHAT?
THE ROYAL FAMILY ACCEPTED MY RACE ...
...BECAUSE THOUGH WE ARE FEW, WE HAVE GREAT COMMAND OVER DARK ENERGY.
ZSSH...
THAT'S ...
...SO CRAZY.
I'M NOT INTERESTED!
HE...
...WAS CREATED BY BLACK?!
WHAT ARE YOU SAYING ...?

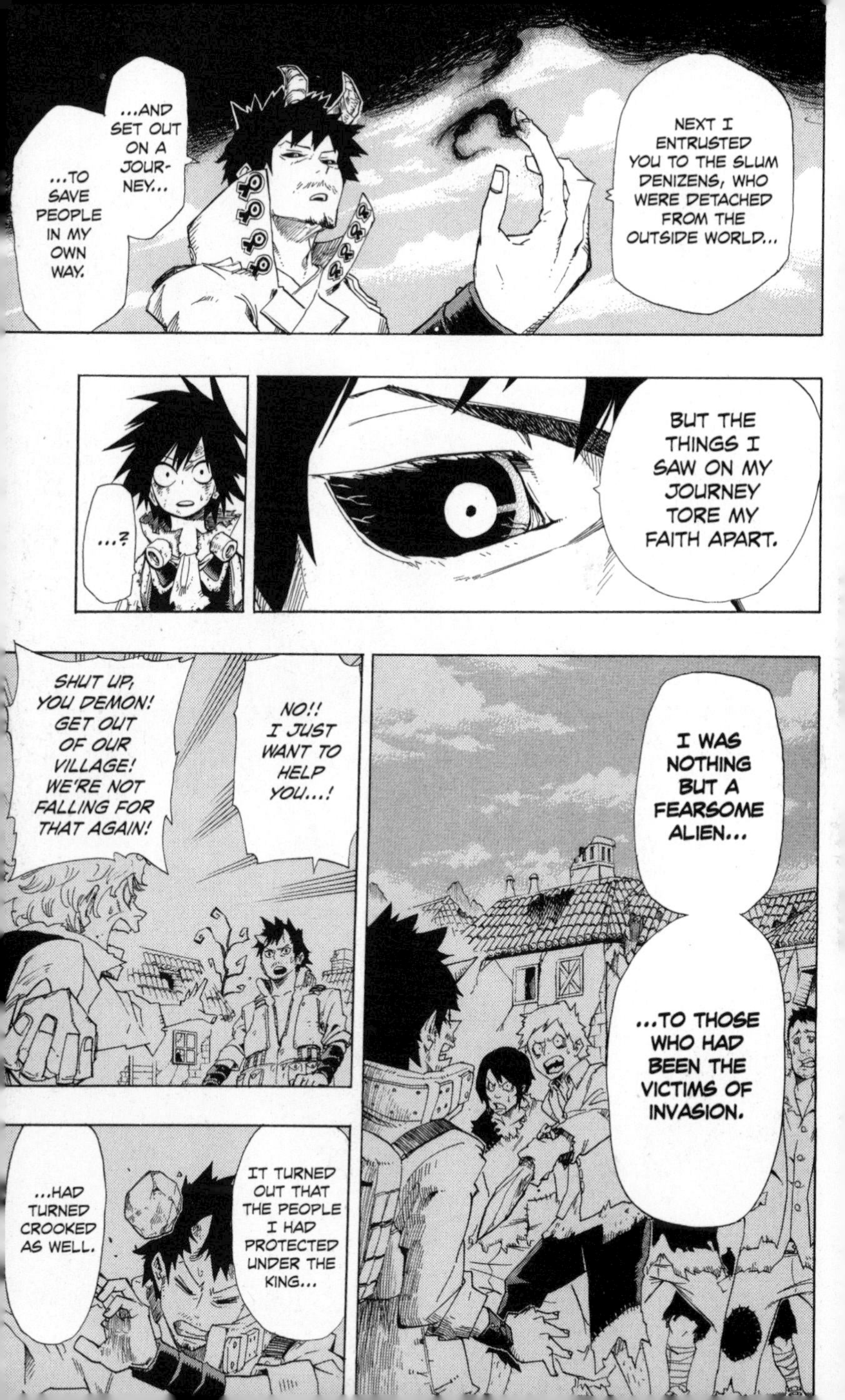
NEXT I ENTRUSTED YOU TO THE SLUM DENIZENS, WHO WERE DETACHED FROM THE OUTSIDE WORLD...
...AND SET OUT ON A JOUR-NEY...
...TO SAVE PEOPLE IN MY OWN WAY.
BUT THE THINGS I SAW ON MY JOURNEY TORE MY FAITH APART.
...?
I WAS NOTHING BUT A FEARSOME ALIEN...
...TO THOSE WHO HAD BEEN THE VICTIMS OF INVASION.
NO!! I JUST WANT TO HELP YOU...!
SHUT UP, YOU DEMON! GET OUT OF OUR VILLAGE! WE'RE NOT FALLING FOR THAT AGAIN!
IT TURNED OUT THAT THE PEOPLE I HAD PROTECTED UNDER THE KING...
...HAD TURNED CROOKED AS WELL.

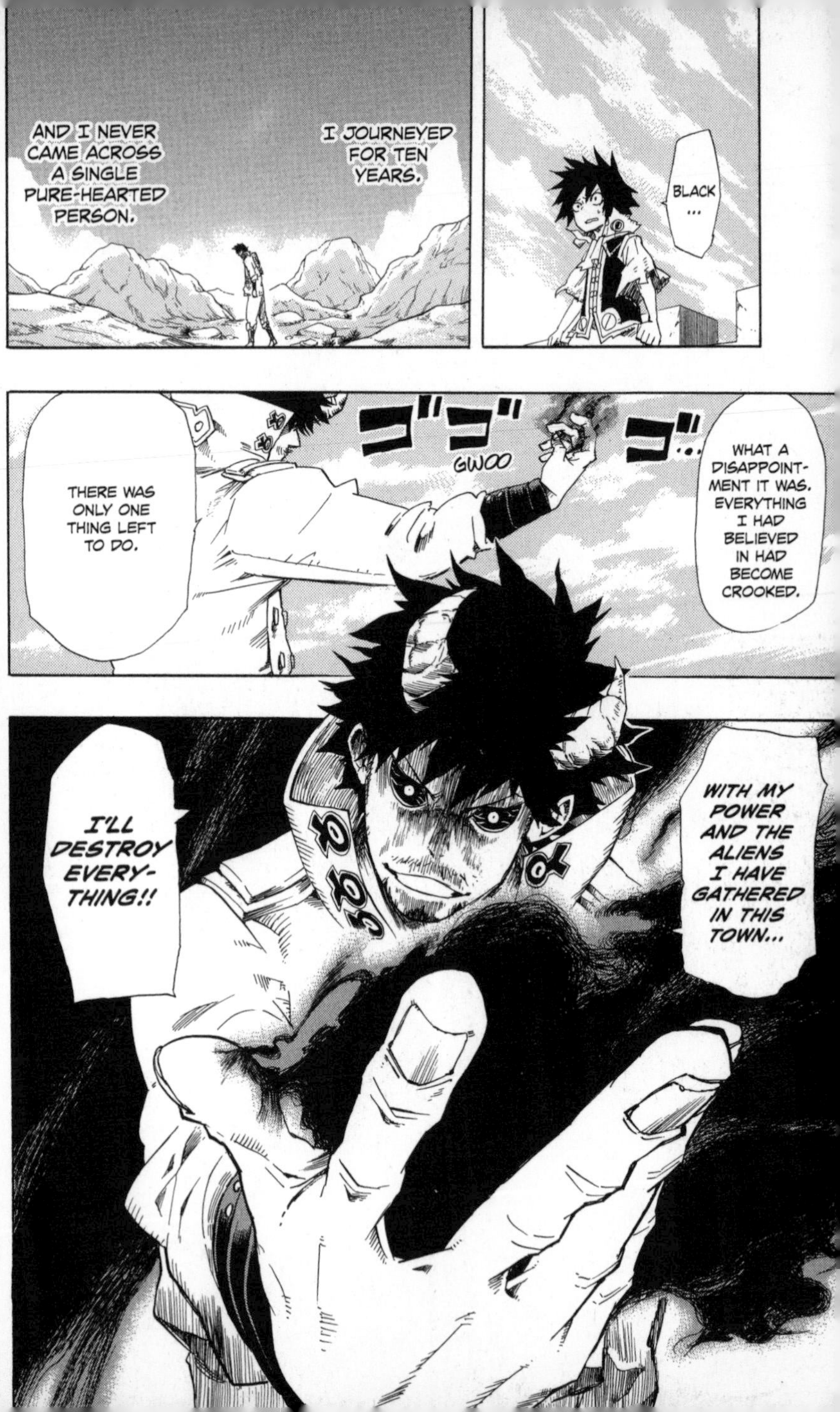
BLACK ...
I JOURNEYED FOR TEN YEARS.
AND I NEVER CAME ACROSS A SINGLE PURE-HEARTED PERSON.
WHAT A DISAPPOINTMENT IT WAS. EVERYTHING I HAD BELIEVED IN HAD BECOME CROOKED.
ゴゴゴ…
GWOO
THERE WAS ONLY ONE THING LEFT TO DO.
WITH MY POWER AND THE ALIENS I HAVE GATHERED IN THIS TOWN...
I'LL DESTROY EVERYTHING!!

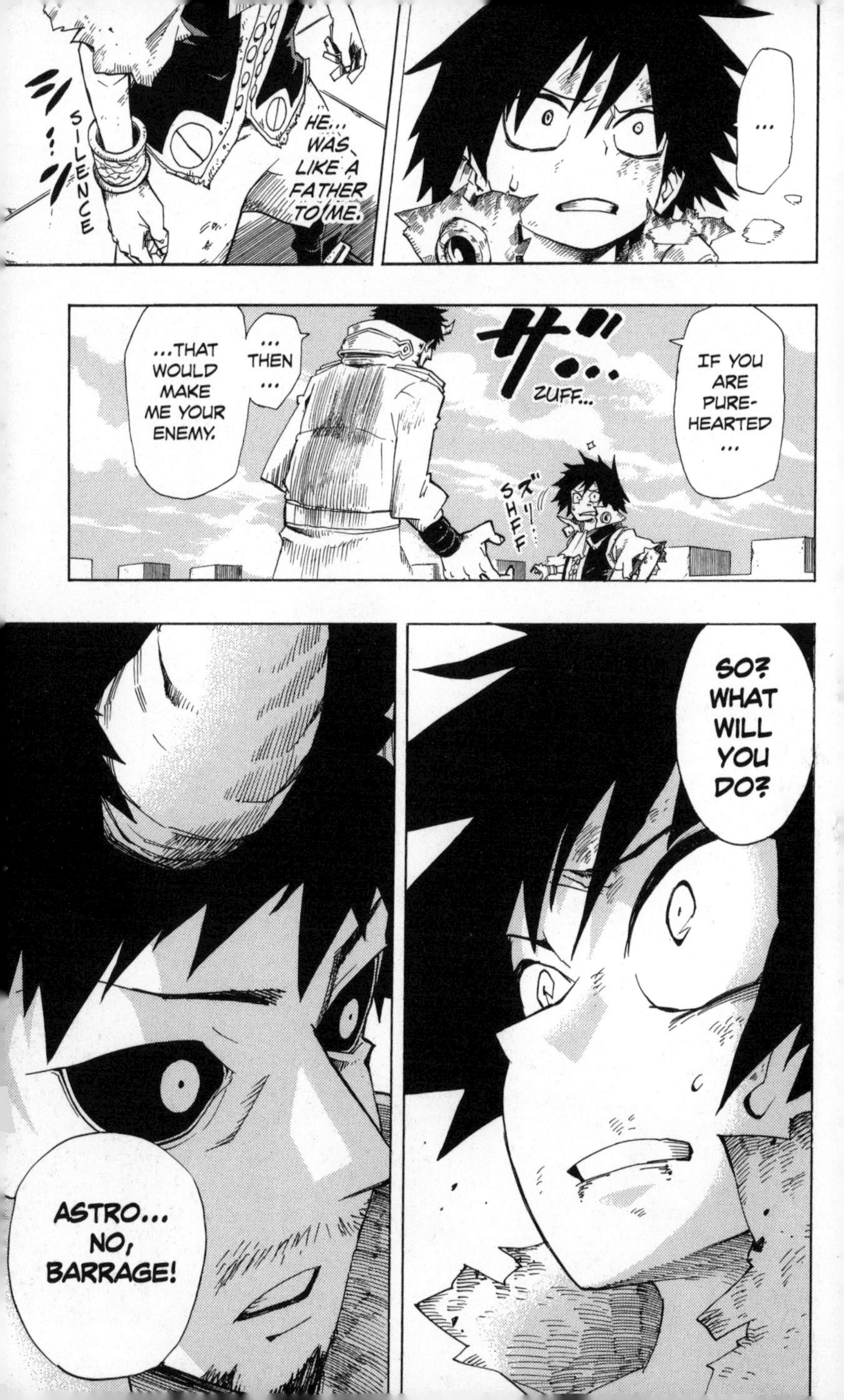
...
HE... WAS LIKE A FATHER TO ME.
SILENCE
IF YOU ARE PURE-HEARTED ...
ZUFF...
SHFF
... THEN ...
...THAT WOULD MAKE ME YOUR ENEMY.
SO? WHAT WILL YOU DO?
ASTRO... NO, BARRAGE!

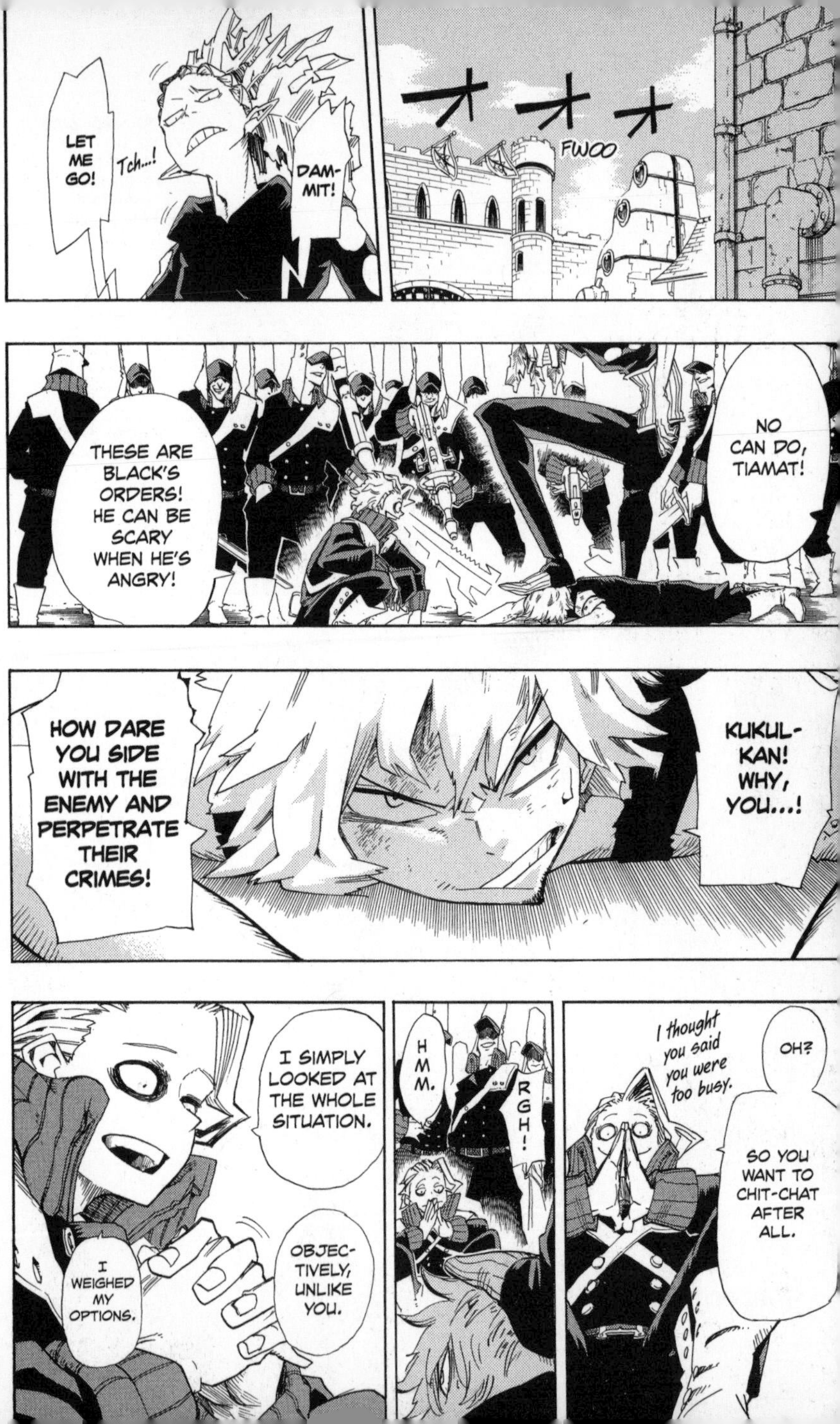
オオオ
FWOO
DAM-MIT!
Tch...!
LET ME GO!
NO CAN DO, TIAMAT!
THESE ARE BLACK'S ORDERS! HE CAN BE SCARY WHEN HE'S ANGRY!
KUKUL-KAN! WHY, YOU...!
HOW DARE YOU SIDE WITH THE ENEMY AND PERPETRATE THEIR CRIMES!
OH?
I thought you said you were too busy.
SO YOU WANT TO CHIT-CHAT AFTER ALL.
HMM.
RGH!
I SIMPLY LOOKED AT THE WHOLE SITUATION.
OBJEC-TIVELY, UNLIKE YOU.
I WEIGHED MY OPTIONS.

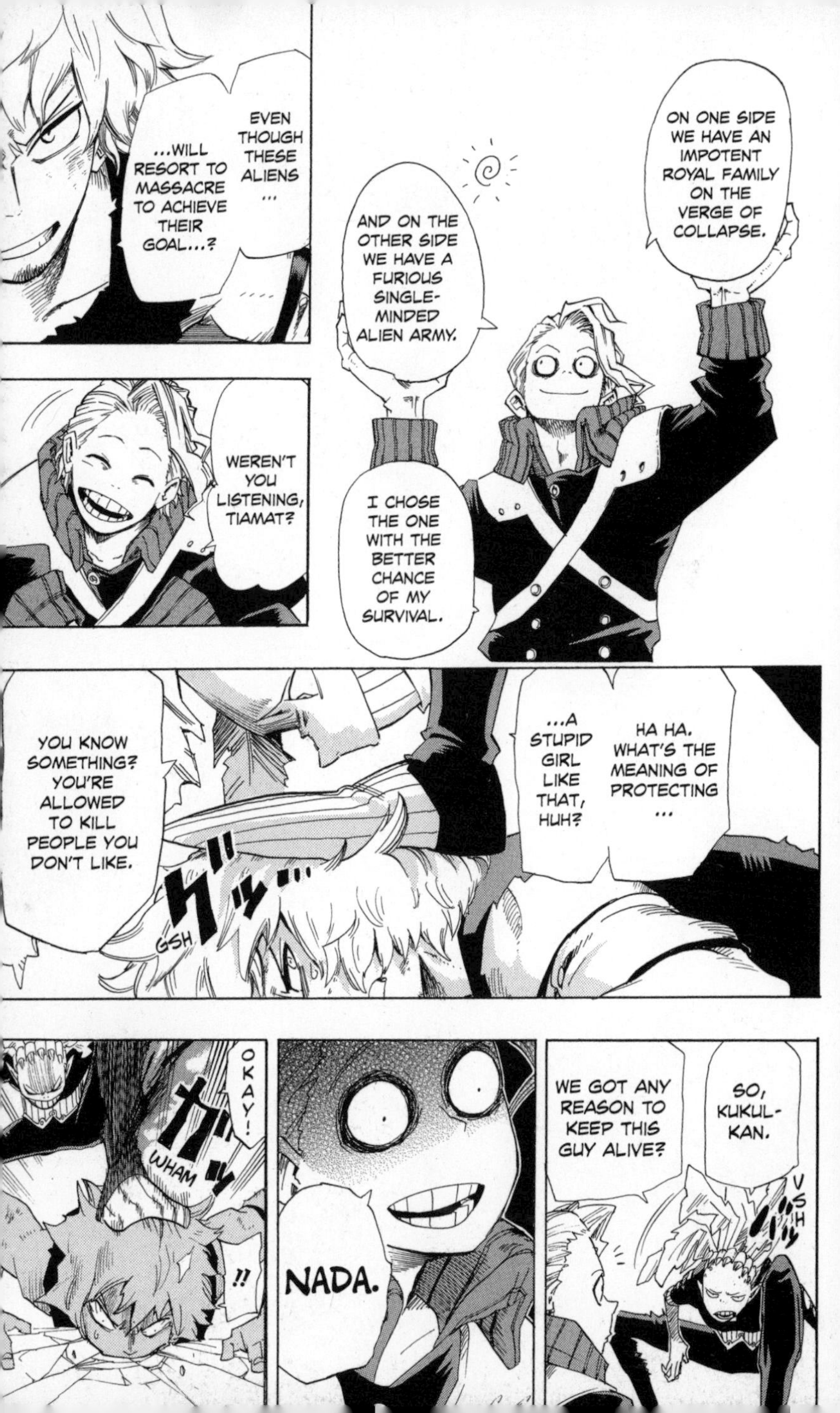
ON ONE SIDE WE HAVE AN IMPOTENT ROYAL FAMILY ON THE VERGE OF COLLAPSE.
AND ON THE OTHER SIDE WE HAVE A FURIOUS SINGLE-MINDED ALIEN ARMY.
I CHOSE THE ONE WITH THE BETTER CHANCE OF MY SURVIVAL.
EVEN THOUGH THESE ALIENS...
...WILL RESORT TO MASSACRE TO ACHIEVE THEIR GOAL...?
WEREN'T YOU LISTENING, TIAMAT?
HA HA. WHAT'S THE MEANING OF PROTECTING...
...A STUPID GIRL LIKE THAT, HUH?
YOU KNOW SOMETHING? YOU'RE ALLOWED TO KILL PEOPLE YOU DON'T LIKE.
GSH
SO, KUKUL-KAN.
WE GOT ANY REASON TO KEEP THIS GUY ALIVE?
VSH
NADA.
OKAY!
WHAM
!!

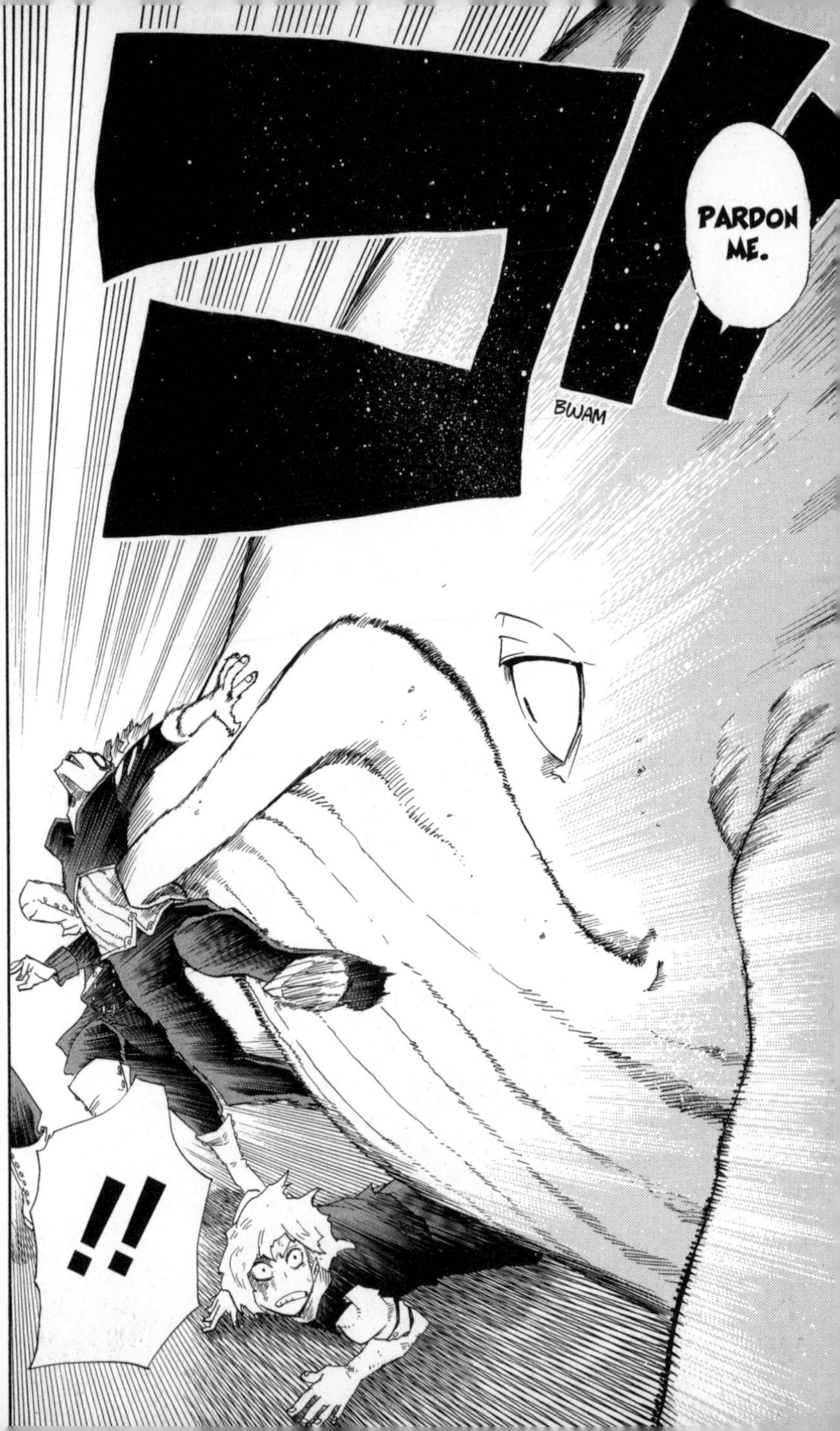
PARDON ME.
BWAM
!!

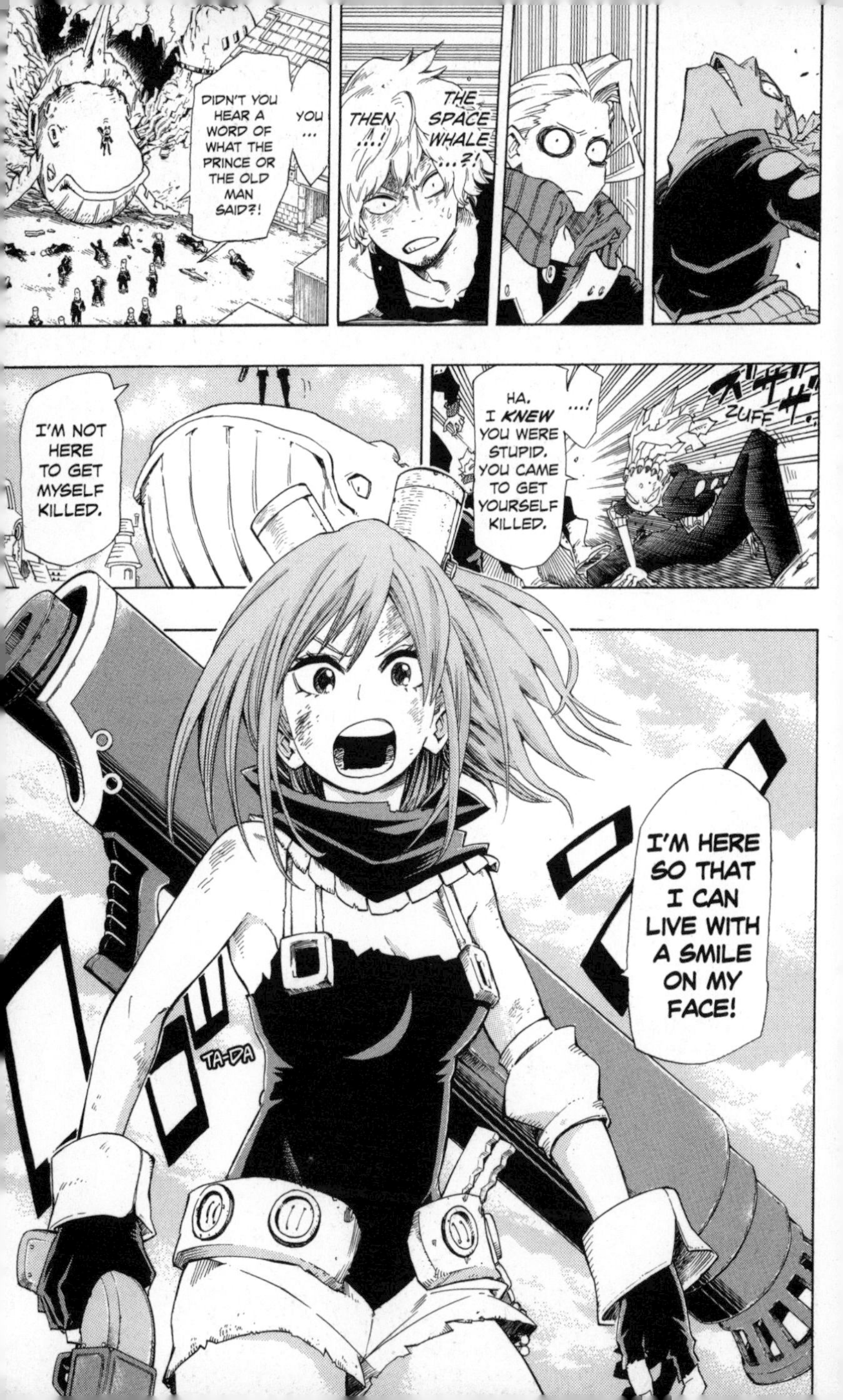
THE SPACE WHALE ...?!
THEN ...!
YOU ...
DIDN'T YOU HEAR A WORD OF WHAT THE PRINCE OR THE OLD MAN SAID?!
ZUFF
...!
HA. I *KNEW* YOU WERE STUPID. YOU CAME TO GET YOURSELF KILLED.
I'M NOT HERE TO GET MYSELF KILLED.
I'M HERE SO THAT I CAN LIVE WITH A SMILE ON MY FACE!
TA-DA

BLACK

Age: 36

Birthday: July 10th
Height: 5'08"

A Horn Alien. I wasn't able to fit this into the story, so although it might seem out of place, I'd like to explain some things about him here. His black eyes are a side effect of using more Dark Energy than his body can handle. Kind of like an overdose. And his horns are twisted because he holds a twisted ideology. There's a saying among Horn Aliens that goes, "The horns say more than the mouth." That's Horn Aliens for you.

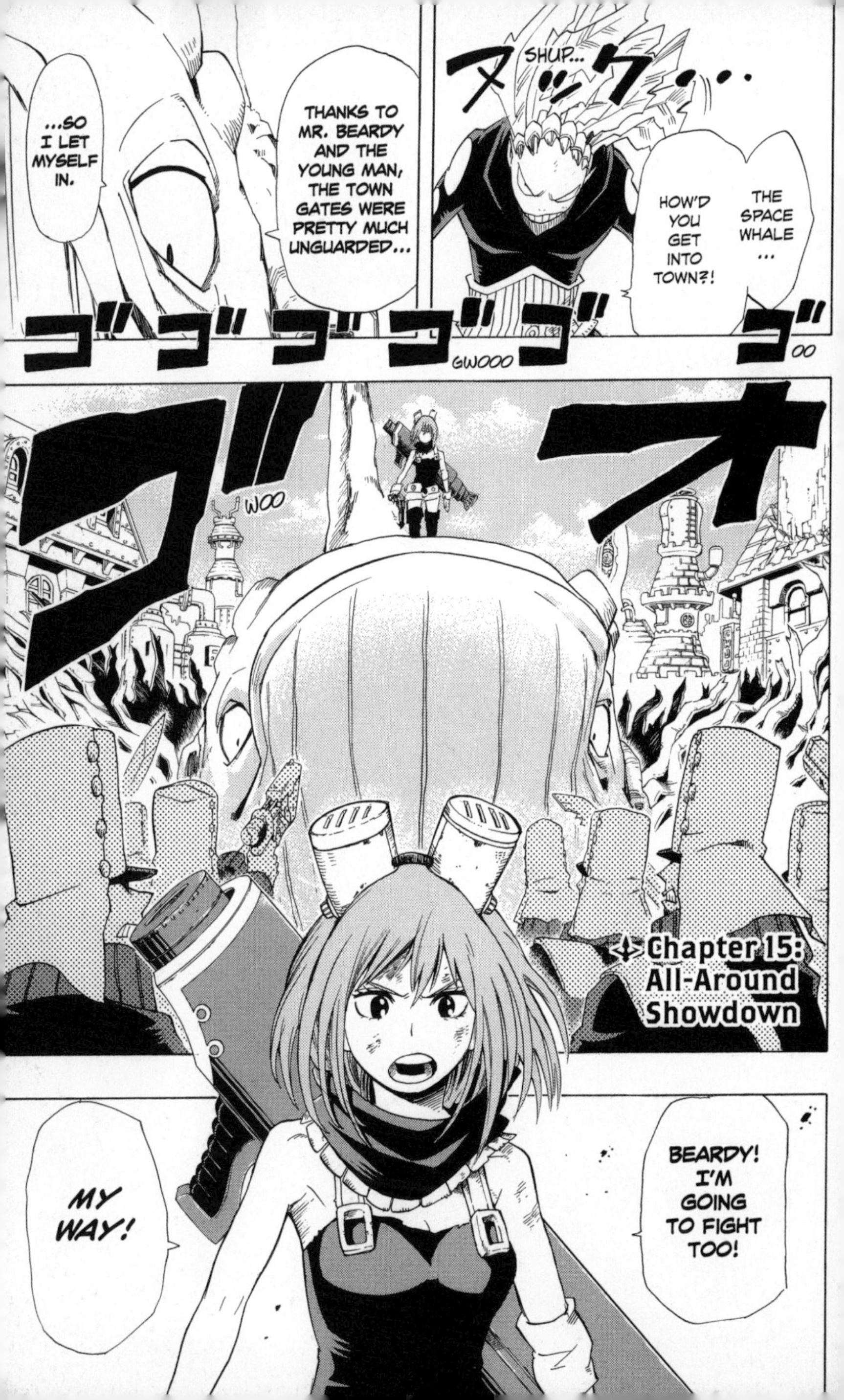

SHUP...
THE SPACE WHALE...
HOW'D YOU GET INTO TOWN?!
THANKS TO MR. BEARDY AND THE YOUNG MAN, THE TOWN GATES WERE PRETTY MUCH UNGUARDED...
...SO I LET MYSELF IN.
GWOOO
OO
WOO
Chapter 15: All-Around Showdown
BEARDY! I'M GOING TO FIGHT TOO!
MY WAY!

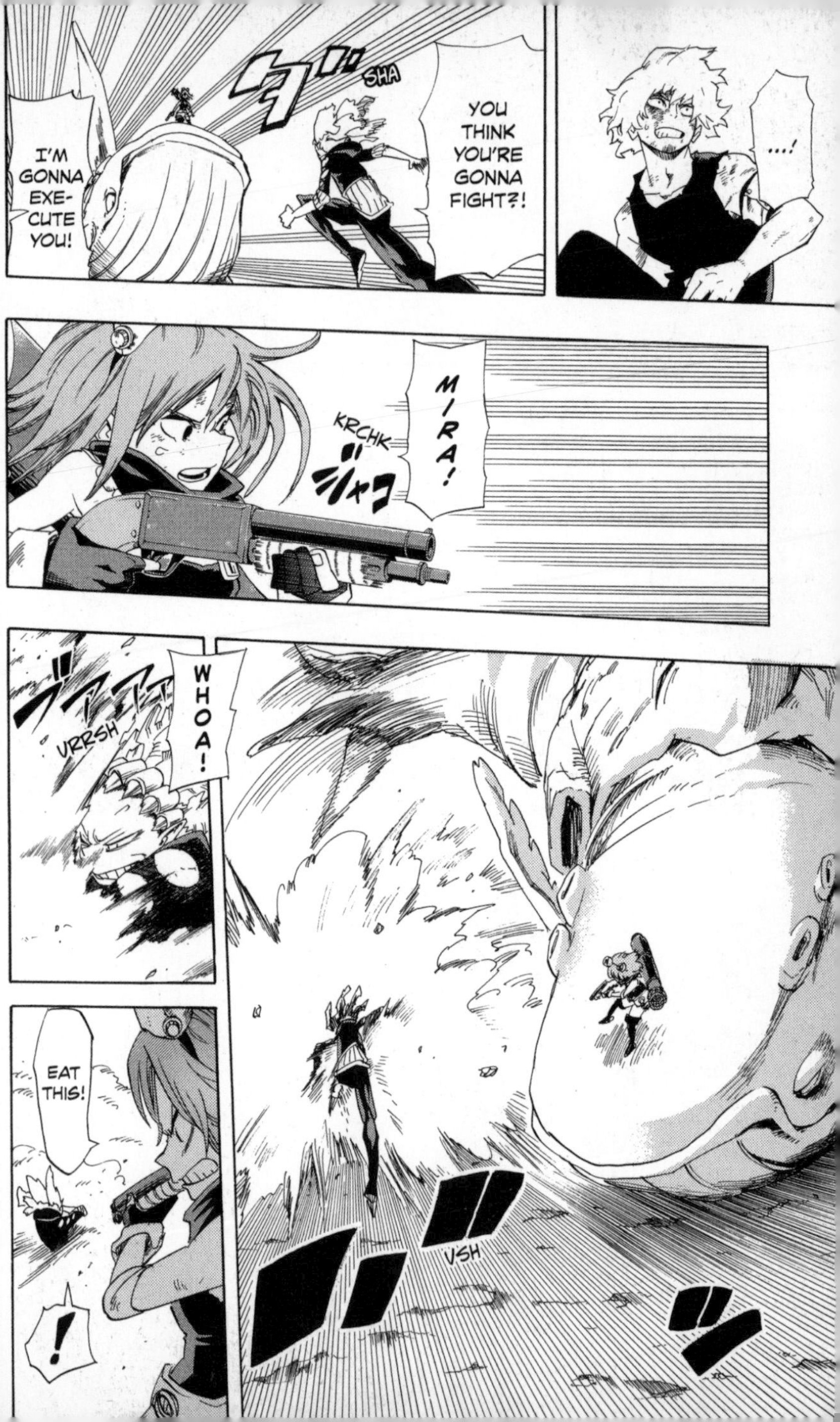
...!
YOU THINK YOU'RE GONNA FIGHT?!
SHA
I'M GONNA EXE-CUTE YOU!
MIRA!
KRCHK
VSH
WHOA!
URRSH
EAT THIS!
!

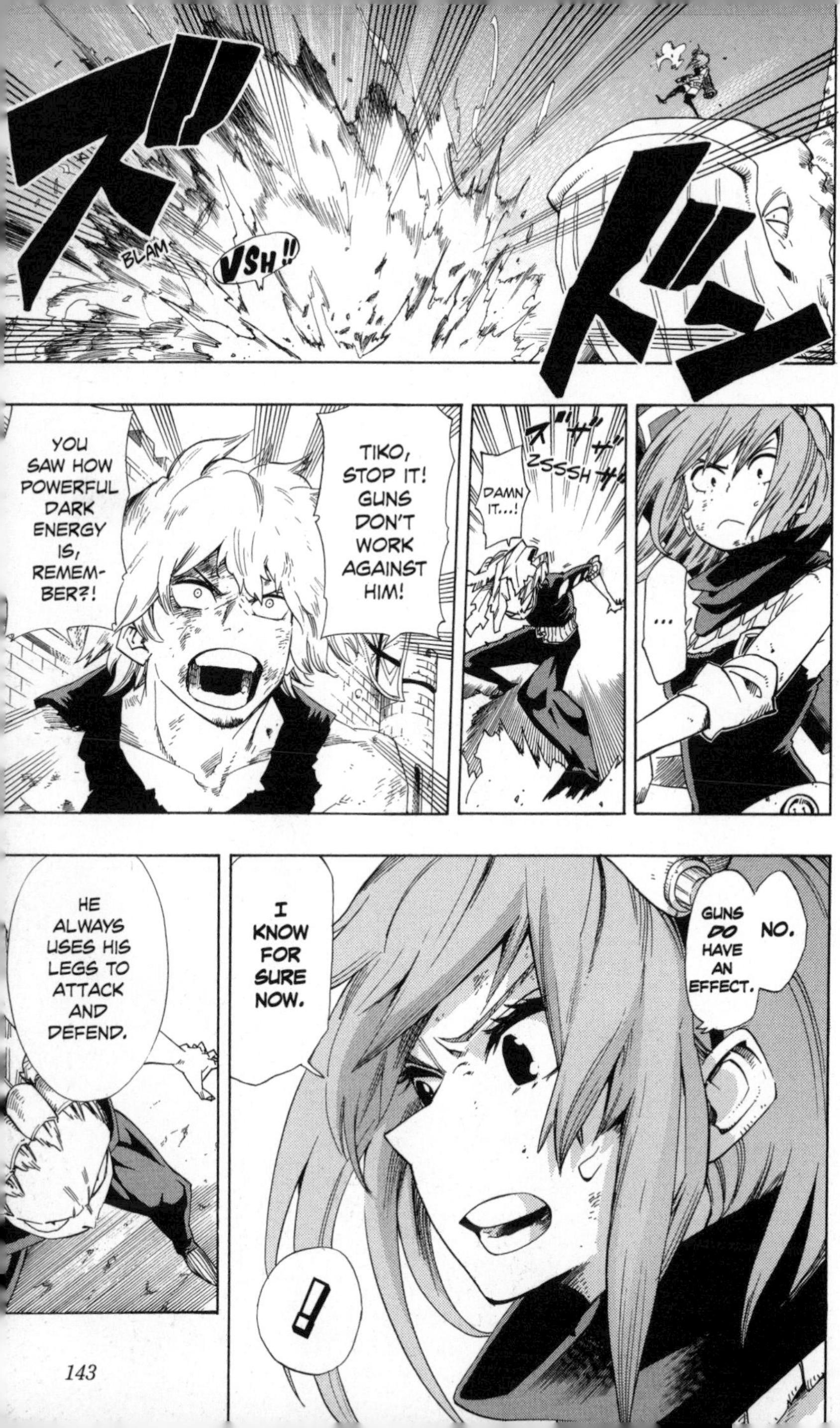
VSH!!
BLAM
...
ZSSSH
DAMN IT...!
TIKO, STOP IT! GUNS DON'T WORK AGAINST HIM!
YOU SAW HOW POWERFUL DARK ENERGY IS, REMEMBER?!
NO.
GUNS DO HAVE AN EFFECT.
I KNOW FOR SURE NOW.
!
HE ALWAYS USES HIS LEGS TO ATTACK AND DEFEND.

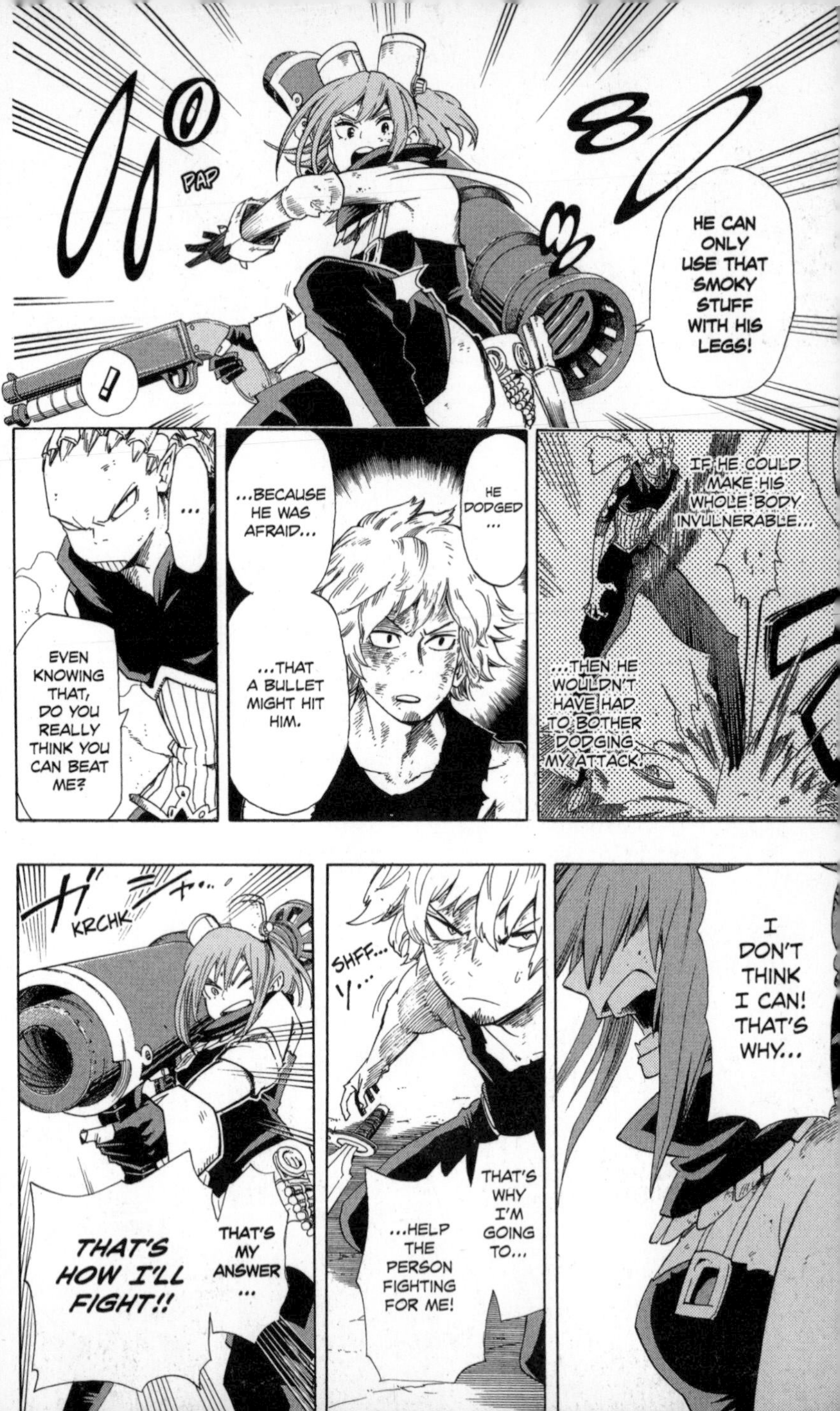
HE CAN ONLY USE THAT SMOKY STUFF WITH HIS LEGS!
PAP
!
IF HE COULD MAKE HIS WHOLE BODY INVULNERABLE...
...THEN HE WOULDN'T HAVE HAD TO BOTHER DODGING MY ATTACK!
HE DODGED...
...BECAUSE HE WAS AFRAID...
...THAT A BULLET MIGHT HIT HIM.
...
EVEN KNOWING THAT, DO YOU REALLY THINK YOU CAN BEAT ME?
I DON'T THINK I CAN! THAT'S WHY...
SHFF...
THAT'S WHY I'M GOING TO...
...HELP THE PERSON FIGHTING FOR ME!
KRCHK
THAT'S MY ANSWER...
THAT'S HOW I'LL FIGHT!!

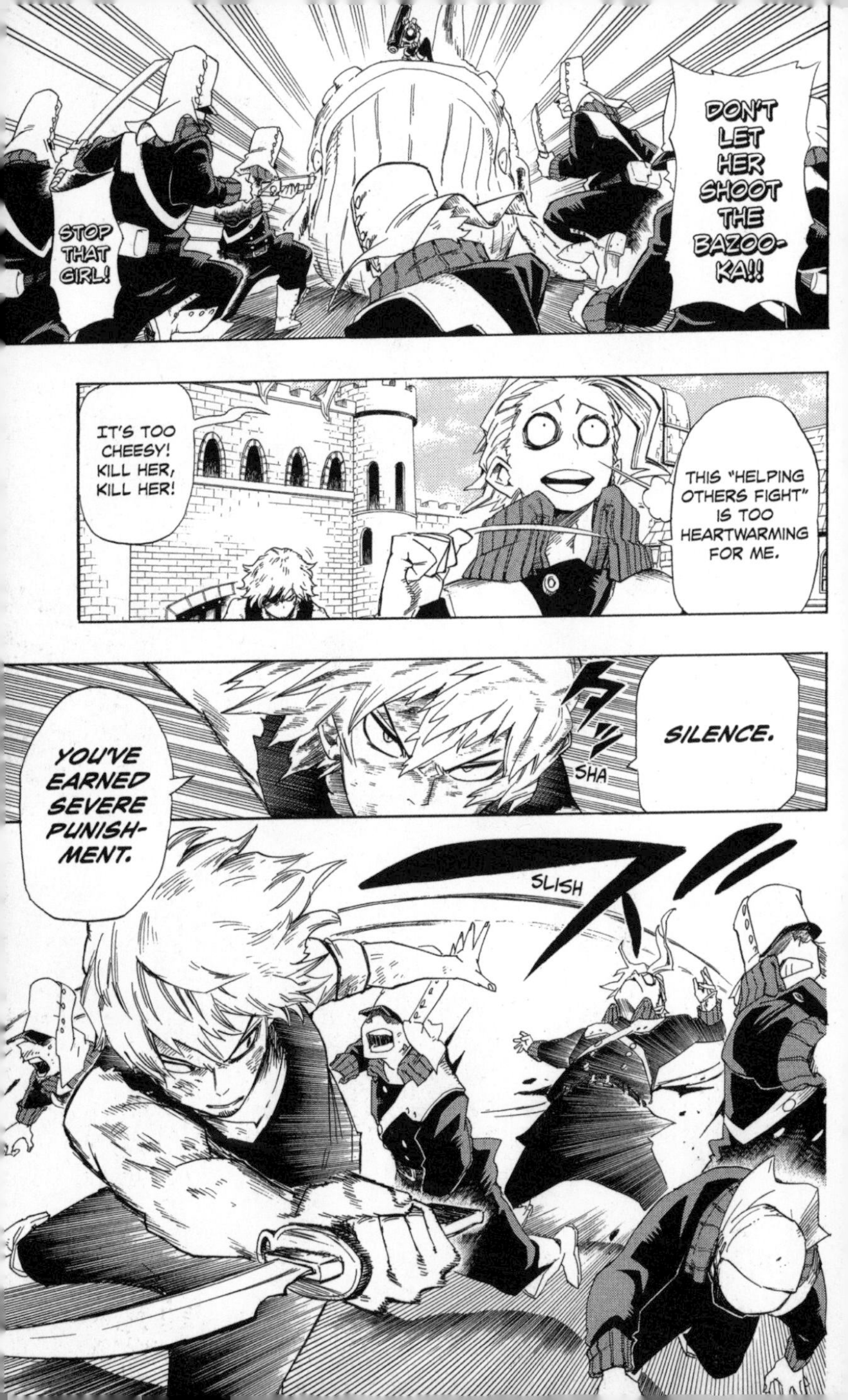
DON'T LET HER SHOOT THE BAZOO-KA!!
STOP THAT GIRL!
THIS "HELPING OTHERS FIGHT" IS TOO HEARTWARMING FOR ME.
IT'S TOO CHEESY! KILL HER, KILL HER!
SILENCE.
SHA
YOU'VE EARNED SEVERE PUNISH-MENT.
SLISH

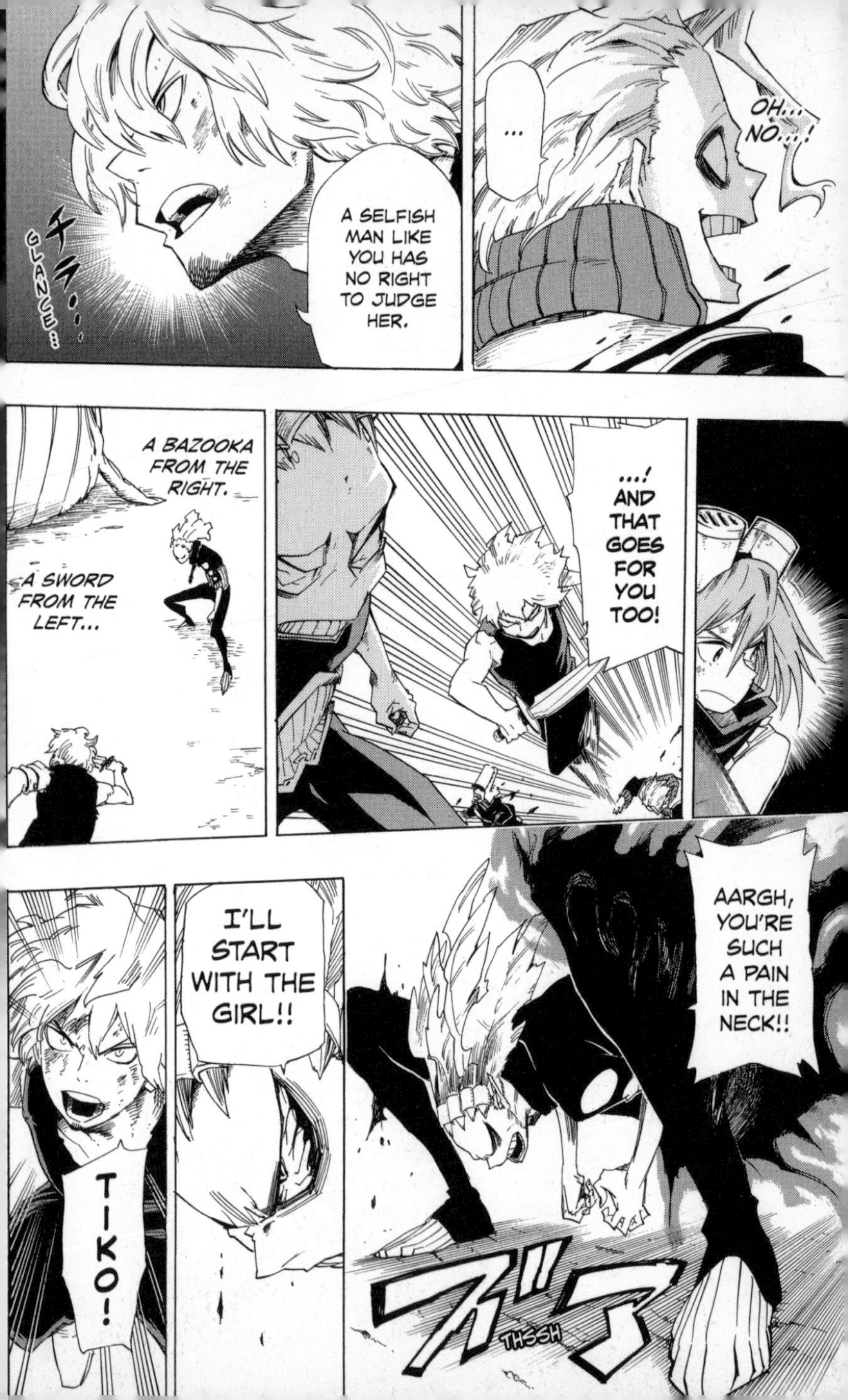
OH... NO...!
...
A SELFISH MAN LIKE YOU HAS NO RIGHT TO JUDGE HER.
GLANCE..
...! AND THAT GOES FOR YOU TOO!
A BAZOOKA FROM THE RIGHT.
A SWORD FROM THE LEFT...
AARGH, YOU'RE SUCH A PAIN IN THE NECK!!
THSSH
I'LL START WITH THE GIRL!!
TIKO!

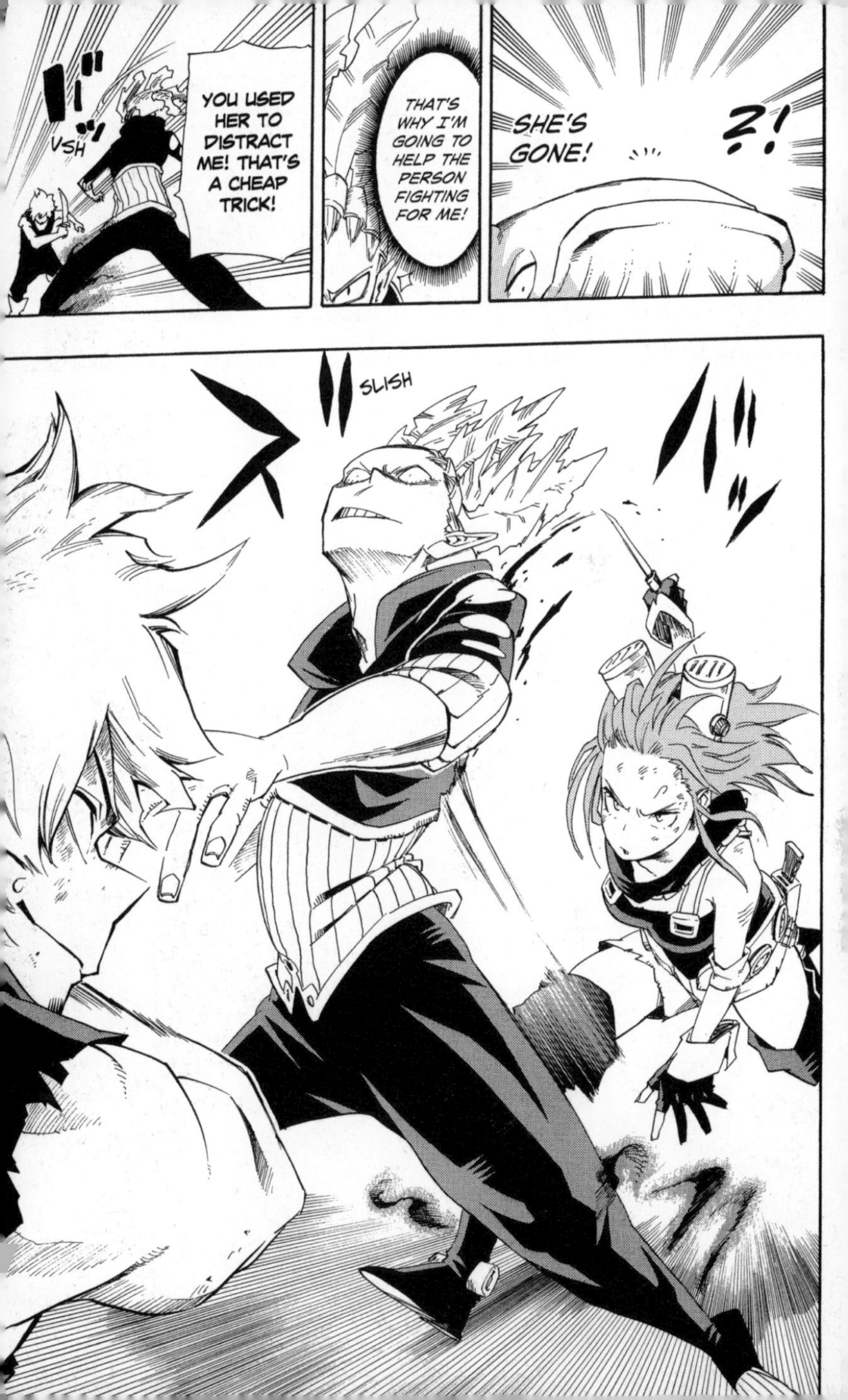
?!
SHE'S GONE!
THAT'S WHY I'M GOING TO HELP THE PERSON FIGHTING FOR ME!
YOU USED HER TO DISTRACT ME! THAT'S A CHEAP TRICK!
VSH
SLISH

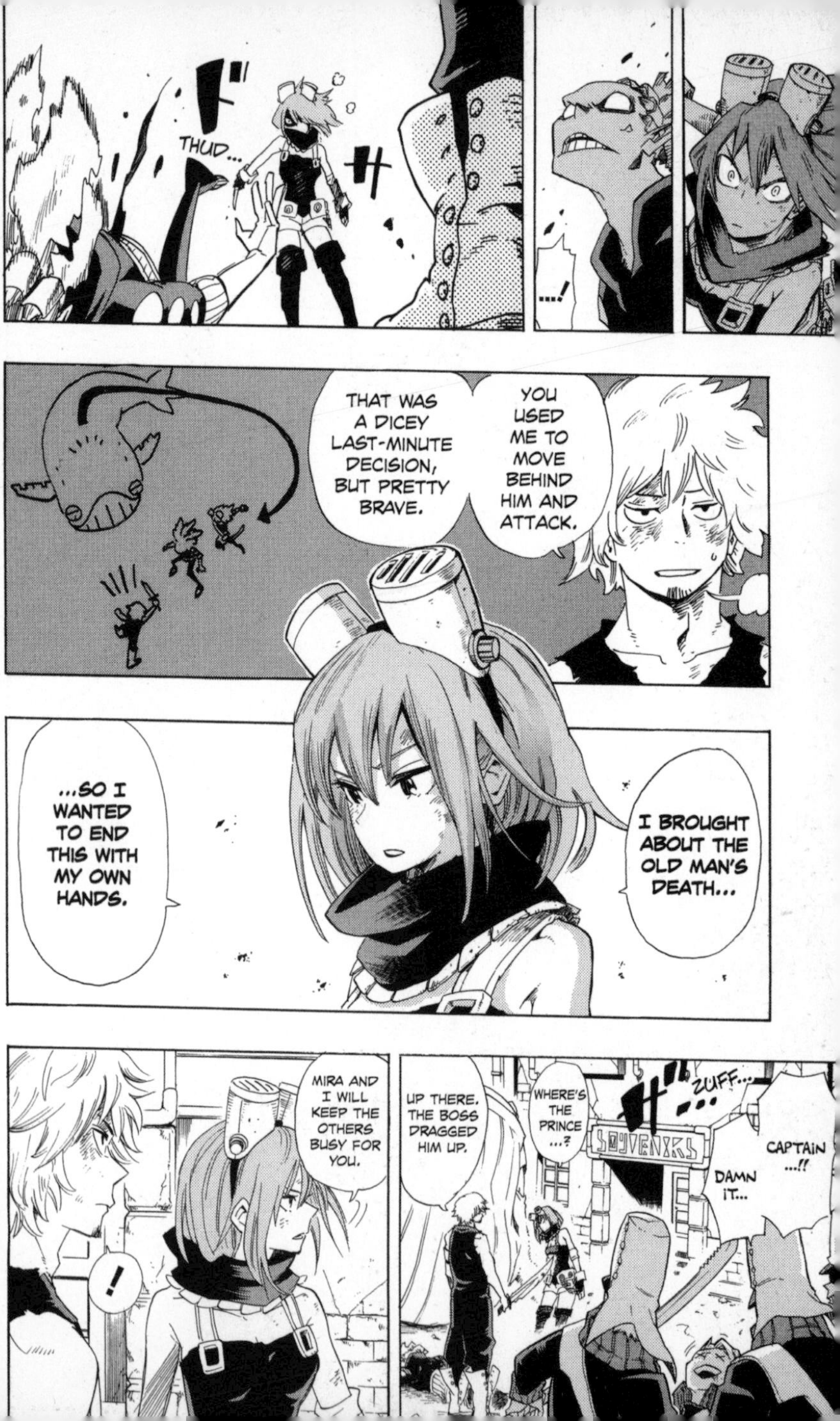
...!
THUD...
YOU USED ME TO MOVE BEHIND HIM AND ATTACK.
THAT WAS A DICEY LAST-MINUTE DECISION, BUT PRETTY BRAVE.
I BROUGHT ABOUT THE OLD MAN'S DEATH...
...SO I WANTED TO END THIS WITH MY OWN HANDS.
ZUFF...
CAPTAIN ...!!
SOUVENIRS
WHERE'S THE PRINCE ...?
DAMN IT...
UP THERE. THE BOSS DRAGGED HIM UP.
MIRA AND I WILL KEEP THE OTHERS BUSY FOR YOU.
!

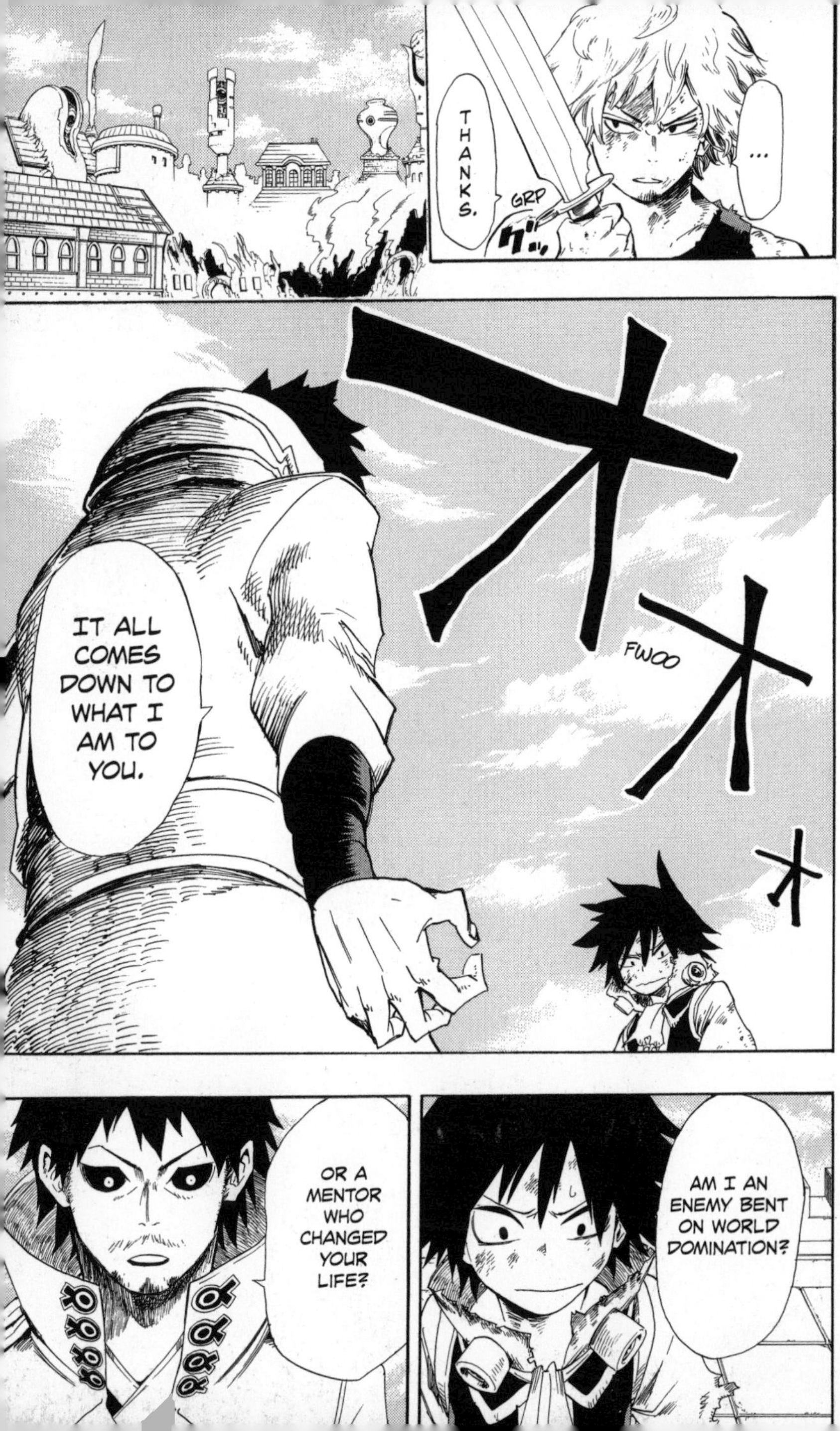
...
THANKS.
GRP
IT ALL COMES DOWN TO WHAT I AM TO YOU.
FWOO
AM I AN ENEMY BENT ON WORLD DOMINATION?
OR A MENTOR WHO CHANGED YOUR LIFE?

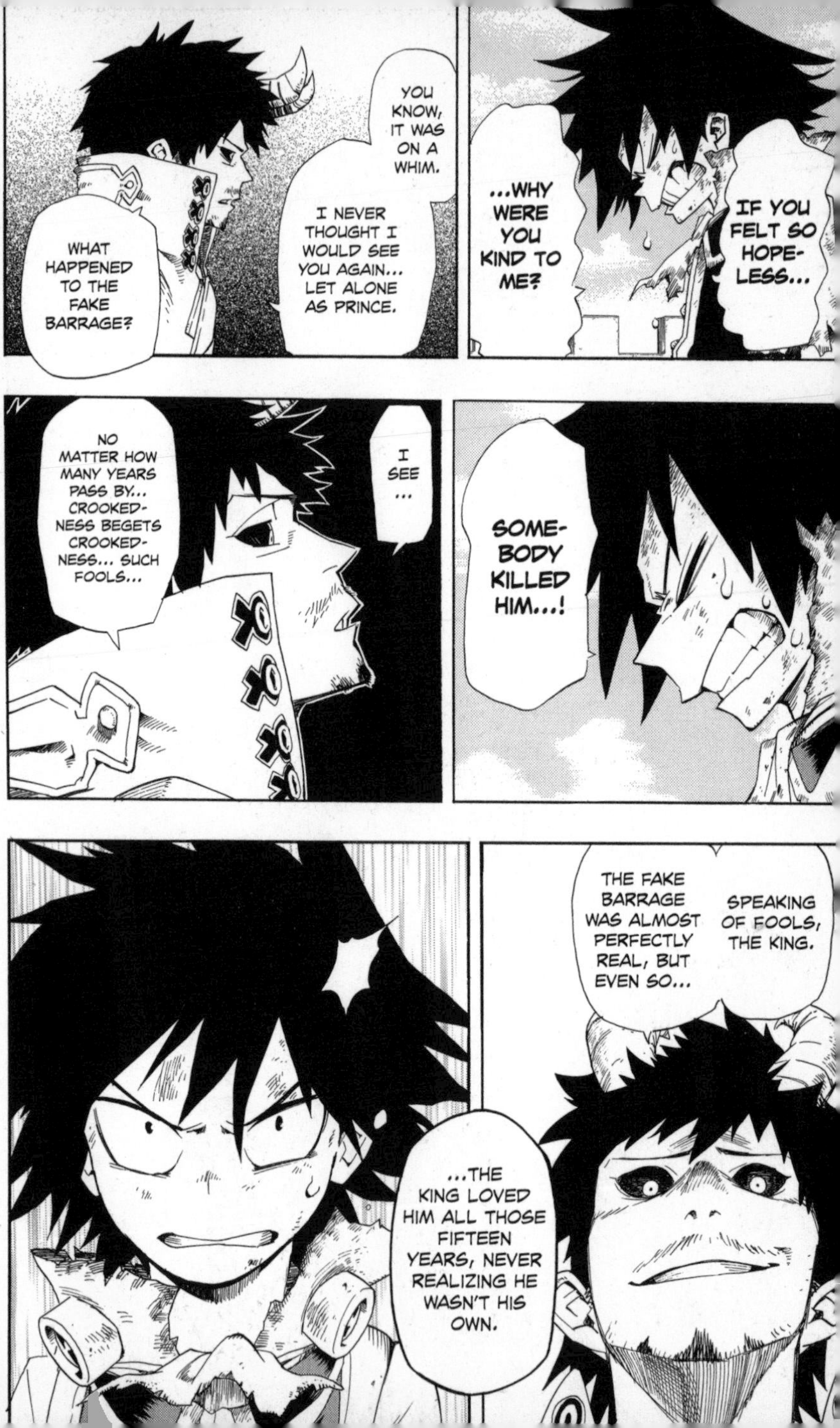
IF YOU FELT SO HOPE-LESS...
...WHY WERE YOU KIND TO ME?
YOU KNOW, IT WAS ON A WHIM.
I NEVER THOUGHT I WOULD SEE YOU AGAIN... LET ALONE AS PRINCE.
WHAT HAPPENED TO THE FAKE BARRAGE?
SOME-BODY KILLED HIM...!
I SEE...
NO MATTER HOW MANY YEARS PASS BY... CROOKED-NESS BEGETS CROOKED-NESS... SUCH FOOLS...
SPEAKING OF FOOLS, THE KING.
THE FAKE BARRAGE WAS ALMOST PERFECTLY REAL, BUT EVEN SO...
...THE KING LOVED HIM ALL THOSE FIFTEEN YEARS, NEVER REALIZING HE WASN'T HIS OWN.

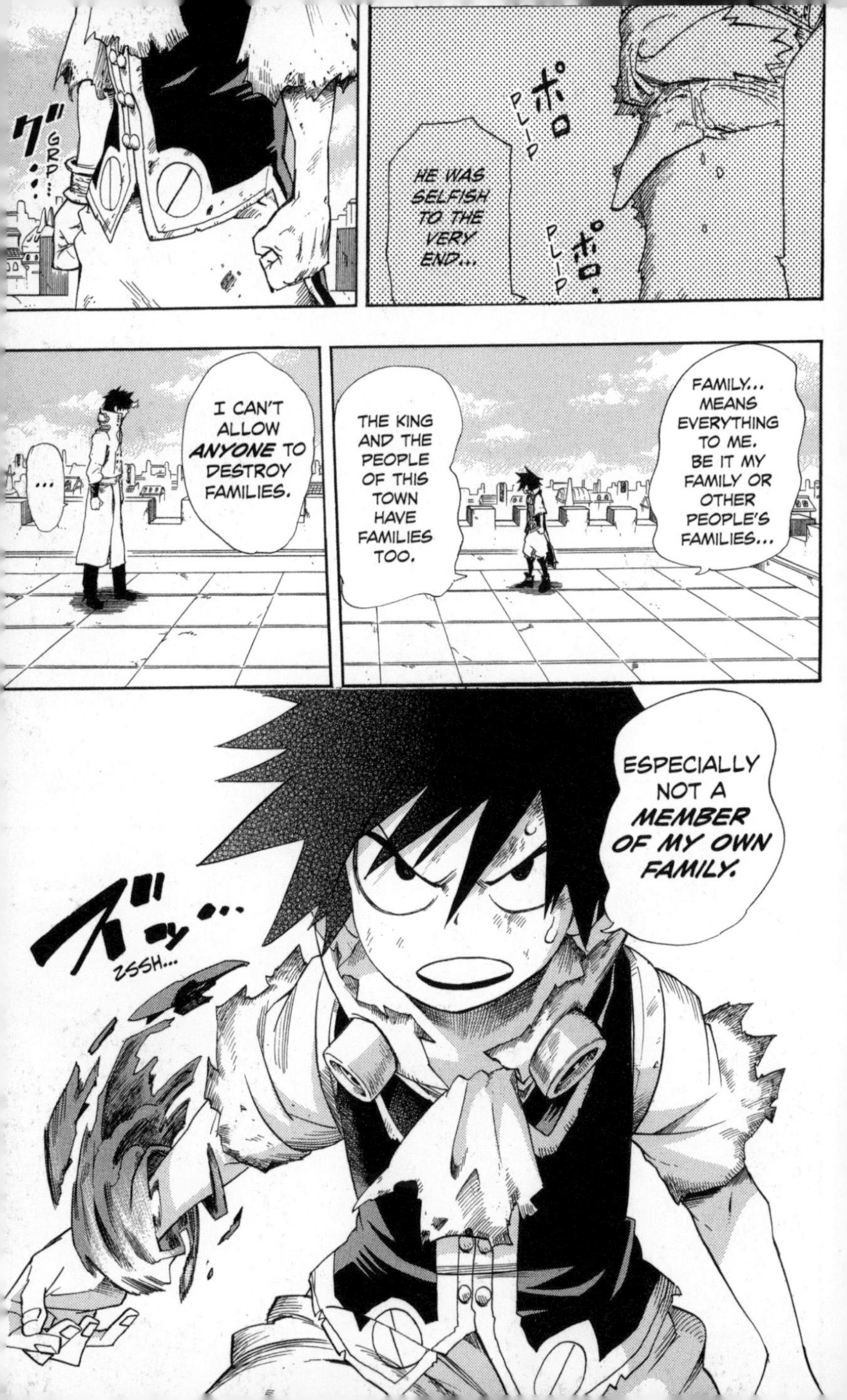

ポロ
PLIP
ポロ
PLIP
HE WAS SELFISH TO THE VERY END...
グ
GRP...
FAMILY... MEANS EVERYTHING TO ME. BE IT MY FAMILY OR OTHER PEOPLE'S FAMILIES...
THE KING AND THE PEOPLE OF THIS TOWN HAVE FAMILIES TOO.
I CAN'T ALLOW ANYONE TO DESTROY FAMILIES.
...
ESPECIALLY NOT A MEMBER OF MY OWN FAMILY.
ズッ...
ZSSH...

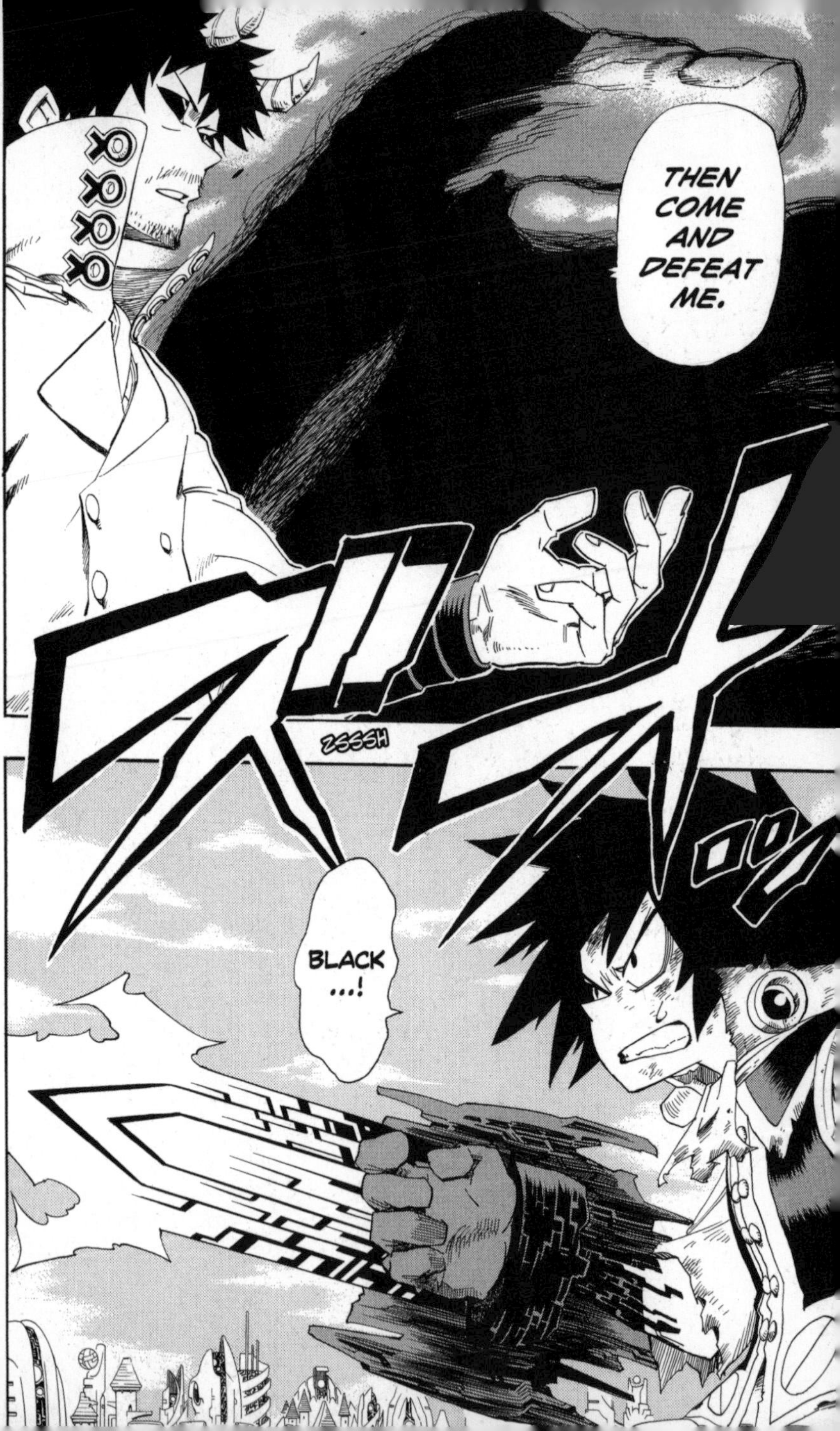
THEN COME AND DEFEAT ME.
ZSSSH
BLACK ...!

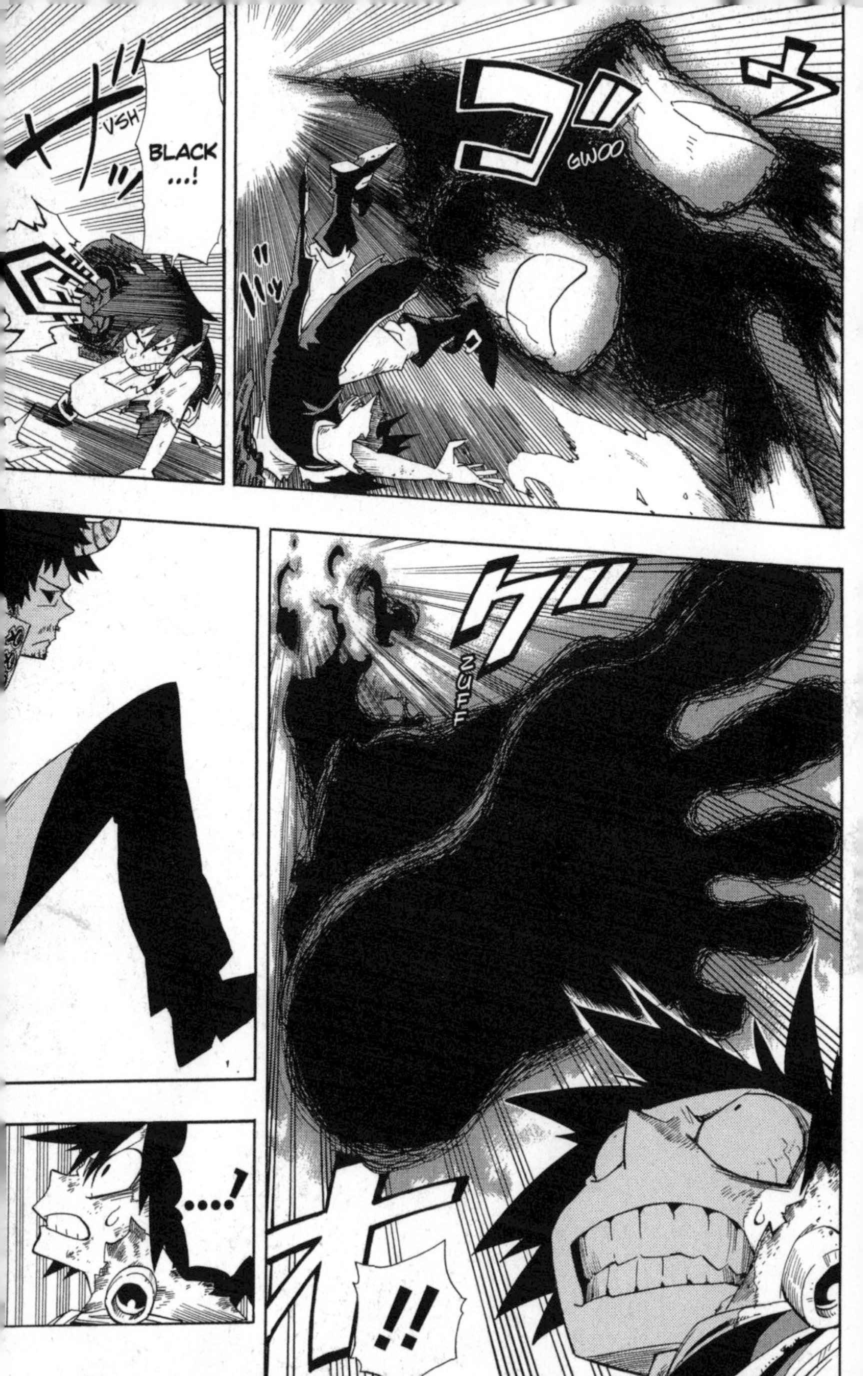
GWOO
VSH
BLACK ...!
ZUFF
!!
....!

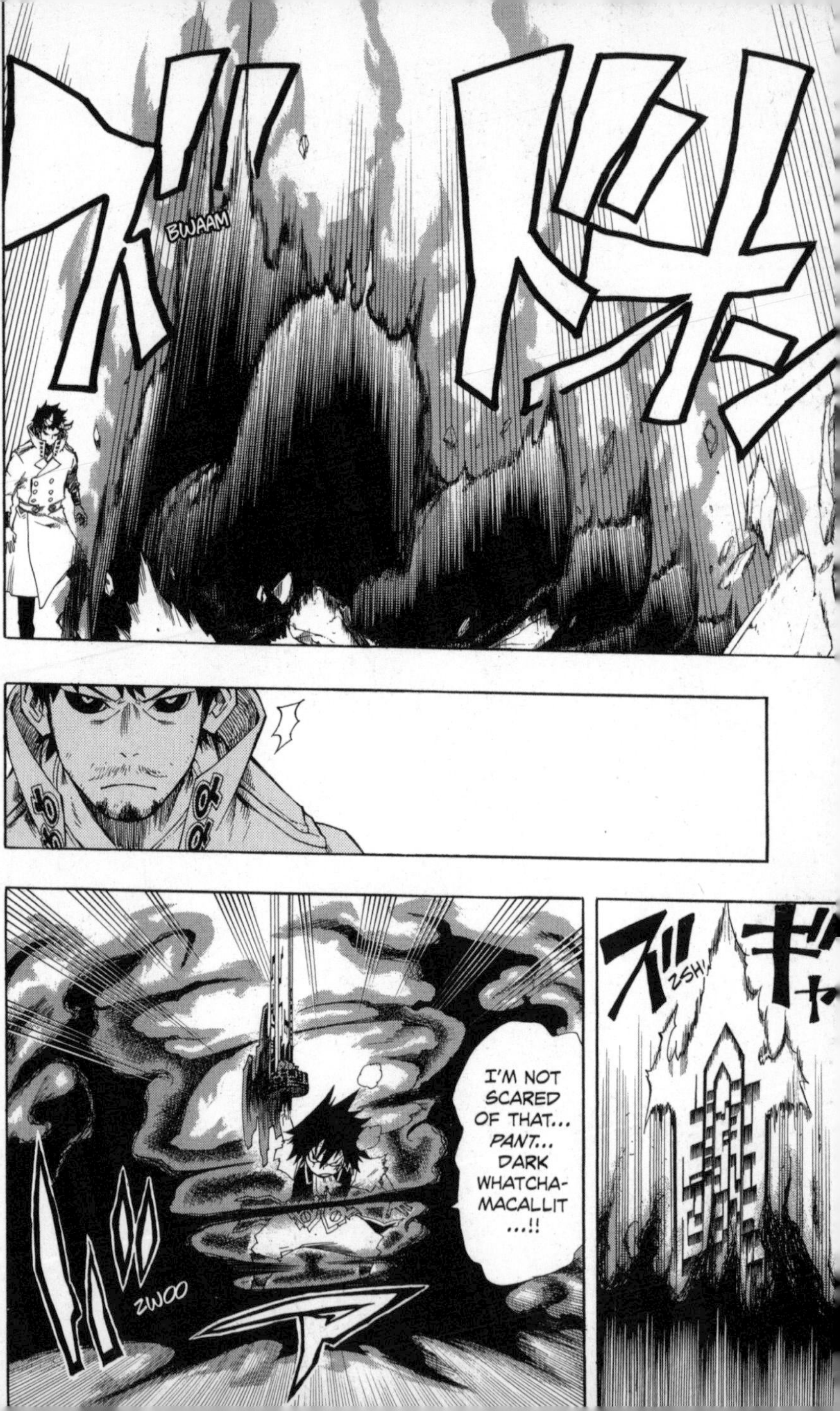
BWAAM
ZSH
I'M NOT SCARED OF THAT... PANT... DARK WHATCHA-MACALLIT ...!!
ZWOO

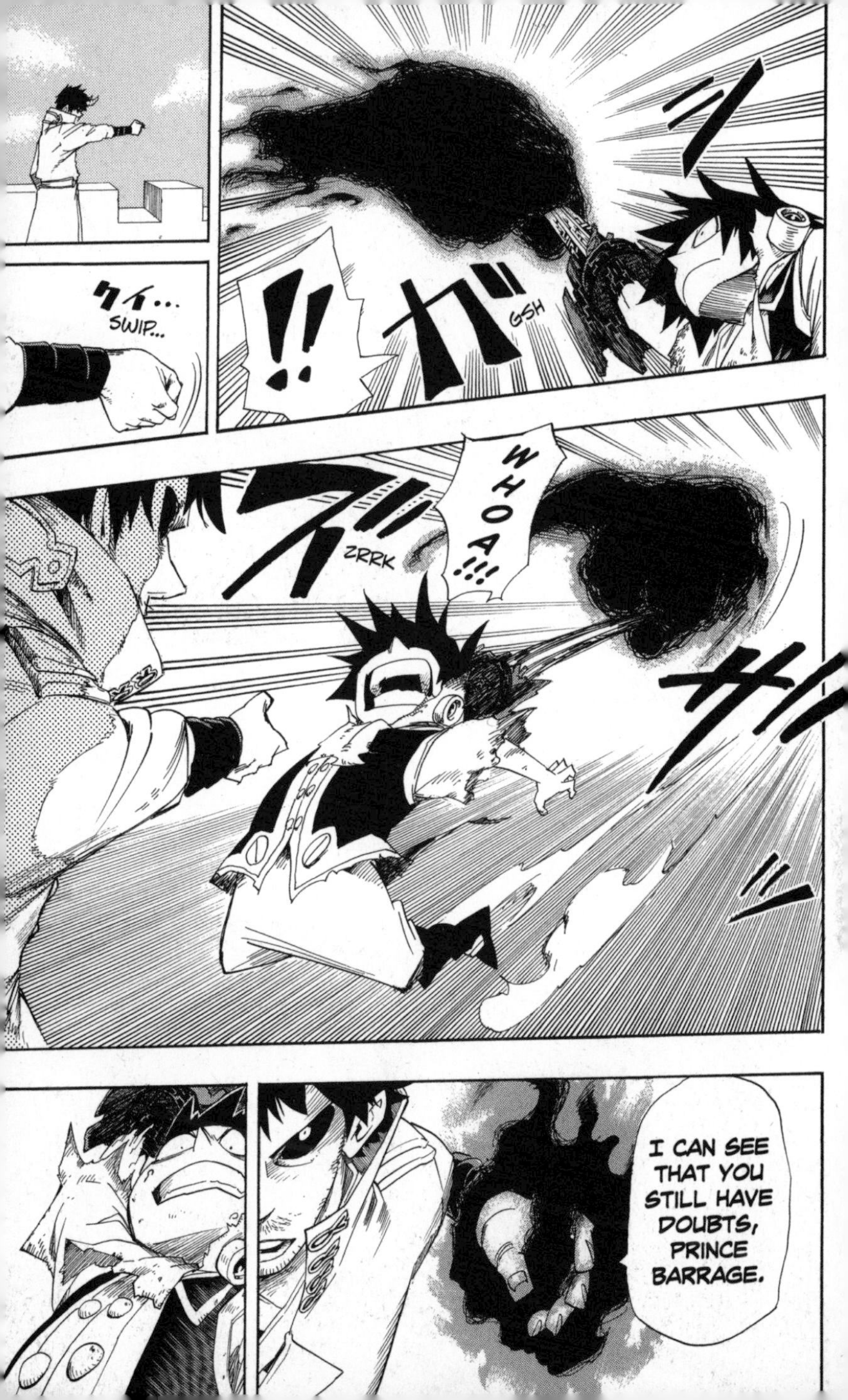
!!
ガ
GSH
クイ…
SWIP...
WHOA!!!
ズ
ZRRK
I CAN SEE THAT YOU STILL HAVE DOUBTS, PRINCE BARRAGE.

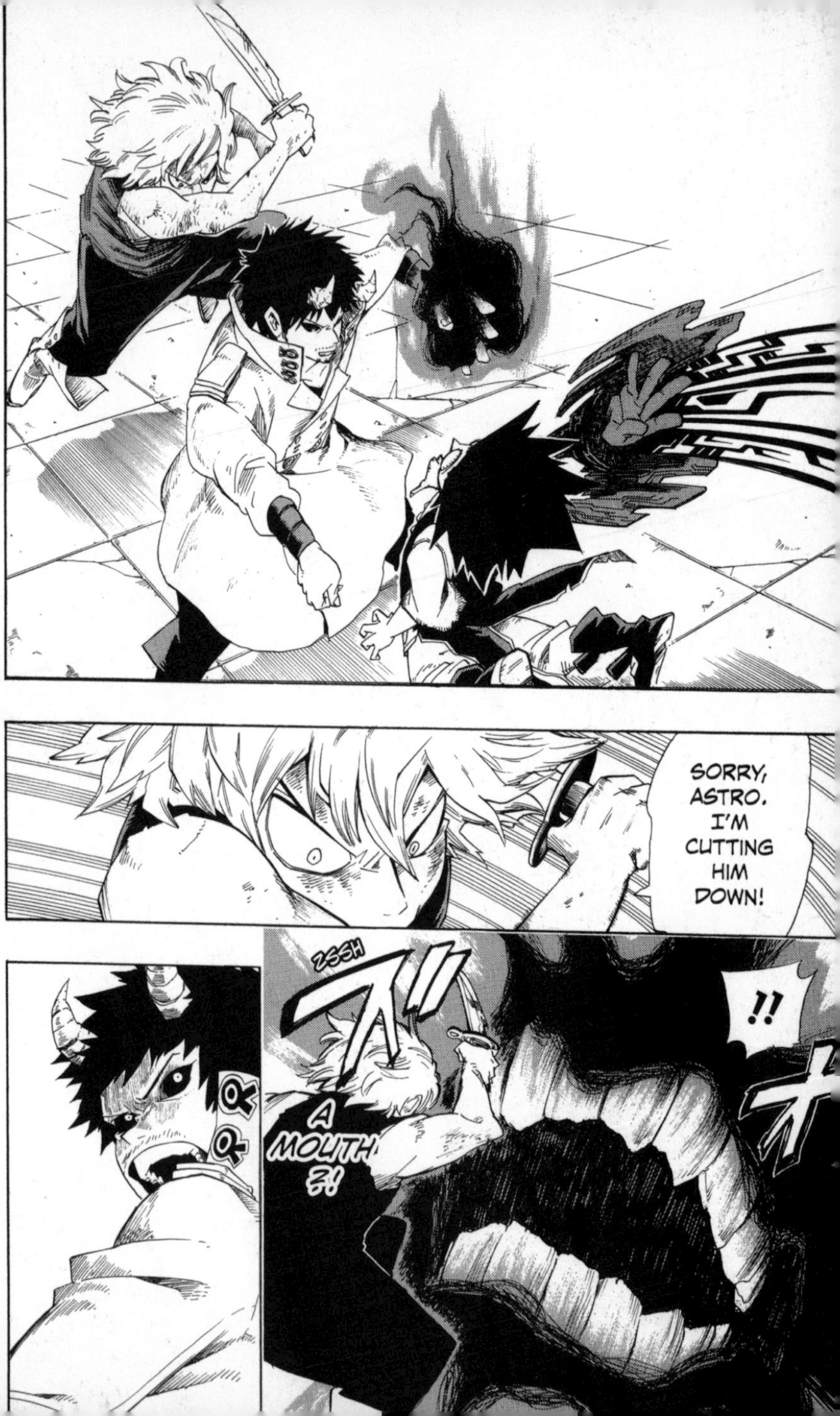
SORRY, ASTRO. I'M CUTTING HIM DOWN!
ZSSH
!!
A MOUTH?!

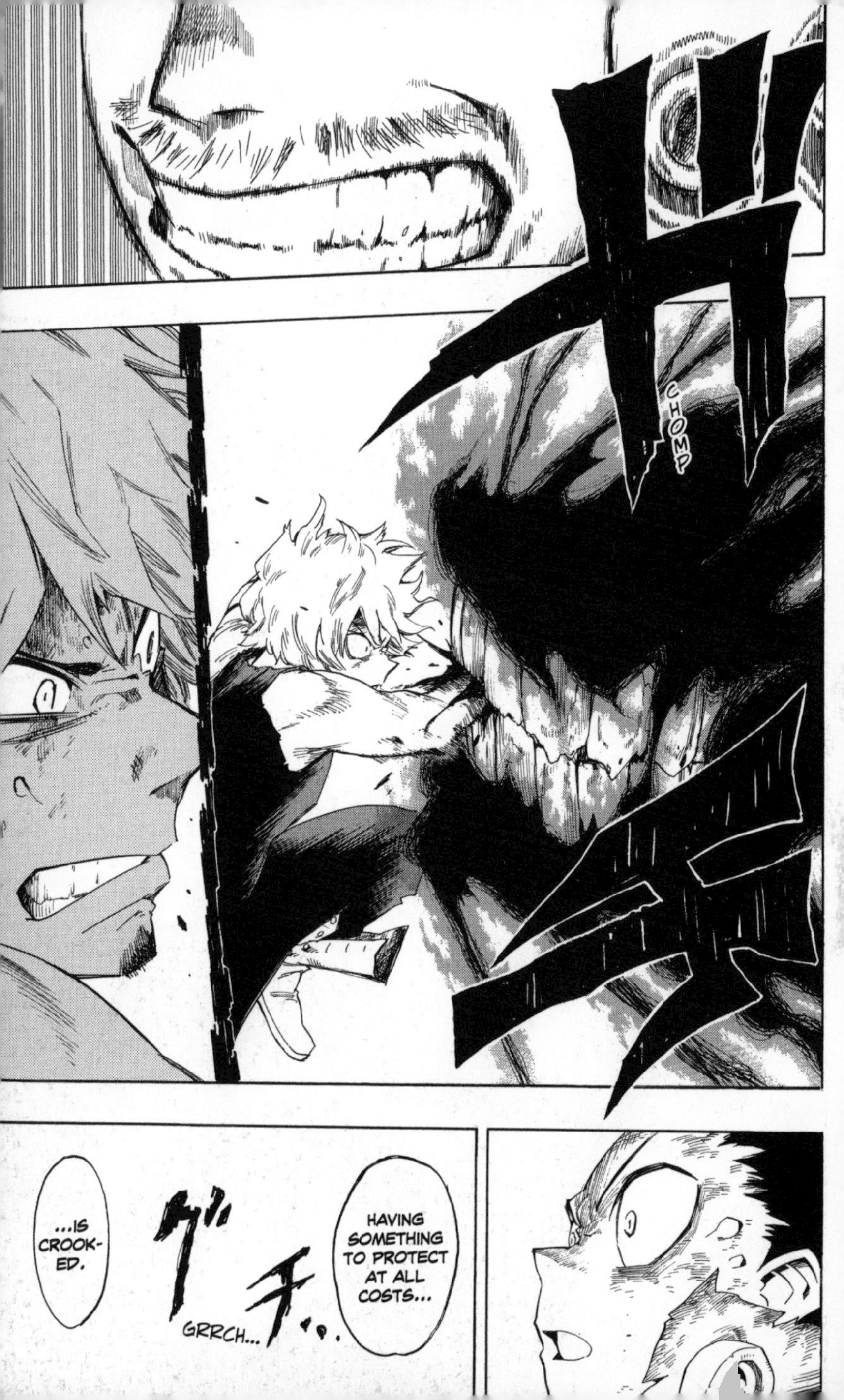
CHOMP
HAVING SOMETHING TO PROTECT AT ALL COSTS...
GRRCH...
...IS CROOK-ED.

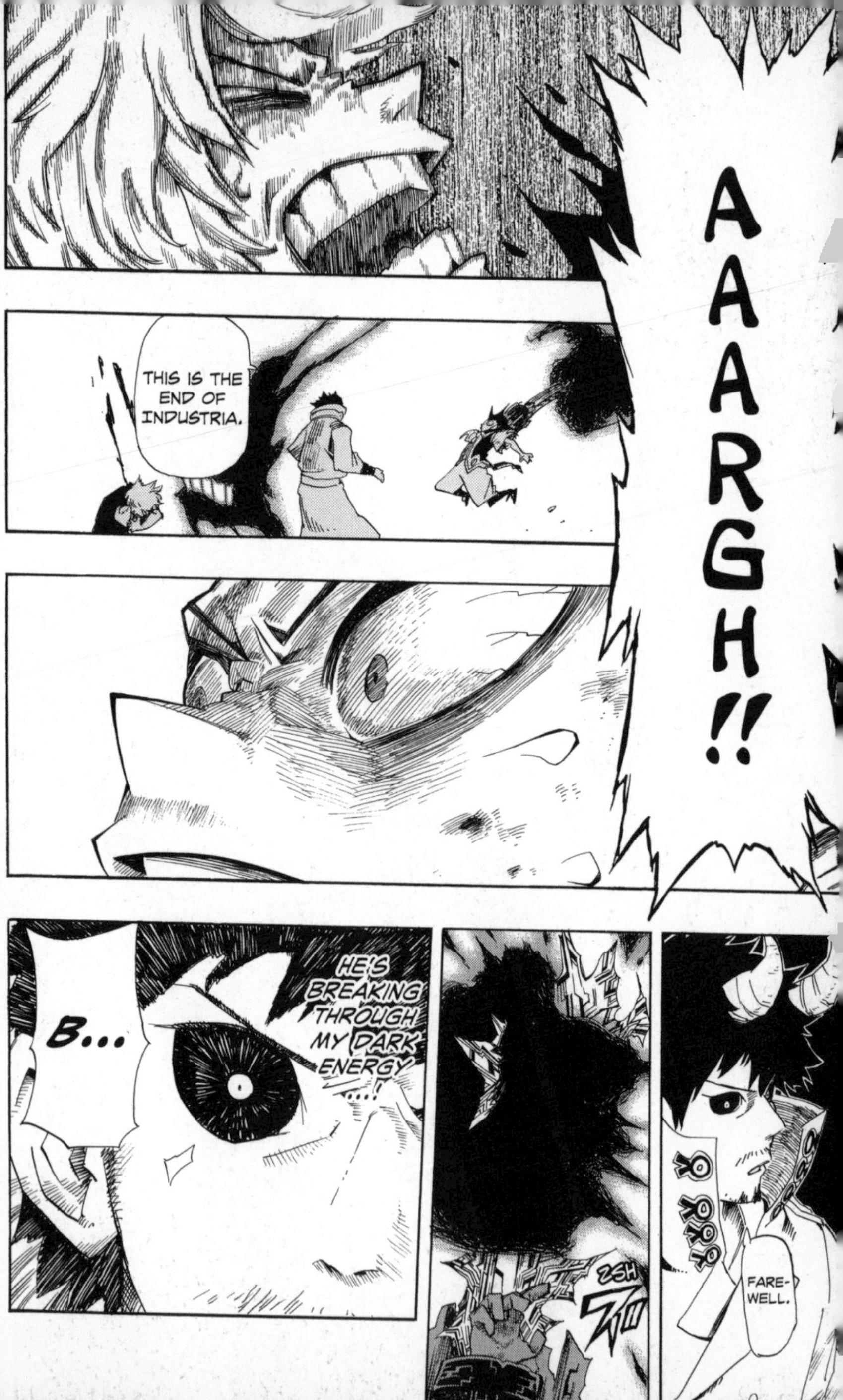
AAARGH!!
THIS IS THE END OF INDUSTRIA.
FARE-WELL.
ZSH
HE'S BREAKING THROUGH MY DARK ENERGY...!
B...

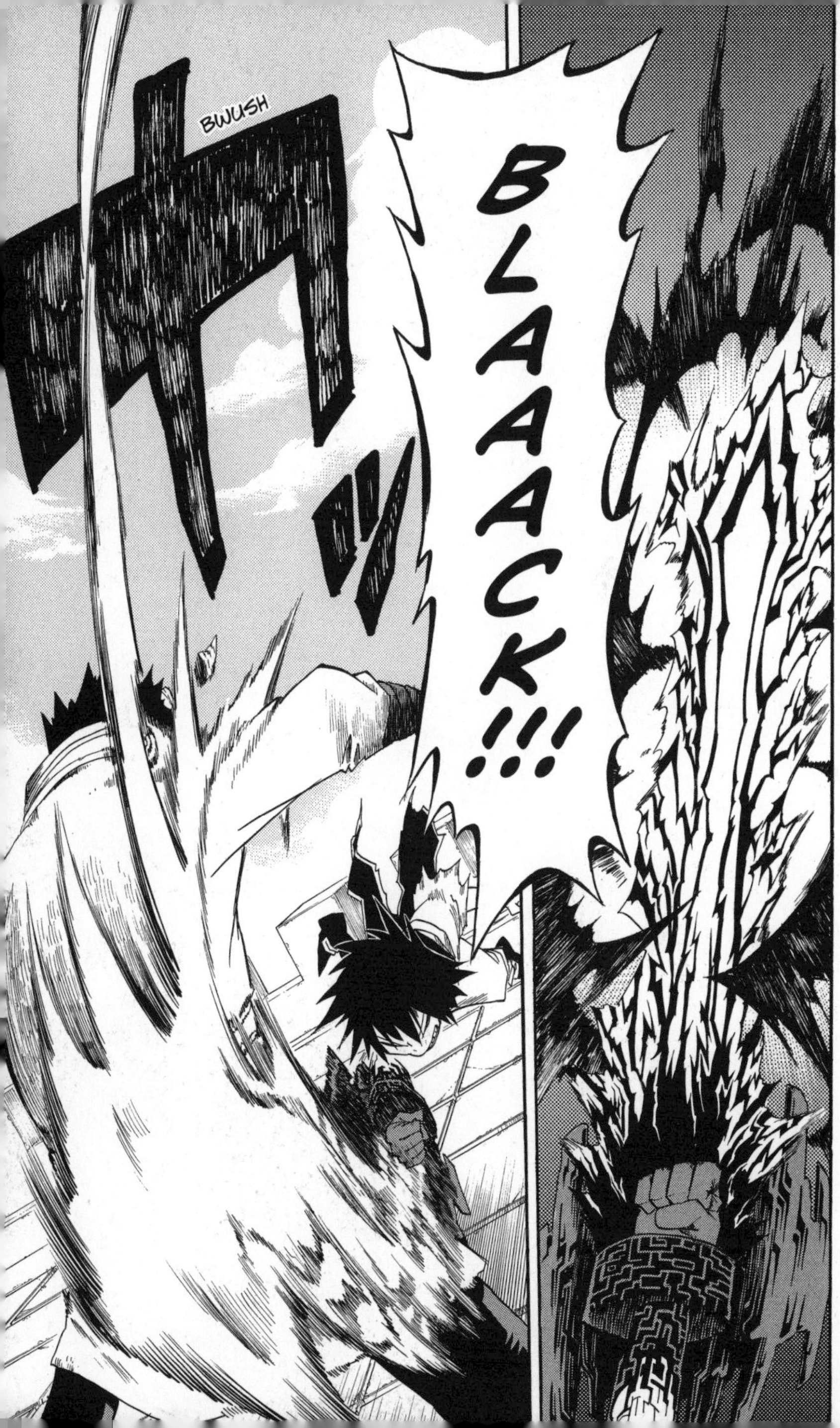
BWUSH
BLAAACK!!!

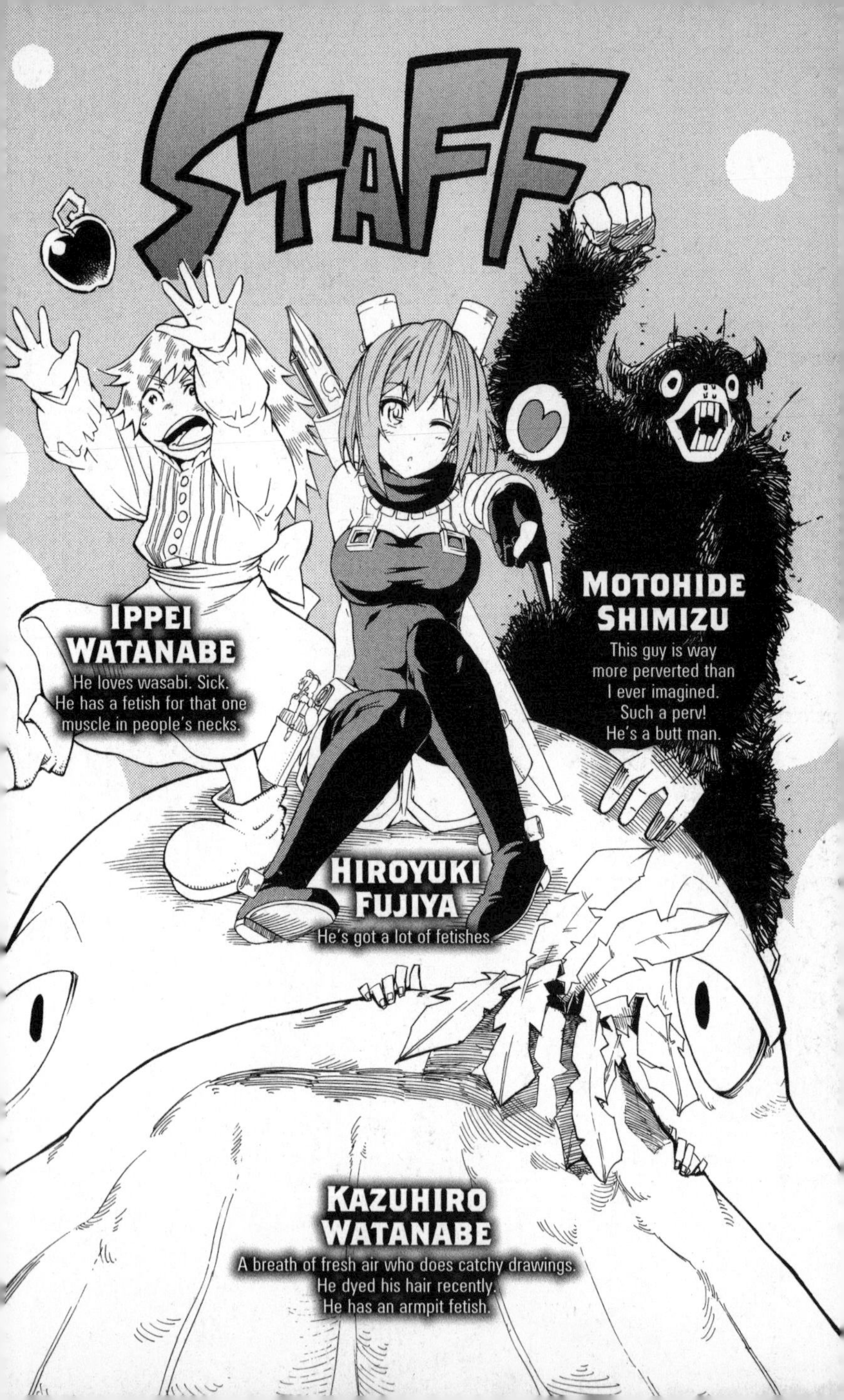
STAFF
Ippei Watanabe
He loves wasabi. Sick. He has a fetish for that one muscle in people's necks.
Motohide Shimizu
This guy is way more perverted than I ever imagined. Such a perv! He's a butt man.
Hiroyuki Fujiya
He's got a lot of fetishes.
Kazuhiro Watanabe
A breath of fresh air who does catchy drawings. He dyed his hair recently. He has an armpit fetish.

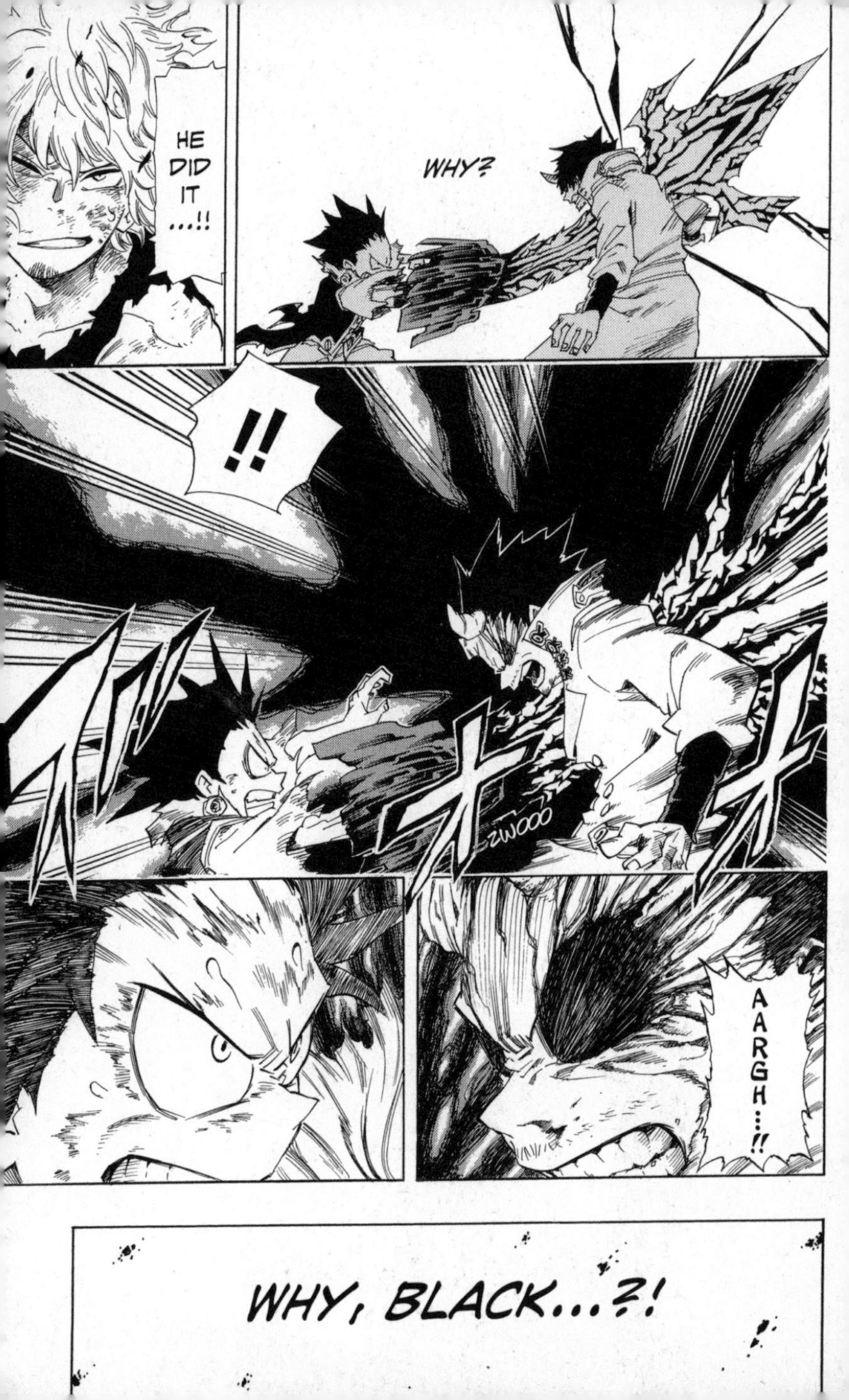
WHY?
HE DID IT ...!!
!!
ZWOOO
AARGH...!!
WHY, BLACK...?!

Final Chapter: Astro of the Warring Planets

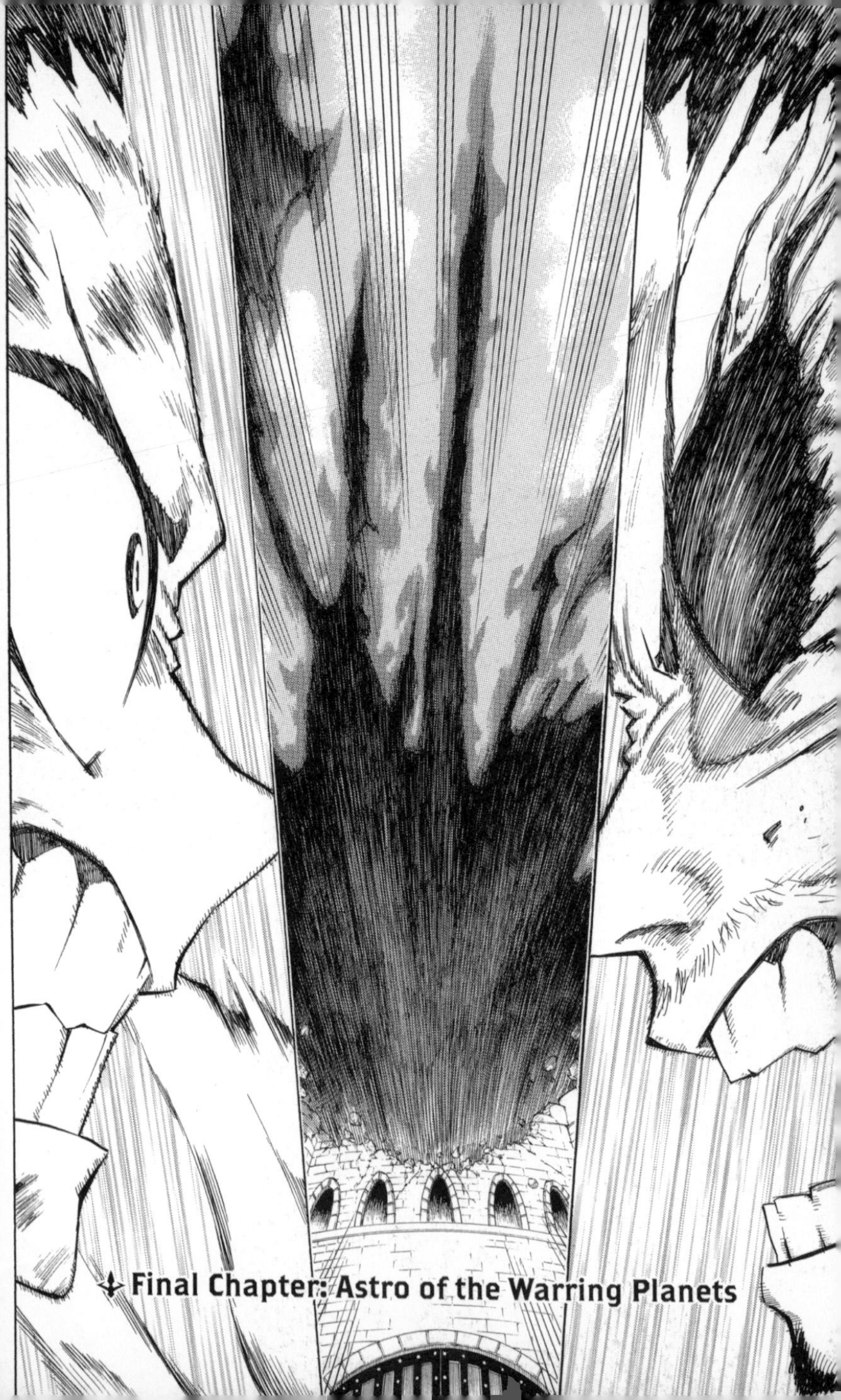

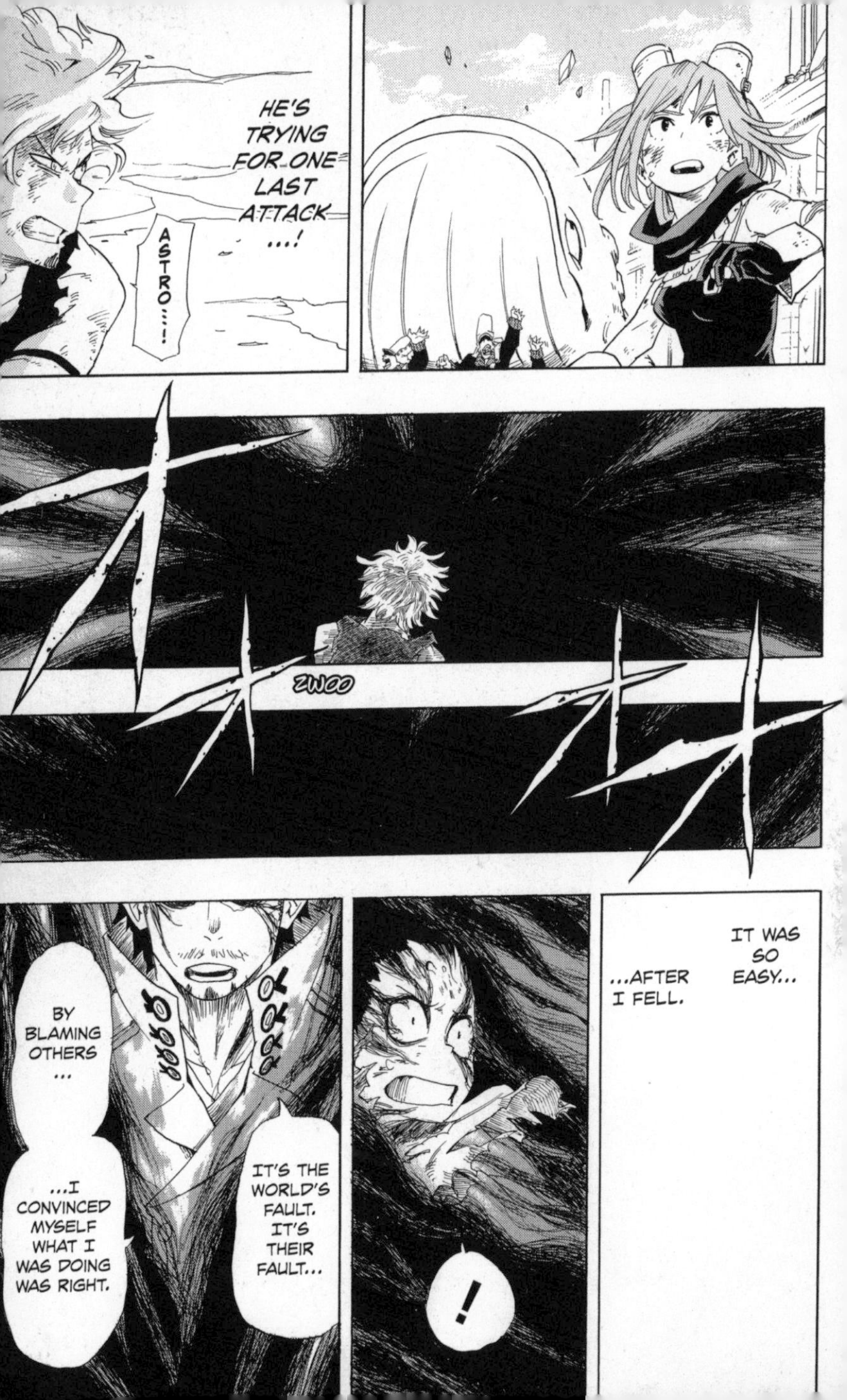
HE'S TRYING FOR ONE LAST ATTACK ...!
ASTRO...!
ZWOO
IT WAS SO EASY...
...AFTER I FELL.
!
BY BLAMING OTHERS...
IT'S THE WORLD'S FAULT. IT'S THEIR FAULT...
...I CONVINCED MYSELF WHAT I WAS DOING WAS RIGHT.

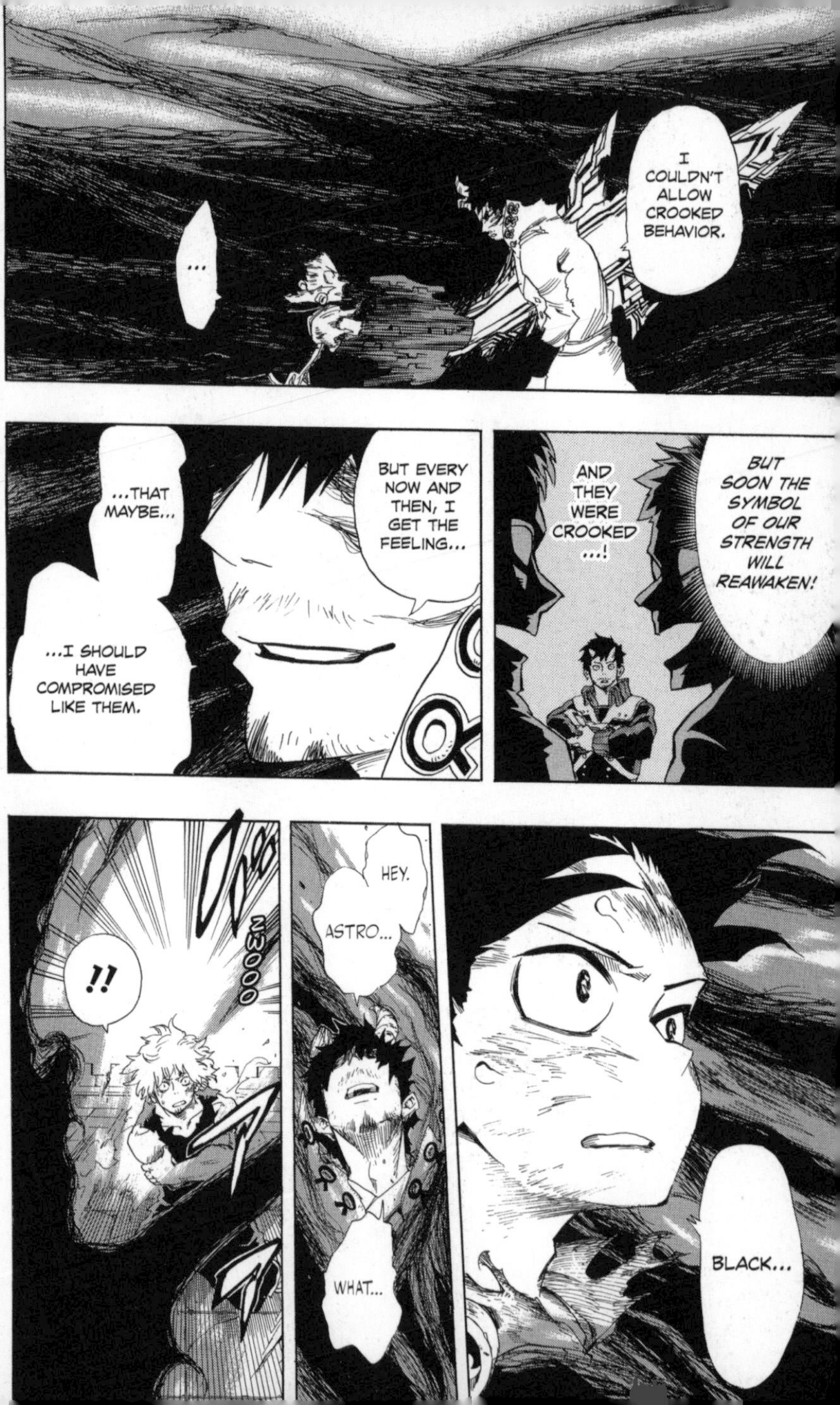
I COULDN'T ALLOW CROOKED BEHAVIOR.
...
BUT SOON THE SYMBOL OF OUR STRENGTH WILL REAWAKEN!
AND THEY WERE CROOKED ...!
BUT EVERY NOW AND THEN, I GET THE FEELING...
...THAT MAYBE...
...I SHOULD HAVE COMPROMISED LIKE THEM.
BLACK...
HEY.
ASTRO...
WHAT...
ZWOOO
!!

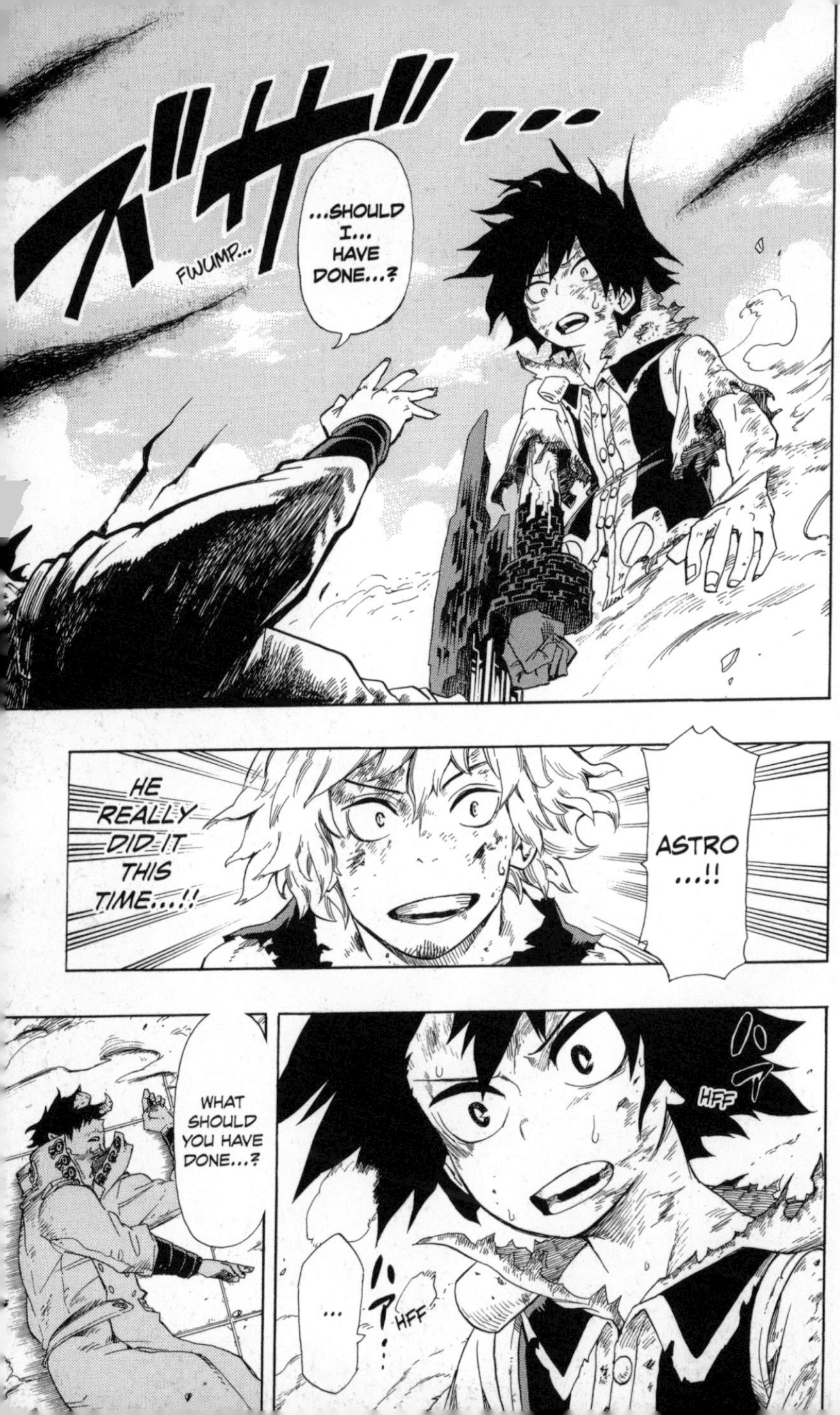
FWUMP...
...SHOULD I... HAVE DONE...?
ASTRO ...!!
HE REALLY DID IT THIS TIME...!!
HFF
...
HFF
WHAT SHOULD YOU HAVE DONE...?

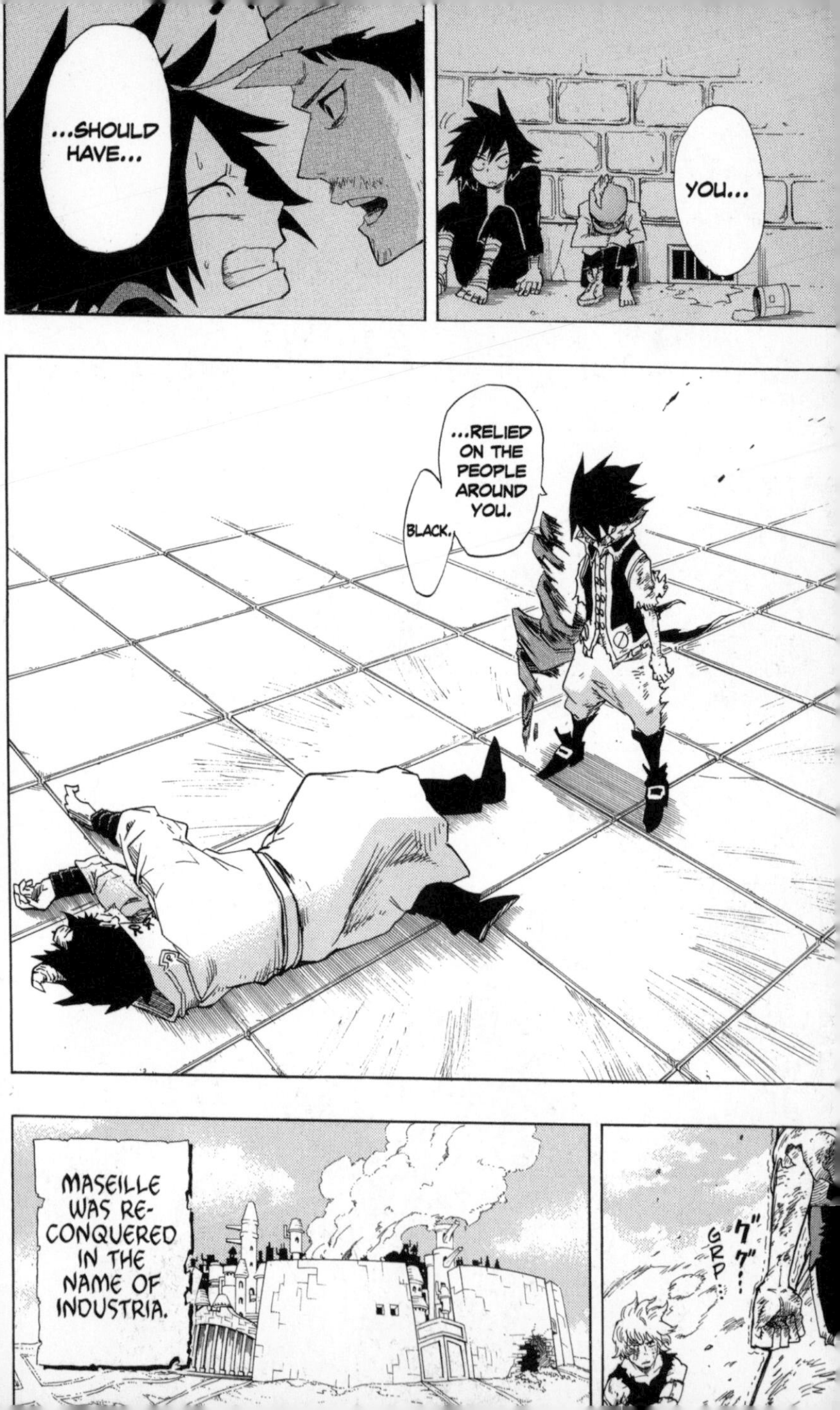
YOU...
...SHOULD HAVE...
...RELIED ON THE PEOPLE AROUND YOU.
BLACK.
GRP...
MASEILLE WAS RE-CONQUERED IN THE NAME OF INDUSTRIA.

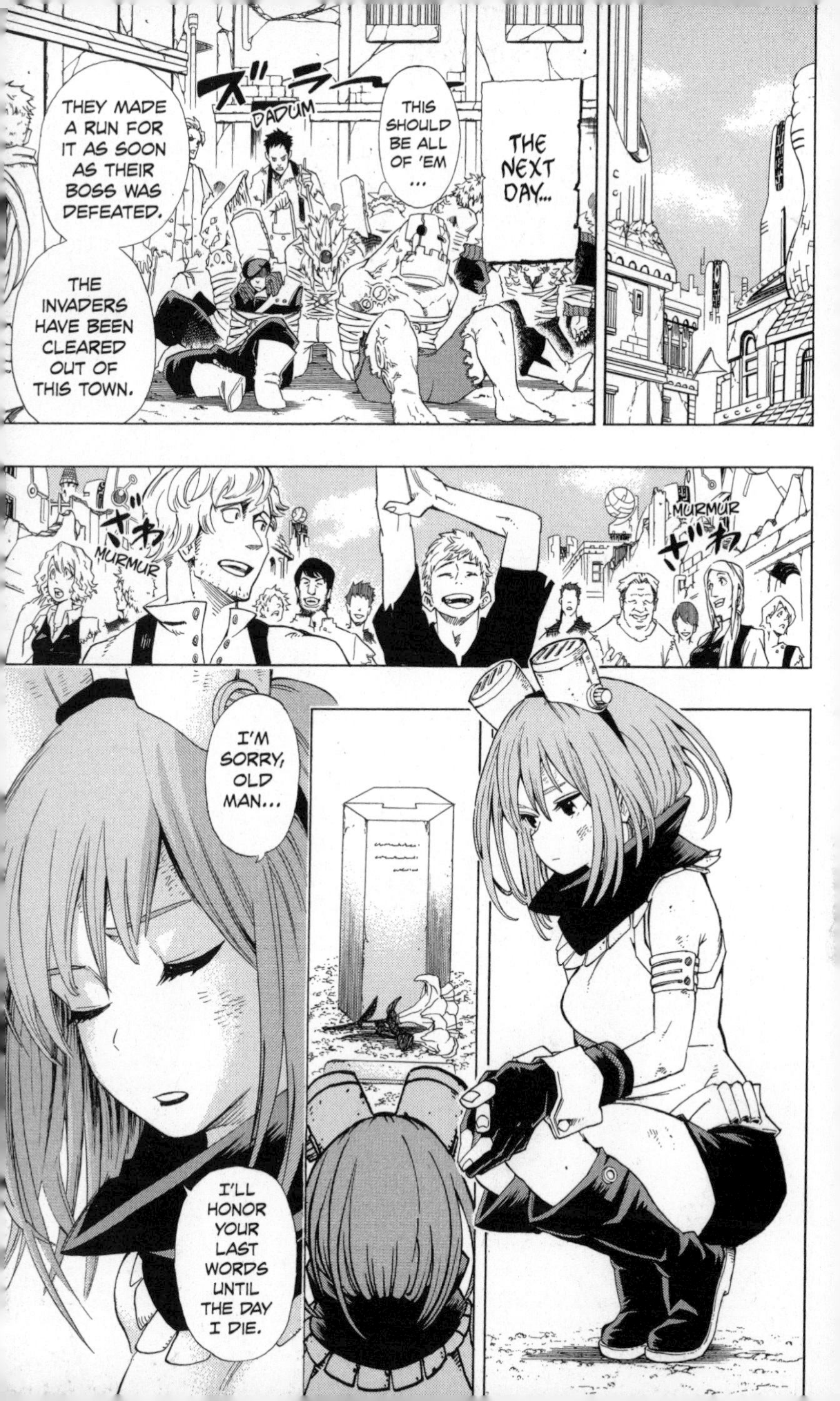
THE NEXT DAY...
THIS SHOULD BE ALL OF 'EM...
DADUM
THEY MADE A RUN FOR IT AS SOON AS THEIR BOSS WAS DEFEATED.
THE INVADERS HAVE BEEN CLEARED OUT OF THIS TOWN.
MURMUR
MURMUR
I'M SORRY, OLD MAN...
I'LL HONOR YOUR LAST WORDS UNTIL THE DAY I DIE.

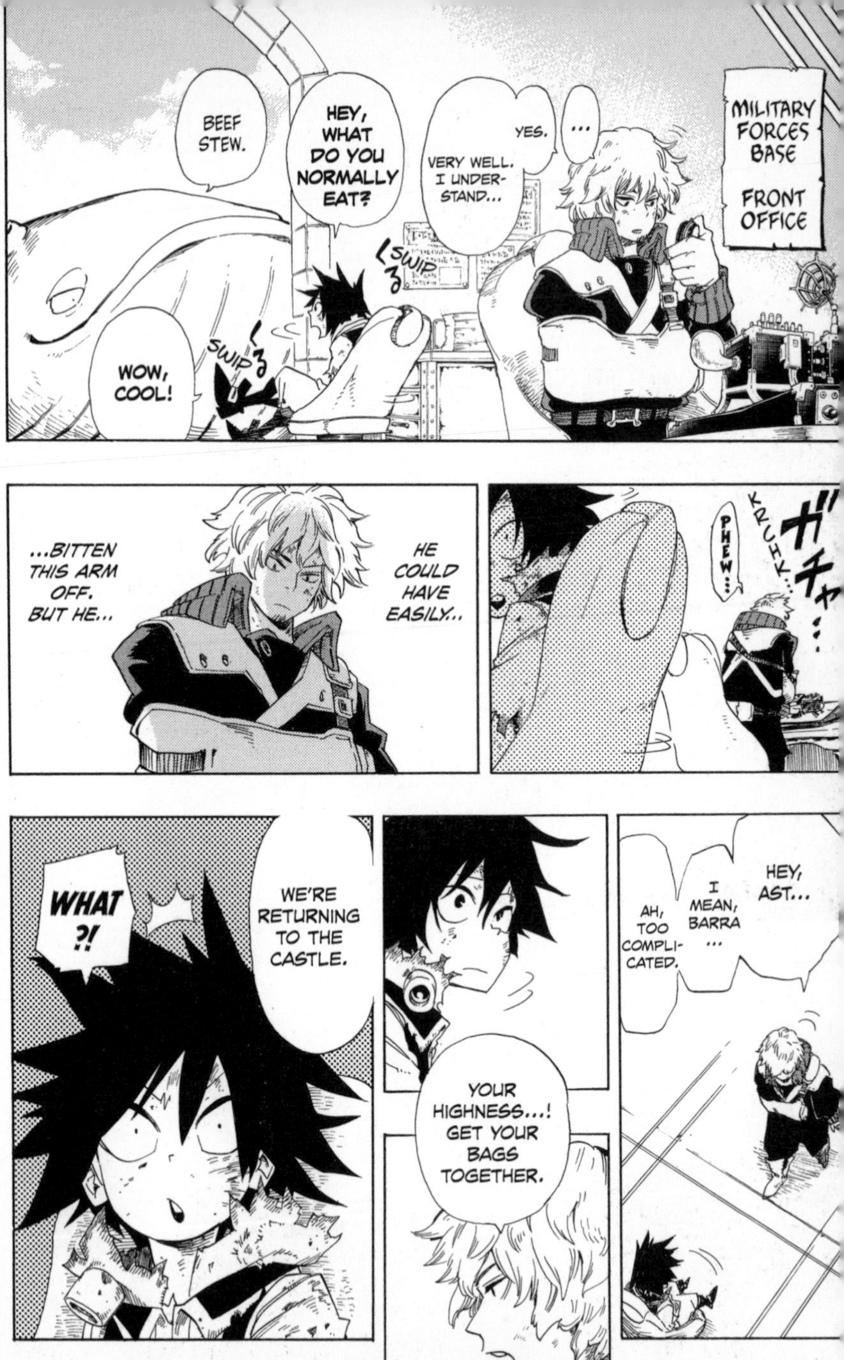
MILITARY FORCES BASE
FRONT OFFICE
...
YES.
VERY WELL. I UNDERSTAND...
HEY, WHAT DO YOU NORMALLY EAT?
SWIP
BEEF STEW.
SWIP
WOW, COOL!
ガチャ
KRCHK...
PHEW...
HE COULD HAVE EASILY...
...BITTEN THIS ARM OFF. BUT HE...
HEY, AST...
I MEAN, BARRA...
AH, TOO COMPLICATED.
YOUR HIGHNESS...! GET YOUR BAGS TOGETHER.
WE'RE RETURNING TO THE CASTLE.
WHAT?!

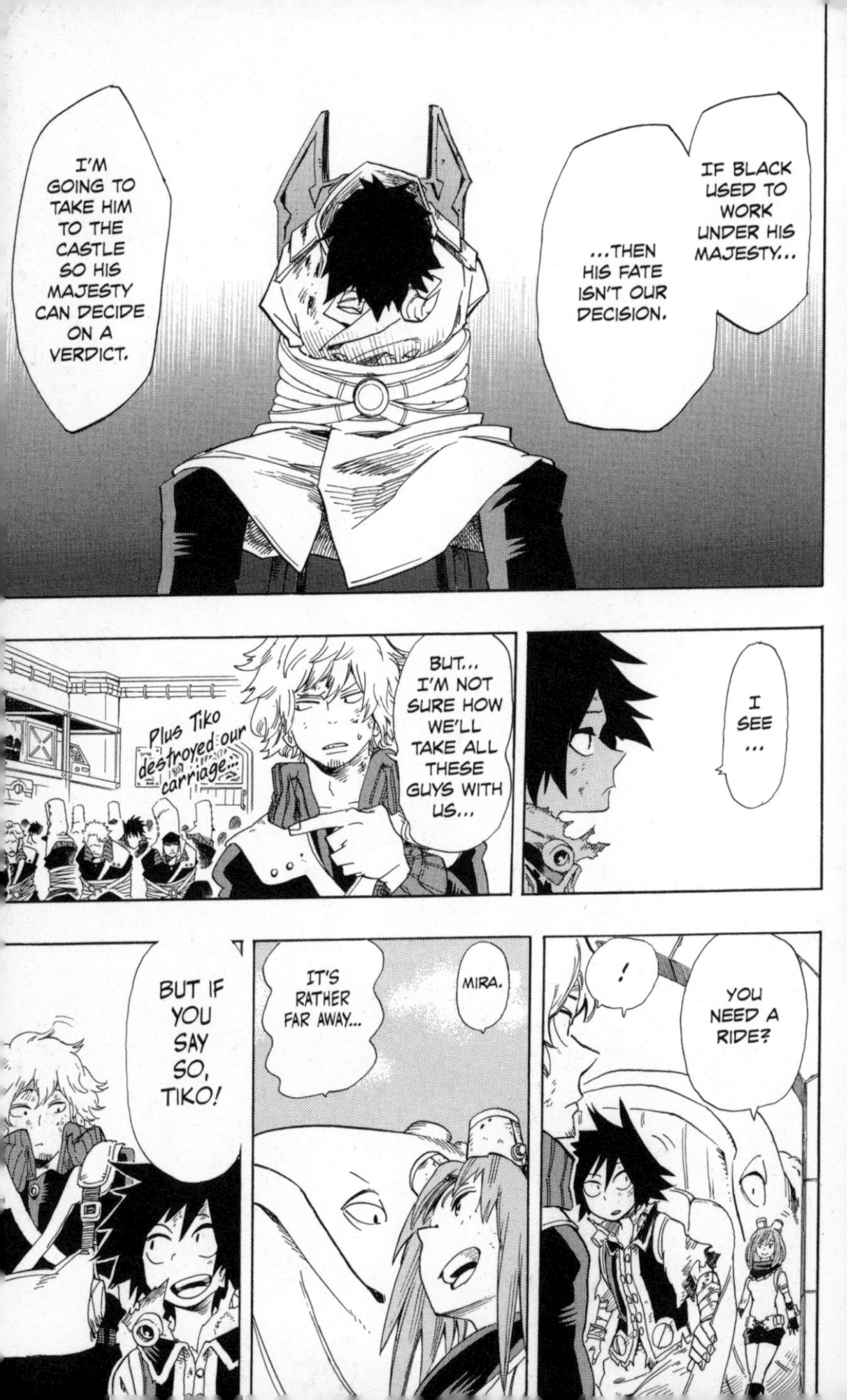
IF BLACK USED TO WORK UNDER HIS MAJESTY...
...THEN HIS FATE ISN'T OUR DECISION.
I'M GOING TO TAKE HIM TO THE CASTLE SO HIS MAJESTY CAN DECIDE ON A VERDICT.
I SEE...
BUT... I'M NOT SURE HOW WE'LL TAKE ALL THESE GUYS WITH US...
Plus Tiko destroyed our carriage...
YOU NEED A RIDE?
!
MIRA.
IT'S RATHER FAR AWAY...
BUT IF YOU SAY SO, TIKO!

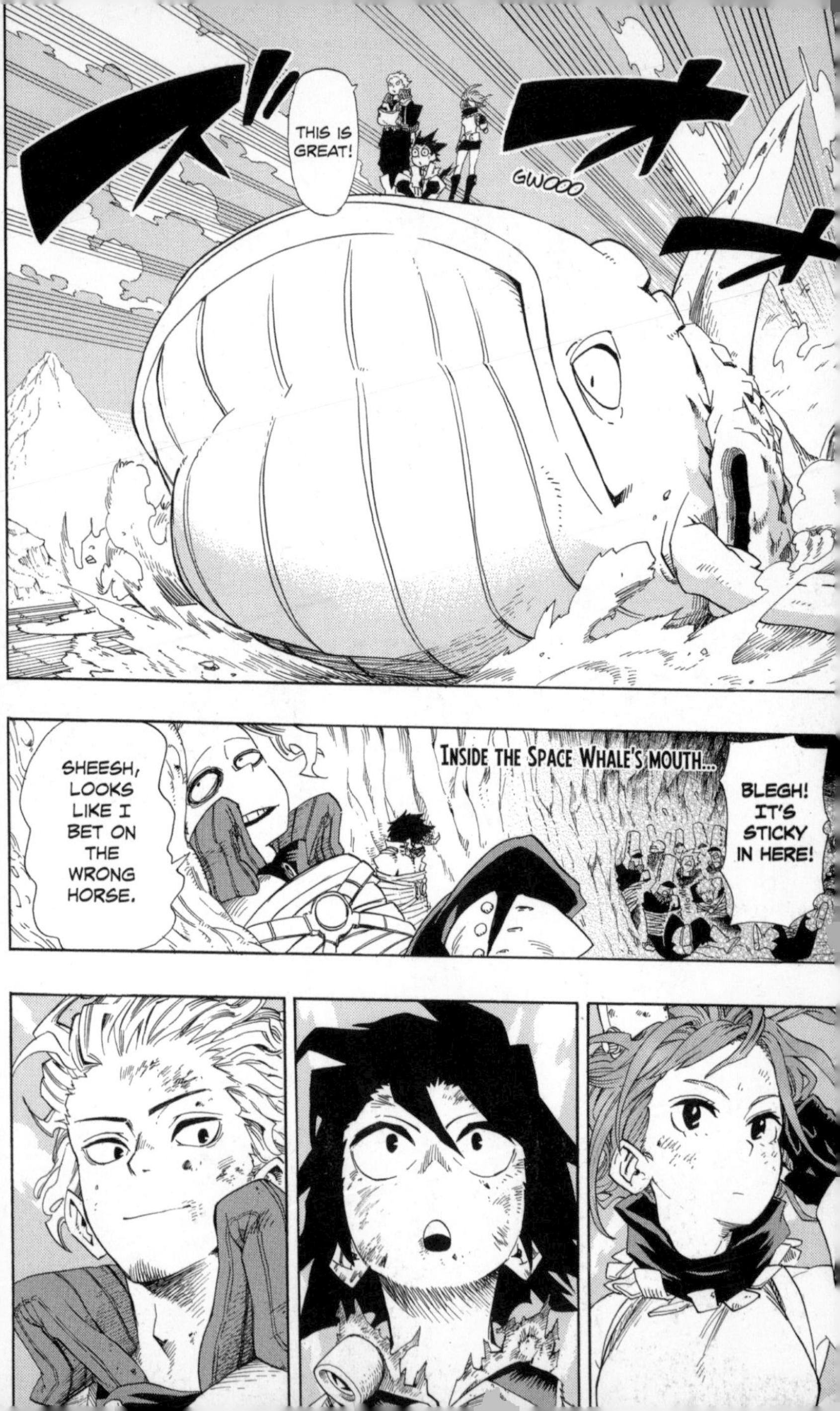

ズオオ
GWOOO
THIS IS GREAT!
BLEGH! IT'S STICKY IN HERE!
Inside the Space Whale's mouth...
SHEESH, LOOKS LIKE I BET ON THE WRONG HORSE.

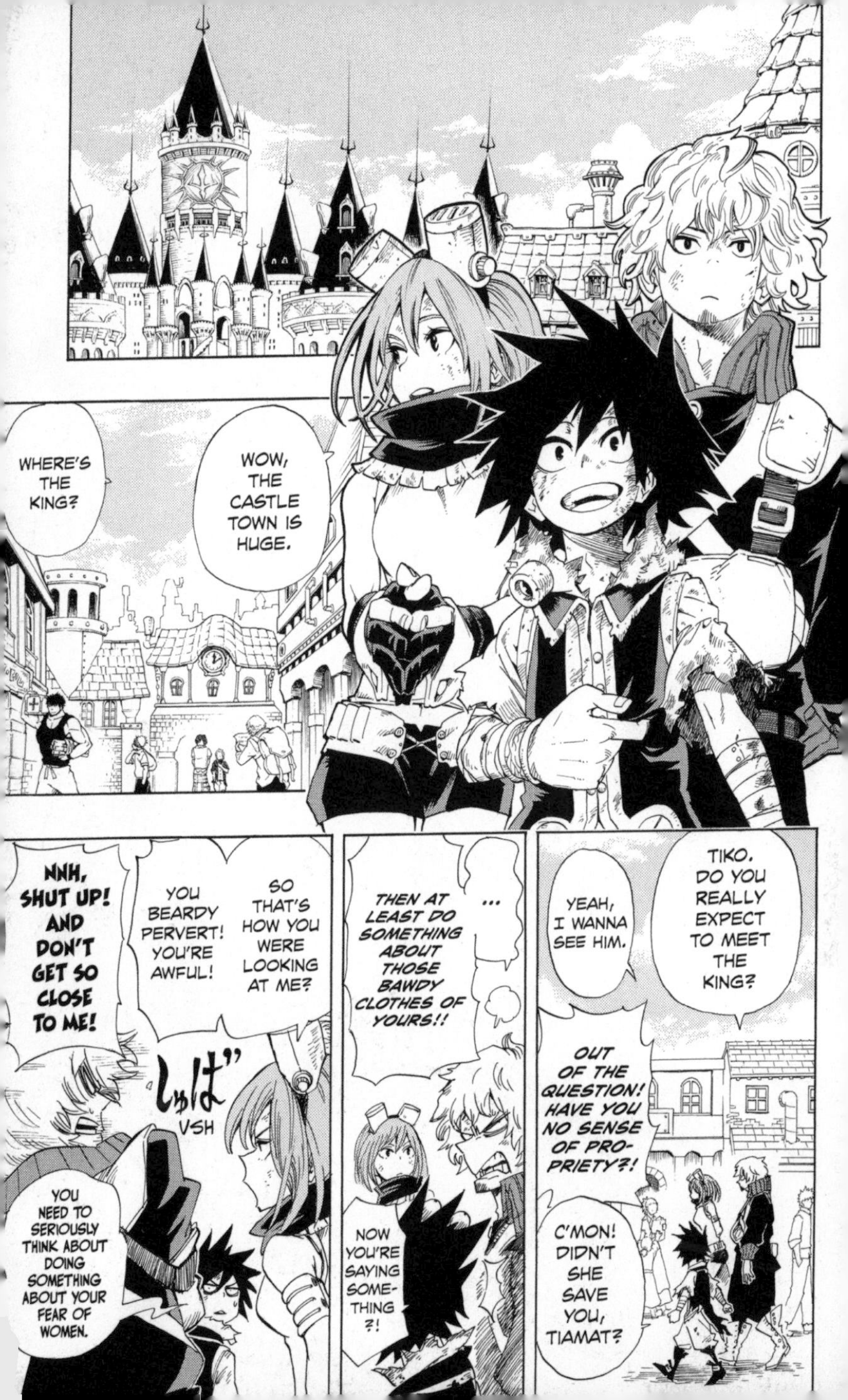
WOW, THE CASTLE TOWN IS HUGE.
WHERE'S THE KING?
TIKO. DO YOU REALLY EXPECT TO MEET THE KING?
YEAH, I WANNA SEE HIM.
OUT OF THE QUESTION! HAVE YOU NO SENSE OF PROPRIETY?!
C'MON! DIDN'T SHE SAVE YOU, TIAMAT?
...
THEN AT LEAST DO SOMETHING ABOUT THOSE BAWDY CLOTHES OF YOURS!!
NOW YOU'RE SAYING SOMETHING?!
SO THAT'S HOW YOU WERE LOOKING AT ME?
YOU BEARDY PERVERT! YOU'RE AWFUL!
NNH, SHUT UP! AND DON'T GET SO CLOSE TO ME!
VSH
YOU NEED TO SERIOUSLY THINK ABOUT DOING SOMETHING ABOUT YOUR FEAR OF WOMEN.

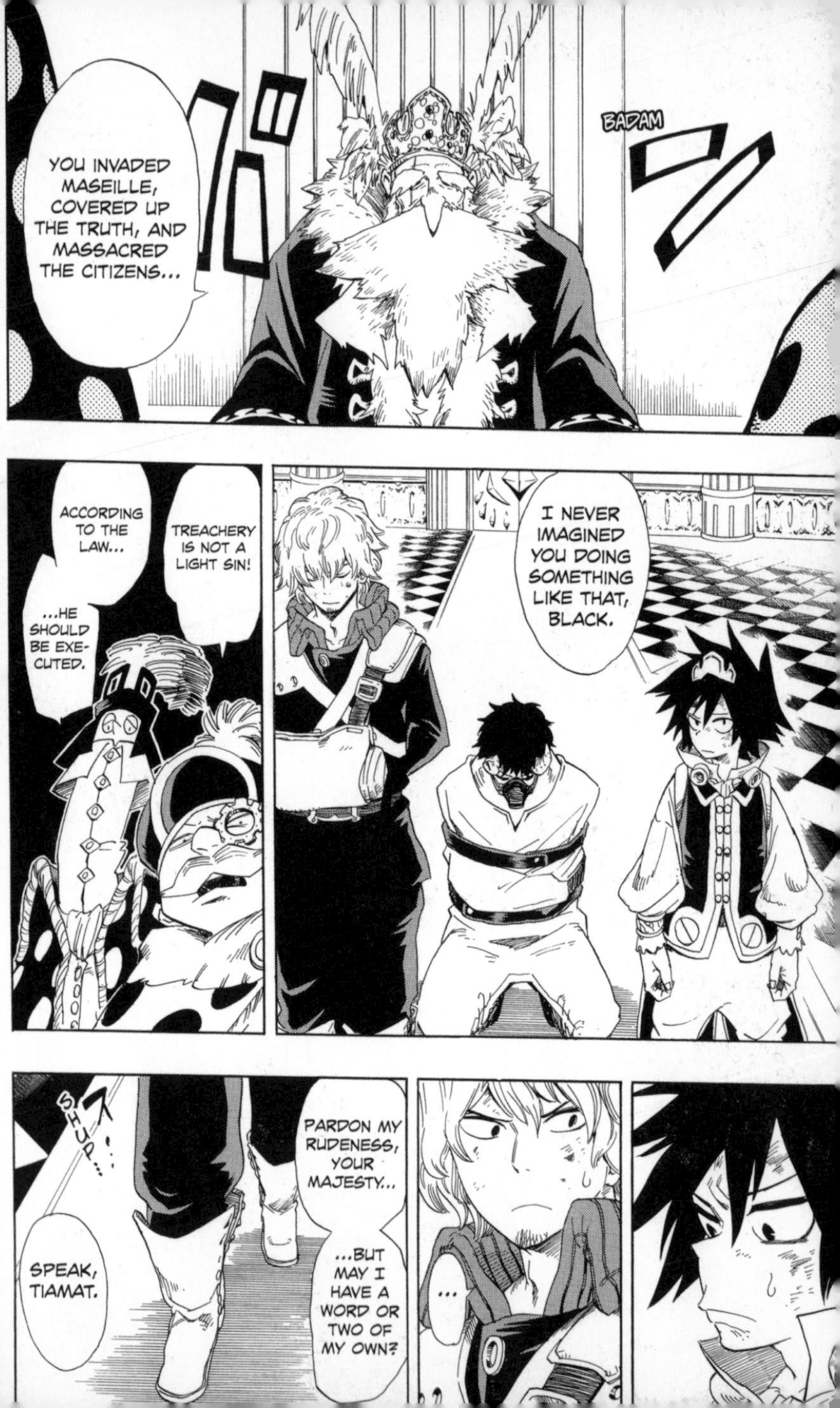
BADAM
YOU INVADED MASEILLE, COVERED UP THE TRUTH, AND MASSACRED THE CITIZENS...
I NEVER IMAGINED YOU DOING SOMETHING LIKE THAT, BLACK.
TREACHERY IS NOT A LIGHT SIN!
ACCORDING TO THE LAW...
...HE SHOULD BE EXE-CUTED.
...
PARDON MY RUDENESS, YOUR MAJESTY...
SHUP...
...BUT MAY I HAVE A WORD OR TWO OF MY OWN?
SPEAK, TIAMAT.

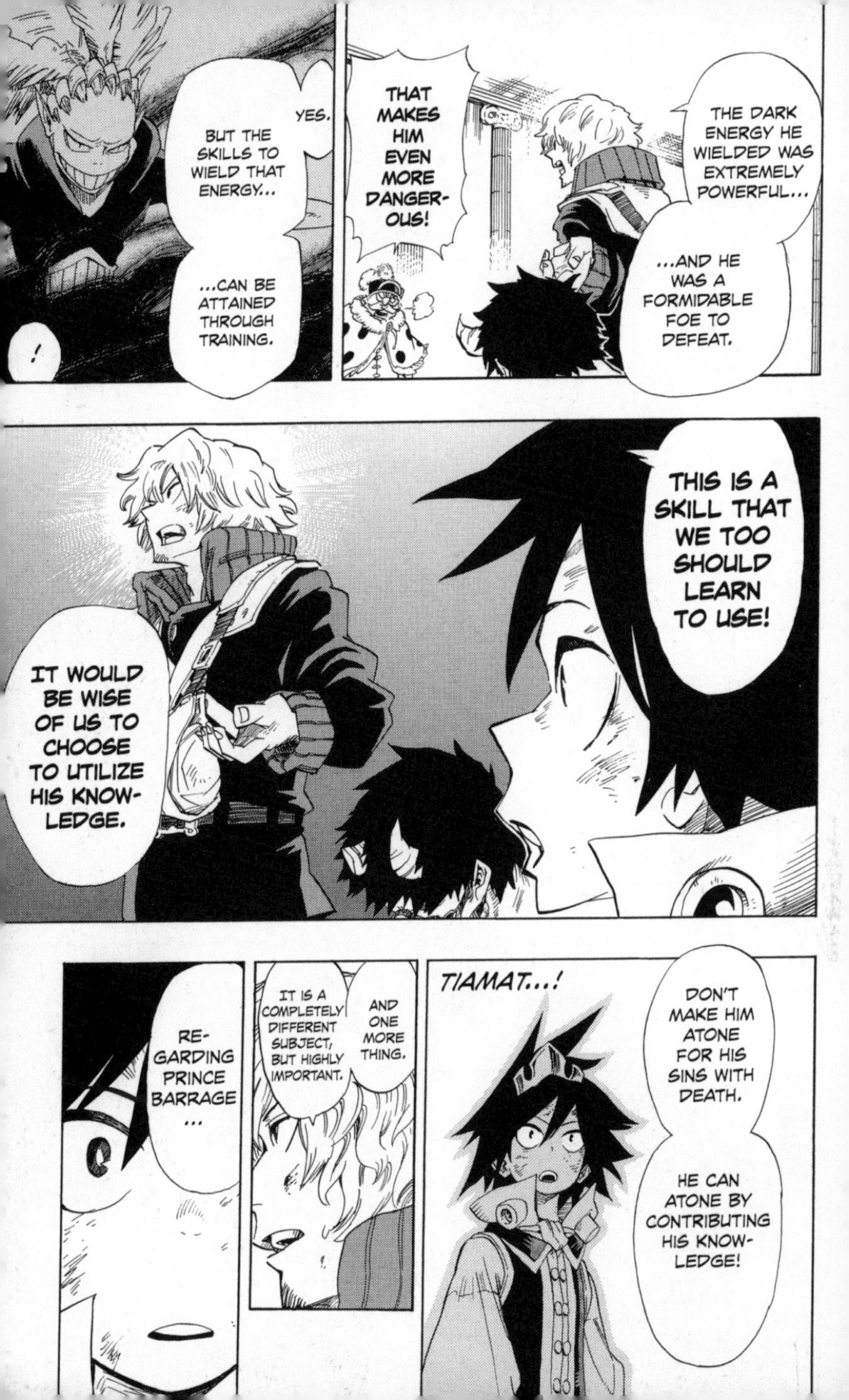
THE DARK ENERGY HE WIELDED WAS EXTREMELY POWERFUL...
...AND HE WAS A FORMIDABLE FOE TO DEFEAT.
THAT MAKES HIM EVEN MORE DANGER-OUS!
YES.
BUT THE SKILLS TO WIELD THAT ENERGY...
...CAN BE ATTAINED THROUGH TRAINING.
!
THIS IS A SKILL THAT WE TOO SHOULD LEARN TO USE!
IT WOULD BE WISE OF US TO CHOOSE TO UTILIZE HIS KNOW-LEDGE.
DON'T MAKE HIM ATONE FOR HIS SINS WITH DEATH.
TIAMAT...!
HE CAN ATONE BY CONTRIBUTING HIS KNOW-LEDGE!
AND ONE MORE THING.
IT IS A COMPLETELY DIFFERENT SUBJECT, BUT HIGHLY IMPORTANT.
RE-GARDING PRINCE BARRAGE...

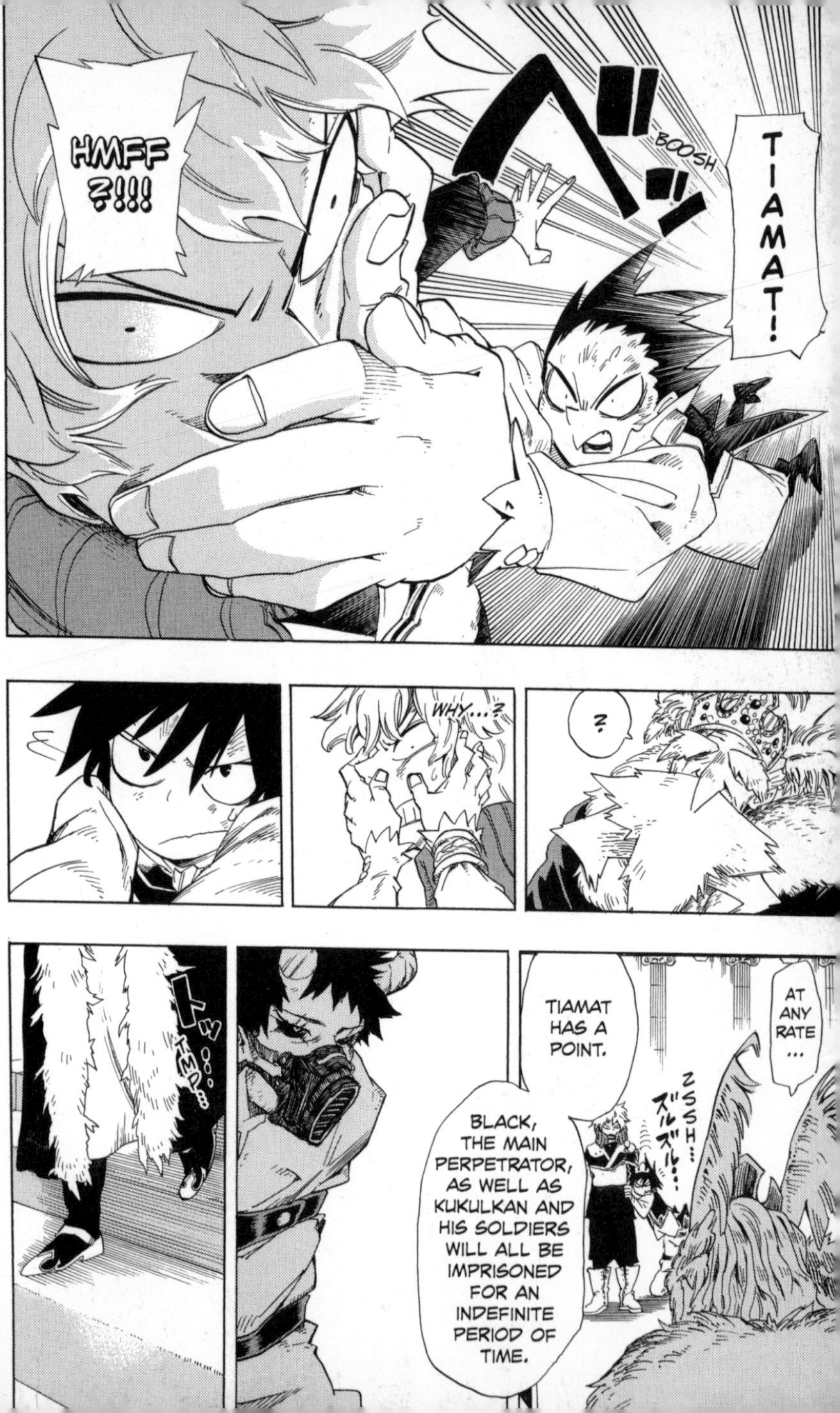
TIAMAT!
BOOSH
HMFF?!!!
?
WHY...?
AT ANY RATE...
TIAMAT HAS A POINT.
ZSSH...
BLACK, THE MAIN PERPETRATOR, AS WELL AS KUKULKAN AND HIS SOLDIERS WILL ALL BE IMPRISONED FOR AN INDEFINITE PERIOD OF TIME.
TMP...

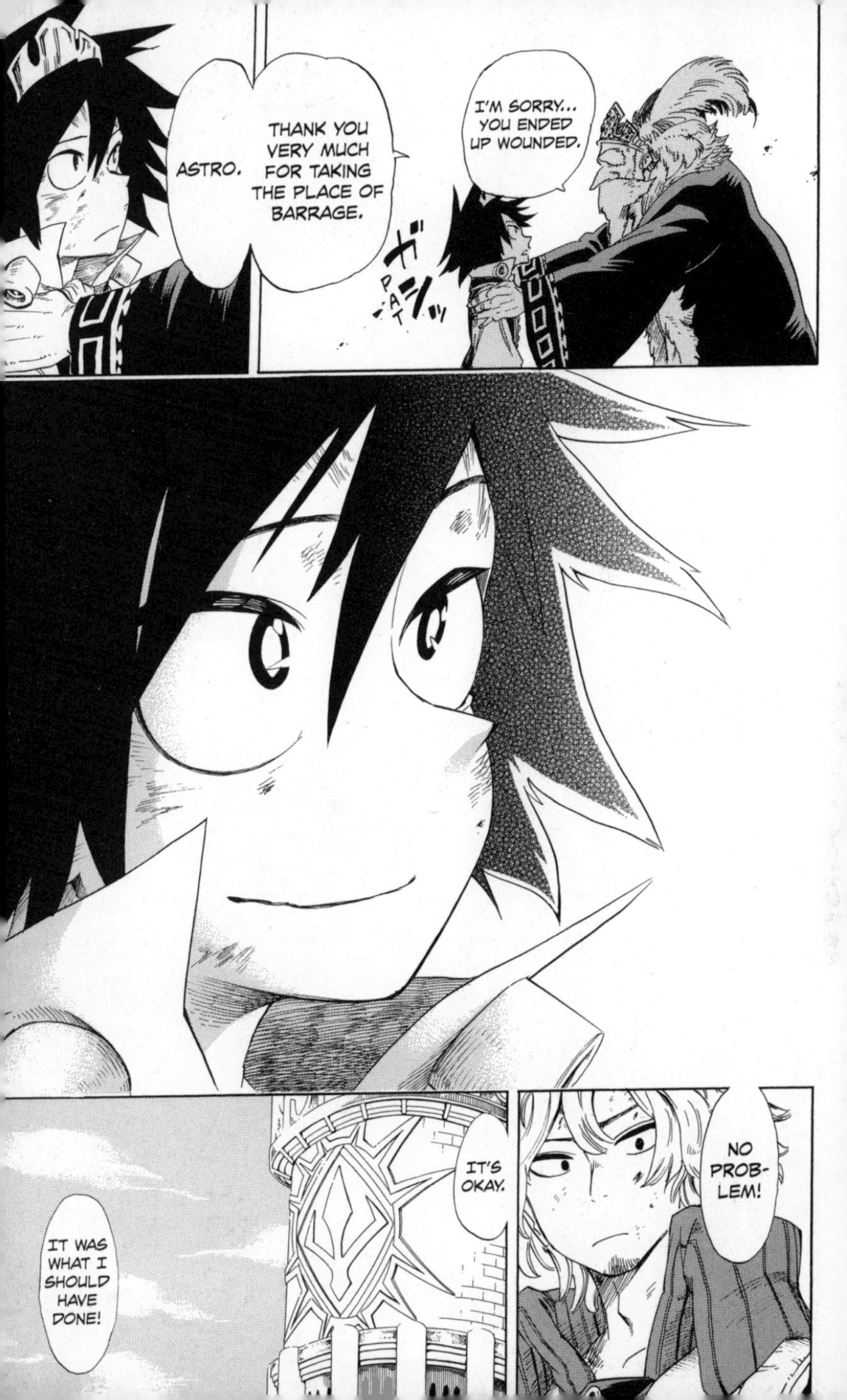
I'M SORRY... YOU ENDED UP WOUNDED.
PAT
THANK YOU VERY MUCH FOR TAKING THE PLACE OF BARRAGE.
ASTRO.
NO PROB-LEM!
IT'S OKAY.
IT WAS WHAT I SHOULD HAVE DONE!

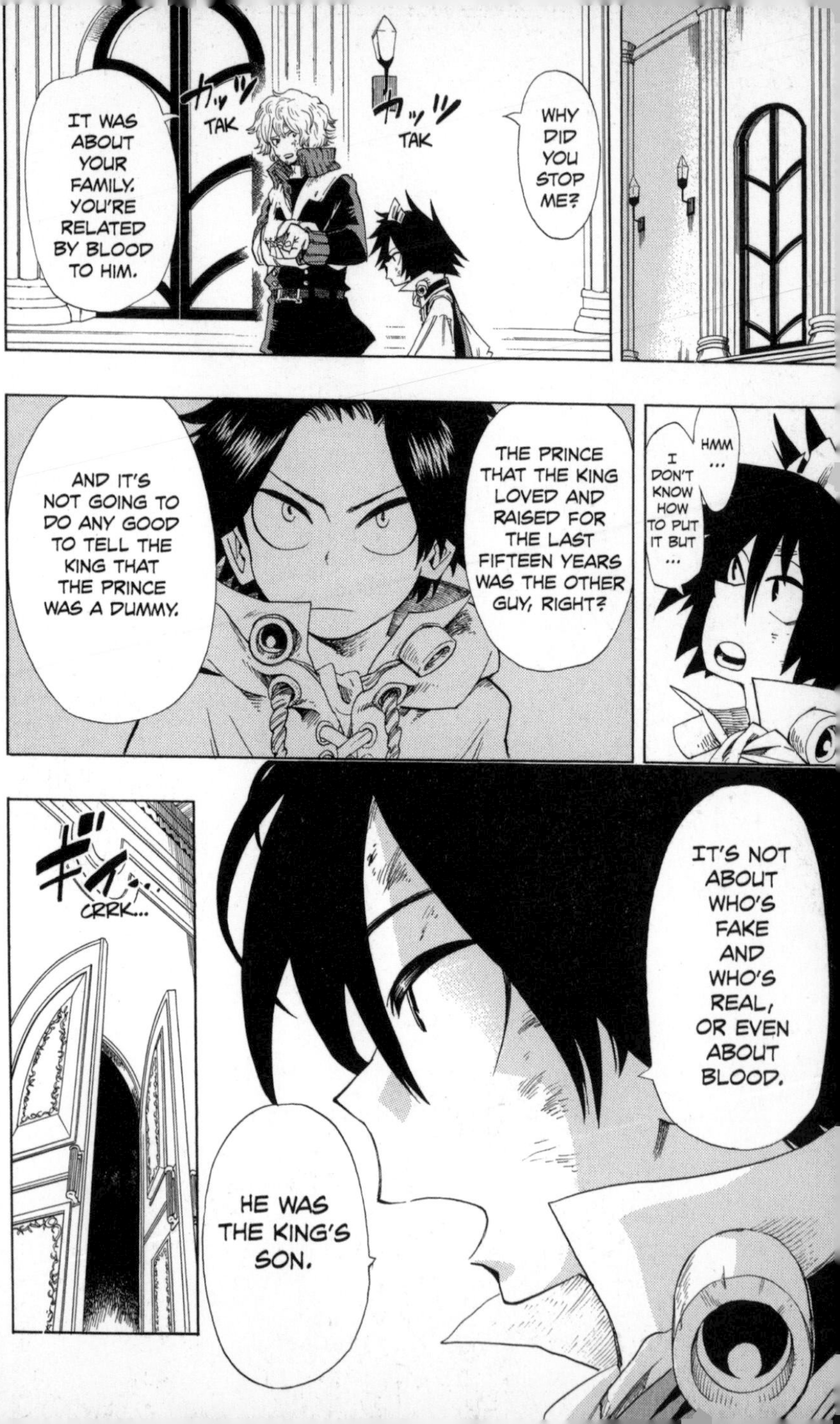

WHY DID YOU STOP ME?
TAK
TAK
IT WAS ABOUT YOUR FAMILY. YOU'RE RELATED BY BLOOD TO HIM.
HMM...
I DON'T KNOW HOW TO PUT IT BUT...
THE PRINCE THAT THE KING LOVED AND RAISED FOR THE LAST FIFTEEN YEARS WAS THE OTHER GUY, RIGHT?
AND IT'S NOT GOING TO DO ANY GOOD TO TELL THE KING THAT THE PRINCE WAS A DUMMY.
IT'S NOT ABOUT WHO'S FAKE AND WHO'S REAL, OR EVEN ABOUT BLOOD.
HE WAS THE KING'S SON.
CRRK...

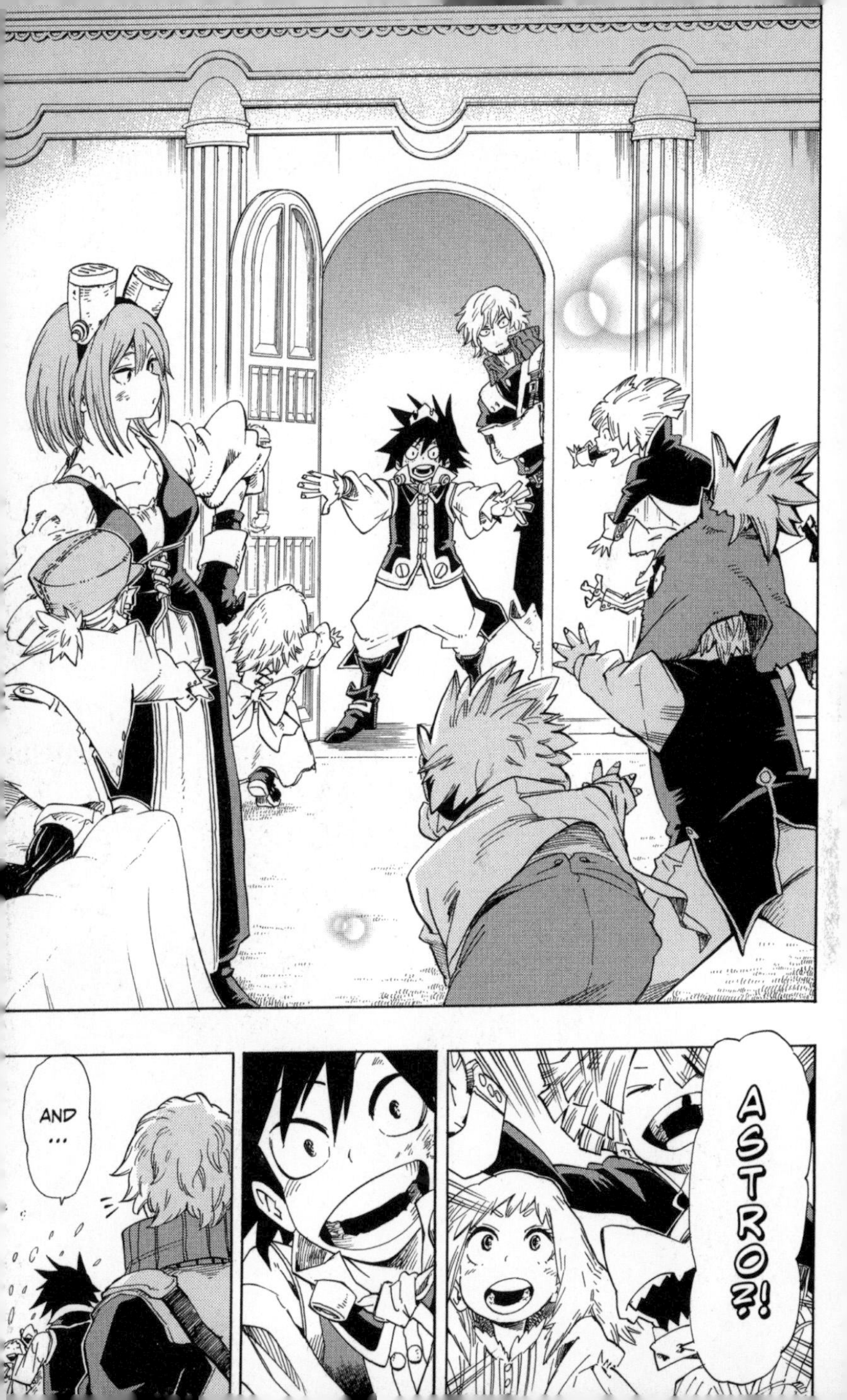
ASTRO?!
AND...

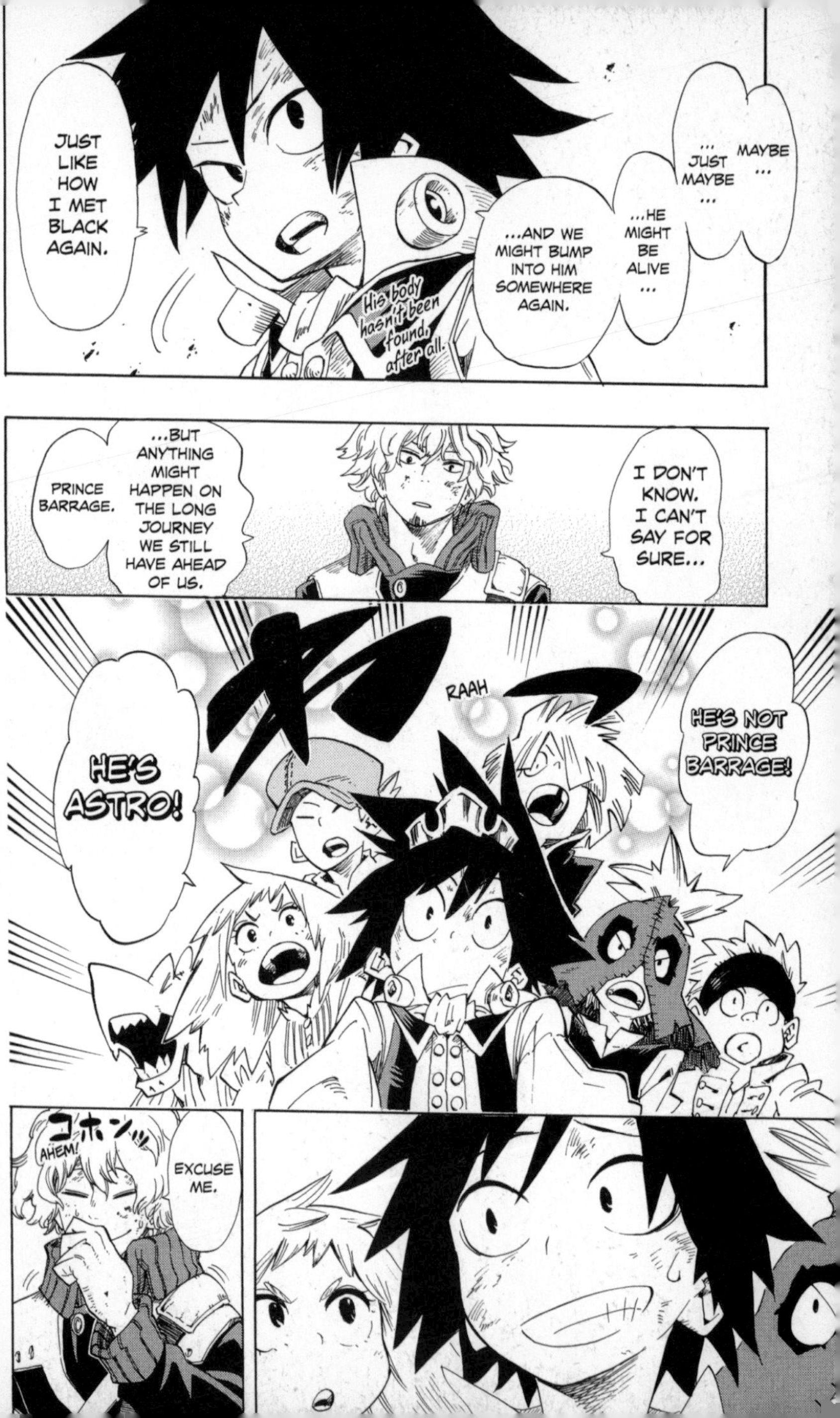
MAYBE ... ... JUST MAYBE ...
...HE MIGHT BE ALIVE ...
...AND WE MIGHT BUMP INTO HIM SOMEWHERE AGAIN.
His body hasn't been found, after all.
JUST LIKE HOW I MET BLACK AGAIN.
I DON'T KNOW. I CAN'T SAY FOR SURE...
...BUT ANYTHING MIGHT HAPPEN ON THE LONG JOURNEY WE STILL HAVE AHEAD OF US.
PRINCE BARRAGE.
HE'S NOT PRINCE BARRAGE!
RAAH
HE'S ASTRO!
EXCUSE ME.
コホン
AHEM!

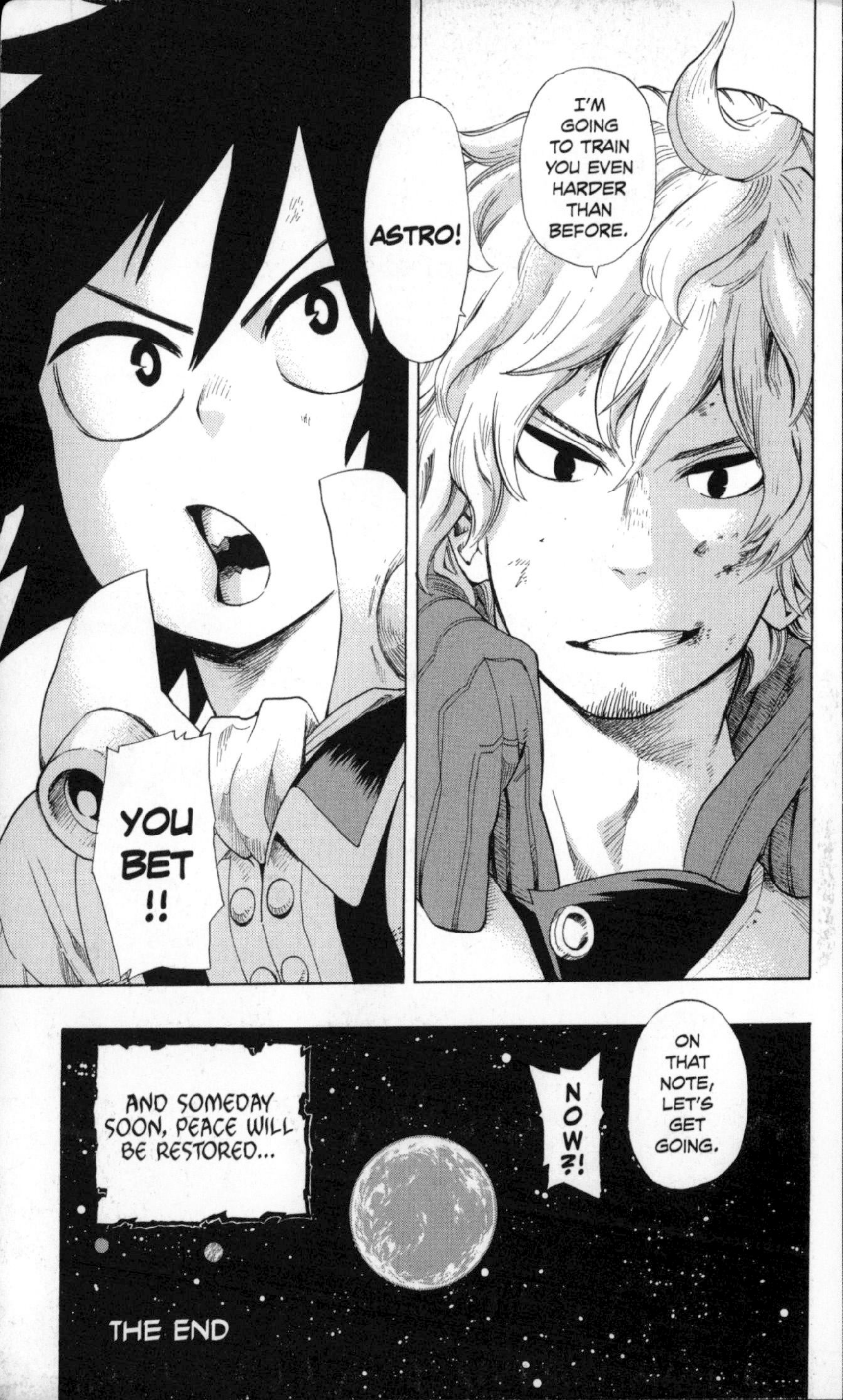
I'M GOING TO TRAIN YOU EVEN HARDER THAN BEFORE.
ASTRO!
YOU BET!!
ON THAT NOTE, LET'S GET GOING.
NOW?!
AND SOMEDAY SOON, PEACE WILL BE RESTORED...
THE END

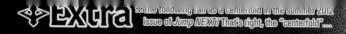

Extra

※The following ran as a centerfold in the summer 2012 issue of *Jump NEXT!* That's right, the "centerfold"...

After Astro's Family Moved into the Castle...

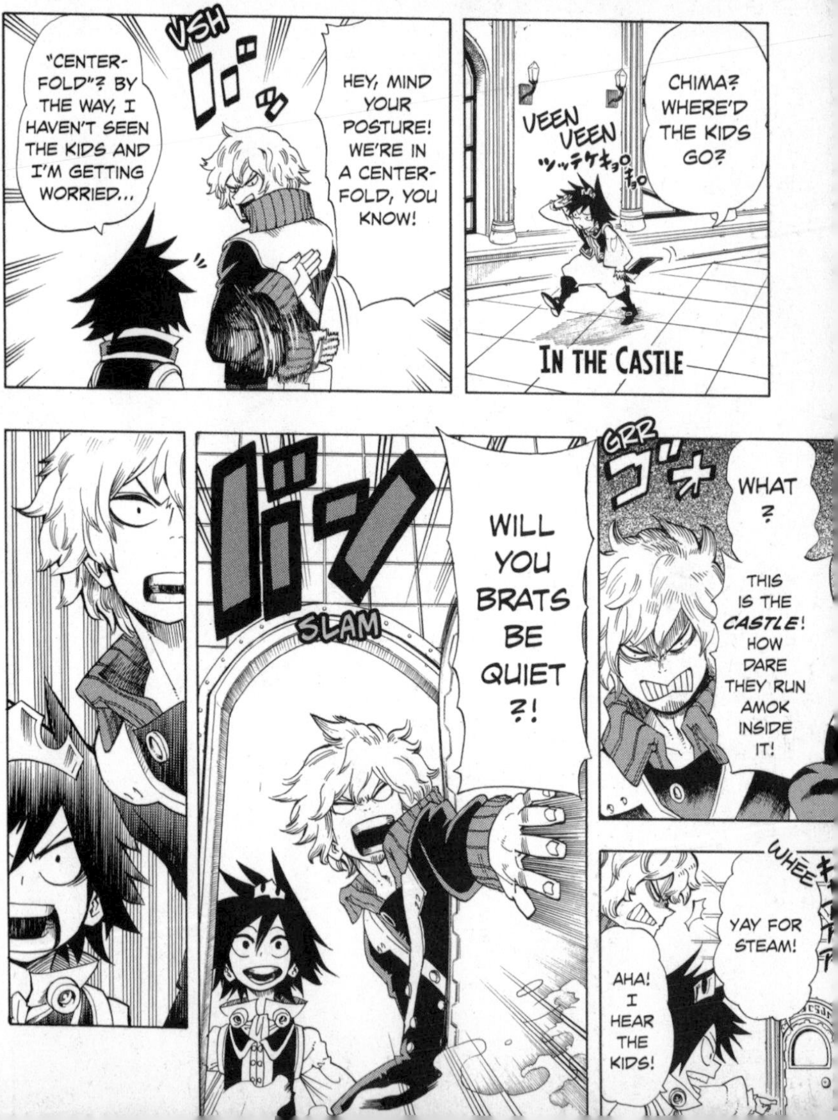
CHIMA? WHERE'D THE KIDS GO?
VEEN VEEN
ツッテケキョ キョ
IN THE CASTLE
HEY, MIND YOUR POSTURE! WE'RE IN A CENTER-FOLD, YOU KNOW!
VSH
"CENTER-FOLD"? BY THE WAY, I HAVEN'T SEEN THE KIDS AND I'M GETTING WORRIED...
GRR
WHAT?
THIS IS THE *CASTLE*! HOW DARE THEY RUN AMOK INSIDE IT!
WHEE
YAY FOR STEAM!
AHA! I HEAR THE KIDS!
WILL YOU BRATS BE QUIET?!
SLAM

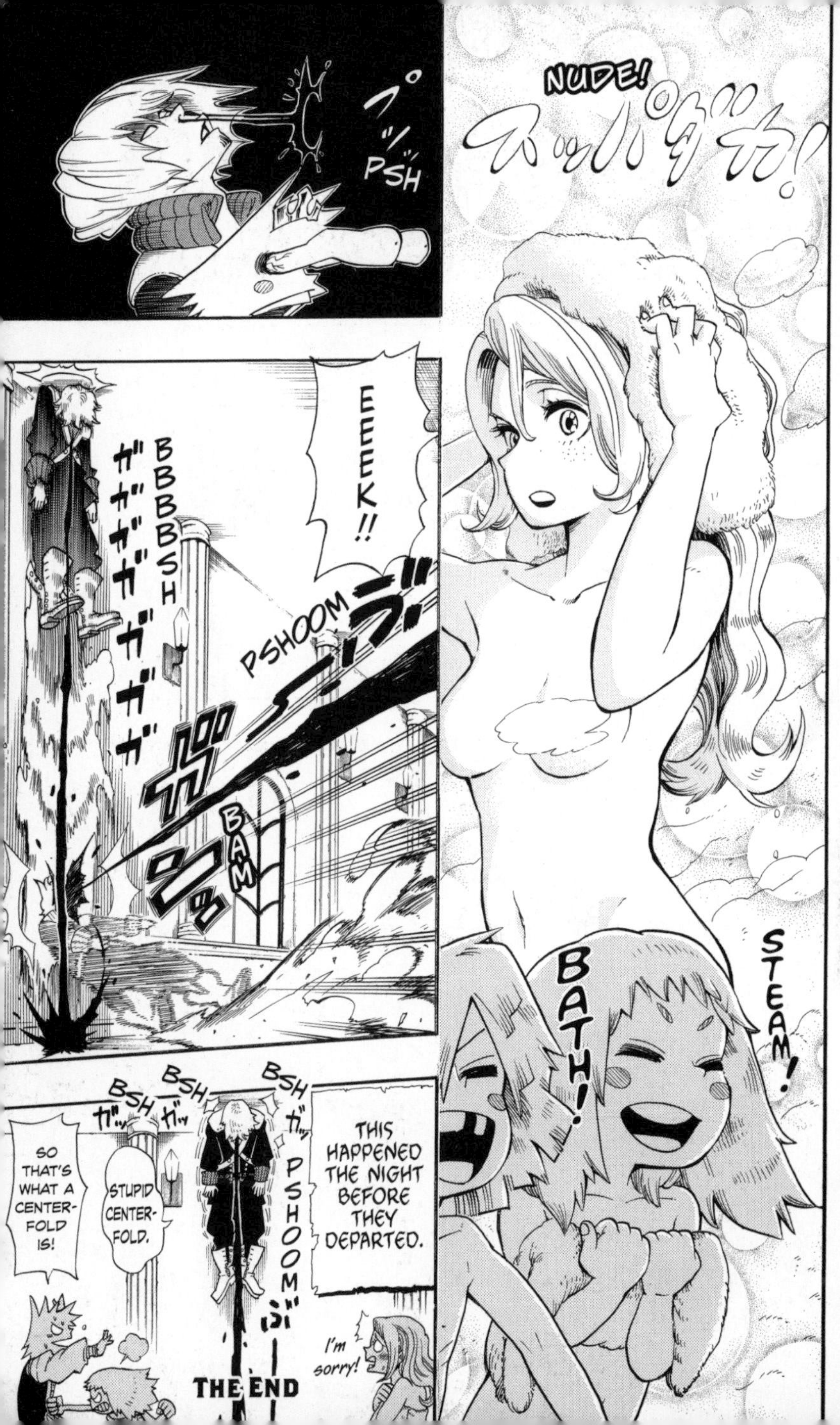
NUDE!
BATH!
STEAM!
PSH
EEEEK!!
BBBBSH
PSHOOM
BAM
BSH
BSH
BSH
THIS HAPPENED THE NIGHT BEFORE THEY DEPARTED.
PSHOOM
STUPID CENTERFOLD.
SO THAT'S WHAT A CENTERFOLD IS!
I'm sorry!
THE END

Bonus Manga
The Party from Hell Arc

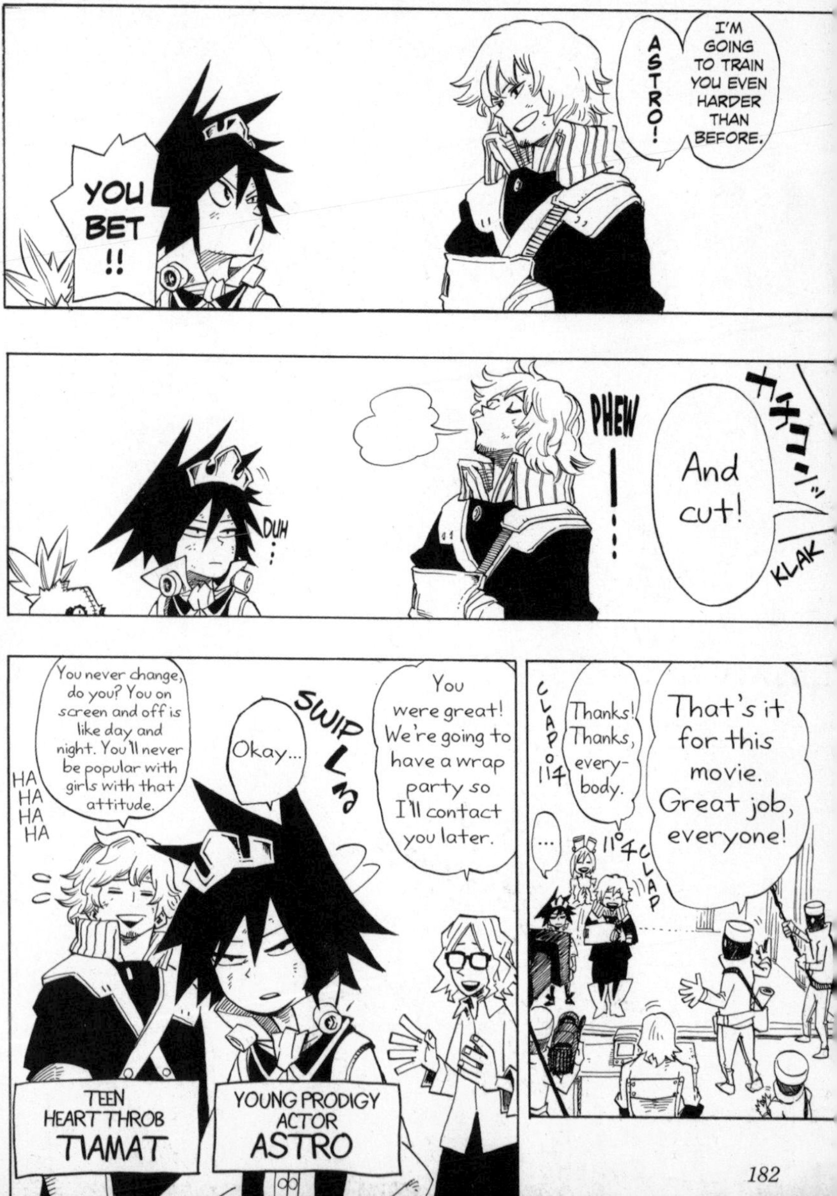
ASTRO!
I'M GOING TO TRAIN YOU EVEN HARDER THAN BEFORE.
YOU BET!!
And cut!
KLAK
PHEW...
DUH...
That's it for this movie. Great job, everyone!
Thanks! Thanks, everybody.
CLAP CLAP
CLAP CLAP
...
You were great! We're going to have a wrap party so I'll contact you later.
SWIP
Okay...
You never change, do you? You on screen and off is like day and night. You'll never be popular with girls with that attitude.
HA HA HA HA
TEEN HEART THROB TIAMAT
YOUNG PRODIGY ACTOR ASTRO

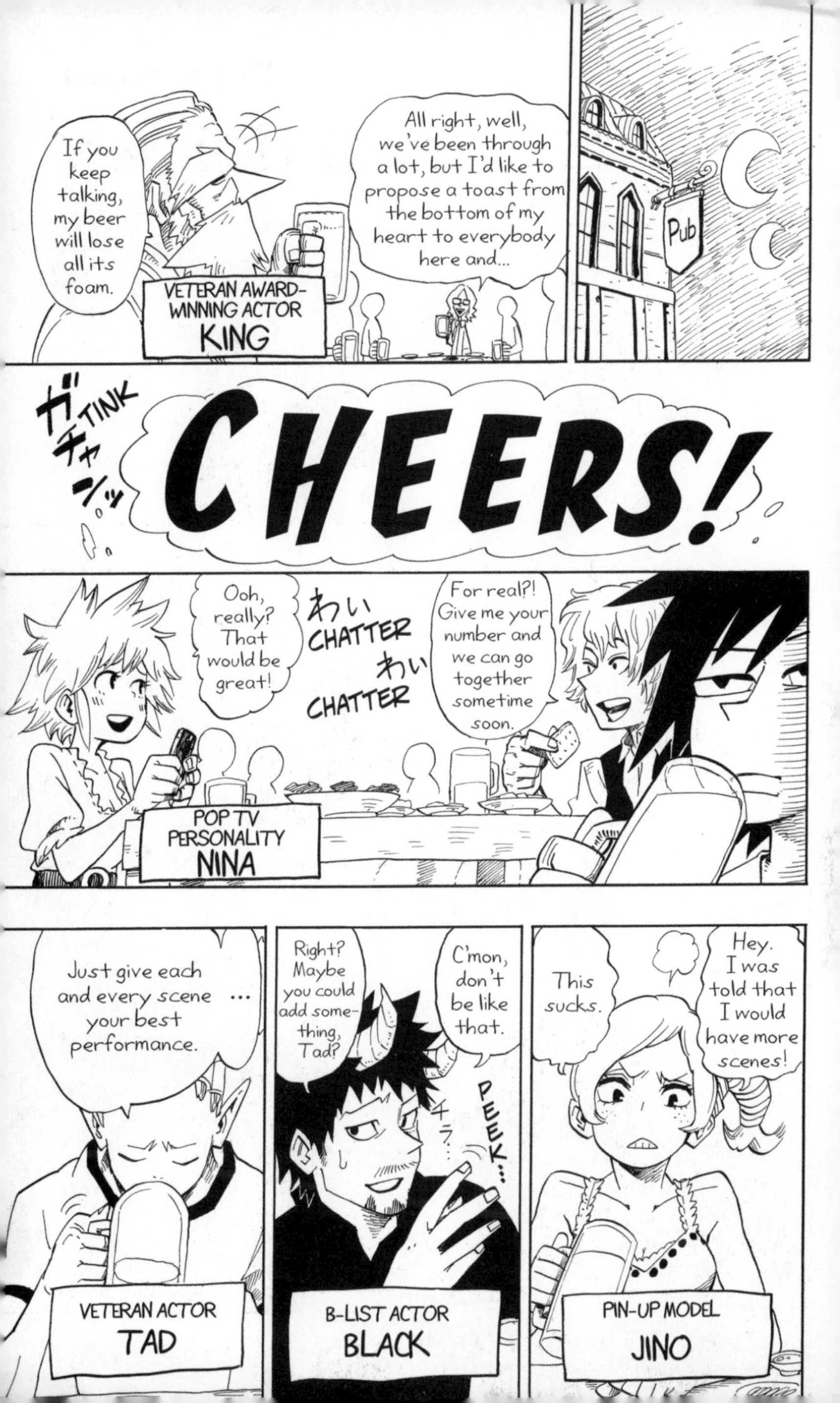
Pub
All right, well, we've been through a lot, but I'd like to propose a toast from the bottom of my heart to everybody here and...
If you keep talking, my beer will lose all its foam.
VETERAN AWARD-WINNING ACTOR KING
ガチャンッ TINK
CHEERS!
For real?! Give me your number and we can go together sometime soon.
わい CHATTER わい CHATTER
Ooh, really? That would be great!
POP TV PERSONALITY NINA
Hey. I was told that I would have more scenes!
This sucks.
PIN-UP MODEL JINO
C'mon, don't be like that.
Right? Maybe you could add something, Tad?
チラ… PEEK…
B-LIST ACTOR BLACK
…
Just give each and every scene your best performance.
VETERAN ACTOR TAD

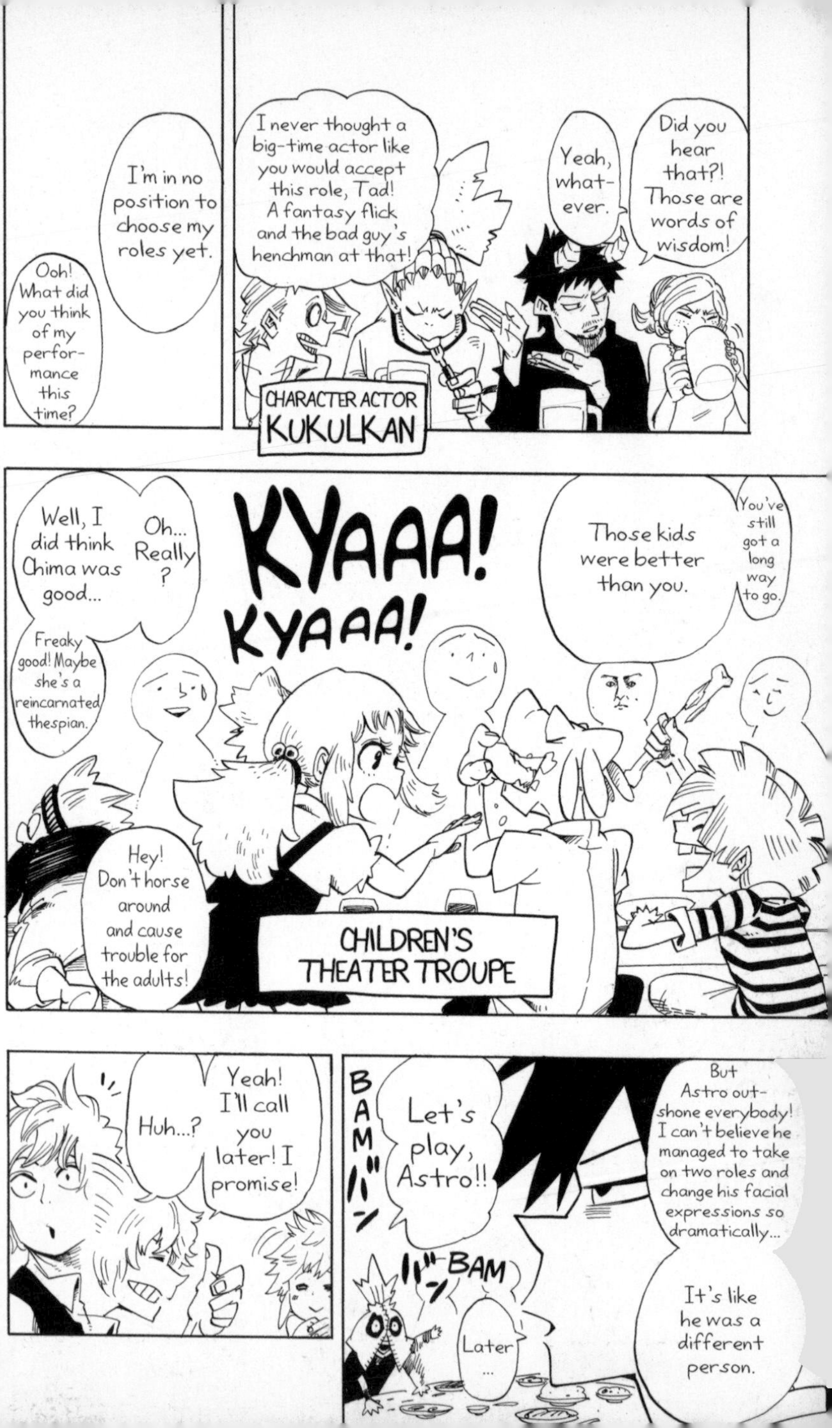
Did you hear that?! Those are words of wisdom!
Yeah, whatever.
I never thought a big-time actor like you would accept this role, Tad! A fantasy flick and the bad guy's henchman at that!
CHARACTER ACTOR KUKULKAN
I'm in no position to choose my roles yet.
Ooh! What did you think of my performance this time?
You've still got a long way to go.
Those kids were better than you.
KYAAA! KYAAA!
Oh... Really?
Well, I did think Chima was good...
Freaky good! Maybe she's a reincarnated thespian.
Hey! Don't horse around and cause trouble for the adults!
CHILDREN'S THEATER TROUPE
But Astro outshone everybody! I can't believe he managed to take on two roles and change his facial expressions so dramatically...
It's like he was a different person.
BAM
Let's play, Astro!!
BAM
Later...
Yeah! I'll call you later! I promise!
Huh...?

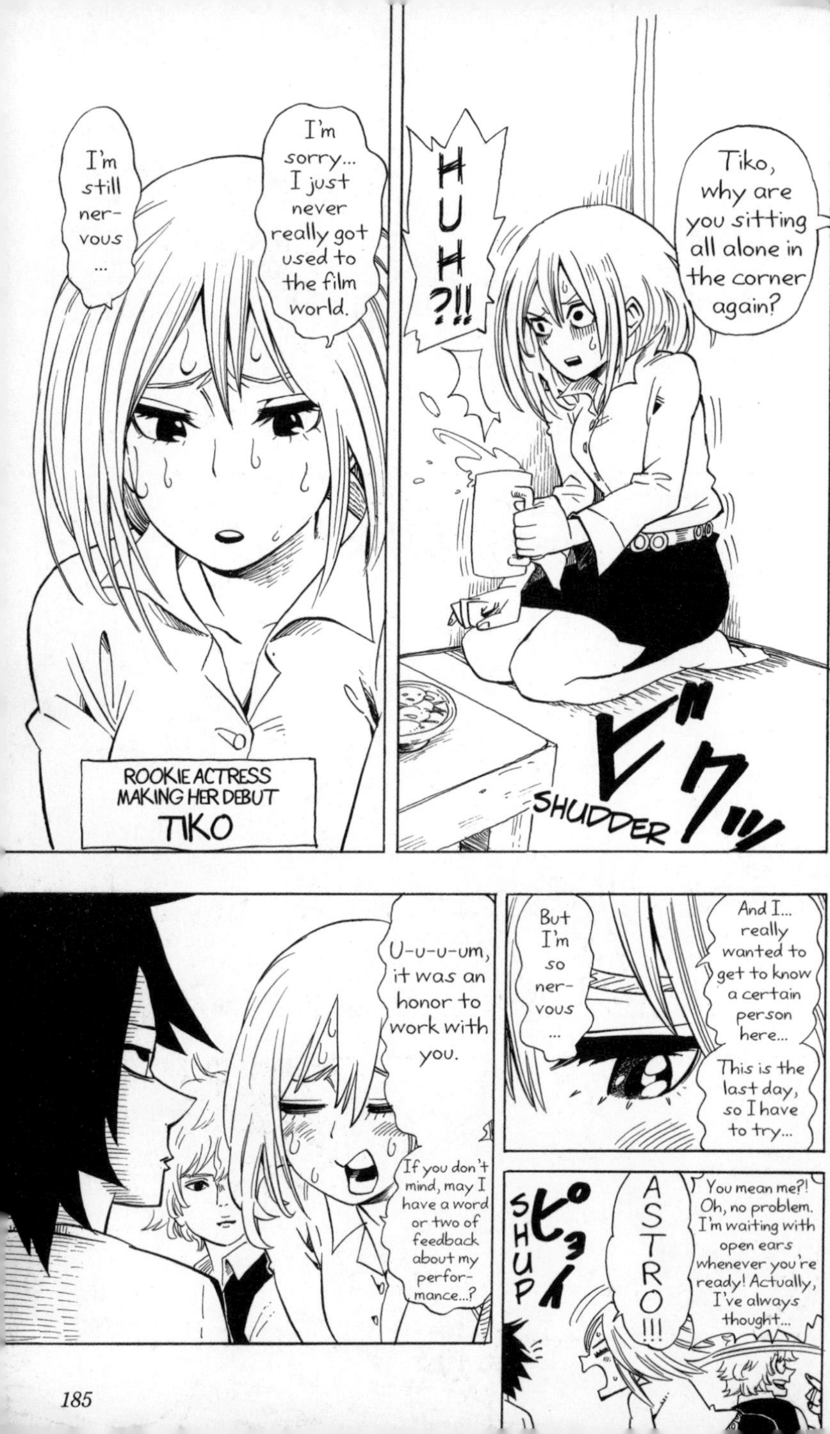
Tiko, why are you sitting all alone in the corner again?
HUH?!!
ビクッ
SHUDDER
I'm sorry... I just never really got used to the film world.
I'm still ner-vous...
ROOKIE ACTRESS MAKING HER DEBUT TIKO
And I... really wanted to get to know a certain person here...
But I'm so ner-vous...
This is the last day, so I have to try...
You mean me?! Oh, no problem. I'm waiting with open ears whenever you're ready! Actually, I've always thought...
ASTRO!!!
ピョイ
SHUP
U-u-u-um, it was an honor to work with you.
If you don't mind, may I have a word or two of feedback about my perfor-mance...?

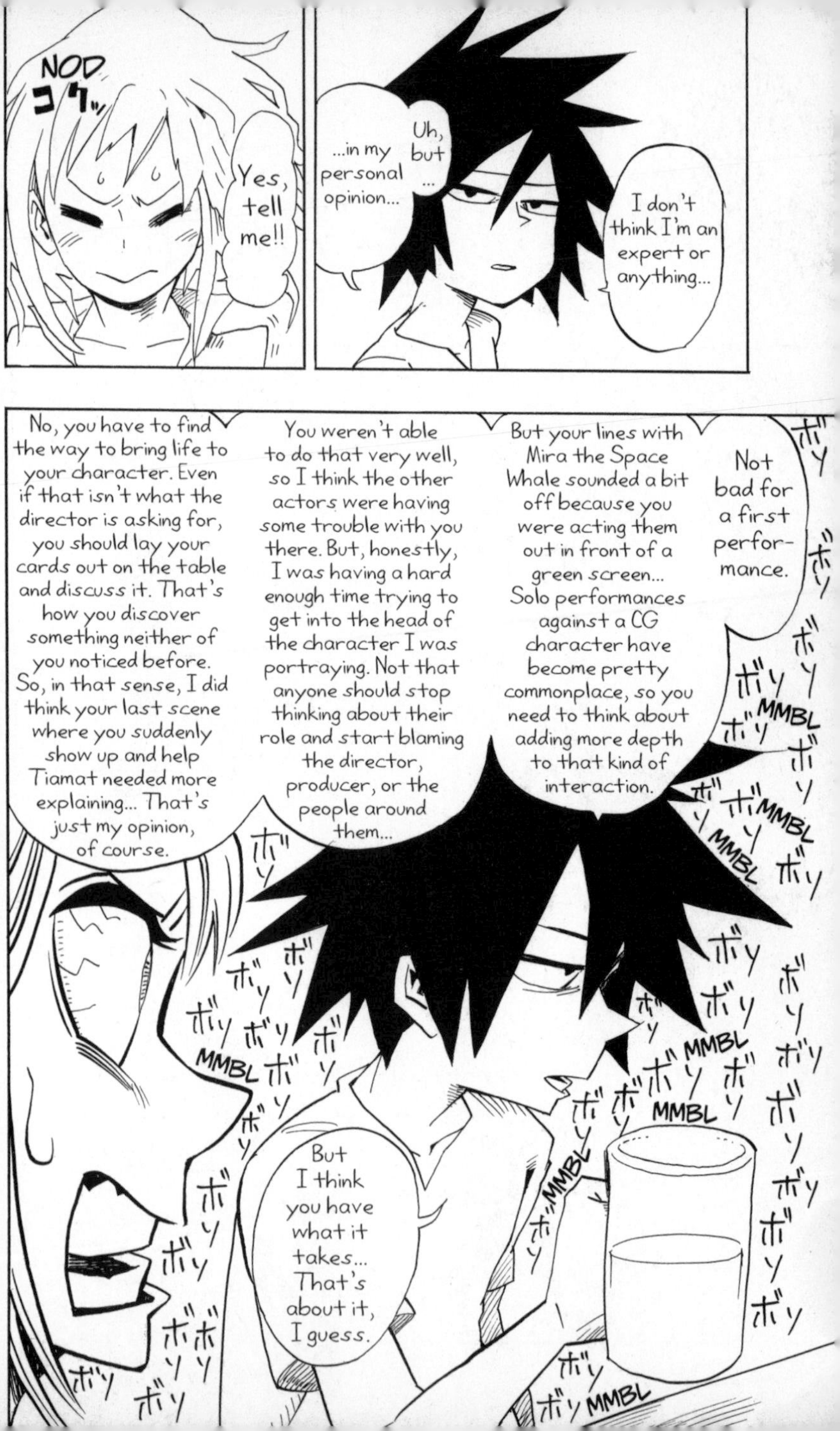
I don't think I'm an expert or anything...
Uh, but...
...in my personal opinion...
NOD
コクッ
Yes, tell me!!
ボソ
Not bad for a first performance.
But your lines with Mira the Space Whale sounded a bit off because you were acting them out in front of a green screen... Solo performances against a CG character have become pretty commonplace, so you need to think about adding more depth to that kind of interaction.
You weren't able to do that very well, so I think the other actors were having some trouble with you there. But, honestly, I was having a hard enough time trying to get into the head of the character I was portraying. Not that anyone should stop thinking about their role and start blaming the director, producer, or the people around them...
No, you have to find the way to bring life to your character. Even if that isn't what the director is asking for, you should lay your cards out on the table and discuss it. That's how you discover something neither of you noticed before. So, in that sense, I did think your last scene where you suddenly show up and help Tiamat needed more explaining... That's just my opinion, of course.
MMBL
ボソボソ
MMBL
ボソボソ
But I think you have what it takes... That's about it, I guess.
MMBL
ボソボソ

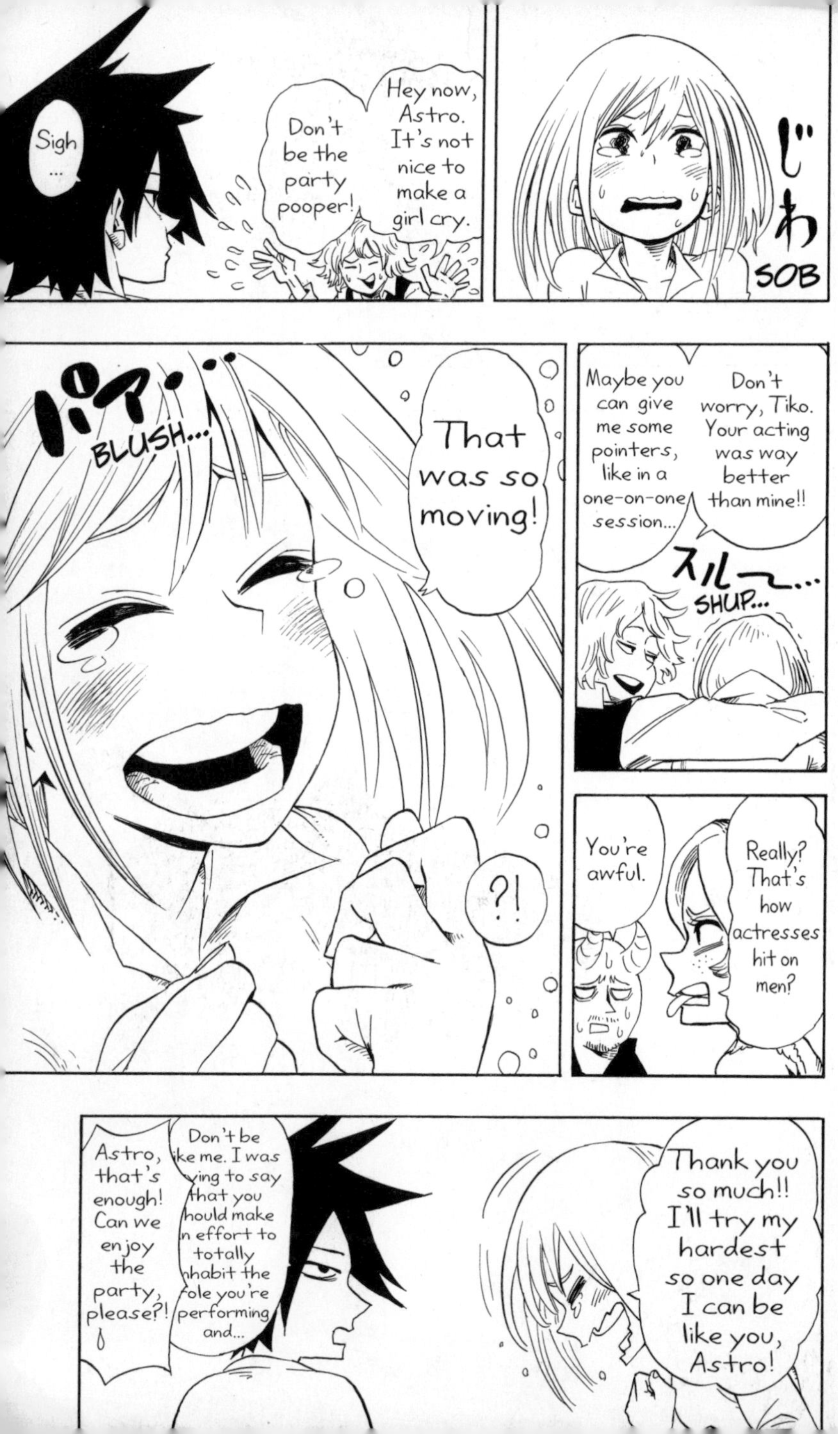
じわ
SOB
Hey now, Astro. It's not nice to make a girl cry.
Don't be the party pooper!
Sigh ...
Don't worry, Tiko. Your acting was way better than mine!!
Maybe you can give me some pointers, like in a one-on-one session...
スル〜…
SHUP...
Really? That's how actresses hit on men?
You're awful.
That was so moving!
パア…
BLUSH...
?!
Thank you so much!! I'll try my hardest so one day I can be like you, Astro!
Don't be ike me. I was ying to say that you hould make n effort to totally nhabit the ole you're performing and...
Astro, that's enough! Can we enjoy the party, please?!

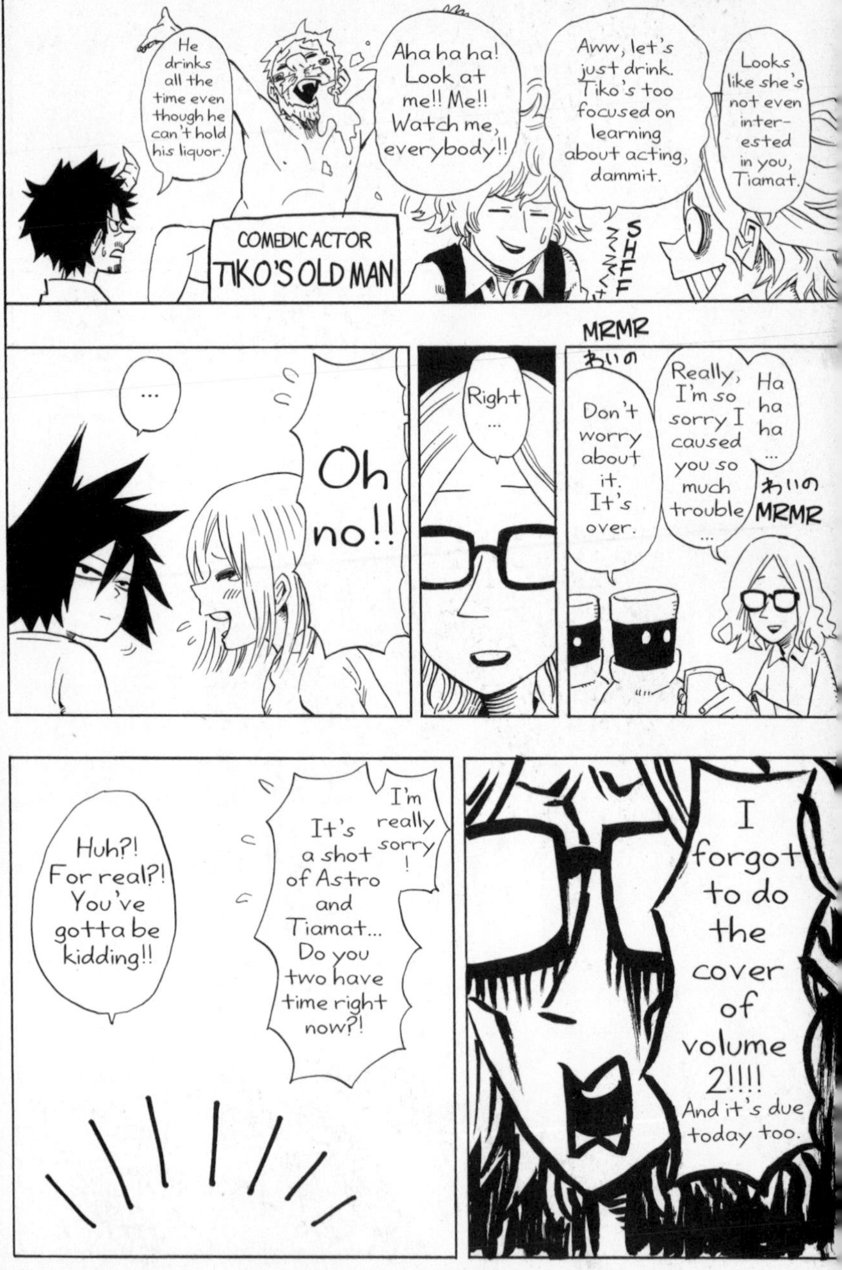

Looks like she's not even interested in you, Tiamat.
Aww, let's just drink. Tiko's too focused on learning about acting, dammit.
SHFF
Aha ha ha! Look at me!! Me!! Watch me, everybody!!
He drinks all the time even though he can't hold his liquor.
COMEDIC ACTOR TIKO'S OLD MAN
MRMR
わいの
Ha ha ha...
Really, I'm so sorry I caused you so much trouble...
わいの
MRMR
Don't worry about it. It's over.
Right...
Oh no!!
...
I forgot to do the cover of volume 2!!!!
And it's due today too.
I'm really sorry!
It's a shot of Astro and Tiamat... Do you two have time right now?!
Huh?! For real?! You've gotta be kidding!!

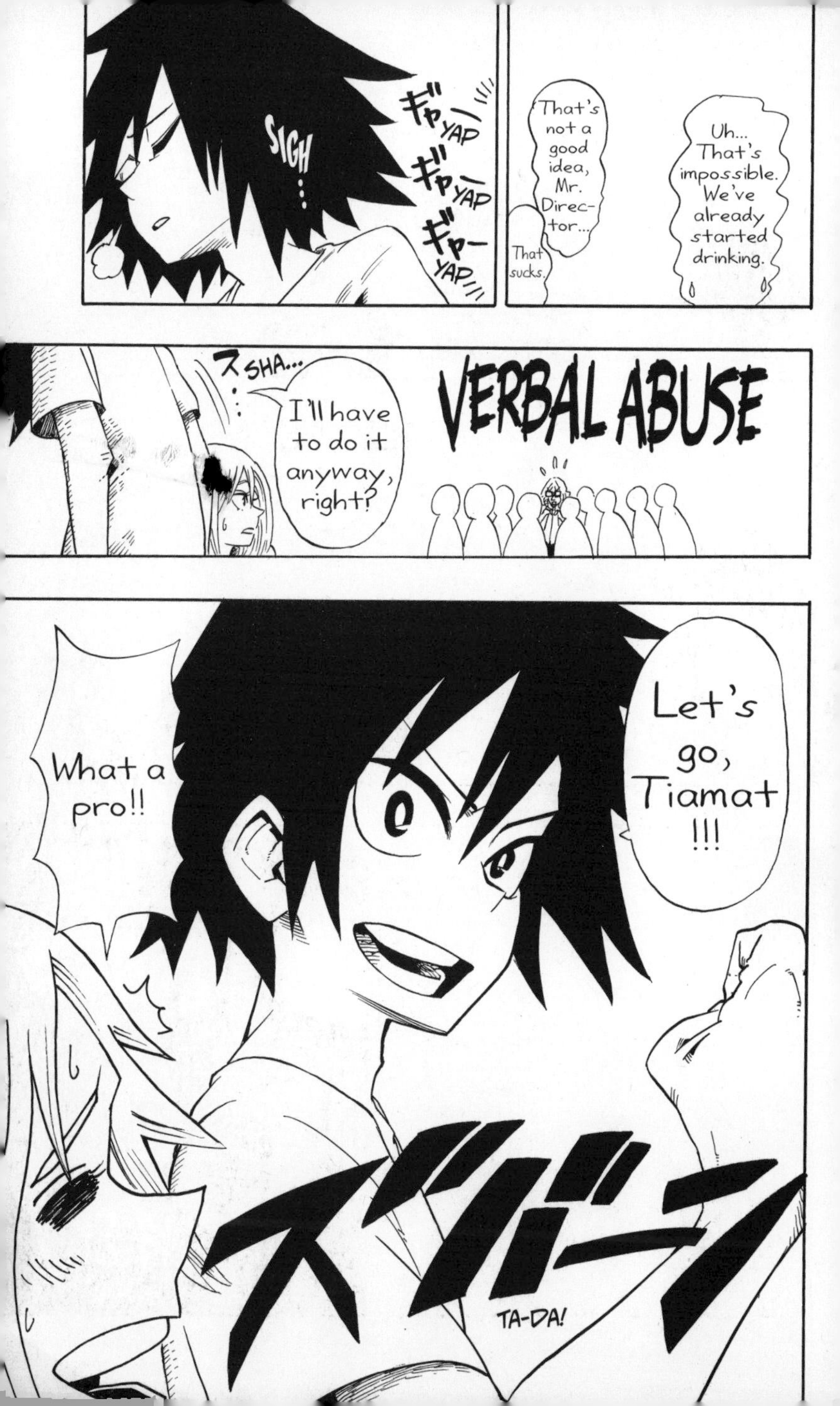
Uh... That's impossible. We've already started drinking.
That's not a good idea, Mr. Director...
That sucks.
ギャー YAP
ギャー YAP
ギャー YAP
SIGH...
VERBAL ABUSE
ス SHA...
I'll have to do it anyway, right?
Let's go, Tiamat!!!
What a pro!!
ズバーン
TA-DA!

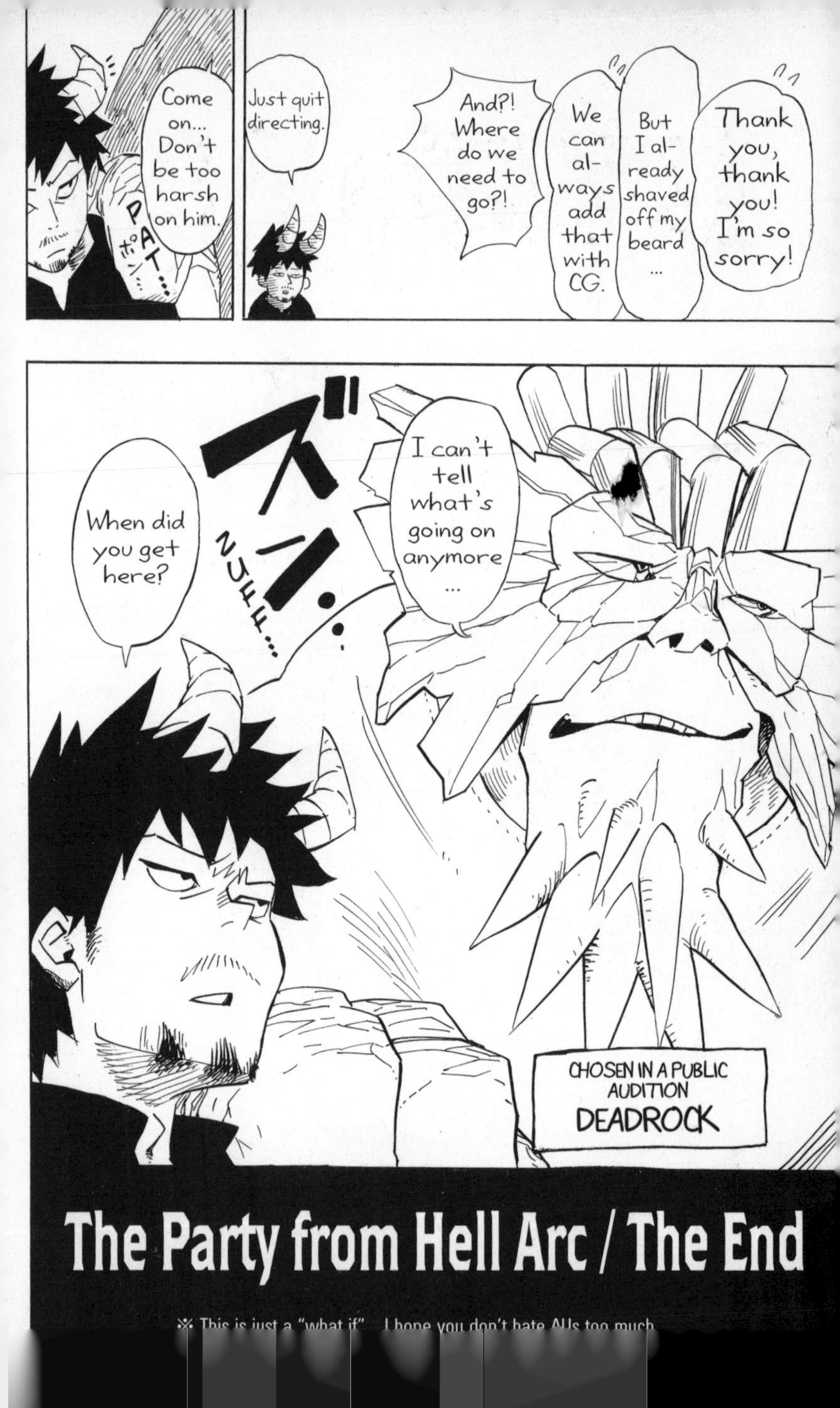
Thank you, thank you! I'm so sorry!
But I al-ready shaved off my beard...
We can al-ways add that with CG.
And?! Where do we need to go?!
Just quit directing.
Come on... Don't be too harsh on him.
PAT...
I can't tell what's going on anymore...
ZUFF...
When did you get here?
CHOSEN IN A PUBLIC AUDITION
DEADROCK

The Party from Hell Arc / The End

※ This is just a "what if"... I hope you don't hate AUs too much.

AFTERWORD

→

What the heck did I just draw? It reeks of the '90s, doesn't it? Like when a manga artist pops up inside their manga. This is what you get when you draw without sleeping or even thinking.

Anyway, thank you very much for reading Barrage.
"Thank you very much" is the only thing I can think of to say.
I'm really grateful. You have no idea how much your support matters...
I'm sorry. Thank you very much.

Okay, see you all around.
Oops, I mean I really hope to see you all again someday. Goodbye...

Kouhei Horikoshi

YOU'RE READING THE WRONG WAY!

BARRAGE reads from right to left, starting in the upper-right corner. Japanese is read from right to left, meaning that action, sound effects, and word-balloon order are completely reversed from English order.

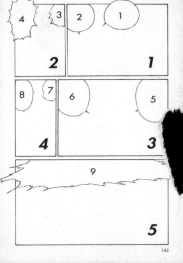